China's Changing Welfare Mix

This book draws attention to two neglected areas in the growing body of research on welfare in China: subnational variation and the changing mix of state and non-state provision. The contributors to this volume demonstrate the diversity of local welfare provision that lies behind broad national policies and programmes. Their focus on local diversity is particularly relevant to understanding the welfare system in China because national state programmes are so often organized by local governments in line with the specifics of their economic and social development. At the same time that economic and social development is itself independently creating an array of different conditions that shape non-state (family, business and third sector) welfare roles.

Through chapters that draw on original research in eight provinces, the book adopts a 'local' perspective to illustrate and explain some of the transformations that are under way and discuss not only local government initiatives and programmes, but also the services and support provided by families, informal social networks and community or third sector organizations, as well as those delivered by private businesses on a commercial, for-profit basis.

This book will be of interest to students and scholars of Chinese society, social policy and Chinese studies more widely.

Beatriz Carrillo is Lecturer in Asian Studies at the University of Technology, Sydney, Australia.

Jane Duckett is Professor of Chinese and Comparative Politics at the University of Glasgow, UK.

Routledge studies on China in transition
Series Editor: David S. G. Goodman

1 The Democratisation of China
Baogang He

2 Beyond Beijing
Dali Yang

3 China's Enterprise Reform
Changing state/society relations
after Mao
You Ji

4 Industrial Change in China
Economic restructuring and
conflicting interests
Kate Hannan

5 The Entrepreneurial State in China
Real estate and commerce
departments in reform era Tianjin
Jane Duckett

6 Tourism and Modernity in China
Tim Oakes

7 Cities in Post Mao China
Recipes for economic development
in the reform era
Jae Ho Chung

8 China's Spatial Economic Development
Regional transformation in the
Lower Yangzi Delta
Andrew M. Marton

9 Regional Development in China
States, globalization and inequality
Yehua Dennis Wei

10 Grassroots Charisma
Four local leaders in China
*Stephan Feuchtwang and
Wang Mingming*

11 The Chinese Legal System
Globalization and local legal culture
Pitman B. Potter

12 Transforming Rural China
How local institutions shape
property rights in china
Chi-Jou Jay Chen

13 Negotiating Ethnicity in China
Citizenship as a response to the state
Chih-yu Shih

14 Manager Empowerment in China
Political implications of rural
industrialisation in the reform era
Ray Yep

15 Cultural Nationalism in Contemporary China
The search for national identity
under reform
Yingjie Guo

16 Elite Dualism and Leadership Selection in China
Xiaowei Zang

17 Chinese Intellectuals between State and Market
Edward Gu and Merle Goldman

18 China, Sex and Prostitution
Elaine Jeffreys

19 The Development of China's Stockmarket, 1984–2002
Equity politics and market institutions
Stephen Green

20 China's Rational Entrepreneurs
The development of the new private business sector
Barbara Krug

21 China's Scientific Elite
Cong Cao

22 Locating China
Jing Wang

23 State and Laid-Off Workers in Reform China
The silence and collective action of the retrenched
Yongshun Cai

24 Translocal China
Linkages, identities and the reimagining of space
Tim Oakes and Louisa Schein

25 International Aid and China's Environment
Taming the yellow dragon
Katherine Morton

26 Sex and Sexuality in China
Edited by Elaine Jeffreys

27 China's Reforms and International Political Economy
Edited by David Zweig and Chen Zhimin

28 Ethnicity and Urban Life in China
A comparative study of Hui Muslims and Han Chinese
Xiaowei Zang

29 China's Urban Space
Development under market socialism
T.G. McGee, George C.S. Lin, Mark Y.L. Wang, Andrew M. Marton and Jiaping Wu

30 China's Embedded Activism
Opportunities and constraints of a social movement
Edited by Richard Louis Edmonds and Peter Ho

31 Marketization and Democracy in China
Jianjun Zhang

32 The Chinese State in Transition
Processes and contests in local China
Edited by Linda Chelan Li

33 China's Governmentalities
Governing change, changing government
Edited by Elaine Jeffreys

34 China's Cotton Industry
Economic transformation and state capacity
Björn Alpermann

35 Serious Crime in China
Policing and politics
Susan Trevaskes

36 The Chinese State's Retreat from Health
Policy and the politics of retrenchment
Jane Duckett

37 China's Changing Welfare Mix
Local perspectives
Edited by Beatriz Carrillo and Jane Duckett

China's Changing Welfare Mix
Local perspectives

Edited by
Beatriz Carrillo and
Jane Duckett

LONDON AND NEW YORK

First published
2011 by Routledge
2 Park Square, Milton Park, Abingdon, Oxon OX14 4RN

Simultaneously published in the USA and Canada
by Routledge
711 Third Avenue, New York, NY10017

Routledge is an imprint of the Taylor & Francis Group, an informa business

© 2011 Editorial selection and matter, Beatriz Carrillo and Jane Duckett; individual chapters, the contributors

The right of Beatriz Carrillo and Jane Duckett to be identified as editors of this work has been asserted by them in accordance with the Copyright, Designs and Patent Act 1988.

All rights reserved. No part of this book may be reprinted or reproduced or utilised in any form or by any electronic, mechanical, or other means, now known or hereafter invented, including photocopying and recording, or in any information storage or retrieval system, without permission in writing from the publishers.

British Library Cataloguing in Publication Data
A catalogue record for this book is available from the British Library

Library of Congress Cataloging in Publication Data
China's changing welfare mix: local perspectives / edited by Beatriz Carrillo, Jane Duckett.
   p. cm. – (Routledge studies on china in transition; 37)
   Includes bibliographical references.
   1. Public welfare – China. 2. China – Social policy. 3. China – Economic policy. I. Carrillo, Beatriz. II. Duckett, Jane, 1964-
   HV418.C444 2011
   361.951 – dc22   2010031448

ISBN 978-0-415-59731-9
ISBN 978-0-203-83277-6

Typeset in Times New Roman by Taylor & Francis Books

Printed and bound in Great Britain by
CPI Antony Rowe, Chippenham, Wiltshire

Contents

List of figures	ix
List of tables	x
List of contributors	xii
Acknowledgements	xv
Glossary of Chinese terms	xvii
Map of the provincial-level administrative divisions of the	
People's Republic of China	xviii

1 China's changing welfare mix: introducing the local perspective   1
JANE DUCKETT AND BEATRIZ CARRILLO

2 Central–local relations in social policy and the development of
urban and rural social assistance programmes   20
XINPING GUAN AND BING XU

3 *Dibaohu* in distress: the meagre minimum livelihood guarantee
system in Wuhan   36
DOROTHY J. SOLINGER

4 Local variation in urban social assistance: community public
service agencies in Dalian   64
DANIEL R. HAMMOND

5 Life goes on: redundant women workers in Nanjing   82
JIEYU LIU

6 'If you can walk and eat, you don't go to hospital': the
quest for healthcare in rural Sichuan   104
ANNA LORA-WAINWRIGHT

7 Regional disparities and educational inequalities: city responses
and coping strategies   126
KA HO MOK AND YU CHEUNG WONG

viii *Contents*

8 Life considerations and the housing of rural to urban migrants: the
case of Taiyuan 151
BINGQIN LI AND MARK DUDA

9 Older people and the (un)caring state in 'China's Manhattan' 171
ANNA BOERMEL

10 Support for the social participation of children and young
people with disability in China: a Jiangxi county case study 193
KAREN R. FISHER, XIAOYUAN SHANG AND JIAWEN XIE

11 Global discourses, national policies, local outcomes:
reflections on China's welfare reforms 211
SARAH COOK

Bibliography 223
Index 249

Figures

2.1	Financial responsibility relations between government and enterprises in the pre-reform period (urban)	21
2.2	Central–local relationships within the governmental system	25
3.1	Number of participants in the MLG (*dibao*) 1997–2007	43

Tables

2.1	Central–local division of expenditure responsibility in the tax reform of 1994	23
2.2	Key responsibility relationships	24
3.1	Cross-city comparison of MLG (*dibao*) norm and per capita GDP, 1998	42
3.2	Cross-city comparison of MLG (*dibao*) line and average wages, 1998	43
3.3	Government spending on MLG (*dibao*) as a share of total spending and GDP, 1999–2007	44
3.4	Number of participants in MLG (*dibao*) 1997–2007	44
3.5	Cross-city MLG (*dibao*) line and average disposable income, July 2002	45
3.6	Cross-city comparison of MLG (*dibao*) line and average wages, 2004	46
3.7	Cross-city MLG (*dibao*) line and average disposable income, March 2004	47
3.8	Cross-city MLG (*dibao*) line and average disposable income, September 2005	48
3.9	Interviewees' household size, *dibao* allowance and income	51
7.1	China's public education expenditure as a percentage of GDP	130
7.2	International comparison of public education expenditure as a percentage of GDP, 2003	130
7.3	Characteristics of the survey sample	136
7.4	Primary and secondary school staffing and student enrolment, Beijing and Lanzhou, 2008	137
7.5	Share of household spending on education in the previous year	138
7.6	Families reporting after-school tuition and activities (primary and secondary education students)	138
7.7	Hardship related to education for households with children studying in primary or secondary school	139
7.8	Hardship related to education for households with children studying in post-secondary education	140
7.9	Non-state educational grants in selected region, 2003	141

List of tables xi

7.10	Education funds per student across regions, 2006	142
7.11	Allocations of places of study in Guangdong, 2003	143
7.12	Annual school fees for migrant children in the Fengtai, Haidian and Chaoyang districts of Beijing, 2002	145
8.1	Migrant employment distribution by industry sector	156
8.2	Housing characteristics	158
8.3	Satisfaction by quality	159
8.4	Housing quality and income	159
8.5	Descriptive statistics for the models	163
8.6	Housing choice logistic regression results	165
8.7	Standard for housing choice	167

Contributors

Anna Boermel is Research and Teaching Fellow in Contemporary Chinese Society at the University of Cambridge. Trained in Chinese Studies and Social Anthropology at the University of Oxford, she has conducted fieldwork in urban China and Taiwan on law, science, governance, sexuality and ageing. She is currently revising her manuscript on the politics of old age in urban China.

Beatriz Carrillo is lecturer in Asian Studies at the University of Technology, Sydney (UTS) and a member of the UTS China Research Centre. She researches social change in contemporary China and is currently working on two projects: one on problems of health-care provision; the other on the evolution of the interaction between the new rich and the state. Her book *Small Town China: Rural labour and social inclusion* is also published by Routledge (2011).

Sarah Cook is Head of the United Nations Research Institute for Social Development (UNRISD) and a former Research Fellow at the Institute of Development Studies at the University of Sussex. From 2000 to 2006 she was a Programme Officer with the Ford Foundation in Beijing. Her research addresses issues related to the social impacts of economic reform in China, including issues of social policy, employment and gender. She recently directed a multi-country research programme on 'Social Protection in Asia' and is engaged in comparative research on informal employment in China and India. Recent publications include papers on social policy in East Asia, rural health reform in China and social protection.

Jane Duckett is Professor of Chinese and Comparative Politics at the University of Glasgow. She has recently completed a book, *The Chinese State's Retreat from Health: Policy and the Politics of Retrenchment* (Routledge, 2010), and has published papers on China's health reforms, unemployment policies and social welfare in such journals as *The China Quarterly, Pacific Review* and *Social Policy and Administration*.

Contributors xiii

Mark Duda is an independent scholar specializing in public policy aspects of homeownership and the single family mortgage market in the US and China. Mark is a Research Affiliate of the Harvard Joint Center for Housing Studies, where he previously held positions as a Research Analyst and Research Fellow.

Karen R. Fisher is Associate Professor at the Social Policy Research Centre, University of New South Wales, Sydney. Her research interests are the organization of social services in Australia and China, including disability and mental health services and community care; participatory evaluation methodology; and social policy process.

Xinping Guan is the head and Professor at the Department of Social Work and Social Policy, Nankai University, China. His main research areas are poverty and social policy, mainly social assistance. His main research topics in recent years include China's social policy transition in the background of globalization, poverty and social assistance in urban and rural China. He is the author of *Urban Poverty in China* (1999), *Introduction to Social Policy* (2003, 2008), and many papers published within and outside China.

Daniel R. Hammond recently gained his PhD at the University of Glasgow. His research interests include social assistance policy in China and theories of the policy process.

Bingqin Li is a Lecturer in Social Policy at London School of Economics. She is also a research associate of CASE (The Centre for Analyses of Social Exclusion) at LSE. Her research is focused on social policies in China. The main string of research includes social exclusion faced by rural to urban migrants, long-term unemployed people and informally employed people. She has also worked on the relationship between urbanization and social policy changes and the relationship between fiscal reform, urban governance and social policy.

Jieyu Liu is an Academic Fellow in the White Rose East Asia Centre, University of Leeds. She is the author of *Gender and Work in Urban China: Women Workers of the Unlucky Generation* (Routledge 2007) and the co-editor of *East Asian Sexualities: Modernity, Gender and New Sexual Cultures* (Zed Books, 2008). She is interested in gender, sexuality, work and organization, and labour-market changes, and is currently working on a project examining the sexualization and aestheticization of white-collar work in urban China.

Anna Lora-Wainwright is a University Lecturer in the Human Geography of China, School of Geography and School of Interdisciplinary Area Studies, University of Oxford. Her research concerns perceptions of health and health-care provision and, more recently, their interplay with experiences of environmental pollution in the Chinese countryside. Her forthcoming xiv *Contributors*

monograph offers a bottom-up account of how families strive to make sense of cancer and to care for sufferers in the context of changing social and economic relations in contemporary rural China.

Ka Ho Mok is Chair Professor of Comparative Policy and Co-Director of the Centre for Governance and Citizenship at the Hong Kong Institute of Education. He has researched and published extensively in comparative education and policy studies in East Asia and Contemporary China. He is also Editor of *Journal of Asian Public Policy* (Routledge) and Book Series Editor of Comparative Development and Policy in Asia (Routledge).

Xiaoyuan Shang is a Senior Research Fellow in the Social Policy Research Centre, University of New South Wales. She specializes in research about the social welfare provision to orphans, and other vulnerable children, people with a disability and older people in China.

Dorothy J. Solinger is Professor of Political Science at the University of California, Irvine. She is beginning a project on the urban poor and the state's treatment of them. Her most recent publication is *States' Gains, Labor's Losses: China, France and Mexico Choose Global Liasons* (Cornell University Press, 2009).

Yu Cheung Wong is Assistant Professor in the Department of Social Work and Social Administration, University of Hong Kong. His major research interests are digital inclusion, social welfare and education in China. He is also Programme Leader of the Master of Social Work programme at the University of Hong Kong.

Jiawen Xie is a doctoral student at Beijing Normal University. Her research interests are in the experiences and welfare status of children with disabilities in rural China.

Bing Xu is a PhD candidate at the Department of Social Work and Social Policy, Nankai University, China. Her academic area is China's social policy, particularly its social assistance and child welfare.

Acknowledgements

This book grew out of a workshop held in late October 2008 at Nankai University in Tianjin. The workshop was jointly organized by the China Research Centre of the University of Technology Sydney (UTS), the Scottish Centre for Chinese Social Science Research (based at the University of Glasgow), and the Department of Social Work and Social Policy at Nankai University. We are grateful to Louise Edwards, Director of the China Research Centre at UTS for supporting the workshop, and to its administrator, Claire Moore, for her hard highly efficient work organizing it. We are equally grateful to Nankai University, our hosts, and to all the colleagues and students in the Department of Social Work and Social Policy, led by Professor Xinping Guan, for all the work they put into its smooth running. Finally, we would like to thank all those who participated in the workshop for their very valuable contributions as discussants and paper givers, and for lively discussions around all the papers. Notably, David S.G. Goodman provided sound guidance and, along with Tim Oakes, Louisa Schein, Sun Wanning and Carolyn Cartier, brought wisdom and experience from long leadership of and involvement in Provincial China workshops. We would also like to thank the contributors to this book for so quickly and professionally revising their papers and so enabling a speedy publication. Finally, we are grateful to Sarah Cook for both her valuable contribution to the workshop discussions and for agreeing to write this book's concluding chapter.

In organizing the workshop and producing this book, our aim has been to draw attention to two relatively neglected areas in the growing body of research on welfare in China: sub-national variation and the changing mix of state and non-state provision. We wanted to highlight the local, or sub-national, variation that lies behind broad national policies and programmes, and that is growing from divergent local government and non-state activities. In doing this, we hoped to contribute to the 'localizing' project pioneered for over a decade at UTS through a series of annual Provincial China workshops and publications. But we also felt this approach to be particularly relevant to understanding welfare provision in China because national state programmes are so often organized by local governments in line with the specifics of their economic and social development, while at the same time that social and xvi *Acknowledgements*

economic development itself is independently creating differential conditions for non-state (family, business and third sector) provision.

In organizing the workshop we hoped to develop understanding not only of welfare provision but also of people's 'responses' to any gaps in state or societal programmes. As Sarah Cook rightly notes in her chapter, this tends to lead us to focus on the weaknesses in the state system and the problems people in China face as they experience both industrialization and marketization. She is right to point to the many signs of progress and the commitment of people within and outside the Chinese state to tackling problems and meeting the needs of the most vulnerable. We think, too, that many of the contributions to this volume are valuable not just for giving us insights into the local welfare picture across China but also for their revealing portrayals of ordinary people and the stoicism, persistence and initiative with which they face often difficult circumstances, as well as the generosity, compassion and dedication they bring to helping others. We hope that together these nuanced accounts contribute to understanding China as it is experienced locally by its people, and that in doing so this book might in some small way contribute to developing new means of identifying and assisting those least able to cope with the upheavals of rapid economic and social change.

Jane Duckett
Beatriz Carrillo
Glasgow and Sydney
June 2010

Glossary of Chinese terms

Pinyin terms are in bold, followed by the English translation.

chengzhen zhigong jiben yiliao baoxian   urban employee basic medical insurance

hezuo yiliao zhidu   cooperative medical system (CMS)

jiedao banshichu   neighbourhood office, or street office

san wu   'Three Nos'

shehui baoxian   social insurance

shehui baozhang   social security

shehui fuli   social welfare

shehui jiuji   social assistance

shequ   community

shiye baoxian   unemployment insurance

wubaohu   'Five Guarantee Households'

yanglao baoxian   old-age insurance

zuidi shenghuo baozhang (dibao)   'Minimum Livelihood Guarantee' (MLG)

Map 1.1 Provincial-level administrative divisions of the People's Republic of China (PRC)

1 China's changing welfare mix
Introducing the local perspective
Jane Duckett and Beatriz Carrillo

After three decades of marketization and high-level economic growth China is incomparably richer, but its social problems have changed rather than diminished.[1] While average incomes have risen, so have inequalities between individuals, between countryside and cities, and between coastal and interior regions (Khan *et al.* 1992; Khan and Riskin 1998; Khan *et al.* 2001; Khan and Riskin 2005; Sato and Li 2006). And while the number of rural dwellers in absolute poverty has fallen, urban poverty has been on the increase (Leung 1994; Guan 1995; Leung and Wong 1999). In the cities, meanwhile, average living standards have climbed but so have unemployment and people's expectations.

How is China dealing with its changing social problems and what do they mean for its welfare system and its most vulnerable people?[2] A growing body of work has set out and assessed state policies introduced to tackle the problems nationwide (for an overview see Saich 2008; Song and Appleton 2008). There have been studies of policies in the spheres of poverty alleviation (Chen and Ravallion 2008), housing (Wang and Murie 1999), social insurance (Saunders and Shang 2001; Duckett 2003), health (Hindle 2000; Liu 2002; Duckett 2010), and unemployment and laid off worker provision (Solinger 2002; Solinger 2005).

The focus on national state policies and public provision is understandable: China's pre-reform welfare system was embedded in, and premised on, an economic system of state planning and was dominated by the state. But the state's predominance has been weakened by economic marketization and political liberalization over the last three decades, and as a result China's 'welfare mix' – the balance of state, market, family and third-sector provision – has changed.[3] First, as economic policies have increased the role of markets and private business have reduced that of the state in the economy, labour has become more commodified while private for-profit provision is emerging in some parts of the welfare system (Zhang 2003; Zhang 2006; Hou and Coyne 2008). Second, although studies have often understated the supporting welfare role that the family played under the command economy, the commodification of labour and the marketization of welfare provision have increased its role. Third, political liberalization (although limited) has led to

2 *Jane Duckett and Beatriz Carrillo*

the emergence of a civil society that includes not-for-profit organizations and informal community groups working in the welfare sphere (White *et al.* 1996; Howell 2003; Read 2008; Saich 2008).[4] Overall, then, China's mix of state, market (private sector), family and third sector in the provision of welfare has been reconfigured from one dominated by state and family, to one with a growing role for private provision and third sector involvement (Wong and Tang 2006).[5] At the same time, the nature as well as extent of state and family provision has changed.

But China's welfare mix will vary between localities.[6] As we discuss at more length below, there are two well-established reasons for this. First, since 1978 there has been decentralization within the state of many of the public resources and responsibilities for delivering welfare (Wong 2000; Lin 2004; Hussain 2007; Zhang and Shih 2008). While the central government still defines the national public policy framework, local governments now have more space to adjust policies during implementation and encourage or discourage non-state provision. Second, local economies have diverged in terms of wealth (measured in per capita gross domestic product), development (measured in degree of industrialization and growth of the tertiary sector) and private-sector development (the importance of the non-state sector to the local economy), as well as amounts of foreign trade and investment. This in turn has increased the differences between localities in terms of public and private (business and family) resources for welfare, social problems (patterns and rates of poverty, unemployment, migration and demographic change) and the likelihood of the private sector filling gaps in state provision. While there was sub-national variation under state planning, it has increased – and continues to increase – in the era of market-oriented reform.

Growing variation in sub-national experience means we need to build our understanding of China's changing welfare mix from the bottom up as well as from the top down. This book therefore adopts a 'local' perspective, showing not only local government initiatives and programmes, but also the services and support provided by families, informal social networks and community or third-sector organizations, as well as those delivered by private businesses on a commercial, for-profit basis. Its ethnographic chapters also reveal the experiences, attitudes and responses of often vulnerable people across China. The book cannot, and does not intend to, be comprehensive in its coverage. But through chapters that draw on original research in eight provinces, it shows and explains some of the transformations that are under way. From the thriving coastal city of Dalian (in Liaoning province) to a poor village in the interior province of Sichuan, from the centre of wealthy Beijing to a poor county in Jiangxi, the chapters cover a wide range of social welfare provisions, examining social assistance (that is benefits for people on low incomes), rural health and health insurance, education, housing for migrants, and benefits, social services and support for redundant women, elderly people and young people with disabilities (for a map of China showing the provinces and cities discussed in this volume, see p. xviii).

China's changing welfare mix 3

The book is multidisciplinary. It includes chapters by political scientists, sociologists, anthropologists and social policy researchers that take an array of approaches to the issue of understanding China's changing welfare mix. Reflecting their different disciplinary perspectives, the chapters also vary in their purposes. Some are written with the scholarly goal of explaining social policies or the experiences of social groups, while others focus more on showing the problems and gaps in provision and offer policy advice. All inevitably reflect the values and expectations of their authors, as well as perhaps the social welfare discourses of these authors' diverse home countries. Together, they demonstrate the breadth of disciplinary approaches and research methodologies being used to research social policies and welfare in China today. Some chapters (by Guan and Xu; Hammond; Solinger) focus on policies and their implementation, seeking to explain what shapes them locally. Others use quantitative population surveys to assess the impact of marketization and privatization on people in different localities (Mok and Wong) or the needs of particular social groups (Li and Duda). Almost half the chapters (Solinger; Liu; Lora-Wainwright; Boermel; Fisher, Shang and Xie) take an ethnographic approach and focus on the experiences, attitudes and resources of vulnerable people and communities in a context of changing public policies.[7] Sarah Cook's concluding chapter considers the other contributions and gives a thoughtful, balanced and informed overview of both the progress China has made and the enormous social welfare problems it continues to face.

This book is aimed at a wide readership, including not only scholars of Chinese social policy and welfare but also researchers, policy makers, journalists and others with an interest in understanding welfare and social change in China. For those readers unfamiliar with its historical origins and contemporary context, this chapter therefore first introduces China's welfare mix under the state planning system that operated from the 1950s into the 1980s and then discusses the welfare implications of economic marketization since the 1980s. It also considers the consequences of market-oriented policies and practices introduced into parts of the welfare system itself, wider political liberalization and the emergence of civil society.

The chapter then sets out the two main contributions that this book makes: first to explaining local variation in the welfare mix, and second to understanding its societal consequences and responses. It argues that chapters in this volume show the need to go beyond the currently dominant focus on fiscal decentralization and divergent local economies to explain variation in policies and the role of the state. First, Anna Boermel and Jieyu Liu show state provision to be variable even in the richest cities, where hierarchies of entitlement and industrial-sector successes and failures shaping intra-local variations. Second, Xinping Guan and Bing Xu, Daniel Hammond, Dorothy Solinger and Liu demonstrate how national and local governments and elites, their ideas, and the 'games' they play, as well as the legacies of pre-reform provision, also shape local policy innovation and implementation.

4   *Jane Duckett and Beatriz Carrillo*

This chapter also sets out how the quantitative, survey-based and ethnographic chapters enrich our understanding of people's attitudes and individual and collective responses to their problems in a context of (often limited) local public welfare provision. These chapters (particularly Liu; Mok and Wong) show both the unequal impact of marketizing policies and the unequal distribution of individual and family resources to deal with the insecurities those policies have brought. But they also (particularly Liu; Fisher, Shang and Xie) demonstrate the emergence of informal and more organized community and third-sector support.

The final section of this chapter summarizes and assesses China's changing mix of state, private, family and third-sector welfare provision and examines the gaps in our understanding of its evolution. It calls for more research to map and explain local variation in the welfare mix and in particular for more attention to be paid to understanding the impacts on families and women, as well as the factors behind the growth of private- and third-sector provision.

The welfare mix from plan to market

State and family welfare in the era of planning and full employment

Following the creation of the People's Republic of China in 1949, a nationwide welfare system was gradually established in tandem with the planned economy that nationalized urban industry and collectivized agriculture. Premised on full employment that virtually eradicated labour markets, and on highly restricted geographical mobility, welfare was delivered by the state primarily through the organizations that formed the foundation of economic activity, urban work places (or work units, *danwei*) and rural communes and production brigades. Although actual delivery was handled by workplaces and communes and funded locally, the entire system was founded on state plans that meant the state organized or subsidized provision, though more so in the cities than in the countryside.

This was a bifurcated system in which the welfare mix differed substantially between urban and rural areas. Urban work units were subsidized by the state to provide not only jobs for life, but also pensions, housing, education and health care to employees and their dependants – the so-called 'iron rice bowl'. The level of provision varied between employers dependent on whether they were state or collectively owned, or beneath central or local government.[8] But in the context of almost full employment and with many women in work, the vast majority of urban dwellers had access to state-backed welfare and high levels of security. The family was, however, a key supplementary institution for those without work – notably children, disabled people and those elderly people without a former work unit. Only people with 'no work, no family and no other means of support' (the so-called 'Three Nos', or *san wu*) were eligible for state support that usually took the form of very minimal material assistance and some social services organized and delivered by local government agencies. The state often tried to provide work for people with disabilities, establishing enterprises aimed primarily at employing them (Wong 1998).

In rural areas, welfare was delivered through the communes (state-organized collectives consisting of a number of villages) and production brigades (often the equivalent of a village) that were part of the state's organization of society and agricultural production at the sub-county government level. Rural welfare was very different from that provided in the cities. There were no pensions and the state did not provide housing, but the communes in the 1960s and 1970s, usually with some county government financial support, funded some basic education, cooperative medical schemes and health care, effectively ensured people had work, and gave some minimal support to households in the most absolute poverty (the so-called '*wubaohu*', or 'five guarantee households', 'guaranteed' a roof over their heads, clothing, food, basic medical care and burial expenses) (Dixon 1981). Here, too, however, the family remained a key institution that provided support for children, elderly and disabled people, and others unable to work.

In both urban and rural areas therefore, the mix was state (including the collective provision it organized) plus family, and there was no role for provision by private for-profit businesses or third-sector organizations. Private business was eradicated by the mid-1960s and with the state dominating all forms of social organization, genuine community or third-sector provision was stymied or taken over by the mid-1950s. In the cities for example, residents' committees, so-called grass-roots organizations actually dominated by local government, were used to deliver state support to the poorest and neediest (Dixon 1981).

Marketization, commercialization, privatization and China's welfare mix

The shift from state planning to 'socialist market economy' since the early 1980s has involved enormous changes in China's welfare system. State enterprises were at first given powers to make redundancies, eroding the full-employment system and enabling the commodification of labour. Then, as markets for goods and services replaced state allocation, enterprises also began to experience competitive pressures and lay off workers in significant numbers. Unemployment rose, particularly in the late 1990s and into the twenty-first century (Liu in this volume; see also Solinger 2001; Duckett and Hussain 2008). Moreover, market-induced competition also led state and urban collective enterprises to cut back or renege on pensions, health payments and housing for their employees (Davis 1988; Shan 1995; Selden and You 1997; Song and Chu 1997; West 1999; Zhuang 2002; Béland and Yu 2004; Frazier 2004; Saunders 2004). Similarly, planning era enterprises set up specifically to provide work for disabled people began to close because they were uncompetitive in the emergent market environment.

6   *Jane Duckett and Beatriz Carrillo*

Although national policies have promoted the replacement of work unit provision with local government-organized social insurance for old-age, medical treatment and unemployment, participation rates are well below the pre-reform levels and many urban dwellers are without pensions or pay for much of their health treatment out of their own pockets (Gao *et al.* 2001; Hu *et al.* 2008; Duckett 2010).[9] Participation rates are lower in part because as state and collective enterprises have been reformed, restructured, downsized and privatized, the share of the population working in them has declined. As a consequence, the numbers of unemployed and self-employed, as well as those working in the growing private and informal sectors has risen. Workers in these latter categories often do not participate in the local government schemes because their employers do not enrol them. As Boermel's chapter in this volume shows, some elderly and retired workers have also experienced difficulties as local governments or *shequ* (so-called 'communities' that are local government agencies) have taken over responsibility for them from work units.

In the countryside, as collective farming and the communes were dismantled in the early 1980s and household farming introduced, some of the state-backed collective safety nets for rural dwellers were cut. Although in some places rural industrial firms sustained collective income and provision into the 1990s, many experienced difficulties from then on and have been closed or privatized. Families, now in a household-based farming system, are taking on more of the burdens of care, particularly where cooperative medical schemes (CMS) that had provided basic assistance with the costs of medical treatment have still not been re-established. As Anna Lora-Wainwright's chapter shows, recent efforts to re-establish CMS may have begun to help some households, though the scheme is not (at time of writing) generous enough to cover the costs of more expensive treatments.

There has been some marketization and growing private, for-profit provision in welfare. While the private provision of certain former public goods and services has increased their quality and supply, it has at the same time reduced equality of access. In education, for example, while state schools remain widespread, private provision has expanded. Moreover, the costs to families even of state provision have been high in the late reform period because schools charge fees if not for tuition then for certain teaching materials and such things as uniforms, school trips and computer use (see Solinger's and Mok and Wong's contribution, as well as Kwong 1996; Mok 2001). Meanwhile, in health, although there are still relatively few private hospitals, small private practices are widespread, particularly in the countryside and urban public hospitals are now commercially oriented, with most of their income deriving from private, out-of-pocket payments. Lora-Wainwright vividly depicts the impact this has had on poor rural dwellers' attitudes toward doctors and seeking hospital treatment.

Urban housing is another sphere in which the state has retreated and markets have been allowed to emerge. As a result, the cost of housing has begun to rise and many urban residents have been forced to relocate to cheaper suburban districts because of the large-scale demolition and rebuilding perceived as critical to economic progress by Chinese urban planners (see Boermel in this volume, and Wang and Murie 1999). Marketization has nonetheless meant the growth of a supply of commercial housing for rural migrants drawn into the cities (Li and Duda's chapter) – important since newcomers often have been denied access to urban public housing and other public goods (Solinger 1999). Where some city governments have begun to provide migrant housing, however, Bingqin Li and Mark Duda argue that they have done so poorly on the basis of incorrect assumptions about the needs and wants of migrants. Their chapter shows that the options for migrants are limited in the relatively poor city of Taiyuan, the capital of Shanxi province, where there is as yet no state provision.

Up until the late 1990s, government policy towards private providers and public–private cooperation in the provision of public goods remained ambiguous (Meng *et al.* 2000). Meanwhile, ideological reformulations vis-à-vis the private sector by the central party-state allowed the promotion of private provision of public services and resultant emergence of 'welfare entrepreneurs' (Carrillo 2008). Yet, contrary to the claims of a 'shrinking state' and outright privatization (Blumenthal and Hsiao 2005), public-service supply in China has often resulted in a more complex pattern of provision in which state providers of health and education charge fees on a commercial basis and have incentives to generate revenues and new public-private partnerships are formed (Mok and Wong in this volume; Xu and Jones 2004; Carrillo 2008). However, there are yet no clearly articulated government strategies on just how private (both for-profit and not-for-profit) provision might complement public provision – even in health where hospital ownership has been hotly debated in recent years.

Political liberalization and the emergence of the third sector

While marketization and privatization have facilitated private provision of welfare, most notably in education, health, housing and social services, political liberalization has opened up some space for the 'third sector' activity in welfare that further adds to the diversity of the social welfare mix. Particularly since the 1990s, there has been substantial discussion of the emergence of civil society – organizations and activity in the interstices of state and family (White *et al.* 1996; Howell 2003; Saich 2008). While initially in the sphere of environmental activity, non-governmental or third-sector participation has now been found in the provision of health services for sex workers and support for AIDS orphans, as well as support and advice to people with particular illnesses such as HIV/AIDS, hepatitis, haemophilia and tuberculosis. Some of these organizations have also begun to extend their activities into lobbying for policy change (Duckett 2007b; Zhou 2009). Other research has shown third-sector education for the children of

8 *Jane Duckett and Beatriz Carrillo*

migrant workers. These include studies of grassroots attempts to provide education to migrant children in Guangdong and in Chengdu (Froissart 2003; Kwong 2004), and Carrillo's research on county social welfare provision in Shanxi (Carrillo 2011). Wong and Tang (2006) discuss third-sector provision for elderly people. In this volume, Karen Fisher, Xiaoyuan Shang and Jiawen Xie add to this literature with their study of the neglected area of not-for-profit provision of welfare and social services for young people with disabilities.

A changing state role

At the same time as marketization and liberalization have resulted in an expansion of non-state welfare provision, the state's role has changed. It has responded to labour commodification and marketization that it set in train, and to the rising unemployment and growing urban poverty (or at least their political consequences) that ensued, by transforming its own contribution to the welfare mix in some policy areas. As described by Liu in this volume, political imperatives have stimulated policies to reform the corroding system of work unit provision in the late 1990s and give responsibilities to local governments. With state enterprise reform and privatization high on the agenda, some protection for former state-sector employees now losing their jobs was politically important and resulted in reforms that set up social unemployment insurance run by local governments as well as enterprise-based 're-employment service centres' (RSCs). These were accompanied by policies establishing social old-age and health insurance in the cities. In the countryside, cooperative systems of health risk protection are being rebuilt (see Lora-Wainwright in this volume) and pensions, too, have been introduced, though they are spreading only slowly, so that the rural–urban divide remains. Nevertheless, local governments have taken from work units the responsibility for providing mandatory social insurance (that is financed by employers and employees), as well as financing public education and health services. They now also finance or part-finance (together with central government) means-tested social assistance. Welfare reforms have thus shifted responsibility for much welfare provision down from the centre and up from urban work units and rural collectives so that they have converged on local governments.

The replacement of work unit provision with local government-run social insurance and services for the unemployed indicates a transformation of the state's role rather than a simple withdrawal. But protection under these schemes remains lower than it was under the work unit system. This is in part because of poor government capacity to enforce employer participation or 'compliance' in old-age, unemployment and health insurance schemes (Duckett and Hussain 2008), but it may also be due to people's reduced understanding of their entitlements. In Liu's chapter, redundant women are unclear about the benefits they are due, and have a much weaker sense of

China's changing welfare mix 9

entitlement to those that the local government provides than to those delivered through their work units.

The central state also has established new programmes of social assistance (that is, monetary benefits provided by the state or local governments to people on low incomes). The 'Minimum Livelihood Guarantee' (MLG, in Chinese *zuidi shenghuo baozhang*, often abbreviated to '*dibao*') is the most important of these and is discussed in the chapters by Guan and Xu, Solinger and Hammond. The means-tested MLG is a fundamental safety net now financed by both central and local governments and in place across both urban and rural China. In the cities, MLG evolved, like RSCs and unemployment insurance, in part as the state tried to negotiate the political minefield of state enterprise reform. Hammond argues in his chapter that it won political support among the top leadership in the late 1990s as other systems of provision to compensate unemployed and 'laid off' workers encountered problems. Solinger's and Liu's chapters, however, show how efforts to reduce poverty have been undermined by other parts of the governmental system. Local government departments tasked with keeping city streets clean, for example, often remove people trying to earn a living as street vendors. Guan and Xu show MLG to have developed more slowly in the countryside where it lags in terms of both geographical reach and generosity apparently because it has been less politically pressing.

Finally, the state has announced that it is extending provision of social services for elderly and disabled people. This is part of a new '*minsheng*' initiative targeted at protecting people's livelihood in part by using social services to tackle some social inequities.[10] But provision seems to remain limited. Boermel's chapter concludes that the social services provided by the state even in wealthy central Beijing play only a very small part in the lives of the overwhelming majority of older residents. Similarly, Fisher, Shang and Xie in their chapter on a poor rural county, show the Disabled Persons Federation, a 'government-organized non-governmental organization', to be providing virtually no support for young disabled people and their families.

Overall, therefore, the state is providing more programmes through local governments as compared with the 1990s, though far from comprehensively. As Guan and Xu remind us, it also retains a dominant role in terms of policy making, though they show policy development to be often the outcome of interactions and relationships among a range of state institutions within central and local governments. Like Hammond, who looks at the role that intra-state policy sponsors played in the development of a variant of MLG, Guan and Xu indicate that academic researchers can play an important part in developing and supporting policies. They also show the stimulus that 'public opinion' can sometimes play. However, direct non-state influences on policy are limited. While private businesses and third-sector providers may lobby for policy change, their influence as yet seems relatively slight (see also Howell 2003; Duckett 2007b).

Explaining local variation in the welfare mix

Fiscal decentralization and divergent local economies

China's welfare mix has become increasingly varied between localities in the post-Mao period in part because of intra-state fiscal decentralization and divergent local economies. It is now widely accepted that fiscal decentralization from the early 1980s, while successfully encouraging local governments to focus on economic growth, also gave them responsibility for funding social provision (Wong 2007). Thus, although all provinces have experienced economic growth in the decades since 1978, the economies of some (mainly on the coast) have grown much faster than others (for example Unel and Zebregs 2006). These differing rates of economic growth have in turn increased differences between local governments in terms of fiscal capacity (e.g. Wong *et al.* 1995; World Bank 2002).

Differential fiscal capacity and its impact on welfare provision is evident not only at provincial level but right down to the lowest – county and urban district – levels.[11] Duckett (2002), for example, has demonstrated how fiscal capacity as well as economic development resulted in variable welfare provision across urban district governments in the wealthy city of Tianjin. Solinger in her chapter adds to this in her study of the MLG programme's implementation in the city of Wuhan, which she compares with other cities. Although the MLG is mandated nationwide by central policy, the levels of subsidy are set city by city, usually based on the local cost of living (though precise methods for establishing the subsidy vary from locality to locality). Other aspects of the programme can also vary: how eligibility criteria are defined (for example whether some informal work is permitted), and how strictly assessments of need are made. In considering what shapes the programmatic differences between localities, Solinger suggests the local finances and economy play a role. She examines the role of differential central subsidies or earmarked funds for localities (poorer provinces often receive more, somewhat offsetting inequalities) and the extent of poverty problems due to the local economic situation. Like Duckett, she finds fiscal decentralization and the local economy to be important even within cities, and sees some parts of Wuhan experiencing a downward spiral as deprivation limits employment and business opportunities, implying that local variation and divergences are reinforcing and difficult to reverse.

Local economies and their trajectories of development not only affect the social welfare mix through their impacts on local government resources and capacities, however. They also shape private and community resources. Adams and Hannum (2005: 100), for example, conclude their study of children's access to health insurance and education by saying that local resources 'conditioned the provision of social services, and that dimensions of community level of development and capacity to finance public welfare increasingly mattered for some social services'. Ka Ho Mok and Yu Cheung Wong in this volume show the greater private resources available for children's education in economically developed Beijing as compared with poor Lanzhou.

Thus fiscal decentralization and divergent local economies produce different social problems, different levels of state provision and different balances in the welfare mix. In poor localities, for example, there are likely to be high levels of poverty, fewer state resources for schooling, health and social services, and fewer private resources to compensate. The burden of family care is therefore likely to be higher. Fisher, Shang and Xie find limited state provision for young people with disabilities in their study of a poor county in rural Jiangxi, for example, and show the pressure on families to be high. Encouragingly, however, they also find valuable low-cost support delivered by local community organizations.

People in wealthier localities, however, may expect greater public support for their elderly relatives or children with disabilities. And in rich localities decentralization may protect resources that make innovations in welfare provision possible. Certainly, innovation and leading edge reforms seem to take place in the wealthier parts of the country. Lee and Warner (2004) have shown Shanghai's experimentation with re-employment services, for example, while Chow and Xu (2001) have set out Guangzhou's social security reforms. For richer areas, however, wealth can bring social problems and new welfare needs. Life expectancy is much greater in rich provincial-level cities such as Shanghai, for example, and puts greater pressure on pensions and health systems, while richer localities attract migrants with varying needs.

Beyond decentralization and local economies: actors, ideas and the legacies of state planning

As the discussion above indicates, local variation in state provision and the balance in the welfare mix is not simply a question of the wealth of a locality. While MLG may sometimes be more generous in richer cities, this is not necessarily the case, as Solinger's comparison of Wuhan and Lanzhou indicates. Guan and Xu's chapter, which provides important context for other chapters in this volume by sketching out the national institutional framework for social policy making, also shows how in the institutional context of fiscal decentralization social policies can evolve and be implemented variably through the interactions of both central and local government actors. They show how central and local governments have played games in efforts to try to get the other to finance the means-tested MLG programme, with local governments unwilling to implement policy until have been given central government financial support. The result has been slow and uneven implementation of the programme across China. Note, too, that Guan and Xu's arguments are relevant not only to the MLG. Urban social insurance schemes (old-age, health and unemployment insurance) introduced in the same decade also have been influenced by similar central–local games.

12   *Jane Duckett and Beatriz Carrillo*

Hammond, too, develops an actor-based explanation of the emergence in Dalian in the late 1990s of a local variant of the national MLG policy. He discusses Community Public Service Agencies' (CPSAs), 'self-organizations' of MLG recipients aimed at getting them involved in community work. He agrees that institutional factors – decentralization and the autonomy brought by Dalian's status as a city that for planning purposes lies directly beneath the central government – gave it leeway for policy innovation. But Hammond also shows the CPSAs to have been the product of the combined actions of three kinds of policy sponsors: Mayor Bo Xilai (an 'elite sponsor'), the city's Civil Affairs Bureaux (charged with administering MLG, 'an administrative sponsor') and academic researchers from outside Dalian ('ideas sponsors'). This explanation chimes with Solinger's claim that variation in the generosity of MLG was linked to city leadership views about their city's appearance, as well as to officials' interpretations of the goals of MLG and perhaps also to their perceptions of what motivates individuals to seek work and what the state's role in supporting the poor should be. Relatedly, Hammond found that affluent Dalian officials were motivated to develop CPSAs in part as a means to reduce benefit fraud.

Jieyu Liu, meanwhile, reveals how legacies of the pre-reform system shape intra-local variation in public provision in the twenty-first century. Liu recounts how even in the relatively economically developed city of Nanjing, state enterprise restructuring has left many women in very difficult circumstances and often with only informal support. But she also shows how some of the legacies of the state planned economy fed through to shape the provisions to workers. Notably, the nature of a workplace (whether it was an industrial workplace, a non-enterprise workplace or a part of the government administration) and its industrial sector affected the generosity of provisions.

Boermel, on the other hand, shows hierarchies of entitlement that are less a planning system legacy and more simply a matter of preferential policies for elites. Her chapter examines social services for older people in Jianwai, a prosperous area in Beijing's central business district with a high proportion of retired residents. She argues that despite some recent improvements in service delivery for this group, because of the economic importance of the business district, priority has been given to commercial redevelopment there, resulting in the demolition of many older residents' homes. She finds that the pursuit of a new socio-economic order in Jianwai has marginalized and displaced less well-off older people, while privileged civil servants retired from central government ministries are insulated from such changes and better provided for.

Taken together, these chapters therefore suggest the need to look beyond fiscal decentralization and differences in local economies to explain China's changing welfare mix. Local variation in state and non-state provision is often shaped by elites and their ideas, their 'games' and their interests, as well as by the legacies of Mao era planning, and the extent to which privatization and the third sector have been able to develop. Local variation in state provision may also be shaped by culturally driven past local practices not captured in this volume but demonstrated, for example, by Vivenne Shue's (2006) study of philanthropy in Tianjin and Carrillo's (2008) example of welfare provision by a Catholic congregation in a county in Shanxi province. Local clan and lineage practices and organizations may also affect the resources and capabilities of local communities. As yet these, like other non-economic factors, are little understood and deserve more research.

Societal consequences of the changing welfare mix

Growing family responsibilities

But what does the change in state, private and third-sector contributions to China's local welfare mix mean for the most vulnerable people in Chinese society? We can begin to explore this by looking at the implications of marketization and welfare system variation for the family, an important but often neglected source of China's social welfare provision. It is interesting that studies of China's welfare system tend to pay little attention to the family, though Chinese researchers and policy makers sometimes do argue that a significant role for the family is a particularly 'Chinese' cultural or Confucian phenomenon (Chan *et al.* 2008). Several contributions to this volume help fill this gap in understanding by examining the experiences of households or families and their role in supporting their children, sick and elderly, disabled and unemployed members. Mok and Wong analyse data from a 2004 survey of household spending on education to show the high levels of family spending on their children's education. Fisher, Shang and Xie show a family's efforts over many years to secure education and other support for their disabled son. Li and Duda's study of migrants' housing choices in Taiyuan finds that they are in part the result of their wider household strategies and marital status. Liu shows spouses sometimes sharing their social capital – networks of contacts – to help each other find work, while Boermel shows families providing care for the elderly.

But these works also reveal the poorest families struggling to provide adequately. Mok and Wong show that low-income households, especially in the relatively less well-developed city of Lanzhou, spend very high proportions of their income on educating their children, and much higher proportions than households in Beijing. Fisher, Shang and Xie also show the difficulties poor families have providing an adequate education for their disabled children. Li and Duda show migrants often living in very poor, unhealthy housing conditions. Solinger highlights the inter-generational impacts of limited state provision when poor families are unable to provide sufficiently for their children, arguing that children in poor families are unable to improve their chances because state provision through MLG policy is restricted to financial supplements and recipients are not linked into programmes to help with schooling, training and retraining. Liu, too, shows that all too often family members are equally poor in terms of the social networks that might help them find work.

14 Jane Duckett and Beatriz Carrillo

Lora-Wainwright's chapter demonstrates that even where families may be able to afford medical treatment for family members, they may decide against it in a poorly functioning health system. Her illuminating study of the perceptions, attitudes and health-seeking behaviour of poor villagers in rural north Sichuan explores the family dynamics of support for the sick. She shows that family (and individual) responses to illness are shaped not only by the high cost of treatment and the lack of trust in medical practitioners, but also by historical, social and cultural factors including Confucian notions of filial piety. These factors have combined in some cases to discourage people suffering from cancer, and their families, from seeking hospital-based medical treatment.

Looking within and beyond the family: individuals, gendered informal care and social networks

The ethnographic chapters in this volume remind us that reliance on the family alone is regressive because families have differential resources and capacities on which to draw. But to what extent are 'families' the right unit of analysis? And what are the consequences of increasing family responsibilities? Lora-Wainwright shows individual identities in the context of family and community as also important not only for the dynamics of family support but also for people's willingness to seek medical treatment. Solinger and Liu similarly show how people feel ashamed or demoralized by their inability to contribute to the family through work and how this is detrimental to their self-esteem.

Significantly, Liu's study of the experiences of redundant women workers in the city of Nanjing reveals the limitations of focussing on the family. Liu shows women to sometimes be disadvantaged in finding work by unchanged expectations in their families about their role in the home. She also finds women sometimes to retain the double burden of paid work and domestic unpaid work and child care even when their husbands are unemployed. In both Liu and Solinger's chapters, we see elements of a gender division of informal provision of care (care for children and disabled people), which has consequences for women's access to formal work and consequently to various kinds of social insurance. But this is unsurprising: as Kirk Mann (2008: 9) points out in relation to informal care (so-called because it is unpaid and not formally organized), 'the pattern of caring responsibilities has demonstrated considerable continuity over time and between countries', with the bulk of the care undertaken by women. Arksey and Glendinning (2007) thus argue that the concept of informal welfare needs to be recognized as a specific form of welfare provision and dependency (cited in Mann 2008: 9).

Several chapters show disadvantaged and vulnerable people across China often make careful calculations about their options so as to make the best of their situation. They indicate how rarely people turn to the state and how instead they draw on social networks – another informal safety net for those without access to state or private welfare provision. Lora-Wainwright reveals people using their networks to find trustworthy doctors in a semi-privatized health system perceived as profit-oriented, while Liu shows their uses in finding work where state re-employment services are lacking. Li and Duda reveal, too that for migrants to the city, who are excluded from public provision of goods, proximity to social networks is an important factor in shaping housing choices. Similarly, Boermel points out how in the face of limited social services and the threat of relocation from redevelopment the elderly, too, resort to using social networks and even create new ones.

Again, however, these informal networks, like families, have different capacities to assist: the well-off usually have better networks than the poor and thus better routes to employment and medical care. As other chapters also show, the elderly, the indigent and women tend to have the poorest networks. This is a point made particularly by Liu, but which is also evident in the situation of the recipients of MLG, as described by Solinger. Using their own words, she demonstrates recipients – often sick, disabled and elderly people – to be short of not only financial but also social capital, and to be marginalized or excluded from mainstream society.

Towards an understanding of China's welfare regime

For industrialized democracies the mix of state, market, family and third sector in the provision of welfare and security has been used to identify national welfare 'regimes' (Esping-Andersen 1990; Gelissen 2002; Mann 2008). Though we use the welfare-mix concept, however, we do not wish to imply that China's welfare system resembles its Western counterparts, or that it is converging with them. Indeed, we think it premature to pronounce on where China fits in the range of types that have been identified internationally. Documenting and explaining variation in the mix as it evolves across China is an enormous task and one that this volume can only begin to tackle. We cannot therefore go so far as to comprehensively characterize China's welfare system or even identify emergent local variants in particular localities. But we do venture some concluding remarks on the trends that emerge from our bottom-up as well as top-down explorations. We also identify where the most glaring gaps in knowledge indicate scope for further research.

Pre-reform China had what might be termed a 'state socialist-conservative' regime that privileged the urban working classes, provided less comprehensively and invested less in the countryside, and retained the family as an important if secondary element. It was conservative in that, like Bismarckian Germany, it provided segmented programmes mainly for key (urban) political support bases and relied significantly on the family. But it was state socialist in delivering public, almost universal, egalitarian security for urban workers, and in attempting to provide collective security (albeit much less generously) for the rural population. There was no role for the private or third-sector provision in either city or countryside.

16   *Jane Duckett and Beatriz Carrillo*

The balance of that mix has shifted significantly towards one today in which the state is providing not through fundamental organizations of production but through local governments, while private-sector (and joint public–private) provision has grown substantially in education, health services and housing. The third sector has grown, though it is constrained, patchy, localized and has few resources. The result is that the role of informal support through families and social networks has expanded, disadvantaging the poorest and many of the most vulnerable, such as women and elderly and disabled people. Thus there has been a retreat of the state-socialist, redistributive element of the mix and an increase in its conservative elements, with provision increasingly segmented as new programmes are added to existing ones. Reliance on the family – and the burden on women – remains higher than in the pre-reform period, particularly in rural areas.[12]

But the particular mix will vary for different spheres of welfare and in different localities depending on private and community as well as local government resources. In addition, decentralization of resources has provided space for policy innovation through which local governments have found their own strategies for balancing public–private provision within the framework of national policies and regulations. There, closer relationships between state and market and between government and society (Goodman 2001) may have fostered greater cooperation between local governments and the private sector, to undertake tasks previously deemed solely within the state's sphere. Thus the mix is not simply about mutually exclusive provision that is zero sum. As Fisher, Shang and Xie show, state and non-state may work together and certainly interact as they have in the Jiangxi county they have studied. There, deaf people have set up organizations which have also become an indispensable intermediary between disabled people and local government agencies in charge of delivering state support.

Local strategies – both public and private – continue, however, to be influenced by changes in national policy, which since the late 1990s have shifted the emphasis away from economic growth alone towards a growth strategy that is more socially responsible. This approach has recently been publicized using the slogan of 'building a harmonious society', and would seem to be a deliberate strategy by the Chinese Communist Party (CCP) leadership to regain trust from a society experiencing growing inequality. Formally endorsed by the CCP Central Committee in October 2006 this formulation distinguishes the current top leadership's commitment to tackling a series of social problems, including the growing wealth gap, corruption, access to education and health, and pollution (Kahn 2006). A year later, during the 17th Party Congress, the government reiterated its commitment to building a harmonious society by promoting the acceleration of social development with an emphasis on improving people's livelihood or *minsheng* (Hu 2007, see also Boermel in this volume).

While the relationship between centrally dictated polices and local circumstances will continue to influence welfare provision throughout China, a changing mix will also shape individuals' perceptions of the state and its role as provider and guarantor of welfare. Yet China's evolving welfare mix is also shaped by the attitudes of local decision-making elites toward such issues as the place of markets and private sector, and notions of social justice and equity. Some of these attitudes are revealed by Hammond, for example, who shows widely-held views among the urban elite that the poor are more deserving of state assistance if they work. More recently, these views have also been influenced by popular discourses on 'population quality' (*renkou suzhi*), which are used as markers of social distinction that create a complex social hierarchy of deserving and undeserving members in the urban environment (Anagnost 2004; Murphy 2004; Shue and Wong 2007a). But attitudes are shaped by debates conducted in the media (even though they are often controlled or delimited by state actors), within think tanks and within state agencies as well as by ideas that filter up through these institutions and from more direct action from wider society. They may also be influenced by external actors – not only the international organizations operating in China but also Chinese and international researchers such as those writing in this volume, whose own values and attitudes underpin their analyses and policy recommendations. Liu, for example, is critical of state policies that have disadvantaged women workers, Mok and Wong see privatization as a pragmatic state response to the problems of supplying education through the state alone, and Lora-Wainwright contests Fan's (2006) argument that pre-reform collectivist and egalitarian commitments should be supplanted by a Confucian medical professionalism that can function morally within a profit-driven market economy.

Changes may also come from socio-economic pressures. As experiences elsewhere have shown, low employment rates and financial strain can heighten in society a sense of government responsibility for economic provision and redistribution of income (Blekesaune 2006) and potentially create demand for state interventions. Yet, conversely, a problematical condition *per se* may not be sufficient to bring an issue to the fore (Skocpol 1994) or to create the necessary incentives for reform (Geva-May and Maslove 2000), particularly if it involves vulnerable sectors of society without powerful backing.

Given these multiple influences and China's size and diversity, a single volume cannot hope to capture the full range of social problems and local patterns of welfare provision. We still have, for example, a poor understanding of the range of local experiences of social problems – from unemployment, to poverty, inequality and ill-health – and of how and why local governments and communities are (or are not) tackling them. And we have just as limited an understanding of how some people experience the problems and provisions in the changing welfare mix. To take just one example, there is a glaring gap in our understanding of the perspectives of the better off. While Mok and Wong and Boermel's chapters offer glimpses of their situation, most studies (understandably) look at the most vulnerable. Similarly, we have only

18 *Jane Duckett and Beatriz Carrillo*

begun to understand the extent and range of private and third-sector provision. Moreover, China's national and local policies are changing quickly, the balance of market and state in some policy arenas has become a subject of debate, the role of third-sector provision continues to grow, while family structures and relationships are in flux. Clearly, then, the opportunities for further research are enormous. We hope that this book – through both its omissions and its revelations – demonstrates not only the possibilities for locally grounded research in Chinese social welfare but also the fascinations and rewards of that endeavour.

Notes

1 The literature on this topic generally is growing (Lee 1993; Guan 2000; Gu 2001; Saunders and Shang 2001; Shue and Wong 2007b).
2 We use 'welfare system' and 'welfare' to refer to provision of material social assistance for the poor (income support benefits), social (old-age, health and unemployment) insurance, social services, health care, education and housing.
3 The concept of 'welfare mix' has been used to compare Western welfare system variation in the combination of state, market and family provision (Esping-Andersen 1990). The 'third sector' is that part of civil society that delivers welfare on a not-for-profit basis and which can play a political role in shaping welfare regimes (Evers 1995). The welfare mix was referred to as the 'social division of welfare' by Titmuss (1958), as discussed in Mann (2008).
4 Although there is some debate over use of the term 'civil society' in contemporary China, it is often used to refer to the emergence of new kinds of societal organizations.
5 Although conceived to help understand welfare provision in democratic states with well-developed market economies and civil societies, given the economic and political transformations in China over the last three decades, the concept of 'welfare mix' is useful for exploring that country's welfare system change. 'Welfare mix' is more appropriate for China than the 'welfare pluralism' that others, including Wong and Tang (2006) use. This is because the term welfare pluralism itself has been associated with normative approaches that advocate voluntary welfare provision and a reduced state role (see Beresford and Croft 1983).
6 'Locality' is conventionally used to describe provincial and sub-provincial areas of China, usually defined using administrative jurisdictions in the governmental hierarchy (province, prefecture, county, township, with cities at provincial, prefecture and county levels).
7 It is because some chapters, most notably Dorothy Solinger's, span both policy and ethnographic research that we have not divided the book into sections.
8 State-owned enterprises and central government work units had more resources and so provided more generously than urban collective enterprises and local government units.
9 Medical expenses have been shown to be one of the main causes of rural poverty (Lindelow and Wagstaff 2005) and to have direct consequences on intergenerational equity on most other socio-economic indicators (Fitoussi and Saraceno 2008).
10 Thanks to Anna Boermel for this point.
11 Note, however, that the degree of fiscal decentralization varies between localities, and this too can affect welfare provision. Hiroko Uchimura and Johannes Jütting (2007), testing the specific link between fiscal decentralization and health outcomes,

found that counties in more fiscally decentralized provinces showed lower infant mortality rates, though outcomes were also dependent on the fiscal capacity of each county government.

12 See Esping-Andersen (1990) on conservative welfare regimes: key features of such regimes, even in democratic political systems, is their segmented provision, with better provision for elites, and a strong emphasis on the role of the family. Both the new rural CMS and urban residents health insurance programmes are examples of new programmes grafted onto the existing system in recent years.

2 Central–local relations in social policy and the development of urban and rural social assistance programmes

Xinping Guan and Bing Xu

Social welfare in China has experienced many changes in recent years that reflect in turn changes in government social policy. Social policy can be seen as the outcome of a series of government institutional actions to provide social welfare for people in need, and include pensions, health care, education, housing, social assistance and social welfare for the elderly, disabled and children. In China, as in many other countries, such social welfare provisions are financed not only by government, but from a mixture of different sources. For example pension programmes are financed by both employers and employees, education is paid for mainly by the government but with some user payments, and social assistance, including the Minimum Livelihood Guarantee (MLG), is paid for entirely by the government. This mixture of sources of finance means the involvement of many actors in the social policy arena, including governments at both central and local levels, enterprises and non-governmental organizations (NGOs), as well as welfare beneficiaries themselves.

In social policy making and implementation, actors play out their roles in the context of institutional relationships. The success of a social policy action – the action taken in making or implementing a social policy – will depend not only on top government leaders' political will, but also on the nature of institutional relationships, and on the effect and efficiency of the interactions between actors. Three kinds of relationship between key social policy actors are important for a successful social policy action: the relationship between central and local governments; among governments, enterprises and NGOs; and among ministries and government departments at various levels. In contemporary China, social policy issues and debates are mainly conducted through these three kinds of relationship. But the most important relationships shaping China's social policy are those between central and local governments.

A brief review of central–local relations in social policy

In the centrally planned economic system that existed before the reforms began, state power was centralized, almost all social policies were made by central government and local governments were merely subordinate agencies who were required to straightforwardly implement the central government's policies. Although the over-centralized policy-making model was criticized in

1950s, it was not fundamentally changed until the reform era, especially in social policy. In the pre-reform period, moreover, social welfare benefits and other social services were paid for either directly by governments or state enterprises, or in rural areas by collective economic organizations (such as communes or production brigades), but many were ultimately backed by the central government through the planning system (see Figure 2.1).

Since the early 1980s, however, central–local relations in the social policy arena have changed significantly. Decentralization in social policy has gone hand-in-hand with the process of economic marketization. At first, in the early 1980s, the central government decided to increase the managerial autonomy of enterprises that had hitherto funded some social provisions. In 1983, the central government decided to replace the former enterprise 'profit sharing' system with a new tax system. This meant that enterprises should pay taxes to the government, and keep and make use of all the after-tax profits (Liu 2004).

The next important action impacting on central–local relations in social policy was the tax reform of 1994, by which the central and local governments

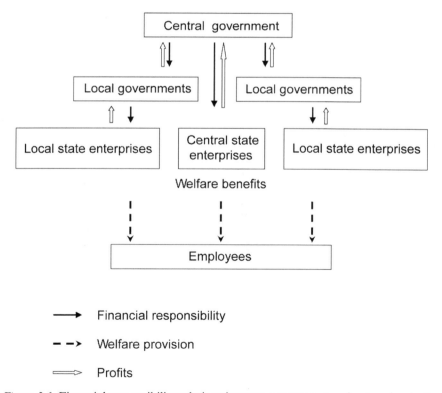

Figure 2.1 Financial responsibility relations between government and enterprises in the pre-reform period (urban).

22 Xinping Guan and Bing Xu

divided their tax sources so that each had its own sources of tax revenues (State Council 1994) (see Table 2.1). At the same time, the expenditure responsibility was also divided between central and local governments. Under this new tax system, most social expenditures were paid for by local governments with the exception of those for the employees of the enterprises and other organizations directly under the central government. The central government then further localized many former central government enterprises and organizations, including education, science and cultural organizations, thus concomitantly further decentralizing social expenditure responsibilities. This put a significant burden of responsibility for social welfare on local governments (World Bank 2002), and is one of the main causes of declining welfare in the 1990s.

Central–local relations in the Chinese governmental system today

A country's central–local relations in the sphere of social policy are fundamentally influenced by its governmental system. As a first step to understanding central–local relations in China's social policy, it is therefore helpful to outline three key sets of relationships in its governmental system: the responsibility relationships that govern who bears responsibility for policy-making and financing; the organizational relationships that govern the interactions among various actors involved in social policy making and implementation; and the authority relationships between central and local governments that govern who has actual decision-making power. We will look at each of these in turn.

Central–local responsibility relations

There are several dimensions to consider in analysing the responsibility relations between central and local governments in the public administration system. Of these, three are the most important: those relating to policy making, implementation and financing (see Table 2.2). These three dimensions are common to many public policy areas, but are particularly important in social policy where many joint governmental actions are needed and many actors may be involved.

These three dimensions are crucial for a successful social policy action. And in a good governmental system, there should be consistency in the allocation of responsibility across them all. In a centralized governmental system, all dimensions should consistently place responsibility with the central government; while in a local model, responsibility across all the three dimensions should be with the local government; and in a shared system, responsibility should be shared by central and local governments in the same or similar ratios. For instance, in a centralized system where the policy decision is made mainly by the central government there should be centrally organized implementation as well as central responsibility for finance. Many problems in

Table 2.1 Central local division of expenditure responsibility in the tax reform of 1994

Central financial expenditure	*Local financial expenditure*
1. Central administrative costs	1. Local administrative costs
2. Police/procurator/judiciary (central share)	2. Police/procurator/judiciary (local share)
3. Armed police under the centre	3. Local armed police
4. Military	4. Local militia
5. Construction investment under centre	5. Construction investment at local level
6. Technical innovation and new product trials in centrally enterprises	6. Technical innovation, new product trials and manufacture in locally-owned enterprises
7. Agriculture (central share)	7. Agriculture (local share)
8. Culture/education/health/science expenditures for the organizations directly owned by central government and their staff.	8. Culture/education/health expenditures for all the local people and the organizations owned by local governments.
9. Diplomacy & foreign aid	9. Urban public utilities and construction
10. Geological exploration	10. Price subsidies (public subsidies to keep the prices lower, and some cash subsidies to local employees to compensate for such things as higher food prices caused by price reforms).
11. Repayment of state debt	And some other local expenditures.

Source: State Council (1994).

24 *Xinping Guan and Bing Xu*

social policy actions appear when there is inconsistency among the three dimensions. For instance, a social policy is likely to encounter big problems if a policy is made by central government but the responsibility for financing it is given to local governments. In the following we set out how this kind of problem has affected social policy in China and offer suggestions about how it should be resolved.

Central–local and cross-sectoral organizational relations

Central–local relationships are much more complicated if not only central and local governments as a whole but also individual central ministries and local government bureaus are taken into consideration (see Figure 2.2). The central government, that is the State Council, has mandatory authority over provincial governments and then provincial governments over the next level of government below them and so on down through the hierarchy. But at the central level, there are several ministries in charge of social services of various kinds, including the Ministry of Civil Affairs (MCA), which handles social welfare and social assistance; the Ministry of Human Resources and Social Security (MHRSS), which handles employment and social insurance; the Ministry of Education (MOE), which handles education; the Ministry of Health (MOH), which handles health services; and the Ministry of Housing and Urban-Rural Development (MHURD), which handles housing policy. All these ministries have their counterparts (bureaus) at local levels – that is within local governments. Ministries in social administration, however, usually have no mandatory authority directly over the local governments, and can only advise provincial bureaus and the subordinate bureaus in their own vertical 'systemic' hierarchy (*xitong*).

Second, at the central level, the State Council has mandatory authority over ministries and at the provincial level the provincial governments have

Table 2.2 Key responsibility relationships

Decision-making	Who takes prime responsibility for making decisions in public policy, or at which level are public policies mainly made? Do local governments have the right to make a decision to set up a public policy programme, or refuse to implement a programme that has been formulated or suggested by the central government?
Implementation	Who will take the responsibility in organizing and administering the implementation of public policy programmes?
Financial responsibility	How is the financial responsibility divided among central and local governments? Is it entirely a central responsibility, entirely a local responsibility, or is it shared by central and local governments at different levels? If shared, then what is the ratio of central to local?

Central–local relations in social policy 25

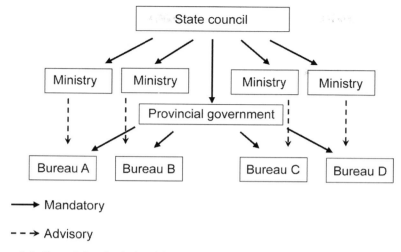

Figure 2.2 Central–local relationahips within the governmental system.

mandatory authority over their bureaus. And at the lower levels there are the same mandatory relations between governments and their bureaus.

Third, ministries or bureaus at the same level have in principle the same administrative authority – that is they are of the same rank, but they have different responsibilities in dealing with public affairs and have significant power in their own administrative fields. Due to their different relationships to key resources, notably public finance, the actual authority or power of ministries or bureaus at the same level can be different.[1] Since the ministries usually play very important roles in putting policies on the agenda it is meaningful to take them as important independent actors in the analysis of central–local relations in social policy making and implementation.

In addition to ministries with direct social policy responsibilities, there are some ministries and central government commissions and offices that control the distribution of public resources and policy-making procedures. These include most notably the Ministry of Finance (MOF), which allocates public financial resources; the National Development and Reform Commission (NDRC), which directs overall economic and social development planning and approves major social programmes; the State Commission Office for Public Sector Reform (*zhongyang jigou bianzhi weiyuanhui bangongshi*, SCOPSR), which controls the establishment of government bodies and their personnel quotas; and the Legislative Affairs Office of the State Council (LAO), which directs legislative procedures in policy making. These four ministry-level bodies control four crucial resources and sets of procedures in policy making: finance, planning, organization and personnel, and legislative procedures. All other ministries have to work with them when making policy in their own fields. These four government bodies are replicated at each level of provincial and sub-provincial governments.

26 *Xinping Guan and Bing Xu*

Actual authority relations

The above discussion relates only to the formal administrative relationship between the central ministries and local bureaus. In practice, the actual relationships between them are also importantly influenced by the central ministries' deployment of resources. Although local bureaus have no formal obligation to directly obey a ministry, they usually tend to follow ministry's advice because the latter not only represents central authority, but also controls resources, mainly financial resources. For example, ministries have much influence over decisions to distribute central funds to local social welfare programmes. And those provinces that perform well in social welfare programmes under the guidance of central ministries may be rewarded with more central funds. The ministries also have some so-called 'policy resources', notably the power to permit a special 'favourite policy' that allows localities to go beyond the national regulations. This was especially relevant in the early reform period when central regulations were very rigid.

Local government autonomy in social policy

In spite of the centralized governmental system, local governments still have some autonomy in making and implementing social policy, as well as in many other public policy arenas. But the scope of local autonomy has been different in different periods. Before the reforms began, local autonomy was very limited, and most, if not all, social policies were made by the central government. Local governments only had to implement them. In the reform period, local governments have gradually acquired more space to innovate and develop their own social policies. Local innovation in social policy began with policy implementation, as local governments often added details to the policies made by the central government, and sometimes made changes to the central-made policies so that they fit the local situation. But there has also been local innovation in social policy making, with local governments making new policies based on their own needs. The central government and its ministries usually agree or give tacit consent to local innovations if they are not violating the core principles of central policy, or even publicly encourage local innovations if they are in keeping with the central government's aspirations. Indeed some locally developed policies have been recognized and extended to the whole country by the central government, and have thus become national policies. The MLG is one example of this, as we shall see below.

Current characteristics of central–local relations in the social policy process

China has a centralized, multi-level governmental system in which the central government holds supreme power. There are five main levels of government from the top to the bottom: centre, province, prefecture, county and township.

Central–local relations in social policy 27

Cities can be situated at provincial, 'semi-provincial',[2] prefectural or county levels. This means analysing central–local relations is far from straightforward, perhaps especially in relation to social policy because it often involves joint public spending from governments of various levels.

Central–local relations in social policy making

First of all, both central and local governments at various levels have authority to make a social policy within their jurisdiction, although lower governments' policies cannot contravene higher level ones. It is not stipulated in national laws and regulations, but it has become common practice that many new social policy programmes and initiatives have been first set up by particular local governments, independently or at the suggestion and under the guidance of central government ministries.

Second, ministries often play a significant role in promoting new social policy initiatives by making policy suggestions, spreading local initiatives, organizing policy research and experiments, drafting policy documents, and drawing up the technical norms for a social policy. The ministries have strong authority in making technical norms and supervising local governments' implementation of a social policy according to laws and state regulations, but they usually cannot independently make a compulsory decision to initiate a significant new social programme, because the making and implementation of most of major social policies are beyond a single ministry's domain. In other words, local governments can make decisions about whether or not and in what form to follow a ministry's policy suggestion. Note that most social policies fall within the domain of several key ministries and it is a common practice that several ministries jointly issue a social policy document. When a compulsory national policy is needed, it is usually the State Council that issues an authoritative document.

Third, it is the State Council that normally issues official documents that set out nationwide social policy decisions. This is usually done when the policy practice has 'matured' through some local experiments. Local governments cannot refuse to implement a State Council social policy decision, but, in most cases, they have authority to decide on certain details, including the timing, scope, benefits level and scope of expenditure. Often, after a social policy has been set up and implemented nationwide, the State Council will issue a state regulation to bring into line local government implementation practices.

Central–local relations in social policy implementation

As noted above, lower-level governments are obliged to implement higher governments' compulsory social policy decisions – this includes State Council decisions, but sub-provincial governments must also implement provincial government decisions and so on down the hierarchy. Lower-level governments first make concrete plans to implement the policy, in which some necessary

28   *Xinping Guan and Bing Xu*

adjustment may be made to enhance implementation, but adjustments must not contravene the main principles of the policy. The implementation of social policies is organized and administered by the relevant local government bureau (for example the Bureau of Human Resources and Social Security or the Bureau of Civil Affairs). Where a policy is beyond a single bureau's administrative capacity, cross-departmental bodies may be set up to coordinate them.

Organizational systems in the social policy process

First, as shown in Figure 2.2, there are various vertical lines of central–local organization, but the vertical governmental relations between central and local governments are not the same as the vertical departmental relations between ministries at central level and bureaus in the localities. While the State Council requires the provincial governments to implement a social policy by issuing a compulsory policy document, usually a 'decision' (*jueding*) or a 'notification' (*tongzhi*), and the provincial governments in turn require the lower-level governments to do so, the ministries usually provide technical guidance to the bureaus at provincial or lower levels in the same ministerial system and supervise their implementation.

Second, because the administrative relations between central ministries and local bureaus are weaker than those between levels of government, but are the main channels from central to local in technical design and social policy details, local governments still have space to decide whether or not, or to what extent, to accept the detailed arrangements of a social policy set out by central government ministries. Therefore, in many cases, with the agreement of the head of the local government, bureaus may, to some extent extend or modify ministerial policy details so long as they do not violate the main principles of central government's policy.

Central–local relations in fiscal arrangements in the social policy process

Central–local fiscal relations are one of the most important and complicated aspects of wider central–local social policy relations. According to institutional arrangements created in the 1994 taxation reform, almost all the social projects at provincial and sub-provincial levels should in principle be paid for by local governments (State Council 1994). But it has become common practice in recent years for the central government to share part of the financial burden, and in some cases even share a high percentage of that burden by providing central funds to provinces with fiscal difficulties. However, so far there has been no formal legislative or governmental administrative regulation for central government financial transfers to local governments. Without institutional regulation, the central government has a large free space in the decision on the total central payments to local welfare projects, and its distribution to each province. But while central funds have played an important role in promoting social welfare projects at local level in recent years, especially in less-developed regions, the lack of institutional regulation also causes complicated bargaining between central and local governments and, to different degrees, the dependency of some local governments on central funds. As a result, some local governments are not active in setting up a social policy programmes by themselves until the central government has promised to pay for it.

Thus there are actually three kinds of financial arrangements in relation to social policy: wholly central funding, wholly local funding, and a mixture of both central and local sources. Actual arrangements are made mainly through central–local negotiations, which do not follow a formal policy process. In other words, they are not governed strictly by formal regulations. Instead, central and local governments negotiate the financial arrangement for each individual project. These kinds of fiscal structures and the related inter-governmental negotiations are not restricted to the social policy arena, but are more common for social policies. While this kind of practice gives the central government more manipulating space and thus more targeting in many cases in the allocation of central transfers, it may have a higher risk of 'rent-seeking' from lower-level governments. As some researchers have pointed out (Wong, C. 2009: 942), it may even cause some central–local tensions or some breakdown of central–local relations, which may in turn hinder the implementation of national policies.

Central–local relations in the Minimum Livelihood Guarantee

The MLG is a core programme in China's social assistance system. It provides poor families with basic cash benefits so that their income reaches a locally defined minimal level. Unlike the enterprise-based social welfare provisions that have been discussed earlier in this chapter, MLG is not delivered or financed by enterprises, but is a direct responsibility of the government. The MLG programme has been one of the most successful in China's social policy system since the 1990s, and now plays a very important role in providing social security in both urban and rural areas. By analysing and comparing the development of MLG in urban and rural areas since the early 1990s, we can see how central–local relations – both formal and informal – shape social policy making and implementation.

The urban Minimum Livelihood Guarantee

There were several steps in the establishment and development of the urban MLG system, from which we can see some of the key characteristics of central–local relations in social policy making and implementation. The first stage involved the preparation of the MLG (from the late 1980s to the early 1990s). Before the reform period, there was only a small social assistance programme in urban China to provide cash benefits to urban poor people categorized as the 'Three Nos' (*san wu*). During that period only a small group of urban people were entitled to this benefit. After the economic reforms began, especially in the late 1980s and early 1990s, however, urban unemployment and poverty increased as a result of state enterprise reform, but the old social relief system could not deal with the rising poverty because of its strong entitlement constraints. A new universal social assistance programme was therefore necessary to help families on low incomes. For this reason, some researchers suggested from the early 1990s that a new social assistance programme be developed (Tang 1992, 1994).

In the second stage, from 1992 to 1997, local governments pioneered new practices. It was not the central government, but some local governments who first responded to the new poverty problem and took up researchers' suggestions for a new social assistance programme. Shanghai and some other cities were the first to establish a new universal social assistance system, the MLG (Zhang 1994). Shanghai pioneered the programme in 1993 but was followed soon by some other provinces and cities with the support of the Ministry of Civil Affairs (MCA), which was in charge of social assistance. The MCA played an important role in promoting the new programme, disseminating pioneer cities' experiences to other cities, preparing the national programme, and suggesting the State Council require all cities set up the new system.

In the third stage, from 1997 to 1999, the programme was promoted nationwide. After several years of local pioneering, the State Council in 1997 issued an important document that asked all cities nationwide to set up MLG (State Council 1997). All cities then did this according to the State Council's requirement over the next two years. However, because the State Council's document only set a compulsory requirement for local governments to set up MLG, but did not issue regulations detailing of the programme until 1999, local governments initially had a great deal of leeway in how MLG actually operated. This meant that where local governments were unwilling to spend significantly on MLG, the average population coverage and benefits level were often low, and the local programmes were run in different ways.

In the fourth stage, from 1999 to 2002, MLG was subject to regulation by the State Council. In 1999, following two years of national expansion, the State Council issued a new set of MLG regulations in which most of the main institutional arrangements were set out (State Council 1999). These central government regulations were compulsory administrative regulations and all local governments were required to comply with them. Under these regulations, the urban MLG was established as mainly a local government responsibility, and most importantly, it was stipulated that it should be paid for by local governments. The general practice in that period was that the financial costs for the MLG in a city were shared by the municipal government and its districts governments. Since in most cities the local governments, especially those at the district level, had financial difficulties, they tended to strictly control entitlement and the average benefit level so that actual coverage in most cities was very small. Up to 2000, there were only around four million beneficiaries nationwide (MCA 2000). Although there was a big increase in 2001, the total number of MLG beneficiaries that year still stood at only 11.7 million across all Chinese cities (MCA 2001). This is despite researchers' estimates that no less than 30 million urban dwellers were in poverty in the late 1990s and early 2000s (Guan 2003). Thus the urban MLG did not adequately tackle urban poverty.

The fifth stage, from 2002 up to now, has been characterized by significant central government financial involvement. Since the new MLG could not reach enough of the poor because of local governments' poor fiscal capacity, and yet there was an increasingly serious poverty problem in the cities – especially in the old industrial cities of the northeast, central and western areas of China – the central government hoped to reinforce the MLG so that it could play a more effective anti-poverty role in cities. In the early 2000s, the government found that the MLG could help balance its two supreme goals: reforming the economic system reform and maintaining social stability. It could play an important role in maintaining social stability by reducing poverty while not impeding economic system reform and economic growth because it cost much less than many other social security programmes, most notably social insurance. From this understanding, in 2002, the central government decided to reinforce the MLG by restating its importance, further regulating local government implementation and increasing the central government's financial contribution. As a result, the number of beneficiaries grew significantly, reaching more than 20.6 million in 2002 (MCA 2002). Since then there has been a slight further increase.

The sixth stage, from 2007 to 2009, involved the renewal of state regulations. Since 2002, there has been a small increase in the number of MLG beneficiaries, and its average benefit level increased significantly between 2002 and 2008. Moreover, during this period, the whole urban social assistance system, which includes not only the MLG but also other social assistance benefits for such things as poor people's medical care, housing and education, has also developed very quickly. In the rapid expansion of the social assistance, however, a lot of new needs and administrative problems appeared that the old regulations of 1999 could not deal with. For example, the central government's financial involvement, although helping extend urban MLG, contravened the state regulation of 1999 according to which urban MLG should be paid for by local governments. Also, according to the 1999 regulations, the root management of MLG should lie with local government Neighbourhood Offices (*jiedao banshichu*), but actually many such Offices were unable to manage the volume of applications and have had to hand over the management work to Residents' Committees (*jumin weiyuanhui*). To deal with the new problems, many local governments developed new local regulations in relation to their MLG programmes. Since the central government has become deeply involved in the MLG, and its financial input has accounted for more than one half of the total expenditure on it nationwide, it hopes to unify these local practices into a national system. Therefore, with the authorization of the State Council, the MCA in 2007 started work on revising the regulations.

32 *Xinping Guan and Bing Xu*

The rural Minimum Livelihood Guarantee

Compared to its urban counterpart, rural MLG took longer from the first local pioneer initiatives to becoming national policy, and it is still institutionally at a very early stage. Some central–local 'games' reflecting different levels' attitudes to and expectations of financial responsibility can also be seen by reviewing its processes of initial establishment and development.

In terms of background, it is important to understand that poverty in rural areas has long been more serious than in urban areas and that most poor people have lived in the countryside where economic development has been much lower than in the cities. It has been estimated that there were about 125 million rural people living in poverty in the mid-1980s. At around that time, the Chinese government initiated a large-scale rural anti-poverty programme. This was called the 'Supporting the Poor and Development Programme', and was basically a state-funded economic development programme for poor rural regions. Through it, most of the rural poor in poor regions became better off, but still millions of rural people, including vulnerable individual families in villages not designated as a 'poverty region', were not able to benefit from it. Since these individual poor families could not get better off through regional economic development programmes, social assistance programmes were necessary to relieve their poverty. In this context, rural MLG was initiated from the mid-1990s.

In the first stage, from 1992, rural MLG was pioneered at local level. One year before the first urban MLG programme was pioneered in Shanghai, the first rural MLG project was initiated in Zuoyun County, Shanxi Province, neither a rich nor a very poor region. Much like its urban counterpart, rural MLG was not initiated by the central government, but by local government. It was a local response to helping individual poor rural families (Sun 2008) by providing cash benefits to the families with income lower than the local MLG standard.

In a long second stage, from 1992 to 2004, there was a slow development and expansion of the rural MLG. Unlike its urban counterpart, the local implementation of rural MLG in other places developed slowly over several years following the first initiatives in Shanxi province. The MCA was keen to promote rural MLG and in 1996 issued a document 'Suggestions for accelerating the rural social security system', in which it put rural MLG at the core of the whole rural social security system. In spite of the MCA's support, however, rural MLG developed slowly after Shanxi's early pioneering practice. Although nearly 1000 counties, or about one-third of the total, had joined the 'experimental' rural MLG project by 1997, most of them had only very small coverage and very low benefits, and actually did not run it according to MLG principles. By the end of 2004, only eight provinces and 1206 counties had set up rural MLG programmes, and the total beneficiaries of rural MLG were just 4.88 million (MCA 2004).

The slow development of rural MLG in this period was not due to the financial difficulties of central or local governments as it may have seemed,

Central–local relations in social policy   33

but mainly to the central government's attitudes towards it and central–local 'games' over it. Because the central government at this time did not think rural MLG politically important, it was reluctant to take financial responsibility for the establishment of a national MLG system. And many local governments, expecting the central government to pay for it, chose not to act by themselves but just to wait for the central government to act.

From the late 1990s, however, there were criticisms of the government for not sufficiently emphasizing the establishment of rural MLG. Into the twenty-first century, public criticism became more vocal, and many people thought that it was unfair not to set up MLG in rural areas when the urban poor were able to enjoy its benefits. Under these circumstances, some provinces began to set up MLG in rural areas. In spite of that, the development of rural MLG was still very slow in the early 2000s. By 2004, only eight provinces (and provincial-level cities) out of a total of 31 had implemented rural MLG across their entire jurisdiction, with another four having established it in some areas. Highly motivated to support rural MLG, the MCA originally decided to promote it nationwide in the early 2000s, but without the State Council's formal encouragement and financial backing, the Ministry had to slow it down, and turned to promoting a less beneficial alternate programme of 'rural social relief for extreme households', which ran on a different rationale: not for all the poor families below a local MLG income line, but just for very small groups of the extreme poor; and not to guarantee all the poor families' income up to the local minimal standards, but just subsidize them with very low fixed benefits (Xu *et al.* 2007).

In the third stage, from 2005 to 2007, the central government encouraged rural MLG. Facing stronger and stronger criticism from the public, and influenced by the new top leadership's promotion of a 'harmonious society' the central government in the mid-2000s began to change its attitudes towards the rural MLG. From 2005, in some important documents, the central government encouraged local governments in regions with adequate conditions to set up rural MLG, but it still hesitated at this stage to issue a compulsory state requirement for all local governments to set it up. In any case, the more active attitude of the central government had some effect, and more and more provinces set up MLG in their rural areas from 2005, so that actually almost all provinces had set it up by the summer of 2007. At this stage, there were many discussions and negotiations between local and central governments and among different central government ministries about the financial arrangements for rural MLG. Naturally, there were some debates because each side had different opinions and attitudes towards this issue, but under the central government's guidance an agreement was eventually reached.

In the fourth stage, from 2007, the central government required rural MLG to be set up nationwide. Following discussions and debates among several ministries over several years, in June 2007, the State Council finally issued a document requiring all local governments to set up rural MLG, in other

34 *Xinping Guan and Bing Xu*

words turning former individual local practices into a national system (State Council 2007). When this document was issued, almost all provinces had in fact established or begun to establish rural MLG. It had taken 15 years from the first pioneer programme in Shanxi Province in 1992 to the State Council's document in 2007, while for the urban MLG it had taken just five years. Slow development of the MLG in the countryside was due not only to the central government's reduced enthusiasm in developing the rural MLG before the mid-2000s, but also to many local governments' reluctance to implement it without a financial subsidy from the central government.

Conclusion

From the establishment and development of both the urban and rural MLG, the basic characteristics of the 'central–local games' in these processes can be summarized as follows. First, from the MLG development in both urban and rural areas, we can observe how the responsibility relations between central and local governments affect the social policy process. The urban MLG did not work well when the central government set it up as a national programme but asked local government to implement and pay for it. The inconsistency in the allocation of responsibility across all the three responsibility dimensions – policy making, implementation and financial – between central and local governments delayed the development of urban MLG in late 1990s and early 2000s. The rural MLG's long-term slow development can also be attributed to inconsistency and disagreement in the allocation of responsibility between central and local governments, especially in financial arrangements.

Second, in a big country like China with multiple levels of government, social policy can be successful only if there is a good relationship between centre and localities, and good cooperation between the relevant ministries and bureaus. Any disagreement among the main actors on key issues, such as financial arrangements, may slow the policy-making process.

Third, in the development of MLG, in both urban and rural areas, the different attitudes towards urban and rural MLG can be explained to some extent by differences between central and local governments in their views of the programmes' political and economic significance. For the central government, social and political stability was more important than for the local governments, and thus the MLG was seen as more necessary by the centre. But the centre saw it as more important in cities than in rural areas. That was why the urban MLG got greater support from the central government in late 1990s and early 2000s than did its rural counterpart. In contrast, local governments tended to consider the financial costs of the MLG in both urban and rural areas and were less concerned with social and political stability.

Fourth, without formal regulation of the central–local financial share in social policy financing, the 'games' between the centre and localities continue when financial arrangements are being established. Both central and local governments have been motivated to set up a rural MLG, but neither side wanted to pay for it by itself. Both sides hoped the other side would bear the bigger financial burden. Thus the absence of institutional regulation has caused this central–local game, in which the local governments always tend to seek more financial subsidy from the centre while the central government hopes local governments take more responsibility. This slowed the development of the rural MLG for some years.

Fifth, although the central government has now taken more financial responsibility in many social policy programmes, including both the urban and rural MLG, old regulations have not yet changed the stipulation that the financial responsibility should be assumed mainly by local governments. This inconsistency between official regulations and actual practice may cause problems in financial arrangements. To have a better social policy-making process and to avoid unnecessary delay, it is vitally important to pass new regulations that fix central–local financial responsibilities in social policy. Considering the enormous internal differences in economic development and in local governments' fiscal capacity across regions in today's China, the central government should take a greater financial responsibility than it promised in the 1994 tax reform.

Notes

1 For policies involving more than one ministry, inter-ministry joint actions may be initiated, for example through *ad hoc* 'leading groups' (*lingdao xiaozu*). For key studies of policy making in China see Lieberthal and Oksenberg (1988) and Shirk (1993).
2 In addition, some cities are also designated '*jihua danlie shji*', or directly beneath the centre for planning purposes (an example is Dalian, discussed in Hammond's chapter in this volume).

3 *Dibaohu* in distress

The meagre minimum livelihood guarantee system in Wuhan

Dorothy J. Solinger

> A problem in the development of the *dibao* system is that it's a relief system, but very many people consider it social welfare; everyone wants it. If they can't get it, they feel uncomfortable in their hearts. ... There are widespread errors of understanding of the system. The *dibao* standard is not based on expenditures. So if you spend a certain amount of money each month to buy medicine, you can't on this account compare yourself with other people who are getting more *dibao* funds.
>
> (Interview, Community [*shequ*] V, Wuhan, 27 August 2007)

This confounding of two forms of assistance is alluded to here by a member of the tiny personnel corps charged with taking care of the *dibao* (*zuidi shenghuo baozhang*, Minimum Livelihood Guarantee; hereafter, *dibao* or MLG) in a 'community' (*shequ*) office in Qiaokou, one of Wuhan's seven city-centre districts, in summer 2007. The confusion may or may not be genuine; just as likely, it could be feigned. The point the cadre hoped to convey was that those whom she (and the state) see as greedy, troublesome *dibao* designees are inclined to demand more funds for their subsidy allotment just because their mandatory monthly expenses surpass the amount the allocation can cover.

But the underlying issue might have escaped the official: according to a number of interview subjects in Wuhan that summer, the standardized setting of the city *dibao* norm really ought to be calibrated to the specific requirements of individual households, or at least to the varied characteristics of different types of families. Homes in which the chronically diseased or disabled lie prone on a bed day and night often, for instance, can just barely afford the minimal medicines that will keep these sick people breathing; in other cases consumption needs depend a great deal on the age structure of the family members.

And yet, according to national regulations announced in 1999 (Chengshi jumin zuidi shenghuo baozhang tiaoli 1999), the *dibao* is determined according to an inflexible criterion: each recipient household each month is to receive the difference between its average per capita income and its city government's calculated minimal level of income needed to survive (but do nothing more than to survive!) in that city – the amount, that is, necessary for purchasing basic necessities at the prices prevailing locally. The funds distributed are 'just enough to keep body and soul together', in the words of the *dibao*'s leading scholar within China, Chinese Academy of Social Science (CASS) social policy researcher Tang Jun (Tang 2002b: 4; Hussain *et al.* 2002: 59). The crux of the trouble is that most beneficiaries aspire to more than that.

Should we view the system as beneficent or miserly, as charitable or churlish? And how do practices in the city of Wuhan measure up comparatively, as revealed statistically, as described by officials there and as experienced by the people who get the outlays? I begin by outlining the programme at the national level, its history and purposes. I go on to appraise how that city stacked up originally and stacks up now against other similar municipalities. The assessment, we will see, is not straightforward.

Last, I offer findings from at-home, face-to-face interviews with 53 *dibaohu* (MLG recipient households, also termed *dibao duixiang*, or *dibao* targets) conducted in three different districts in Wuhan: Hanyang, a low-to middling-income area; Qiaokou, a lower-income section; and Qingshan, the wealthiest of the seven districts making up the urban core. The residents in the communities covered could be questioned because of personal connections with community officials. The 'sample' consists of those *dibaohu* at home and willing to speak with me and/or three graduate students who assisted me. Besides the interviews with recipients, I also spoke with city-level bureaucrats in charge of the programme in Wuhan and Lanzhou, and with community cadres at several Wuhan community offices.

My documentary data come from the following sources. For 1996 through 2002, I used all articles on the *dibao* in the journal of the responsible ministry, the Ministry of Civil Affairs, *Zhongguo Minzheng* (China Civil Affairs). For 2003 to 2006, I consulted statistical yearbooks and annual social development 'blue books' published by CASS; and for 2006 and 2007, I read official government work reports, 50 official articles found on the Internet, and sundry documents collected in Wuhan and Lanzhou in August and September 2007.

The *dibao* programme: history and purposes

The Chinese regime's switch in force to market incentives and competition-based compensation in the mid-1990s is widely recognized as having yielded increasing income differentials and – less often recognized – newborn urban poverty. Indeed, the incidence of urban indigence shot upward once state and collective enterprises were enjoined to cut back drastically on their workforces in and after the mid-1990s; at the same time, with the total overhaul of the socialist economy and its institutions, the traditional welfare entitlements were also taken away (Wang 2004: 60, 71–87; 'Zhongguo chengshi' 2006), leaving losers at a total loss.

In the 1990s, China's leaders agonized over what they perceived as the potential impact of these deprivations on their regime's hallowed objectives of

38   *Dorothy J. Solinger*

social stability and a successful project of state enterprise reform. As explained in 1996 by Wuhan's Qiaokou district government office vice chairman, Wang Mingxing (also the City's Finance Bureau chief), 'Urban *dibao* work concerns social stability; it's not only economic work, even more it's a political task' (Liu 2002: 4). Accordingly, the political elite initiated a special poverty-assistance approach to handle the people most severely affected by economic restructuring – supplementing an earlier programme to care just for the '*san wu*' (or 'three withouts', sometimes referred to in English as 'Three Nos') persons, those lacking work ability, people to support them, or any source of livelihood, and adding to a contemporaneous project whereby still-extant firms that could afford to do so provided monthly allowances to their laid-off workers. Once the new administration of Premier Wen Jiabao had got under way, concern for the poor became linked to the new catchword, 'harmony' (Di shi'erci quanguo minzheng huiyi zai jing juxing 2006).

The rhetoric of the rules for the programme – especially its language of rights and self-reliance – belie its actual outcomes. The empowering 1999 Regulations proclaim that those households whose members, living together, have an average per capita income below that needed for a minimal livelihood 'have the right to obtain material assistance with their basic livelihood'. The statute also alleges that the policy is meant to 'encourage self-support through labor' (Chengshi jumin zhuidi shenghuo baozhang tiaoli 1999: 16). Yet little, in fact, is heard either of rights or of spurs to economic autonomy in the speeches of top leaders; nor are these ideas present in the great majority of government documents. In Wuhan in particular these principles have not been in evidence.

The case of Wuhan

Wuhan in the context of **dibao** *history*

Wuhan initiated its *dibao* programme in March 1996, a full three years after Shanghai had devised the original version. In that year the Government Work Report presented at the Fourth Session of the Eighth National People's Congress called for gradually establishing the system nationwide during the Ninth Five Year Plan (from 1996 to 2000). This was also the year that state industry for the first time experienced an overall loss (Rawski 1999: 144). Wuhan, a city where heavy industry was prominent, and where much factory equipment was long obsolete (Solinger 1991: Chapter 3), by then already contained laid-off and unemployed workers from firms in the red or which had disappeared, whether sold off or bankrupted. In 1998 and 1999, researchers led by Tang Jun investigated the implementation of the *dibao* in five cities, including Wuhan (the others were Shanghai, Tianjin, Chongqing and Lanzhou), finding the city a place where '*xiagang* [layoffs] and unemployment are a widespread social problem' (Yang and Zhang 1999: 102; Tang 2002b: 10). Street cadres told the study team that:

> Recently state-owned enterprises are commonly in recession, especially textiles, printing and dyeing. Staff and workers are being laid off in droves and those not laid off are having a tough time too. Once they're laid off, they're immediately without a source of livelihood, especially those older ones. If they have no special skill, it's hard for them to find work. Doing business is more difficult; if you mess up, the capital won't be returned. If we didn't establish the *dibao* system, many families would not be able to eat even rice. If there are a lot of such families in the city, how can there be social order?

As of early 1998, the traditional *sanwu* targets in Wuhan amounted to just 4.2 per cent of the total *dibao* recipients; labour-age unemployed people with working ability constituted another 45 per cent, while still at-work and laid-off staff and workers stood at 25.6 per cent. Thus, the lately impoverished urbanites together accounted for about 70 per cent of the targets, whereas such people had amounted to only 58.15 per cent two years before. In Jiang'an district, in particular, the district hit hardest by firms' failures, unemployed people as a percentage of the total helped by the MLG shot up from 34.4 per cent to 59.8 per cent of beneficiaries two years later. If the laid-off and still at-work poor were added in, these new poor climbed to 76.2 per cent of the recipients in that district that year (Yang and Zhang 1999: 100, 101, 102).

Wuhan, situated in the second set of cities starting the project, might have copied earlier examples, but instead claims to have set up its own model. But the documentation I found on this 'model' is sparse: it mentions only that it 'took the city district as the business accounting unit, the street as the contracting unit, and the residence committee as the unit that accepted and heard cases in the first instance'. Its chief principle was that the government – as opposed to the enterprises, as in earlier experiments elsewhere – took responsibility (Meng and Tan 1996: 19; Yang and Zhang 1999: 99; Tang 2002b: 31). Among cities, the funds-sharing formula among administrative levels varied – Lanzhou, for instance, got 65 per cent of its funds from the centre, 15 per cent from Gansu province, and had to contribute just 20 per cent itself, with its districts (as a group) throwing in a portion of the city's total (Interview, *dibao* section head, Lanzhou, 5 September 2007; Tang 2002b: 25). As of 2002, the city-to-district share was 30 to 70 in Dalian; but in Qingdao, 70 to 30; and in Shenyang, Wuhan and Chongqing, 50 to 50 (Hussain *et al.* 2002: 71). In my interview in summer 2007, the director of the *dibao* office at the Wuhan city Civil Affairs Bureau told me that the city was by then contributing close to 60 per cent, with the central government putting in about 40 per cent. Each district was to contribute half of what it got, though the City sometimes supported a district if necessary (Interview, Wuhan, 28 August 2007).

This 'Wuhan model' was later publicized nationwide and had some influence on other municipalities. Chongqing, though, removed Wuhan's limits on working-age residents, using local urban registration (the *hukou*) as the only

40 *Dorothy J. Solinger*

qualification, regardless of a person's unit's ownership status, and without reference to whether the person was at work, laid off, or unemployed (Tang 2002b: 12, 14, 27). Tianjin also altered the model, determining that, 'because of illness, disability, having lost work ability and being older, some people have more difficulties, so we can be more lenient' (Tang 2002b: 19). At this early stage – as was to remain the case – Wuhan unabashedly declared that its aims were 'to help the enterprises throw off their worries and solve their difficulties' and 'to lighten the enterprises' burdens' (Meng and Tan 1996: 19).

Wuhan's programme considered comparatively

Despite that Wuhan's rhetorical formulation was typical, in line with the right given to cities in the national regulations to design the details of their own programmes, Tang Jun's group found conspicuous variations in the approaches taken by the different municipalities it investigated. Its study of 2,354 poor families discovered that the *dibao* line was respectively 31, 21, 21, 27 and 28 per cent of the average local income in these cities, with Wuhan tied with Tianjin for lowest (Tang 2002a). After an elevation of the norm in autumn 1999, Shanghai's rate went up to 40 per cent, but in Wuhan it remained low, at 27 per cent.

Reflecting these disparities, when *dibao* recipients were asked whether they felt the funds they got were insufficient, in Wuhan as many as 67 per cent replied that they were, whereas in the other cities the percentage went from 44 per cent for Lanzhou to 59 per cent in Tianjin and Chongqing (Tang 2002b: Chapter 8). And, perhaps an indication of the greater stinginess in Wuhan, as many as 46 per cent of the targets admitted that they 'didn't like to interact with their neighbours or colleagues', while the same inquiry got affirmative rates ranging from just 34 (in Shanghai) up to 42 per cent (in Lanzhou) (Tang 2002b: Chapter 8, p. 33). Thus, the team's report characterized Wuhan as particularly miserly, using the words of a street office official there as illustration:

> In giving out funds we need to be very strict and eliminate those who don't meet conditions. We can't follow our personal feelings; we must consider the overall picture, compare the various residence committees [in our street area], and strive to solve [just barely, was the implication] the problems of the poorest families.
>
> (Tang 2002b: 12)

Two scholars at the Wuhan University Research Institute of Social Security noted that before executing the system, the city Bureau of Civil Affairs submitted a report to the city government judging that the poverty-stricken portion of the city's populace amounted to four per cent of all registered residents. But at first, in 1996, only a tiny 0.05 per cent of urban residents entered the system, at a time when 10 million yuan was budgeted, meant to

Dibaohu *in distress*   41

assist 1.2 per cent of the city's population, and the norm was pegged at 120 yuan per person per month (Yang and Zhang 1999: 103; Tang 2002b: 14, 13). Contemporaneously, in Tianjin, the norm was set at 185 yuan, which could accommodate 1.8 per cent of the city's people and in Chongqing, where 130 was the norm, 2.8 per cent of the non-agricultural population was being covered (Tang 2002b: 15, 32; Anon., Xiao ziliao 1999: 26). Clearly metropolises are free to allow idiosyncratic factors to determine the local poverty lines that administrators in the city finance, statistics, price and civil affairs bureaucracies set ('Shi renmin zhengfu' 2004: Chapter 2, Article 4, 3).

By early 1998, the proportion of the populace actually serviced in Wuhan had risen (but just to 0.15 per cent), although some in-kind benefits were thrown in, such as subsidies for grain, housing rentals, and a few other basic necessities (Yang and Zhang 1999: 103). Revealing the dire situation in Wuhan, in February 1997, the City Education Commission and the Bureau of Civil Affairs jointly issued a ruling allowing that *dibao* families with children attending nine-year compulsory schooling need not pay miscellaneous school fees. The regulation also decreed that each primary school student in these households was entitled to a subsidy of 50 yuan for book copying; junior high students got 100 yuan for this (Yang and Zhang 1999: 100).

The Wuhan University researchers also noted that, 'The results of several internationally used methods of estimating the poverty line are all higher than Wuhan's line'. According to the 'income proportion' approach, which takes 50 per cent of the local average per capita income as the poverty line, Wuhan's line in 1995 should have been 174 yuan, and according to the 'proportion of expenditure' method (presumably indicating a certain proportion of local average per capita expenditure), it should have been 169 yuan. Or, sample statistics of residents' spending showed the minimum per capita outlay as 144.25 yuan. But the Wuhan Bureau of Civil Affairs relied on a so-called, undefined 'vegetable basket' method for calculating poverty (estimating the cost of the minimum foods needed to survive), and set the line at a mere 120 yuan. It was only in mid-1998 that this standard was raised, and then just to 150 yuan (Yang and Zhang 1999: 103).

A 2001 study examining 35 cities' 1998 implementation of the *dibao* featured a formula representing a city's generosity, while also illustrating the disparity among cities in how they decided on how high to make their norms: this is the ratio between its *dibao* norm and its average wage for the year 1998. The value for these cities ranged from 20 to 30 per cent; Wuhan's percentage was just 21.35 (Wu 2001: 38). Similarly, in a listing of 36 cities' 1998 *dibao*, 24 municipalities had levels above Wuhan's 120 yuan (the highest was Xiamen, at 250 yuan; seven were the same as Wuhan; and only five were lower) (Anon., 'Xiao ziliao' 1999: 26).

Another exercise tells the same story: Wuhan's 1998 per capita gross domestic product (GDP) was in the middling range among 19 special municipalities and provincial capitals, at just under 14,000 yuan. The range went from Shenzhen at 33,300 down to Chongqing at just 4,700 yuan (see Table 3.1).[1]

42 *Dorothy J. Solinger*

Compared with other cities with similar per capita GDP levels, such as Shenyang (13,900), Jinan (14,800), Qingdao (12,700), and Fuzhou (14,800), Wuhan was low in its *dibao* to GDP per capita ratio, at 10.32 per cent: Shenyang stood at 12.93 per cent, Jinan at 11.33 per cent, Qingdao at 15.12 per cent, and Fuzhou 13.76 per cent. In the same year, Wuhan's *dibao* accounted for just 17.4 per cent of its average wage, while Shenyang's was 23 per cent, Jinan's was 20.2 per cent, Qingdao's was 23.6 per cent, and Fuzhou's 23.3 per cent (see Table 3.2).

The numbers of *dibao* targets nationwide and the funds for their assistance rose in 2001 and 2002, but there were no large leaps thereafter (see Figure 3.1, and also Tables 3.3 and 3.4). Perhaps Wuhan's management shifted around this time: comparing four cities' *dibao* as a percentage of average disposable income in mid-2002, Wuhan's ratio was 32.2 per cent, above both Jinan (27.8 per cent) and Qingdao (28.2 per cent). Of these four cities, only Shenyang, where dismissed workers were by far the most numerous nationally and where the central government was especially generous with welfare money (Feng *et al.* 2002: 26; 'New Social Security System 2001) was higher than Wuhan, at 34.9 per cent (see Table 3.5). These and later data suggest that Wuhan's

Table 3.1 Cross-city comparison of MLG (*dibao*) norm and per capita GDP, 1998

City	MLG line (yuan/month)	Annual MLG line (monthly × 12)	Annual av. per capita GDP (yuan/year)	MLG line as % of per capita GDP
Beijing	200	2400	18,478	13
Tianjin	185	2220	14,800	15
Shenyang	150	1800	13,922	13
Dalian	165	1980	17,251	11
Changchun	130	1560	8,866	18
Harbin	140	1680	8,504	20
Jinan	140	1680	14,834	11
Qingdao	160	1920	12,699	15
Shanghai	205	2460	28,240	9
Hangzhou	165	1980	18,600	11
Nanjing	140	1680	15,537	11
Wuhan	120	1440	13,957	10
Chongqing	130	1560	4,700	33
Chengdu	120	1440	11,107	13
Xi'an	105	1260	8,425	15
Lanzhou	100	1200	9,196	13
Fuzhou	170	2040	14,828	14
Shenzhen	245	2940	33,289	9
Xiamen	250	3000	31,727	9

Sources: For the *dibao* norm: 'Small material: Nationwide various cities' residents' minimum livelihood guarantee norms' (*Xiao ziliao: Quanguo ge chengshi juimin zuidi shenghuo baozhang biaojun Shehui*), *Society*, 1999, 26; for the average per capita GDP: *Wuxi Statistical Yearbook 1999*; China data online accessed 29 May 2009

Dibaohu *in distress* 43

decision makers increased their payments to the *dibao* fund as a percentage of the city's budget in the 2000s. For instance, in 2004, comparisons between Wuhan and other provincial capitals make the city look rather better, though just in a relative sense. By then, Wuhan's *dibao* as a per cent of the average wage

Table 3.2 Cross-city comparison of MLG (*dibao*) line and average wages, 1998

City	MLG line (yuan/month)	Annual MLG line (monthly × 12)	Annual av. wage	Annual MLG as a % of annual av. wage
Beijing	200	2400	12,285	20
Tianjin	185	2220	9,946	22
Shenyang	150	1800	7,811	23
Dalian	165	1980	9,275	21
Changchun	130	1560	7,869	20
Harbin	140	1680	6,603	25
Jinan	140	1680	8,326	20
Qingdao	160	1920	8,125	24
Shanghai	205	2460	12,059	20
Hangzhou	165	1980	10,194	19
Nanjing	140	1680	10,661	16
Wuhan	120	1440	8,255	17
Chongqing	130	1560	5,710	27
Chengdu	120	1440	8,248	17
Xi'an	105	1260	6,922	18
Lanzhou	100	1200	7,736	16
Fuzhou	170	2040	8,772	23
Shenzhen	245	2940	18,381	16
Xiamen	250	3000	12,799	23

Sources: 'Small material: Nationwide various cities' residents' minimum livelihood guarantee norms' (*Xiao ziliao: Quanguo ge chengshi juimin zuidi shenghuo baozhang biaojun Shehui*), *Society*, 1999, 26; for the average per capita GDP: *Wuxi Statistical Yearbook 1999*; China data online accessed 29 May 2009

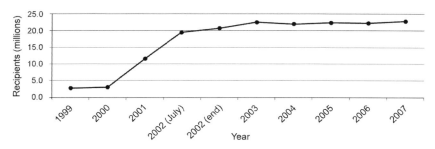

Figure 3.1 Number of participtants in the MLG (*dibao*) 1997–2007.

44 *Dorothy J. Solinger*

had decreased, to 16.5 per cent, but Shenyang's had dropped much more, to 14.2 per cent. Qingdao's had also gone down, to 20.5 per cent, while Fuzhou's by then was 15.2 per cent (see Table 3.6, and Tables 3.7 and 3.8).

Yet despite the improvement in comparative quantitative measures, it seems that the style of Wuhan's management remained grudging. In the five-city investigation in 1998–99, researchers had found that Lanzhou adopted a more 'mobilizational' approach to its indigent than did Wuhan (Tang 2002b: 25), a

Table 3.3 Government spending on MLG (*dibao*) as a share of total spending and GDP, 1999–2007 (unit: billion yuan)

Year	Total MLG expenditure	Total gov't expenditure	MLG as % of gov't expenditure	GDP	MLG as % of GDP
1999	2	1,319	0.11	8,968	0.02
2000	3	1,589	0.19	99,215	0.03
2001	4	1,890	0.22	10,966	0.04
2002	11	2,205	0.48	12,033	0.09
2003	15	2,465	0.69	13,582	0.11
2004	n.a.	2,849	n.a.	15,988	n.a.
2005	20	3,393	0.57	18,387	0.11
2006	20	4,042	0.50	21,181	0.10
2007	28	4,957	0.56	24,660	0.11

Sources: For the *dibao*, figures are either taken from or estimated from the following sources: Tang Jun 2002a, 2006. For government expenditures (1999–2006): *China Statistical Yearbook2007*: 279. For GDP (1999–2006): *China Statistical Yearbook 2007*: 57; and for 2007: Wen Jiabao 2008; Ministry of Finance 2008
Note: Figures are rounded to two significant digits

Table 3.4 Number of participants in MLG (*dibao*) 1997–2007 (unit: million)

Year	Number of participants
1999	2.8
2000	3.2
2001	11.7
2002 (July)	19.3
2002 (end)	20.6
2003	22.5
2004	22.1
2005	22.3
2006	22.4
2007	22.7

Sources: For 1999: Tang Jun 2002a: 15–16; for 2000: *ibid.*: 18; for 2001: Hong Zhaohui 2002: 9–10; for 2006: *2006 nian 10 yuefen quanguo xian yishang dibao qingkuang*; for 2007: 'National urban and rural residents, the minimum livelihood guarantee system for equal coverage' 2008. For 2002, 2003, 2004, 2005, 2006: *China Statistical Yearbook 2007*: 899

Dibaohu *in distress*   45

Table 3.5 Cross-city MLG (*dibao*) line and average disposable income, July 2002 (unit: yuan per month)

City	MLG line (yuan/month)	Av. disposable income (yuan/month)	MLG line as % of av. disposable income
Beijing	290	1039	28
Tianjin	241	778	31
Shenyang	205	588	35
Dalian	221	683	32
Changchun	169	575	29
Harbin	200	584	34
Taiyuan	156	615	25
Jinan	208	748	28
Qingdao	205*	727	28
Shanghai	280	1104	25
Hangzhou	285*	982	29
Nanjing	220	763	29
Wuhan	210	652	32
Changsha	190*	752	25
Chongqing	185	603	31
Chengdu	178	748	24
Xi'an	156	599	26
Lanzhou	172	n.a.	n.a.
Shenzhen	317*	2078	15
Xiamen	290*	981	30
Guangzhou	300	1115	27

Sources: for the *dibao* line: 'General survey of 36 cities' minimum livelihood guarantee norm' (*Quanguo 36ge chengshi zuidi baozhang biaozhun yilan*), http://china.com.cn/city/txt/2006-11/25/content_740675\hich\af0\dbch\af13\loch\f08_2.htm (accessed 17 August 2007); for urban residents' average disposable income: *Chengdu Statistical Yearbook 2003*, China data online (accessed 29 May 2008)
Note: * indicates that figure is average of upper and lower figures for *dibao* norm for city for that year

tendency that the city appears to have retained over the years (Gansusheng renmin zhengfu bangongting 2002: 58–69). Officials there 'emphasized arousing the *dibao* targets' activism for production, organizing them to develop oself-reliance' (Tang 2002b: 25).

This approach was still evident in the city again in 2007, when Lanzhou was showing considerably more leniency toward the sidewalk business of the indigent than Wuhan then was. A talented but hard-up woman in Wuhan complained that the fees for advertising her artwork on the streets had escalated substantially over time, so that she was forced to abandon any effort to make sales outside (Interview, Wuhan, 26 August 2007). And, unlike in the past, after around 2000 nowhere in the city could shoe repair specialists be found outside, apparently banned by the authorities. In Lanzhou, by way of contrast, all manner of curbside business was going on unobstructed in 2007,

46 Dorothy J. Solinger

Table 3.6 Cross-city comparison of MLG (*dibao*) line and average wages, 2004

City	MLG line (yuan/month)	Average monthly wage of staff and workers	Annual MLG as a % of annual av. wage
Beijing	290	2473	12
Tianjin	241	1813	13
Shenyang	205	1444	14
Dalian	276*	1643	17
Changchun	169	1159	15
Harbin	200	1161	17
Qingdao	230	1120	21
Shanghai	280	2490	11
Hangzhou	285*	2408	12
Nanjing	220	2172	10
Wuhan	220	1331	17
Chongqing	185	1196	15
Chengdu	178	1463	12
Xi'an	180	1275	14
Shenzhen	317*	2661	12
Xiamen	290*	1712	17
Guangzhou	300	2633	11
Fuzhou	210*	1382	15

Sources: for the *dibao* line: 'General survey of 36 cities' minimum livelihood guarantee line' (*Quanguo 36ge chengshi zuidi baozhang biaozhun yilan*) http://china.com.cn/city/txt/2006-11/25/content_740675\hich\af0\dbch\af13\loch\f08_2.htm (accessed 17 August 2007); for wages: *Wuxi Statistical Yearbook 2005*, China data online (accessed 29 May 2008)
Note: * indicates that figure is average of upper and lower figures for *dibao* norm for city for that year

including stalls for fixing footwear as well as hawking by young men vending political picture posters (Author's observations, Lanzhou, 3 September 2007).

Indeed, the section chief of the *dibao* office in the Gansu provincial civil affairs department admitted that summer that, 'If the *chengguan* [the police in charge of maintaining order in public spaces]' – the very same body that has often chased poor and unemployed persons off the avenues of Wuhan – 'is too strict, the *dibaohu* cannot earn money. And letting them earn money is a way of cutting down their numbers. If their skill level is low, their only means of livelihood can be the streetside stalls they set up themselves' (Interview, Lanzhou, 5 September 2007). He claimed that complaints to their communities from the unemployed had secured the greater leniency. Lanzhou also set up a phone hotline at every administrative level for the poor to report their dissatisfactions, with the goal of rectifying errors in officials' workstyle, a practice not mentioned in Wuhan. In recent years, too, Lanzhou established an organ in each community, entitled the 'democratic assessment small group' (*minzhu pingyi xiaozu*) to judge whether applicants qualified for the MLG. And also unlike in Wuhan, the Bureau of Labour and Social Security set a goal of eliminating the phenomenon of families having no employed members

Table 3.7 Cross-city MLG (*dibao*) line and average disposable income (yuan per month), March 2004

City	MLG line (yuan/month)	Av. disposable income (yuan/month)	MLG line as % of av. disposable income
Beijing	290	1303	22
Tianjin	241	956	25
Shenyang	205	744	28
Dalian	276*	865	32
Changchun	169	742	23
Harbin	200	745	27
Taiyuan	171	779	22
Jinan	208	1000	21
Qingdao	230	924	25
Shanghai	290	1390	21
Hangzhou	285*	1214	23
Nanjing	220	967	23
Wuhan	220	797	28
Changsha	200	918	22
Chongqing	185	768	24
Chengdu	178	866	21
Xi'an	180	712	25
Lanzhou	172	640	27
Shenzhen	317*	2300	14
Xiamen	290*	1204	24
Guangzhou	300	1407	21

Sources: For the *dibao* line: 'General survey of 36 cities' minimum livelihood guarantee line' (*Quanguo 36ge chengshi zuidi baozhang biaozhun yilan*) http://china.com.cn/city/txt/2006-11/25/content_740675\hich\af0\dbch\af13\loch\f08_2.htm (accessed 17 August 2007); for the urban residents' average disposable income: *Chengdu Yearbook 2005*, China data online (accessed 29 May 2008); for Lanzhou: *Lanzhou Statistical Bureau* (ed.) (2007) *Lanzhou Statistical Yearbook 2007*: 297

(*ling jiuye jiating*), aiming to guarantee that at least one person per household had work (Interview, Lanzhou, 5 September 2007).

Another distinction between the two cities is the relative severity with which the needy are excluded from the programme. In Lanzhou, a directive from the end of 2001 barred from receiving *dibao* funds only three kinds of people: the labour-able who without good reason refuse to take a job; those with working ability who decline to participate in public service work assigned to them by the community; and those whose household's actual livelihood level is obviously higher than the local minimum livelihood norm (Gansusheng 2002: 59), whereas Wuhan's regulations disqualified people engaged in 18 different kinds of behaviour.

In at least one Wuhan community in 2007, households, however poor, were prevented from getting the *dibao* if their members engaged in any of these 18 sorts of forbidden behaviour, including being in possession of or even using a motorized vehicle; buying a refrigerator; having obtained air conditioning or

48   *Dorothy J. Solinger*

Table 3.8 Cross-city MLG (*dibao*) line and average disposable income (yuan per month), September 2005

City	MLG line (yuan/month)	Av. disposable income (yuan/month)	MLG line as % of av. disposable income
Beijing	300	1471	20
Tianjin	265	1053	25
Shenyang	220	842	26
Dalian	240	1000	24
Changchun	169	839	20
Harbin	200	839	24
Taiyuan	183	873	21
Jinan	230	1132	20
Qingdao	260	1077	24
Shanghai	300	1554	19
Hangzhou	300*	1383	22
Nanjing	230*	1250	18
Wuhan	220	904	24
Changsha	200	1036	19
Chongqing	210	854	25
Chengdu	195	947	21
Xi'an	200	802	25
Lanzhou	190	711	27
Shenzhen	344	1791 [*sic.*]	19
Xiamen	290*	1367	21
Guangzhou	330	1524	22

Sources: For the *dibao* line: 'General survey of 36 cities' minimum livelihood guarantee line' (*Quanguo 36ge chengshi zuidi baozhang biaozhu yilan*, http://china.com.cn/city/txt/2006-11/25/content_740675\hich\af0\dbch\af13\loch\f08_2.htm (accessed 17 August 2007); for urban residents' average disposable income: *Chengdu Statistical Yearbook 2005*, China data online, accessed 29 May 2008; for Lanzhou, for Lanzhou: *Lanzhou Statistical Bureau* (ed.) (2007) *Lanzhou Statistical Yearbook 2007*: 297

a computer in the recent period; spending more on electrical fees than 15 yuan per month, or more than 40 yuan on phone fees; having a family member who uses a cell phone or other hand-held communication gadget (even if having acquired it as a gift or a loan); or having a member at work outside the city whose income is hard to verify (Interview, Wuhan, Community X, 27 August 2007).

Also forbidden was arranging for one's children to select their own school, enrolling them in special classes for study or training; or arranging for them to study with a foreigner. Some grantees took these guidelines seriously, as did a mother of a 16-year-old boy:

> This year his grades could qualify him to transfer to the Number 3 Senior High School, a provincial-level 'keypoint' institution. But I don't have the money, and secondly, if it's discovered that there's a child in the family who has transferred to a 'keypoint' high school, our *dibao*

qualification would be eliminated. We can't take this risk. He really wants to study in that school, but he knows the family's conditions, so he doesn't demand it of me; I feel I have really let my son down.

(Interview 6)

Several Wuhan interviewees found their families' *dibao* funds cut back or even cut off when a member took on some wage-earning work. In one representative case, the wife in a family of three bravely reflected that:

The family has one person working, so our subsidy was lowered a lot. We're not thinking of arguing about it, we all are very submissive people, so we don't think of haggling over money. If you give us 200-plus yuan it still can be of use.

(Interview 11)

Speaking to another woman, aged 34, the questioner pointed out that the woman's husband was out of the city doing odd jobs (*dagong*), and that she was managing a stall, and inquired whether their monthly *dibao* quota was therefore decreased. 'Yes,' she replied, and continued:

It's a no-way affair (*mei banfa de shiqing*). In my stall in one month I can earn only so much money, his work also isn't stable, but now our work is calculated into our income, and then they have to cut our subsidy. But this income fluctuates, sometimes we have it and sometimes we don't, only relying on the *dibao*, that little money, means that basically there's no way to live.

(Interview 12)

In 2007, when Lanzhou was providing 7.75 per cent of its urban population with the *dibao,* Wuhan was underwriting a mere 4.8 per cent of its own residents (Interviews, Wuhan, 28 August 2007 and Lanzhou, 5 September 2007). But Lanzhou probably received substantial financial subsidies from the central government as a part of the Party's post-2000 programme to develop the west, and so perhaps had more wherewithal to offer to the needy. And in some sections of Wuhan the proportion served matched Lanzhou's average: in Community X, in Hanyang district, about 7.9 per cent got it and in Community V, in Qiaokou district, 7.84 per cent did (Liu 2002: 5).

Whatever the differences, in the two cities, as in others throughout the country, the average payment of the *dibao* supplement varied among urban districts as of 2007. Though each city had just one *dibao* standard, in the more productive, well-off districts (where high-tech, capital-intensive, high-paying firms predominated), the average supplement per household was higher than in poorer districts. As officials in both Wuhan and Lanzhou explained, this discrepancy occurs because in the poorer districts, where the numbers of recipients are higher, the average stipend can be lower at least in

50   *Dorothy J. Solinger*

part because these districts tend to have more tertiary sector employment opportunities and so less may be needed to make good the difference between a family's income and the city's *dibao* norm.

Not only was the financial income of Qingshan, Wuhan's wealthiest district, higher than in other city districts, but it had comparatively fewer *dibao* targets to subsidize, allowing larger allocations per recipient. Qingshan also had fewer aging plants, so unemployment was lower: in 1998, its unemployed constituted the lowest proportion of total MLG recipients (where it was just 38.6 per cent), as compared with their percentage in the other districts of Wuhan, such as Jiang'an, where 60 per cent of all *dibao* recipients were unemployed (Yang and Zhang 1999: 102). Moreover, in industrial districts, prices are higher, and the consumption standard is higher, so *dibaohu* needed more funds. This relationship held in both Lanzhou and Wuhan, according to informants (Interviews, Wuhan, 28 and 30 August 2007 and Lanzhou).

In sum, it is clear that localities have definite leeway in the treatment of their *dibao* targets. While Wuhan emphasizes beautiful, unencumbered thoroughfares, Lanzhou values more highly allowing its poor to have a chance at prospering, if possible. Such variation complicates the evaluation of the worth and generosity of the MLG programme.

Insights from interviews in Wuhan

My 2007 Wuhan home visits discovered people getting the *dibao* to be living in precisely the same state of duress in which Tang Jun's group had found such folks nine years before: ailing, fearful about expenses and the future, and eating poorly. The description penned by one of my assistants about the first *dibao* domicile she visited is both poignant and precise:

> The home is very small and narrow, the facial colour of the wife is yellowish white; she's always lying on the small, short bamboo bed, the daughter is sitting at the bedside chatting with the mother, the father is cooking food. The kitchen has no ventilator so the air throughout the whole home is filled with the mist of oil soot. It looks like the health of the wife is not too good.

Among the 53 households interviewed, several grievances cropped up repeatedly. Though only a few informants complained about the paucity of the funds the supplement supplied, this fact was at the root of all their troubles. From the information provided me, the average per capita income in most households, after adding in the money from the *dibao* allotment, was usually in the range of 220 to 240 yuan, about the amount they were supposed to be receiving at the time, assuming the speakers were telling the truth (see Table 3.9). Granted, some refused to reveal their financial situations and perhaps some were not directly asked. But if they truly took in that sum, their total take amounted to about one US dollar per day, according to the current exchange rate.

Table 3.9 Interviewees' household size, *dibao* allowance and income (unit: yuan)

Case #	No. of Household Members	dibao	Other income/ from	Total income	Income per capita
1	3	200+	500/n.a.	700+	233+
2	3	415	218/pension	633	317
3	4	200+	900/pension	1300+	325+
4	3	n.a.	n.a.	n.a.	n.a.
5	2	300+	none	300+	150+
6	1	n.a.	n.a.	n.a.	n.a.
7	3	200	odd jobs, darning clothes	n.a.	n.a.
8	4	100+	several 100/ odd jobs	400–600	100–150
9	3	n.a.	no work	n.a.	n.a.
10	2	n.a.	no work	n.a.	n.a.
11	3	n.a.	n.a.	n.a.	n.a.
12	3	n.a.	n.a.	n.a.	n.a.
13	3	n.a.	150	n.a.	n.a.
14	1	170	n.a.	n.a.	170
15	3	210	severance pay	n.a.	n.a.
16	3	150	n.a.	n.a.	n.a.
17	4	n.a.	pension/ severance pay	n.a.	n.a.
18	3	100	400/sanitation work; odd jobs; severance of pay	n.a.	n.a.
19	3	80	severance pay; odd jobs; dept. store job	n.a.	n.a.
20	4	200+	700/pension; severance pay	900+	225
21	2	200	200/basic allowance from work unit; odd jobs	n.a.	n.a.
22	3	n.a.	n.a.	n.a.	n.a.
23	3	210	400/odd jobs	610	203
24	1	120	severance pay	120	120
25	3	290	nursemaid;80/ work unit;300/ sister 670+300/sister		n.a.
26	3	210	460/severance pay	670	223
27	4	200	odd jobs	n.a.	n.a.
28	3	n.a.	600/odd jobs; 100 relatives; 100 work unit	n.a.	n.a.
29	3	300	100/work unit; 200/brother	600	200
30	2	460	0	460	230
31	3	420	severance pay	n.a.	n.a.
32	3	150	small stall	n.a.	n.a.
33	3	160	500/wages; severance pay	660	n.a.
34	3	300	400/odd jobs/100 relatives	800	266
35	3	180	400/wages;70/work unit	650	217
36	2	319	120/housing subsidy	439	220

(continued on next page)

52 Dorothy J. Solinger

Table 3.9 (continued)

Case #	No. of Household Members	dibao	Other income/ from	Total income	Income per capita
37	4	240	600/odd jobs	840	210
38	1	160	80/work unit	240	240
39	3	300	400/odd jobs	700	233
40	3	260	400/wages	660	220
41	3	n.a.	600/pension; odd jobs	n.a.	n.a.
42	4	n.a.	both adults do odd jobs	n.a.	n.a.
43	2	n.a.	n.a.	n.a.	n.a.
44	3	n.a.	sanitation work; job in a welfare company	n.a.	n.a.
45	3	n.a.	unstable construction work	n.a.	n.a.
46	2	n.a.	n.a.	n.a.	n.a.
47	4	n.a.	odd jobs	n.a.	n.a.
48	4	100+	400–500/temporary work	500–600	125–150
49	3	n.a.	n.a.	n.a.	n.a.
50	3	136	300/work unit	436	136
51	3	234	odd jobs	n.a.	n.a.
52	3	n.a.	stall; odd jobs	n.a.	n.a.
53	2	200	195/work unit	395	197.5

Source: 53 interviews in dibao homes in 3 districts of Wuhan, August 2007
Note: n.a. indicates that the information was not available for 1 of 3 reasons; since I participated in only 7 of the interviews (because it seemed subjects were more apt to voice complaints when I was not present), I am unable to state whether in specific cases the reason was: (1) the interviewer did not record the answer; (2) the interviewer did not ask for the information; (3) the subject refused to provide the information

About half the households (26) contained a disabled or chronically ill member, often the victim of some serious malady. In a third of the families (18) the parents were desperately worried about either the present or the future costs of educating their children. Eleven, slightly more than a fifth, spoke of the difficulties of finding work, while over half (31) confided their hopes, virtually all of which seemed to be in vain.

Fears about being able to afford minimal sustenance cropped up in five of the conversations (a tenth), especially in light of the inflation of food costs then under way; only three claimed to be surviving fine. Twelve, just over a fifth, admitted to receiving some assistance from their extended families, and another five spoke of borrowing money to help themselves scrape by. A number were pinning their futures on their children. Four acknowledged they did not want to be *dibaohu,* but saw that they had no other recourse. Three talked of feeling ashamed and seven of them, when queried about their relations with neighbours, disclosed that their situation was so dishonourable (*bu guangrong*) that they preferred not to mix with others.

Six alleged that they couldn't understand the workings of the programme, possibly an indirect form of criticism of its irrationalities and unofficial inequities. Just one openly railed about her lack of power to convey her dissatisfactions to personnel in charge; another expressed dishearteningly that it was of no use to do so. More than a fourth (15) offered negative opinions about the programme and its workings, generally when I was not present, while only 10 families had positive things to say, nearly always – to the contrary – when I was there. Three broke down into tears with me as they described their plight.

The general impression the transcript affords is of an assortment of downtrodden cast-asides, abandoned by the community even as they wilfully absent themselves from it. This decaying fragment of Chinese society, a product of the state's – and Wuhan's – drive to develop, appears to be no more than minimally tethered to life, poised as its members are meant to be – humble tokens of the veneer of compassion celebrating China's alleged 'socialism'. That they are not prone to foment disorder – the ensuring of which appears to be the subtext underlying this shabby benevolence – is not surprising, given their hunger, their isolation, their weakened or wasted bodies, their confusion, their futile hopes and, for a tiny few, their pitiful gratitude. Quiet and subdued, these people will cause no chaos. Below I detail some of these themes.

The most urgent issues: illness, disability and schooling

Illness and disability

In all the cases where someone was in poor health the patient stayed at home, lay on a bed nearly all of the time, was unable to work and contrived to subsist, if barely, by swallowing a minimal amount of medicine, visiting a hospital only in times of dire emergency. Here are several typical examples.

First the husband speaks:

> My wife [aged 44] got uremia [urine poison illness] in 2002; she's from the countryside and has never worked, for her medical funds she's completely dependent on me. Before, when she wasn't sick, she could do household chores, now she can only lie on the bed, can't do anything. The medical fees are very high, she sometimes gets dialysis. We basically despise this illness, everyday she stays home, takes a little medicine, and in this way drags on.

Soon the wife chimes in:

> The doctors in the hospital would let you stay for treatment, but we haven't so much money, basically we can't afford it. Each day I can take some medicine to control the illness, and that's very good, I can't hope to cure the illness, can just live a day and write it off [*huo yitian, suan yitian*], sometimes I think if I can only lie on the bed all day like this, unable to do anything, it's the family's burden, it's not as good as dying earlier.

54   *Dorothy J. Solinger*

As she speaks, there's a tear in her eye and the daughter quietly goes away (Interview 1).

In two other homes it is rheumatism, while elsewhere a husband down with cancer receives a petty 70 yuan from his former work unit (Interviews 6, 23, 33). One man with a vision problem never worked, while his wife's rural *hukou* (household registration) has limited her employment possibilities (Interview 48). Perhaps the most pitiful tale is one related by a young wife in tears: when she married her husband she was not aware of his schizophrenia. Having been hospitalized four times since their 2003 wedding, he takes a medication that renders him dull and stiff, his reactions slowed down, so he is routinely cheated each time he goes out to work (Interview 50).

At yet another home, twin 19-year-old sons had some media training but, without any connections, 'they basically can't find work that fits their speciality'. To raise the money for their education, their mother explains, 'I and their father worked day and night, a year ago we both got so worn out we had to go to the hospital. But as soon as we got in we got right out; it was too expensive, there was nowhere we could afford to go' (Interview 42).

Children, too, are afflicted and unattended to. In one family, a 22-year-old son was born blind and has never worked, but has no way to acquire entree into a work unit for the disabled (Interview 28); in a household that a divorced wife had abandoned, a 59-year-old husband is compelled to stay at home to minister to his 26-year-old son, born with no upper limbs or left leg (Interview 30). In a third, the medical needs of a 'mentally deficient' daughter, now 19, have devoured the family's entire savings (Interview 47).

And then there are aged relatives limping along without a pension, as one whose body just 'gets worse and worse, always running to the hospital to see the doctor ... medical costs are too high; we feel the state should finance her medical care or give her preferential treatment' (Interview 17). Ironically, the chief *dibao* official in Wuhan proudly listed the 12 preferential benefits supposedly accruing to *dibaohu* in the city (two more than Beijing offered), though interviews such as this one clearly indicated they were far from always extended (Interview, Wuhan, 28 August 2007; Yang and Zhang 1999: 100).

Schooling

Dibao parents live in anxiety over how they can finance tuition. One mother, her husband off serving a sentence in labour reform, has become resigned to her son's having dropped out of school: 'He's 16, after finishing junior high he discontinued his studies and is staying at home. There's no money for him to go on' (Interview 39). A father of a 16-year-old boy is determined to put him through higher education: 'There's no question that he'll go on, but when I think about college I get so worried my scalp tingles. When the time comes if I can come up with a solution to this problem, that'll be good I'm considering making him study at a free teachers' college, relying on the *dibao*, but that little money is far, far from being enough' (Interview 46).

A daughter, aged 19, is doing well in senior high, and would 'like to attend a vocational school so she can go out to work sooner and lighten the household's burden. But our family basically can't pay the tuition. We hope we can borrow some money from the bank' (Interview 1). In the home where the husband has cancer the daughter is 20 and in college, but all the tuition is borrowed and her parents 'have no ability to pay it' (Interview 23).

These apprehensions exist not only in families where money must be found for financing higher education. A wife with arthritis is the mother of 10-year-old twins, considered a precious blessing at the time of their birth, when people like their parents were all employed. The mother bemoans her fate:

> Now while they're at primary school it's okay, don't have to spend too much money ... later if they both go on to middle school, expenditures will be too much, their father and I are very worried, can't not let kids go to school or in the future there will be even less of a way out. And both are boys; if they were girls, and found a good marriage we could be done with it, but with boys there are more considerations. These are things we ordinarily don't want to give too much thought to, as soon as we think about them we just worry, so we just pass our days like this and then we'll think about it (Interview 8).

The father of an 8-year-old girl has not yet begun to fret; primary school is not very expensive. 'But primary school and university can't be compared,' he reasoned. 'If she continues to study later on, I don't know if we can do it' (Interview 45). In another household with a 10-year-old, however, the father already had his concerns: 'Okay, we don't need to pay tuition. But the school has so many miscellaneous fees, books, it's all a mess, each semester we have to pay a lot; in the schools today it's impossible to slack off on the fees even a little bit. Later, going to middle school the fees will definitely be higher' (Interview 5). In the family with a retarded daughter, the mother reports that:

> The days are passed in tension. With all our money used up on the daughter, now the son must go to school, and that only adds to our burden. He's about to enter his last year of junior high, and we have no money but still have to help him go to school. I and his father are bitterly working and are all tired out and yet we must provide for him. With his sister in this condition, we're all counting on him and he'll have to fight to do well.
> (Interview 47)

Most hard up is the wife of the schizophrenia-afflicted man, presently tending to an infant. 'Even with the *dibao*, there's still not enough money and the kid will have to go to nursery school [in a few years]. Preferential policies for school won't be enough' (Interview 50).

Even as these parents anxiously wonder how they will ever find the cash to cultivate their children, at the same time many imagine those very same

56 Dorothy J. Solinger

children as their saviours for their own later years. Large numbers among the recipients of the *dibao* – if not every one of them – appear as of this reading to be locked into an inter-generational trap whose long-term label must be 'the underclass'.

Daily sustenance: work, food and borrowing

Work

If at work the woman in the household would usually be doing 'sanitation work' (*weisheng gongzuo*), meaning sweeping the streets. For men, it was 'odd jobs' (*dagong*), quite unreliable, low paid and intermittent. In either case, the take was terribly tiny. Frequently people commented despondently of grave problems getting employment or starting up businesses. Common refrains were their lack of the necessary social connections, the high level of competition among job-seekers, their deficient knowledge or skill, their age or their poor health and failing strength.

A man aged 38 began 'going out' to Guangdong for odd jobs not long after being laid off, prompted by plans to provide for his son's schooling, because in Wuhan he could not get suitable work, and thought he could earn more in the east, where there were also more opportunities. 'But after going out, his circumstances were poor, because without any 'culture' (*wenhua*) and not having mastered any specialized craft, the work he engaged in wasn't secure, the situation was sometimes good and sometimes bad. At times the money he made was just enough to maintain his livelihood while he was out.' His wife tries to accumulate a bit of income by darning clothing, mostly for neighbours, but 'everyone's standard of living is very low, so I can't earn much money' (Interview 7).

A man of 44, reflecting on his potential, despairingly offered this defeatist perspective:

> We all grew up in the city, didn't eat any bitterness and didn't do any heavy physical labour. Now in the labour market there's some construction work and it all demands rather a lot of such labour. They wouldn't want us 40-year-old laid-off workers, and there's some work that, if you give it to us to do we couldn't manage such intensity, eventually we'd just damage our health and have to take medicine, and trying to work would become even more untenable.
>
> (Interview 9)

Several spoke of their time as a pedicab driver, an occupation that Wuhan authorities eliminated in 2002 in the city districts for its unsightly aspect, its suggestion of backwardness, and its interruption of the modern, rapid vehicles of transport taking over the avenues. One man 39 years of age with just a junior high education made his living pedalling a cart after his layoff, but was

Dibaohu *in distress*   57

forced to give it up when the ban was placed. Ever since, he 'very much has wanted to find work, but is always rebuffed' (Interview 29).

Starting one's own business might seem another option, yet lack of start-up capital is a significant obstacle. More fundamentally, however, where these people reside there simply is no market. As one man explained, 'We tried in the past to sell breakfast in the community. We made some hot noodles, things like that. But where we live, the masses everywhere have low incomes, the level of consumption is really low, everyone just eats breakfast at home, so it basically didn't work out' (Interview 4). Another head of household, asked whether he had considered setting up a small shop, had a nearly identical reply: 'Where we live it's rather out of the way, many residents are the nearby state enterprise's laid-off staff and workers. Those who found other good work have basically all moved away, so setting up a retail food and fruit stall is useless – there would be few who would buy. If they have a little money they buy some ordinary vegetables and that's it' (Interview 9).

A web-based analysis frames the problem within a more analytical framework:

> In poor communities the economy creates social segregation, which causes economic units' incomes to fall. So the units leave the area, and capital migrates away, only deepening the poverty. Then there's no way to supply jobs or create tax income for the community. Purchasing power is low, and the return on investment is negligible, so outside businesses won't enter and there's no way internally to generate economic entities. Even if there are those with initiative, they'll leave, so the community will lose their role as a model.
>
> ('Zhongguo chengshi' 2006)

In short, there are simply no spare funds in such locales either for forming or for patronizing commercial ventures.

Eating and borrowing

With income-earning opportunities so scarce, how do the *dibaohu* manage to survive at all? Three answers emerge: they eat minimally, get handouts from family members and borrow money. Statements such as this one, from the mother of the twins, cropped up several times: 'We usually buy the cheapest vegetables, the kids are still little, occasionally buy a little meat, and just give it to them to eat' (Interview 8). In a household without any children, the two spouses refer to 'the food we eat' as 'very dull'; 'after all these years we've gotten used to it', they disclose (Interview 10). Two maiden sisters in their forties residing together just 'swallow the cheapest possible food to sustain [their] lives' (Interview 53). One grandmother, raising her teenage granddaughter, occasionally treats the girl to an egg while she herself survives on nothing but vegetables, unable even to afford any fruit, much less meat (Interview 36). The bottom line here is that the

58   *Dorothy J. Solinger*

families who subsist on the *dibao* have been nearly starving themselves for over a decade (Tang 2003b).

As noted earlier, almost a third of the respondents mentioned financial assistance from friends and relatives. Twelve households had family members outside the household who provided some steady help; the other five only spoke of 'borrowing,' debts very likely to go forever unpaid. If the aid is long term and regularly received the *dibao* managers reduce the family's allowance. But if it is offered just in an emergency or to meet a specific, time-limited need there is likely to be no deduction, according to fund administrators in one community (Interview, Wuhan, Community X).

Relatives might support a child in school (Interviews 4, 12). In one case the loan amount was truly astronomical: a woman's older sister had already invested 10,000 yuan in her niece's college costs by the time we talked (Interview 25). In other cases the money is for expenses like electrical and water fees (Interview 24). Most of the time, though, the sums are trivial, in the range of one to two hundred yuan per month. Yet given their circumstances the recipients may find this small change makes all the difference (Interviews 28, 29, 34).

Taking these hand-outs, however, is by no means without its psychological cost. As one recipient confided, 'Sometimes relatives help some with our ordinary livelihood expenses, but always looking for someone to help feels very bad' (Interview 22). Neither is borrowing an adequate coping strategy, as one respondent made plain: 'We've borrowed a lot and still haven't paid it back; we're embarrassed to ask again. Now our only hope is that our family members can stay healthy' (Interview 7). The two sisters find themselves caught in the same exigency: 'In the past we borrowed money from friends, but now that's hard to do because people fear we won't pay it back' (Interview 53).

Some *dibaohu*, attempting to obtain funds they were not entitled to, falsely report their income, forge documents, or otherwise conceal their earnings or assets. There also are instances of so-called 'mistaken thinking' among the beneficiaries, as when people are said to 'take the responsibility they themselves should bear and push it off to society and to the government', demanding, for example, that the state give their old parent a supplement, 'even when there are five or six siblings who could shoulder the burden'.

One Wuhan community leader explained that without a systematic, societal-wide credit system there is no way to check whether *dibao* targets are also getting a monthly pension. She alluded to 'misinterpretation' of the programme causing inappropriate appeals. In particular, residents in ill health with necessary outlays beyond their means may 'fail to comprehend' that the *dibao* is based on income, not on expenditures, and thus is not geared to help people meet all their costs. Asked whether there were troublemakers, she was quick to affirm it: 'There are some residents who create unusual difficulties,' she reported, who 'clearly don't fit the criteria for getting the *dibao* but still press for it, often running about shouting verbal threats' (Interview, Wuhan, Community V).

Dibaohu *in distress*   59

Opinions and feelings towards the dibao

Positive and negative assessments

In general, voiced negative attitudes somewhat outweighed positive ones. But affirmations were often hedged with caveats and qualms, and negative views tended to include a fundamental acceptance of the system. Here are a few such ambivalent views: 'We very much support the *dibao*, feel it's a good policy, but it absolutely can't solve our family's problems. Our suggestion is that the government should base its work on each family's actual circumstances, not just rely on a household's income to determine the amount to give' (Interview 1).

Another asserted: 'The *dibao* really can solve some of our livelihood expenditures, so it's very necessary, but some of our daily life is very hard to maintain. We're rather satisfied with the *dibao*. But ordinarily the investigation and verification procedures are full of trivial details and complexities; we hope they can simplify it a little in the future' (Interview 4). A third informant, a divorced father raising a 10-year-old son, alleged: 'For use in normal matters of consumption, it's possible but a struggle. Though the money isn't much, it's better to have it than not, it can sustain our livelihood' (Interview 5).

The more purely positive appraisals were voiced with me in the room. One subject, whose mother-in-law had been lying paralysed for half a year, with me listening, stated that she felt that 'the *dibao* is a kind of display of concern for us (*zhaogu*), it's fine (*hai keyi*), the amount is ok, our needs are few' (Interview 3). And a second one, the grandmother living with her granddaughter, letting a few tears fall, expressed her gratitude: 'The government shows a lot of care for us, I really thank (*feichang ganxie*) the government and the Party. Otherwise we'd have to go to the street to beg' (Interview 36). The mother of the blind man with a six-year-old son termed the 'policy pretty good' (*zhengce bucuo*), emphasizing at the end that, 'We're all satisfied, we have no complaints,' once more in my hearing (Interview 48).

As noted, those who grumbled did so when I was not in the room. A man in poor health with a son in junior high criticized the programme thus: 'Now prices are inflating terribly, whatever you buy is very expensive, getting a little *dibao* basically isn't enough, now we're spending it ever faster, only a few days after receiving it – after buying rice and oil – it's gone. We *dibaohu* should get more than we do, it should cover our daily expenses ... they can't just consider the number of people in the family, this way it can't solve any problems' (Interview 11). Asked for their opinion, another couple had just this to convey: 'The *dibao*'s examinations are too strict, each time they come to check it's very upsetting, causes a lot of chaos, the people coming to investigate have no manners' (Interview 13).

Others carp about the insufficiencies of the supplements: 'Every year at new year's they're supposed to give us presents, but I've never gotten any' (Interview 14); and 'They should cut or cancel the kids' high school tuition costs',

60 *Dorothy J. Solinger*

cavilled another (Interview 18). And the mother of a retarded girl noted that the family did not get the amount they ought to have, commenting that, 'Of course the *dibao* isn't enough, recently the days are very tense, all the prices went up ... having a student and a sick person in the family ... they all need money' (Interview 47).

Whether for the programme or against it, almost to a person there is little reflection over state policies' role in leading the individual and his/her family into poverty; most attribute their misfortunes to their age or inadequate strength and skill. But one rare informant, a man of 42 residing alone, places the source of his situation squarely outside himself: 'I'm dissatisfied with my present livelihood, feel it's very unfair. How I got to be living this way is mainly due to social causes [a euphemism for Party policies], otherwise I could not be without work' (Interview 14).

Hopes

The many hopes enunciated seem to lift a bit the mood of dependency and passivity. Frequently uttered are wishes for at least 'a little more subsidy' (Interviews 5, 18, 21, 22, 23, 25, 27, 34, 51, 52); improved health or funds to address sickness – as one woman plaintively put it, 'I hope for free medical treatment, otherwise only can wait to die' (Interviews 7, 17, 21, 33, 35, 42, 47, 52); discounts for children's education (Interviews 16, 18); and for help with job training or introductions to employment. Several speakers dream of having a family member assigned to a work unit for the disabled (Interviews 16, 17, 18, 21, 23, 28, 29, 32). A number of informants – no doubt the specially discontented – verbalized more than just one desire. But only a single speaker, in yearning to see the programme's implementation become fair and open, articulated a longing for an improvement addressing more than her own conditions (Interview 52).

Shame and isolation

The pluckier among the lot made it apparent that, no matter how essential to their wherewithal the *dibao* might be, they would prefer to be able to sustain themselves and their families without it. A few quotations demonstrate this stance: 'I'm a person with a rather competitive personality,' asserted a 44-year-old woman, who had received no regular education, had been unemployed for years, and whose health was poor. 'If I were healthy, I certainly would look for something to do, the family can't go on in such economic difficulty, taking the *dibao* is really no way; if I weren't ill, we all wouldn't want to be a *dibaohu*' (Interview 1). 'We didn't expect to take the *dibao*,' declared another woman. 'Mainly it's because we really don't have the ability to work, can't find stable work, so all we can do is to apply [for it]' (Interview 4).

Behind the discomfort of being a recipient lies a good deal of shame. The wife of the schizophrenic man, though in absolutely dire straits, was 'embarrassed to go to apply, feel[s] too young to take it'. She should be supporting herself, she judged, but saddled with rearing a one-and-a-half-year-old baby, she cannot (Interview 50). And a couple in their late forties, both laid-off workers, 'feel we, as people getting the *dibao*, are not too honourable (*guangcai*); since our son got out of school for the summer he has just stayed home, won't play with other kids, during vacation he rarely goes out, has a sense of inferiority' (Interview 4).

Like this young man, a common sense of disgrace prevents the beneficiaries from initiating exchanges with neighbours. One relates common feelings: 'Ordinarily *dibaohu* talk very little among themselves about how much money they get, generally keep it a secret' (Interview 22). A 67-year-old widow without formal education still had her pride: 'We don't communicate with other *dibao* targets; I basically don't know other people's situation ... I'm also embarrassed to raise the issue with other people, after all, taking the *dibao* isn't a very honourable thing' (Interview 48).

Another woman in her sixties pointed out that a lot of her neighbours also receive the *dibao*, but don't discuss it among themselves (Interview 36). The wife of the schizophrenic man replied in the negative when queried as to whether she speaks about her situation with those living in her community. 'No,' she responds, 'the family's affairs are not easy to speak of much with others, now too many people will look at you and laugh at you' (Interview 50). Obviously, the sense of disgrace these impoverished people feel cuts off any inclination to form a grouping that might protest in unison.

Rebelliousness

Still, among the litany of sufferings – both of the body and of the heart – are the reactions of a mere handful of challengers. Only one revealed spats with the management personnel leading to her estrangement from the community. In general, what could be anger seems to come masked as mystification. A father, asked whether he had been given extra subsidies to deal with recent inflation, refrained from criticizing the system, simply claiming that, 'I've heard that we *dibaohu* are to have a price subsidy of 30 yuan, but actually getting it is not too clear. Each month when they issue us our money, I also don't know concretely how it's calculated. They give us a certain amount, and it's just that amount [*gei duoshao, jiushi duoshao*], haven't inquired' (Interview 5).

The wife of a three-person household, a junior high graduate, seems to have given up in a state of ignorance, though perhaps her perplexity belies some dissent: 'We understand some, but not too much,' she claimed. 'We only know there's some price subsidies, and in winter there's funds for warmth. Concretely it's really not too clear. Anyway, it's such a small amount of money, it's hard to calculate. However much there is, that's it, we don't haggle over the details' (Interview 11).

Two other informants were more straightforward about the futility of expounding upon their grievances. One father, queried as to whether he had

62 Dorothy J. Solinger

any suggestions for the system operators, offered this rejoinder: 'Suggestions I do have, but it's no use. I wish the government would give more money. Now ordinary people (*laobaixing*) don't have the right to speak. Going to the doctor is expensive, studying is hard – how can we solve the problems in a short time? But raising it is useless [*tile ye shi baiti*]' (Interview 46). In the same state of mind, a 34-year-old woman had this to say: 'Suggesting hasn't much use, just hope I can enter a hospital, now seeing a doctor is something I can't afford. ... Basic-level implementation lacks supervision and guarantees, the *laobaixing* don't know much about the actual policy, how the subsidy they issue us each month is really calculated, we're all unclear' (Interview 52).

In the midst of such fatalistic and phlegmatic postures, one pugnacious 67-year-old widow stands out; she dared to wrangle with the administrators in her community. Convinced that her family was not being treated fairly, she charged:

> In 2003, when we got into the system, the subsidy was very transparent, the public bulletin board told how much income each household had every month, what their subsidy was, how much was deducted. But these past two years, it's not this way. Among us *dibaohu* we don't know how much other people are getting.

Questioned as to whether she was being given a larger subsidy after inflation set in, she inveighed, 'It's not like that'. Then she went on to give a fuller explanation:

> Since my daughter-in-law went out to work, and the residents' committee found out, my son's *dibao* was cut back. Getting 100-plus yuan each month is not as good as when it first began. We're a family with an old person [herself], my son can't see and has no labour ability, my daughter-in-law's little money can take care of her son, but [because of this] the residents' committee now deducts our family's allowance. Other families have two people going out to work and their money wasn't deducted. Since I argued opinionatedly with the residents' committee they said I shouldn't compare myself with other people. But our family has no money, no connections, so things can only be this way.

Asked if she has any communication with other *dibaohu*, she ranted on: 'Since my son's subsidy was taken away, I very rarely go to the residents' committee office, don't speak to other *dibaohu*, and when the residents' committee holds a meeting they don't call me, so I basically don't know other people's situation.' Did she get a recent increase, the interviewer wanted to know. Her answer was, again, defiant:

> It increased some, but I don't know why, the *laobaixing* are all very bewildered, sometimes more money comes and we don't know why, when

the total is more we're very happy. I just hope to understand how this subsidy is granted, we ordinary people don't get to see the civil affairs department's documents. The residents' committee ought to treat people equally, everyone should be equal before the regulations, it shouldn't happen that because of a certain family's connections they can do whatever.

(Interview 48)

Of all the informants, only this one older subject had the nerve to give voice to her vexations. And yet, it must be underlined, hushed up among her neighbours by her feelings of humiliation, and pushed aside by her programme managers, she poses no threat to the so-precious stability of the party-state.

Conclusion

The *dibao* programme was admittedly put into place to do nothing more than meet the most minimal requirements of the targeted needy. Its recipients were to be kept alive but muted, in the interest of rendering Wuhan modern without their interference, whether that interference might transpire out on the roadways as they eke out an unsightly sustenance or otherwise venture outside, as in the act of rebelling. Above all, they were not to disturb the forward march of the city onward towards progress, which their uncultured and unwell persons were prone to sully. Given that these objectives are never far from the surface in the minds and the work of officialdom, especially in Wuhan, with its wealth of laid-off workers and its world-class aspirations – counting the *dibao* as poverty alleviation is off the mark. So it would not be surprising if those who receive it might simulate misunderstanding, as they angle for a larger allocation.

And not just the programme itself calls for an ambivalent assessment; the status of Wuhan's version of it is indeterminate comparatively, as well. Granted, placed next to Lanzhou, which receives more central government financial help, it appears harsh. But statistics suggest that its outlays are probably more or less average over time. What is clear from several dozen household chats there, however, is that the recipients of Wuhan's allocations are living on the margin between misery and maintenance, and that is where they and their offspring are apt to remain.

Note

1 Chongqing's very low figure can only be the result of its including in its calculations the incomes of rural residents living within its borders.

4 Local variation in urban social assistance

Community public service agencies in Dalian[1]

Daniel R. Hammond

The provision of urban social assistance in China has experienced a great deal of change during the reform era, and since the mid-1990s has been dominated by the emergence and development of the Minimum Livelihood Guarantee (*zuidi shenghuo baozhang*, hereafter MLG). Initially an initiative developed in the city of Shanghai in 1993, the MLG has evolved into a programme that has been promoted nationwide since 1999. It delivers a means-tested benefit by measuring average per capita household income against a locally set MLG line. The MLG line is set at the amount defined as necessary to sustain a livelihood in the city and the benefit paid to households aims to bring their income up to this amount.

Guan Xinping and Xu Bing's chapter in this book argues that the structure of centre–local relations has provided space for a wide range of local variations in the MLG to emerge, while Dorothy Solinger's chapter has discussed variation in the MLG benefit entitlements between cities. This chapter will discuss a local variant in the management of the MLG in the city of Dalian (Liaoning Province). After 2000, Dalian set up Community Public Service Agencies (*gonggong fuwushe*, hereafter CPSAs) both to filter out MLG recipients who should not be receiving the benefit and to provide psychological support to those recipients who are receiving benefits. This chapter seeks to explain why the CPSAs emerged in Dalian and contribute to a theoretical understanding of why variations in the local welfare mix emerge. Drawing on concepts from Lieberthal and Oksenberg's (1988) fragmented authoritarianism model, public policy and comparative welfare literature, I argue not only that – in line with Guan and Xu – institutional structures of the Chinese state are important (c.f. Lieberthal 1992, 1995; Lieberthal and Oksenberg 1988), but also that policy feedback within and outside of the social assistance policy sphere (Pierson 1994) and the interventions of a number of significant policy sponsors (Kingdon 1984; Baumgartner and Jones 1993) combined to create the circumstances in Dalian within which local policy variation could occur.

This chapter is structured as follows. First, I set out the operation and objectives of the CPSA policy in the city of Dalian. In the next section, I provide some background to the context of the CPSAs' development and then outline the phases of development they went through, highlighting in particular the cooperation between local government and the research community. A section on institutional elements then follows, where I first argue that the decentralized nature of the Chinese state and its institutional structures provided a context where variation could occur. I then argue that feedback from the original MLG policy, in terms of both design and outcomes, and also failings in policy toward laid-off (*xiagang*) workers, provided an agenda for policy change. Finally, I discuss the role of three different policy sponsors and make the case that it was the action of this combination of sponsors, operating in the space and on the agenda created by the institutional features discussed previously, which led to the CPSA policy being implemented. The chapter will conclude with some brief comments on the CPSAs in relation to the moral aspect of social assistance provision.

The CPSA policy

The CPSAs' stated goal was to solve three challenges faced by the MLG policy at a local level. First, they sought to ensure that those on the MLG were not boosting their income in some other way – for example through the non-reporting of work which increased household income above the MLG line. Second, they sought to ensure that those who were receiving MLG benefits participated in the community through altruistic projects, thereby challenging any negative perceptions of the MLG or of those receiving the benefit. Finally, the CPSAs were to provide a means through which those on the MLG could seek work. These last two objectives also sought to build feelings of community, integration and psychological well being amongst the CPSA members (SPRC CASS 2001b: 14; Pei 2002: 51). As Solinger points out in her chapter, the day-to-day pressures faced by MLG recipients are psychological as well as economic. A final wider objective of the CPSAs was to ensure continued social stability by continuing to provide MLG and also counter the specific problems highlighted above. These aims were achieved through the establishing of CPSAs at the 'Community' (*shequ*) level within the urban governmental system. The Communities are not officially a level of government although they do carry out policy on the government's behalf.[2] They are classed as agencies for the Sub-district offices (*jiedao banshichu*) themselves agencies of the District (*qu*) level of urban government (see Derleth and Koldyk 2004).

A CPSA, as defined by those involved in the project, is registered as a non-profit non-governmental (*feizhengfu*) organization (hereafter, NGO) (SPRC CASS 2001a: 10) with the local district Civil Affairs Bureau (CAB) operating as its administrative supervisor (SPRC CASS 2001c: 16). A CPSA is run by and on behalf of the MLG recipients with the support of the local CAB and Community. The MLG recipients themselves organize it, while the CAB and Community provide required funds, space for meetings and community based work. Recipients are required to attend and can be monitored through

66   Daniel R. Hammond

community work projects organized by the CPSAs. Any resident on the MLG who is in employment should be unable to attend required work projects and would forfeit MLG payments after missing three of these community work assignments (SPRC CASS 2003: 3).

In addition, these opportunities to work for the community are perceived by the CPSA designers as helping reduce negative perceptions of MLG recipients. And through the organization of the CPSA it is argued by CAB officials and SPRC researchers that the MLG recipients themselves will begin to view themselves better and feel less isolated because they are working for the community (Interview BJ07–2; SPRC CASS 2003: 4). The CPSAs are also designed to provide a means for MLG recipients to find reemployment. Rather than operating as a formal job centre, they provide a form of mutual help group for those on the MLG. Self-support and learning among MLG recipients is encouraged in the CPSA and CAB officials suggest that this will help the recipients to adapt to their existing circumstances and also to move forward (Interview BJ07–2). It should be noted there is no formal mechanism for finding MLG recipients work. The idea is that job seeking will become easier when people are supported by other MLG recipients seeking work.

After initial start-up funding (to which the United Kingdom government's Department for International Development also contributed[3]), the CPSAs have required little further finance. This is because they are organized and run by the MLG recipients themselves under the supervision of the local Community and Subdistrict office (*jiedao banshichu*) and, therefore, should not have additional overheads as they do not have offices or formally employed staff. Funds generated by compensated public works which the CPSA can carry out on request can also be fed back into the organization. All funds are used under the principle of 'taken for the people, used for the people' (*quzhiyumin, yongzhiyumin*) so that if a CPSA has, for example, cleaned a road and been paid for it, the funds can be used by the CPSA (SPRC CASS 2001d). The Community and Subdistrict also provide the assignments for the community work that the CPSA must carry out (in order to uncover fraud, see above). This does not, rule out the possibility of them providing funding, but neither does it indicate how any funding might be used. But it has been suggested that if local governments were able to provide funding then the CPSAs would be permitted to use it, for example to provide training courses (Ge and Yang 2003: 255).

The CPSA policy initiative is interesting for a variety of reasons. First, in terms of understanding the origins of policy it provides a well-documented example of government and researchers working together. Indeed, this was noted in discussion with a Ministry of Civil Affairs official, who reported that such cooperative opportunities do not arise frequently (Interview BJ07–3). Second, the CPSA policy also emerged at a fascinating point in time as the MLG expanded rapidly not only in Dalian but also nationwide. In the midst of what was a massive mobilization of resources for MLG, Dalian decided on

Local variation in urban social assistance 67

a different direction. Third, the CPSA has a number of interesting characteristics. For example in organizational terms the agencies operate as state sanctioned NGOs. Although such government organized NGOs are not unique – the re-employment centres of the late 1990s are another example (see Cai 2006) – the construction of numerous grassroots NGOs across a city was highlighted in interviews with officials (Interview BJ07–3) and informal discussions with SPRC researchers as potentially controversial. It is also unusual that the policy's objectives do not focus on the delivery of a particular material goal, as many other social welfare and assistance policies do, but instead focuses on the non-material needs of MLG recipients and community relations. Finally, the CPSA policy provides an active solution to one of the issues perceived as facing the MLG – fraudulent benefit recipients. Concerns over the misuse of powers in allocating the MLG and fraudulent recipients are not specific to Dalian and also emerged in discussions with Civil Affairs officials in Beijing and in Anqing City, Anhui Province (Interview BJ06–2; Anqing Field-notes 2006).

Dalian and MLG background

Dalian's geographical and economic position in north east China's Liaoning province has meant it has experienced both the benefits and difficulties associated with the post-Mao reform. Open to outside investment and trade since 1984, Dalian has been in a position to benefit from liberalized economic development, investment and connections with the outside world. It is also the terminus for pipelines serving the Daqing oilfields and the location of associated refinery facilities. In addition, a mix of light and heavy industries has allowed Dalian to successfully develop its economy, particularly in comparison with other localities in the north east. But Dalian's success has not always been assured, and the city's industrial base was the cause of some concern during the late 1990s and into the early twenty-first century as China struggled to cope with the reform of its state owned sector. Today Dalian is an economic success, having begun to diversify into information technology and attracting investors such as Intel, while building on the city's traditional industrial base (People's Daily Online, 2007). Since the turn of the century the city has experienced double digit GDP growth and since 2002 annual increases have consistently been greater than 14.1 per cent (Anon., Yiju Zhongguo Dalian Jigou, 2008; Dalian Bureau of Statistics Online, 2009).

A factor in the development of the CPSAs was the position of Dalian within the Chinese state. Dalian has, since 1985, been given a degree of political autonomy. Although not the provincial capital of Liaoning province, it sits beneath the central government rather than the provincial government in economic planning terms (it is formally a *jihuadanlie shi*, in Chinese) and so enjoys more autonomy than many other cities (Dalian Government Online 2003). Thus while not a provincial-level city like Shanghai and Beijing, it has enjoyed similar economic success and political autonomy. It is also known for

68 Daniel R. Hammond

its policy innovations in social security and social assistance policy (Dalian CAB 1999). The MLG was implemented in Dalian in 1995 marking the city an early pioneer of the policy. This was a response to the suggestion by the Minister for Civil Affairs (the Ministry responsible for social assistance), Duoji Cairang, that the MLG be set up to establish a model for the rest of Liaoning Province (Zhang 2002: 18). The Dalian 'model',[4] as it came to be known, used the emerging Community agencies beneath the local government to administer the MLG and the local government to raise revenues for the policy. This was an innovation on the dominant Shanghai model of the time.

When first set up in Dalian, the MLG line (*dibao xian*) was established at 140 yuan per household member per month. Civil Affairs departments (government departments beneath the Ministry of Civil Affairs) administered the programme through 'residents' committees' (*jumin weiyuanhui*, supposedly grassroots community organizations that are used by local governments to implement certain policies) across the city (Ren 1995). From 1995 until July 1999 the MLG level in Dalian was adjusted upwards six times finally reaching 221 yuan per household member per month (Dalian CAB and SPRC CASS 2002: 81). It should be noted that up to 1999 the MLG as implemented in Dalian was, as one official called it, a small (*xiao*) version of the policy (Interview BJ07–2). By this she meant that it provided for a minimum number of people as interpreted by the Dalian Civil Affairs Bureau.

In June 1999, the Dalian Civil Affairs Bureau reconfigured the MLG system.[5] In order to deal with the increasing numbers of workers affected by enterprise reform and the increasing complexity of urban poverty and problems in the delivery of the laid-off worker 'basic living guarantee', the city introduced a 'Four-in-One' (*siwei yiti*) system of social assistance. The new system broadened the categories of people eligible for the MLG to include households with no incomes but school-age children or long-term sick householders, and it raised the MLG line from 190 to 221 yuan. It also introduced a card system for urban workers with a household income below the MLG line that provided them with an additional 39 yuan a month for food and other essential items. The third part of the system was a call to ensure that the various bureaux involved in social assistance provision cooperated to provide 'one policy for one house' (*yihu yice*). The final part of the new system was a temporary poverty relief provision for those affected by disasters or illness (Dalian CAB 1999). The move to the Four-in-One system can be viewed as another innovation by the city in social assistance but it was also resource intense using 32.4 million yuan per year in 1999 (Dalian CAB 1999). It was in this context of innovation and expansion that Premier Zhu Rongji visited the city in 2000.

Premier Zhu's visit to the city and subsequent comments he made had significant consequences both nationally and locally. Zhu was evidently impressed by the implementation and function of the MLG in Dalian. His opinion was that China should establish a social security system that was independent of enterprises and instead focused on administration and delivery through the

Local variation in urban social assistance   69

community. Previous efforts at social security reform, especially those dealing with the laid-off workers, used their former employers as a means to deliver benefits, but were regarded as having failed (Tang 2003: 23). Nationally Zhu's decision was to be resolved through the mobilization of resources for the 'Ought to Protect, Further Protect' (*yingbao jinbao*) campaign which saw mainly laid-off workers moved onto the MLG. This move was funded by the central government and increased the numbers receiving the MLG significantly. In Dalian, the use of the MLG as a means to provide social benefits outside enterprises to groups like laid-off workers appealed to Premier Zhu faced with the challenge of reforming the social security system.

According to a local Civil Affairs official (Interview BJ07–2), Premier Zhu's approval of the Dalian MLG implementation galvanized the local CAB to resolve the problems facing the policy at that time. The Dalian City CAB contacted the Social Policy Research Centre (SPRC) of the Chinese Academy of Social Sciences (CASS) in Beijing and invited them to participate in the development of measures to resolve the challenges of perceived fraud, social isolation and the need for MLG recipients to find employment. This initiated the first of four distinct chronological phases in the evolution of the CPSA policy. It should be noted that the CPSA is referred to as both a policy (*zhengce*) and a project (*xiangmu*) in documents that refer to the organizations. The Dalian government (after the initial CPSA implementation, see Dalian CAB Online 2008), formal interviewees and informal contacts used the term *policy* when referring to the CPSA initiative and so I use the term policy in discussion here.

The evolution of the CPSAs

The phases that the CPSA policy went through that will be discussed here it demonstrate the high level of cooperation and activities of different policy sponsors. The first phase in the development of the CPSAs ran from May to July 2000, as the CPSA was prepared for a small-scale policy experiment. A survey was carried out by the SPRC research team during May in order to form the basis of policy proposals. The SPRC team then presented the results of this survey and initial policy plans to the Dalian CAB and Dalian Xigang District CAB in two documents: 'The Dalian City Plan for the Community Based Synthesis of the MLG and the Livelihood Guarantee System' (SPRC CASS 2000a) and 'The Dalian City, Xigang District Plan to Complete the Social Security System Experiment' (SPRC CASS 2000b). During the rest of June and into July the SPRC revised the document six times at the request of the Xigang District CAB. These revisions resulted in the 'Xigang District Plan to Complete Social Security System Experimental Work', which was submitted by the Xigang District CAB to the Dalian City CAB and also directly to the district government. Following acceptance of the new revised version of the policy, the CPSAs moved into their next phase with a practical study of the policy in Xigang workers' residence neighbourhood. This

70   *Daniel R. Hammond*

practical phase ran from November 2000 to March 2001 in the Workers' Residence neighbourhood of Xigang District (SPRC CASS 2003: 43–44).

The third phase of the CPSA policy began with the end of the practical phase. This phase saw a rapid exchange of feedback between the CASS research team and various levels of the Dalian City government. Within three months of the practical study ending the Dalian City government published a final version of the policy in the form of the 'Dalian City Bureau of Civil Affairs Circular Regarding Ideas on the Further Completion of the Urban Resident MLG System' (SPRC CASS 2002: 102–6). Feedback exchanges preceding the publication involved a mixture of written reports, small-scale meetings in Beijing and Dalian, presentations made to higher authorities in the city government and also a conference in Dalian (SPRC CASS 2003: 43–44). Perhaps the most significant to the CPSAs' development were two reports produced by the SPRC research team which outlined the main functions of the policy as well as an explanation as to why the policy was designed as it was (SPRC CASS 2001a and 2001b). These meetings and reports consolidated the findings of the study project into a single proposal that was then implemented across Dalian.

The final stage of the CPSA policy was characterized by its consolidation within Dalian, continued assessment by a variety of bodies including the UK Department for International Development (DFID) and the United Nations Education Science and Cultural Organization Management of Social Transition project (UNESCO MOST, which aims to encourage cooperation between social scientists and government policy makers) (SPRC CASS 2003: 44). It is apparent that both DFID and UNESCO MOST provided more than just assessment for the CPSA, notably financing parts of the early project phase of the policy, but in interviews and both the official and SPRC Chinese language documents there was little mention of their input beyond the assessment role. By August 2001 the CPSAs had been implemented in ten cities including Harbin and Shenyang (Ge and Yang 2003: 257).

Explaining the emergence of the CPSAs

The development and implementation of the CPSA policy was a significant addition to the function and impacts of the MLG in Dalian. In many respects the CPSA is a success story. It was developed and implemented smoothly and utilized the cooperation of a variety of different agents. But this is success measured in development and implementation terms rather than in terms of actual provision in relation to the social and training needs of Dalian's impoverished and unemployed population – something I shall discuss later.

But how do we explain the emergence of the CPSAs? I argue that they were developed in Dalian due to a combination of local government institutional arrangements and national policy decisions that facilitated the actions of a number of key policy sponsors.

Institutional elements

The decentralized state

Guan and Xu suggest in their chapter that the decentralized nature of the Chinese state can have a significant impact on social policy. The impact varies depending on the specific policy area but it is possible for a high degree of independent policy development to occur. This was, in the case of Dalian, further facilitated by the relative independence of the city in planning terms after the mid-1980s with the elevation of Dalian's decision-making authority to provincial level. Because Dalian had a high degree of autonomy in policy making this provided the opportunity for developments in the city's MLG system and the later CPSA policy. Examples before the emergence of the CPSA could include the Dalian Model of MLG finance or the Four-in-One set of policies (Dalian CAB 1999). As noted above, the Four-in-One system incorporated additional groups, such as laid-off workers, onto the MLG. The Dalian model of MLG financing was eventually adopted nationally and made funding the MLG a government responsibility. Under previous alternatives such as the Shanghai model some funding had derived from enterprises (Shi 2002).

Fundamentally the structure of the state provided the opportunity or space within which policy could be developed and implemented without it being ordered at a national level, as was the case with both the MLG in the mid-1990s and the CPSA. Without decentralization generally and the flexibility of its status as a city directly beneath the central government for planning purposes (*jihua danlie shi*), Dalian would have been subject to greater provincial government control, which might have reduced its possibilities for policy innovation – note it was the Dalian City CAB, not a provincial level body, that initiated the processes leading to the CPSA.

Structure of the MLG policy

The national MLG policy itself leaves a large amount open for local interpretation in spite of efforts since the 1997 'Circular Regarding the Establishment of a National Minimum Livelihood Guarantee System' (State Council 1997) to standardize the policy further. Both the 1997 Circular and the 1999 'Minimum Livelihood Guarantee Regulations' (State Council 1999) create the space for policy innovations such as the CPSAs by devolving a great deal of the policy administration and financing of the MLG to the local level. The MLG as it developed institutionalized local decision making on financing and administration under an umbrella policy goal. Provided the goal of providing local basic living requirements was dealt with within the fundamentals of the policy, as outlined in the 1997 Circular and 1999 Regulations, little was ruled out. Details focus on who is responsible for managing applications and benefit delivery, where funds come from, and which bureaux are involved in setting the MLG line. There is no specific clause in the 1999 MLG Regulations

72 *Daniel R. Hammond*

or the 1997 Circular excluding the possibility of variation outside of the basic delivery of a locally determined standard of basic livelihood.Rather than being a direct reason for the emergence of the CPSAs, the structure of the MLG policy has, in conjunction with the general trend towards permitting local development of policies, created an institutional background in which policy variation is possible. As one official put it when commenting specifically on the social assistance system in China: 'The openness of the current system in China allows for special adaptations in the localities to occur with regards to how this community level of social assistance is provided' (Interview BJ07–3).

Negative views of MLG recipients

There had been, in Dalian, some negative feedback about MLG recipients from local residents. This feedback was reported up to the CAB by the Community and Sub-district agencies of government (Interview BJ07–2). Officials reported that local residents' views of MLG recipients as isolated from the community, not contributing to society, and defrauding the MLG were one reason that MLG reform was on the agenda (Interview BJ07–2; BJ07–3; Ge and Yang 2003: 242). There was, however, no part of the original MLG policy design which aimed to push those on the MLG off the benefits and back into work unless their income changed (Dalian Municipal Government 1999, Point 13).[6] As the third of the 'Three Security Lines', a policy phrase adopted by Premier Zhu Rongji referring to the minimum wage, unemployment insurance and the MLG, the MLG forms a final safety net and this defines it as different from the other security lines. Whereas social security provisions such as the laid-off worker 'Basic Living Guarantee' (XGBLG), the Re-employment Service Centres (RSCs) and Unemployment Insurance (UEI) have built in time limits for benefits, and in the case of the XGBLG organizational structures which aim to get recipients back into work, the MLG does not. The MLG is for those who have fallen through the social security safety net and receipt of benefits is indefinite and is not accompanied by structured support to find employment. In spite of these differences between the MLG and other provisions, the length of time people received MLG benefits and the employment status of recipients were perceived as important by both local residents and, because of complaints, local officials.

Why was the lack of occupation for those receiving the MLG perceived as a problem? There are two key reasons. The first is that the feedback was in itself a concern for those operating in the city-level bureaucracy. The MLG was originally a policy to ensure social stability. If those who were receiving the policy caused social friction, however small, then the policy would no longer be serving its purpose as set out in the 1997 Circular and 1999 Regulations. Additionally, MCA officials and SPRC researchers demonstrated concerns about welfare dependency amongst MLG recipients. The MLG was seen as an efficient means to resolve social instability and unrest caused by poverty (Interviews TJ06–1 and BJ07–1, BJ06–2, BJ07–2, BJ07–3). Dependency would create a potential problem for the government as it would limit instability but probably at a continuous and increasing financial cost. This long-term commitment would be the logical outcome of the structure of the policy as it stood between 1997 and 1999. Getting those on the MLG into employment, an objective if not a fully supported aspect of the CPSAs, would be ultimately positive for all those involved in the policy. The recipients would work and in theory earn more due to the minimum wage being in place and being substantially higher than the MLG (the MLG benefit is typically set at around 33 per cent of the minimum wage). In addition the state would benefit from a reduction in costs and eventually increased tax returns.

Negative impact of the xiagang and MLG policy

The other issue that had fed back, pushed the MLG onto the agenda in Dalian and contributed to developing the CPSAs was the problem of laid-off workers and the failure of policies aimed at helping them. Laid-off workers are former state-owned enterprise employees who have been laid off by their enterprise during the reform period. They are not formally employed nor are they technically unemployed and they often keep some formal tie with their old employer (Cai, 2006). There were two specific policies designed to support them. The XGBLG was to provide a minimum livelihood to them through their enterprises, and the RSCs that delivered the XGBLG were also to help them find new jobs. The fundamental problem that impacted on the MLG was the failure of these policies to resolve the problems of laid-off workers. This had both political and social aspects that were of concern to those involved in the CPSA initiative.

Fundamentally, the problem was that XGBLG and RSCs had not worked and were being wound down in the early years of the twenty-first century. The number of laid-off workers in Dalian in the early 2000s was substantial (although difficult to quantify, see Solinger 2001), the policies in place were coming to an end, and the government needed to find a means to effectively resolve the problem state enterprise reform had created. One of the key issues in the failure of the XGBLG, as understood by leaders, was the continued connection between the laid-off workers, their benefits, and their former employer (Tang 2003: 23). The policy failed because the economic crisis many state enterprises found themselves in led to benefit funding, such as the XGBLG and for pensions, being absorbed by the enterprises' wider debt issues (Interview BJ07–2). The laid-off population was therefore being failed in two ways: a lack of successful re-employment services and difficulties providing benefits. With the end of the XGBLG policy those previously on the benefit were to be channelled onto the MLG where such 'debt conflicts' (Interview BJ07–2) would not be an issue.

The end of the XGBLG and connections between the various security policies (the UEI, XGBLG and MLG) had created two additional points of

74 *Daniel R. Hammond*

confusion and tension for MLG. First, laid-off workers were believed to be receiving the MLG after being re-employed (Ge and Yang 2003). Second, the increase in numbers receiving the MLG was perceived as putting pressure on resources within the local CAB and their ability to provide MLG benefits adequately (SPRC CASS 2001b: 12). The problem of how to deal with laid-off workers was, therefore, on the agenda for two reasons. First, the original provisions to resolve the problem had failed and this left both local and central government with a significant social and political problem that still needed to be resolved. Second, there was political confusion and fiscal tensions over the potentially huge numbers the MLG might have to absorb. The introduction in Dalian of the Four-in-One policy suggests that in Dalian this problem was particularly acute because laid-off workers were already being channelled onto the MLG before Premier Zhu endorsed the idea in 2000.

Negative social impacts are the second reason why the laid-off worker problem was on the agenda. Officials reported that the suicide rate amongst the long-term unemployed, laid-off and MLG recipients had risen. In addition, criminal activity was being recorded among those who had been on the MLG or laid-off for long periods where there had been no previous such activity. A specific example given was of a woman who had been caught breaking into cars but had no previous criminal record (Interview BJ07–2). This increase, perceived or real, in social instability as a result of shortcomings in both the MLG and XGBLG fed back into the agenda on social assistance as it stood in the early 2000s in Dalian.

Early Dalian MLG precedent

Finally, the early precedent set by Dalian in establishing a MLG system in 1995, two years ahead of national implementation, fed back in two key ways on the policy as it stood in 2000. First, it established Dalian as an innovator in this particular policy area: in 1995 the number of cities with a working MLG system was very small. This willingness to implement new policies and innovate was still in place and influential five years later. In addition, the early MLG model adopted by Dalian had two long-term impacts for the policy further on down the line. The policy design of the original Dalian MLG Model focused on providing a 'small' MLG as noted above (Dalian Municipal Government 1999). This meant that, it provided primarily for those who would have traditionally been eligible for 'Three Nos' (*san wu*) provisions and was not set up with considerations for the needs of other people who may have been impoverished.[7] The 'small' MLG was essentially a like for like replacement of the 'Three Nos' (Dalian CAB 1999).

Second, the Dalian MLG Model was based in the community and this was reinforced by the implementation of additional measures in the 'Four-in-One' (Dalian CAB 1999). The tie between those who were unemployed or laid-off and their work units would not be sustained by the MLG if they went onto

Local variation in urban social assistance 75

the benefit. This lack of connection between work unit and recipient had significant appeal when problems such as those experienced with the XGBLG emerged. The early precedent of the Dalian MLG therefore created both negative and positive feed back. It was negative in terms of the lack of provision, and positive in terms of the absence of work-unit ties. This feedback helped sustain an institutional environment where innovation and new policies were, if not encouraged, then allowed to occur.

Policy sponsors

The institutional setting for the development of the CPSAs created an environment where the possibility of policy innovation was both on the agenda and possible. What made the CPSAs possible was the action and interaction of a number of policy sponsors in the setting that these institutional factors created.[8] In the case of Dalian and the CPSAs, three key kinds of policy sponsors operated together to facilitate the development and implementation of the policy. The case of Dalian is especially interesting because of the interaction and synergy the three different sponsors, from three different parts of the political system, facilitated when developing and implementing the CPSAs.[9]

Officials reported that the involvement of these three policy sponsors was of fundamental importance to the policy emerging both during development and implementation (Interview BJ07–2; BJ07–3). In the case of the Dalian City CPSA the three sponsors who are of key importance are the city's Mayor at the time, Bo Xilai, the CASS research team and the Dalian City CAB. The synergy among these three sponsors ensured the CPSA policy was a success in terms of being implemented and sustained. Differences in how these sponsors operated and what they were able to achieve lend to their categorization as either 'elite', 'administrative' or 'ideas' sponsors.

Elite sponsors

In the case of the Dalian City CPSAs, the elite sponsor was the mayor Bo Xilai, and his influence appears to have been considerable. What is of interest is that although this influence was significant it also did not involve a large amount of activity. In interviews with Dalian and Beijing based Civil Affairs officials, Bo emerged as playing a fundamental role by simply being in a position of enough authority that his support for the policy increased the likelihood of implementation (Interview BJ07–2; BJ07–3). By authority it is meant the authority to make things happen or to allow them to happen. In the case of the Dalian CPSAs, political authority at the elite level allowed the policy to happen. If the top leadership had decided against the CPSA project it would not have taken place. In an interview with a Dalian official close to the whole CPSA policy process Mayor Bo was fundamental to the CPSA taking place even if he appears to have had a particularly passive role (Interview BJ07–2).

76 *Daniel R. Hammond*

Interestingly, in Dalian it is the city's elite leader who has been cited as influential. This means that, if the CPSA policy was to have been sidelined or blocked, such an objection would have had to come from a higher level of authority. In terms of explaining the relatively smooth process from development to implementation the authority supporting the policy, even if it appears to have been relatively passive, was significant enough to ensure policy success. So why did Mayor Bo support the CPSAs? Given the nature of promotion within the state bureaucracy and the assumed ambition of the leader in question the possibilities offered by the CPSAs would have been attractive. This attractiveness could have been because the CPSAs would resolve some local problems and would attract attention if successful. They would also be attractive because they tackled concerns (the MLG and laid-off workers) and policies (the community level of administration) deemed important at the central level. It would also have appealed because the initial project and policy design were low cost.

Administrative sponsors

An administrative sponsor is a policy sponsor whose ability to influence a policy is based on their position within the state administration. An administrative sponsor's influence on a policy is less clear cut than that of an elite sponsor and may require more manoeuvring, negotiation and compromise to achieve particular policy objectives. In the case of the MLG and CPSA in Dalian the administrative sponsors active were within the city and district CAB offices. In the municipal CAB the Director of the Office of Disaster and Social Assistance (*Dalianshi minzhengju jiuzai jiujichu chuzhang*, hereafter 'the Director') fulfilled a specific role in terms of facilitating the policy and also acting as a key bridge between the other two sponsors. The City CAB could act as one of many potential institutional bottlenecks for a new policy to pass through. It is, therefore, very important for a policy to have the active support of or, at the very least neutral indifference, of the local CAB. In the case of the CPSA the local CAB was both a driving force in the events that led to the policy being developed and also a firm supporter of the policy. It was the Director who initiated contact with the SPRC of CASS with the goal of finding a policy that would resolve the issues highlighted previously and the Dalian CAB continued to provide support for the policy throughout the process which followed (Interview BJ07–2). The importance of this particular sponsor was, therefore, vital to the way in which the policy developed.

The Dalian example also demonstrates the influence that lower levels of the administrative structure can have on a policy. At this lower level the Xigang District CAB office can wield much influence. As noted in the background section above, during the development of the CPSAs and before the pilot study the Xigang CAB had the policy revised six times. Although the specifics of these revisions are not available, it can be inferred from differences in language used between the final regulations on the CPSA (SPRC CASS 2001c) and previous drafts of the regulations (SPRC CASS 2001a) that the changes primarily dealt with the supervisory relationships between local governments and the CPSAs; and the incorporation of all MLG recipients with 'activity ability' (*huodong nengli*) rather than 'ability to work' (*you laodong nengli*) into the CPSAs. The rationale for this distinction is unclear but it implies that the district-level officials wanted the CPSA to include and occupy more MLG recipients than the SPRC research team had initially envisaged. The inclusion of those with 'activity ability' implies the CPSAs were more about getting MLG recipients active and improving their image than a policy that had focused on those with the ability to work. But the key point here is that the state administration at this level was able to exert enough influence on the policy as it developed to force revisions which appear to have changed the scope of the policy in a significant manner. The CPSA policy as it appeared and was studied in Xigang went on to become the policy rolled out across Dalian. It is, therefore, important to consider the role of the administrative sponsors and how they deal with potential bottlenecks.

Policy problems and their resolution are the responsibility of administrative sponsors because of the space they occupy in the state structure. There is, therefore, an element of self-interest in supporting a policy which resolves a problem because it will reflect well on them and their ability to do their job. It is also a dangerous game to play as a policy innovation could fail or upset those superior in the hierarchy by introducing unwanted innovations or costs and therefore reflect badly on the sponsor. In Dalian the administrative sponsor's motivations were a result of problems arising in both the MLG and UE/ XGBLG populations which were discussed above. The Director of the Dalian CAB specifically sought a resolution to these policy problems and supported the CPSA throughout its development. Her motivation and sponsorship of the CPSA are clear throughout. The district government had to be convinced of the policy and this reflects the challenge of negotiating different levels of government, even within one city, that policy sponsors in the Chinese system must overcome. A series of revisions and redefinitions of the CPSA over who were to be brought onto the policy, were enough to see the policy through in this case.

Ideas sponsors

The last distinct group of sponsors is based in the research and academic communities. Because they use ideas and research as a means to promote policy this last group will be referred to as ideas sponsors. The authority of ideas sponsors derives from what they can provide rather than any kind of political authority. Ideas sponsors can provide three different things that a policy might benefit from, these are: ideas, evidence and capacity. In terms of ideas these sponsors can provide something new that comes from outside established ways of thinking and doing things. Ideas sponsors can also

78 *Daniel R. Hammond*

provide support for policy ideas being generated within the official discourse. This can be done through the provision of evidence, in the form of case studies, or through the research they do such as the preliminary work and practical study the SPRC carried out for the Dalian CAB (Ge 2001a). Research carried out on behalf of other sponsors, such as administrative sponsors in the CPSA case, is where ideas sponsors contribute capacity. It may not always be possible for a government department to carry out a research project or it may be desired that the project be carried out by someone outside of the department, ministry or organization in question. Such opportunities are, however, rare and in one case two university researchers suggested that potential ideas sponsors spend more time on the outside looking in rather than actively participating in policy making (Interview Grp2BJ06). In the case of the CPSA, ideas sponsors provided ideas, evidence and capacity to the Dalian CAB. The SPRC was able to provide policy recommendations that were outside the official discourse on the MLG, laid-off workers and unemployment. In addition, the volume of evidence to support the policy recommendations they provided was reported as being an invaluable contribution to officials (Interview BJ07-2).

The CPSA in Dalian is seen as special by some of the officials involved (Interview BJ07-2; BJ07-3) because researchers were used by the Dalian CAB and were able to exert a degree of influence on the development and implementation of policy. The SPRC research team was active throughout the process of the policy's development and eventual implementation. This covered a period of three years and involved not just research for the policy but writing up of policy documents and providing training and education to various groups within Dalian (SPRC CASS 2003: 43–44). The SPRC was specifically requested by the Director of the Dalian CAB to co-operate on the development of the CPSA and was, throughout the process, both active and influential. In the initial stages this influence was exerted through the survey and corresponding reports and drafting of policy documents (see SPRC CASS (2003) for a collection of these documents and reports). The content of this work set the initial policy design in place and, arguably, set the parameters of the development and implementation of the policy that followed, including the CPSAs' focus on psychological well-being and the use of community work to expose benefit fraud. A contrast to this can be found in the Shanghai MLG experiments where researchers only became actively involved in the policy during implementation and after the equivalent survey and report stage had been carried out (Interview BJ07-1). The review of the proposed CPSA policy as well as the Xigang District case study and documentation that followed all involved the SPRC research team to varying degrees (see SPRC CASS (2003: 43–44) for example). As active members of the team which brought the policy into being, as well as supporters in terms of publicizing and educating Dalian civil affairs officials, and through meetings about the policy the ideas sponsors in this particular case were very active and exerted considerable influence on the final policy.

Local variation in urban social assistance 79

Sponsor synergy

The three policy sponsors promoted the CPSA but not as a group effort. Instead, they worked in a way which, although not deliberate, complemented each others' efforts and perhaps improved the likelihood of success. Synergy between different policy sponsors is an important element of the policy process in the PRC. The stronger the synergy between policy sponsors the less likely the policy in question will be undermined by conflict with other actors or institutional features in the political system. In the case of the CPSA, lines of communication and authority existed between both the elite and administrative sponsors and between the administrative and ideas sponsors (Interview BJ07–2; BJ07–3). Note, however that two sets of sponsors, as far as I am aware, had no direct contacts. The local CAB operated as a link between the ideas and elite sponsors because it was the only sponsor which had links with both. This meant that the administrative sponsors based in the local CAB provided the key focal point around which the other sponsors operated.

By providing this focus, the administrative sponsors facilitated a situation where both the Dalian top leadership, in this case Bo Xilai, and ideas sponsors, the SPRC research team, could support the development of the CPSA without necessarily having any direct contact. In addition, these sponsors made the administrative sponsorship of the CPSA easier by providing resources that would otherwise not have been available. The elite sponsor provided political authority and financial support for the CPSA project allowing the policy comparatively free rein to develop. Ideas sponsors provided both policy ideas and evidence to support policy ideas; as well as personnel and time to carry out research in support of new ideas. The particular character, design and relatively smooth development of the CPSA in Dalian relied to a great degree on the support and activities of each sponsor type.

Conclusion

The CPSAs emerged in Dalian because of a specific combination of the structure of the Chinese state, the experimental and expansive nature of social assistance in Dalian, the policy impacts of laid-off workers in the local context, and the activities of a number of policy sponsors within the local political environment. Dalian was an economically relatively successful city that was restructuring its state-owned sector and creating tensions in the delivery of the MLG as the number of laid-off workers grew. With a past history of policy innovation, devolved policy making and an MLG that was already absorbing large numbers through the 'Four-in-One' provisions, Dalian found itself in a situation where it was lauded by the Chinese Premier whilst facing significant pressures. The MLG in Dalian was facing increasing numbers and unhappiness amongst residents about the behaviour and contribution of MLG recipients. Whilst variation in the MLG is not unique to Dalian the combination of these features at this particular time created the space,

80 Daniel R. Hammond

innovation and desire for the local CAB to call on the SPRC to help with seeking a solution. It was this combination of policy sponsors that pushed the CPSA through the various phases of the policy process. Innovations have occurred in other cities regarding the MLG and these vary widely from providing additional benefits, for example with child care or lunch costs for workers, to full-blown policy innovations that attract the attention of the MCA in Beijing, such as the special classification measures (*fenlei shibao*) of Daqing (Interview BJ07–3).[10] The CPSAs emerged in Dalian, however, and it was because of the combination of local context and the policy sponsors involved that they did.

The CPSAs also embody a particular set of aims and values. While MLG provides benefits, the CPSAs' aims are to provide for MLG recipients' non-material needs but at the same time push them into work. By requiring recipients to do community work in order to receive benefits, it is implying that people only deserve benefits if they earn them. At the same time, while as intimated in Solinger's chapter, the MLG policy has had the effect of keeping a marginal urban group in a position of quiet subsistence, the CPSAs might be interpreted as a rather different form of social control. Instead of the state merely paying a subsistence benefit in return for a lack of social protest, the CPSAs involve a local government actively organizing a marginal group. In doing this, the state may be reducing the chances that they organize themselves.

The CPSAs may also reflect another concern of the state. The laid-off workers and those receiving MLG are groups that have been viewed as both a social problem and a political challenge since the early 1990s, and the prospect of this group spontaneously organizing would not be welcomed by the authorities. The CPSAs might therefore perhaps be seen as a measure through which the MLG can further placate and monitor the recipients within their communities. The CPSAs do provide a service that is designed to help those on the MLG reconnect with their community and ultimately leave the policy altogether, but it is also based on the coercive power of the state to remove benefits and organize groups as it desires. This dichotomy in social assistance between the expressed desire to help the urban poor and an implied desire to control a perceived threat is both driving the debate amongst interested parties (academics, state researchers and officials) and the development of the most basic provisions of the Chinese state to marginal groups.

Notes

1 Based on fieldwork funded by awards from the Universities China Committee London, 2006, and Glasgow University Department of Politics, 2007. Interviews were conducted during fieldtrips to Nankai University, Tianjin and SPRC CASS, Beijing during 2006 and 2007 respectively. Interviewees were a mixture of officials and researchers/academics in the policy field. Interviewees were, in line with the University of Glasgow Politics Department ethics agreement, afforded automatic anonymity.

2 I use 'Community' to refer to these government-organized agencies and to distinguish them from communities in the usual sense.

Local variation in urban social assistance 81

3 This point was raised during the workshop discussion of an earlier version of the chapter. It has not been possible to discover the exact amount of funding provided. The point remains that the initial project costs were not shouldered entirely by the Dalian city government.

4 The term 'model' is used here to refer to the different local administrative and financing designs of the MLG. The Chinese term often used is '*moshi*'. For example, in his comparison of different MLG models Tang (2003) uses '*moshi*' to distinguish between different administrative and funding mechanisms for the programme in Shanghai, Wuhan and Chongqing.

5 Dalian reconfigured its MLG system three months before the central government announced the national 1999 MLG Regulations. In interviews, local and central government officials made no connection between the two events (Interviews BJ07–2 and BJ07–3). In any case, the Regulations essentially re-iterated the 1997 State Council Circular on the MLG. Thus, the Dalian CAB seems to have been motivated to change by a local rather than national agenda.

6 Income changes have to be reported by recipients, however, and so there is potential for fraud unless officials actively investigate recipients' personal circumstances.

7 The 'Three Nos' was the PRC's traditional social assistance policy. It provided a minimal material benefit to those who filled one of three categories: elderly with no children, children with no parents/carers, workers with no ability to work. The policy was managed by the MCA until the emergence of the MLG in the 1990s.

8 Policy sponsors individual actors who operate within the Chinese system to push a particular policy agenda or policy idea. Based on the idea of policy entrepreneurs (see Baumgartner and Jones 1993; Kingdon 1984) the term policy sponsor is used to reflect the less outwardly confrontational and closed nature of the Chinese political system. The aim of the concept is to build on the concept of the rational bureaucrat core to Lieberthal and Oksenberg's (1988) fragmented authoritarianism model taking into account the increasingly complex and diverse nature of policy making and policy actors in the People's Republic.

9 I focus on the domestic actors involved in the CPSA programme. This reflects the focus on the role of local government actors and the CASS research team that emerged from the documents I had access to and in the interviews I conducted. References to the role of the UK government's Department for International Development and UNESCO MOST were few (and lacked detail) and I have been unable to secure interviews and additional documentation on their role.

10 The '*fenlei shibao*' or special classification measures were a change to the MLG that first appeared in Daqing, Heilongjiang Province. The measures innovated on the MLG by allowing the benefit paid to recipients to be supplemented if the recipient fell into certain categories, for example if the parent of children of school age, someone with dependants such as disabled children, or elderly relatives. Although it appeared as a local innovation, it was endorsed by the MCA through 2002 and 2003 with local Civil Affairs Bureaux encouraged to adopt the measures on an ability to pay basis.

5 Life goes on

Redundant women workers in Nanjing

Jieyu Liu

State enterprises were once the main source of employment for urban workers in China, and provided lifetime employment, housing and welfare. However, under the market reforms of recent decades, many enterprises have been faced with painful choices of mergers, closures or bankruptcy. As a result, millions of state workers have been thrown out of their work units and have gradually become an urban underclass.

A growing body of literature has presented the macro-picture of redundancy, focussing on such things as its causes and characteristics (see Meng 1995; Chang 1998; Gu 2000; Appleton *et al.* 2002; Song 2003; Giles *et al.* 2005). The situation of a few cities has also been recorded so as to explore the processes at a local micro level. Such studies include Beijing (see Cook and Jolly 2000; Price and Fang 2002; Hung and Chiu 2003), Wuhan (Solinger 2001, 2003), Guangzhou (Mok *et al.* 2002), and cities in the provinces of Sichuan and Liaoning (Duckett and Hussain 2008). However, more studies of other localities are needed to enrich our understanding of redundancy[1] in urban China. Therefore, this chapter focuses upon a less studied city, Nanjing, a large provincial capital in East China, to explore the varieties and subtleties of redundant workers' experiences.

First, many of the existing studies follow a top-down analysis, looking how economic restructuring has affected state workers and how the state social security system ineffectively provides for redundant workers (see Li *et al.* 2001; Price and Fang 2002; Giles *et al.* 2006). However, the picture on how local workers have responded to the crisis and managed to live through the unpleasant experiences of job loss is less documented (for an exception, see Cook and Jolly 2000). My study of Nanjing emphasizes local workers' responses and strategies when they were faced with redundancy.

Second, existing studies of other locations (see Mok *et al.* 2002; Solinger 2003) concentrate mostly on the experiences of officially labelled 'laid-off' workers while noting different modes of redundancy (see more discussion on modes of redundancy below). By contrast, my study aims to capture the varieties of experiences of workers who were made redundant via different routes. I find that the experience of redundant workers varies greatly depending upon the nature of their former work unit, industrial sector, the finances of the individual enterprise and the mode of redundancy.

Life goes on 83

Third, in comparison with cities in the old industrial bases and western regions of China, Nanjing is relatively well off and we therefore might expect redundant workers to receive more state assistance. However, by examining how my interviewees were located in formal and informal support systems, I find that many of them relied mainly upon their own support system made up of kinship and other social relationships. By identifying how the workers dealt with the changing relationship with their former work unit as well with the state, I also suggest that their self-reliance strategy exemplified their lack of trust in, and uncertainty towards, the state.

Fourth, most of the existing literature on other localities, with the exception of a few studies in Beijing and Shenyang (e.g. Cook and Jolly 2000), does not consider women specifically. The few existing studies on women and redundancy in China show women to have borne much of the cost of economic restructuring; for example, middle-aged and older women have been most likely to lose their jobs (Wang 2000; Lee 2005) and women have had worse access to social security and been more likely to experience poverty (Cook and Jolly 2000). Similar to the general pattern, women workers in Nanjing were disproportionately hit (Sun and Liang 2000). However, given the economic context of Nanjing, women workers I talked to did not experience the deprivation documented in other cities (see Xia 2001); yet many of them were still institutionally excluded from the formal social provisions for the 'laid-off' workers and the gap between them and other urban working citizens tended to widen. Moreover, a growing sociological literature has indicated the importance of social networks in job-seeking in China (see Lin 2001). Nevertheless, none of the literature on women and redundancy has examined the gendered nature of social networks and how this affected redundant workers' experiences of reemployment. Thus, in order to add to the understandings of women redundant workers in different localities, I focus upon the social disadvantages women workers in Nanjing have experienced and show the gender inequalities inherent in economic restructuring. In particular, I will present new empirical evidence on the gendered nature of social networks and their impact on redundant workers' abilities to find new jobs.

This chapter is based on a qualitative study that took a life-history approach to understanding how women workers responded to state enterprise restructuring in the city of Nanjing. It is based on fieldwork conducted in 2003, 2006 and 2007. In 2003 in Nanjing, I conducted life-history interviews with twenty-seven redundant women workers, five women who had survived or witnessed the economic restructuring but were not made redundant, and one official, and I organized a focus group with another three redundant women workers. These women ranged in age from 37 to 59 years; twenty of the redundant workers were of the so-called 'Cultural Revolution generation', meaning that they had lost their educational opportunities due to the Cultural Revolution in the 1960s–1970s. They all were or had been married; and almost half had spent over twenty years in their work unit. I used informal networking and snowballing strategies to approach potential participants and

84 *Jieyu Liu*

then selected them for interviewing on the basis of their industries so that the industries in which they formerly worked generally corresponded with Nanjing's industrial structure (i.e. petrochemicals, electronics, car manufacturing, machine manufacturing, textiles and metallurgy as major industries). In 2006 and 2007, I talked to officers working at the community committee (*shequ weiyuanhui*) level, in order to get updated pictures of social welfare provision for redundant workers. This chapter mainly focuses upon the experiences of women workers while occasionally referring to the men when interviewees talked about their husbands who were made redundant.

In the next section, I provide a macro-level analysis of labour-market policies and relevant state provisions in tackling unemployment. Second, by initially introducing the economic context of Nanjing, I focus upon my interviewees' diversified experiences of redundancy and then explore their responses and strategies to maximize their interests. Finally, I examine their lives after redundancy and show that informal support systems made up of kinship and other social relationships played an important role as work unit support was withdrawn. I also suggest that their poor quality of social networks and their gender-specific networks has reproduced inequalities during the processes of finding new work.

State enterprise reform and redundancy in urban China

In 1978, the Chinese government adopted an 'opening-up' policy in the hope that this would spur economic development following the social and political upheavals of the Cultural Revolution. Among major developments was the promotion of different types of enterprise ownership. Before the reforms, state-owned enterprises were the major urban employers and providers of essential goods and services, though a minority of collectively owned enterprises played a supplementary role. But state enterprises were more than economic entities. They were also 'work units' (*danwei*): residential and welfare communities guaranteeing lifetime employment and providing workers with services such as housing and health care in addition to wages and retirement pensions.[2]

As the reforms unfolded, the state-run industrial enterprises faced serious competition from new non-state enterprises because they still employed a substantial number of employees and bore the burden of their welfare provision. In part because of this burden their economic performance began to deteriorate rapidly in the late 1980s. By 1992, two-thirds were operating in the red (Gong 2002). In 1992, at its Fourteenth Party Congress, the Communist Party formally decided to establish a 'socialist market economy', indicating that it was to more fully to embrace markets, and endorsed layoffs or *xiagang* (literally 'leaving the post', see below on the difference between lay-offs and unemployment), aimed at enabling state-run enterprises to compete more efficiently with non-state ones. But the scale of redundancies at that time was relatively small, since China adopted a gradual approach to state enterprise restructuring and tended to use mergers rather than bankruptcies as the solution for loss-making firms. But from 1994 onwards, the government started a policy of restructuring small and medium state enterprises while protecting larger ones, and began to extend bankruptcies as well as mergers and 'leases'.[3] Big firms were reorganized in strategic sectors (Lee 2005). At its Fifteenth Party Congress in 1997, the Party confirmed the decision to further reform big state-run enterprises by reducing employees and moving forward with aggressive restructuring. As a result, many state enterprises were permitted to go bankrupt or were privatized, and growing numbers of state workers lost their jobs (Giles *et al.* 2006). By the end of 2004, it was estimated that the number of unemployed state sector workers was as high as 60 million (Solinger 2006). This was close to half of the total state enterprise workforce (140 million) in 1995 (National Bureau of Statistics of China 1999).

In the 1990s, government sources used two terms to denote urban citizens without jobs. According to the National Bureau of Statistics of China (1999: 179), the 'unemployed' (*shiye renyuan*) are urban residents who have no job but desire to be employed and have been registered at the local employment service agencies to apply for a job. Accordingly, unemployed persons include young people unable to find work after graduation and also people who have lost work from the private sector. The second term, 'laid-off employees' (*xiagang zhigong*), was the official term for workers who lost their jobs but retained ties to their former state sector employer. However, as I show below, beyond this official recognition of just two categories of jobless workers, state enterprises adopted a variety of measures to get rid of their employees and invented a range of other categories. So I use the term 'redundant workers' to include any urban workers who have lost their jobs because of state enterprise restructuring – including, but not limited to, laid-off (*xiagang*) workers. As I show below, many redundant workers in categories other than 'unemployed' or 'laid-off' were officially excluded from official statistics.

Because of the growth in joblessness, the central government adopted various measures. First, unemployment insurance was introduced in 1986. Then the 1999 national Unemployment Insurance Rules made it mandatory for all urban employers and their employees to contribute to local government organized unemployment insurance. Employers were required to contribute 2 per cent of their total pre-tax wage bill and individual employees were expected to contribute 1 per cent of their wage (Duckett and Hussain 2008). After losing their jobs as well as severing relations with their work unit, individuals who had paid contributions for at least a year were eligible to receive unemployment benefit for a maximum period of 24 months. However, if redundant workers retained ties with their work unit, they were not eligible for this benefit.

Second, 'Re-employment Service Centres' (RSCs, *zai jiuye fuwu zhongxin*) were set up by enterprises as part of the so-called 'Re-employment Project' launched in 1995 (Gu 2000). Rather than being made unemployed, some workers were to be transferred to these Centres, which were to issue a 'basic

86 *Jieyu Liu*

livelihood allowance' and help them with retraining and finding work. These Centres were a temporary measure, however, and from 2001 began to be closed down. Workers from the Centres who had failed to find work were to become eligible for unemployment benefit. However, many enterprises could not afford to pay their share of contributions for unemployment insurance and for RSCs, and as a result, these programmes were not comprehensively implemented (Cook 2002; Solinger 2002, 2003).

In 2004 as the last of the RSCs were closed, responsibility for supporting newly laid-off workers was legally transferred from the work unit to the state (Information Office of the State Council of the People's Republic of China 2004). Therefore, local governments become the key actors in implementing national policies and their labour departments were expected to provide re-employment services and training. These services were to be offered free of charge to people who registered as unemployed or who were classified as laid-off workers.

Finally, in a related measure (see the contributions by Guan and Solinger to this volume), the state introduced a further safety net. In order to tackle the worst of the rising urban poverty that came with widespread unemployment, a 'Minimum Livelihood Guarantee' (MLG, *zuidi shenghuo baozhang*) was also introduced for urban residents whose income fell below a defined level (see also Solinger 2002).

Enterprise restructuring in Nanjing

Nanjing is the capital of Jiangsu province, a major city and an important industrial base in East China with petrochemicals, electronics and car manufacturing as its key industries; additionally, machine manufacturing, textiles and metallurgy are considered feature industries that absorb large local workforce. These industries were mainly state enterprise based. Nanjing contributes about 1 per cent to China's national gross industrial production (Liu *et al.* 2002). Its GDP grew at about 14.3 per cent per year from 1993 to 1997, 3.3 per cent higher than the national average; from 1998 to 2001, its GDP increased at a rate of 12.2 per year, 4 per cent higher than the average (Liu *et al.* 2002).

Despite the economic growth, aggressive economic restructuring also took place in Nanjing in the 1990s. Large-scale redundancies occurred mostly in Central-West China, old industrial base areas, and areas with relatively rapid market development (Dong 2003). Nanjing falls into the last category: located near Shanghai, Nanjing has experienced the market development that has subjected traditional industries to the dynamics of global economic demand, resulting in the restructuring of many state enterprises. For instance, the share of production from state enterprises dropped dramatically in late 1990s from 77 per cent in 1997 to 41 per cent in 1999 (Liu *et al.* 2002). By 2005, the number of state enterprises in the city had fallen by 60 per cent. According to statistics from the Nanjing Labour Bureau, in addition to 50,000 registered unemployed workers, there were 5.06 million laid-off workers by the end of 1998, comprising 19 per cent of the total work force in the city (Chen *et al.* 2000). By 2003, a national sample survey showed Nanjing to be in a similar position to Tianjin, Chongqing and Xi'an, with redundant workers comprising approximately 20 per cent of the total workforce in the city. This put Nanjing in the middle of the national picture with Shenyang the worst affected (28.9 per cent) and Beijing and Guangzhou the least (less than 10 per cent) (Liu and Deng 2005). However, it is difficult to find local statistical data on lay-offs in the last eight years; the only information available is the unemployment figure (roughly 60,000 people each year from 2003 to 2007) (National Bureau of Statistics 2008), which is likely to exclude large numbers of redundant workers.

Nanjing's healthy economic growth means that the city government is wealthier than many of its counterparts, particularly those in old industrial bases and western parts of China, and it has actively engaged in providing welfare for redundant workers. All the programmes of provision for redundant state workers in national policies have officially been established, though as elsewhere, this does not mean that they are actually fully provided in practice – and the true extent of provision is difficult to determine precisely. Nanjing has been among the earliest to adopt nationally-stipulated programmes. For example, it implemented the 1999 national policy on unemployment insurance that same year, at a rate ranging from 50 to 60 per cent of the minimum local wage for the last ten years, relatively generous compared with some cities in western regions (see Duckett and Hussain 2008, who give a rate of 40 to 50 per cent in Sichuan province). Re-employment Service Centres were set up in many enterprises and districts from 1998 in accordance with other major cities, though the number of workers who entered them is unknown. The city government has often set up job fairs and encouraged re-employment in privately owned enterprises. In particular, it actively promoted the commercialization of domestic service provision – such as cleaning, babysitting and cooking – in residential communities, creating many job opportunities for redundant workers. Therefore, unlike some cities whose economic structure and local economic growth were not helpful in providing financial support and re-employment opportunities, Nanjing was a place where national welfare policies on layoffs were relatively well implemented (Chen *et al.* 2000). This makes it interesting to explore how redundant workers have experienced and responded to state provision.

In terms of the gender picture, Nanjing is known for its strong textile industries that employ many women workers. The number of state enterprises in textile industry comprised roughly 20 per cent of the total state enterprises in Nanjing in late 1990s (Liu *et al.* 2002). In a stratified sampling survey of 775 redundant workers conducted in Nanjing in 1998, women who were formerly working in the textile industries formed 24.13 per cent of the sample (Sun and Liang 2000). It was difficult to identify how many women the textiles industry employed before restructuring but it was a highly feminised

88   *Jieyu Liu*

industry according to my interviewees. Because most redundant women workers come from the machinery and textiles industries nationwide (Zhang 1999), my case study has wider relevance for the situation of redundant women workers in urban China.

Experiences of redundancy

In Nanjing, my data showed that there were five main ways in which workers were made redundant. The first was by putting them on extended maternity leave. This practice involved indefinitely extending the statutory maternity leave period of fifty-six days and was adopted from the late 1980s and early 1990s as a means of making women redundant. The second way of effectively making workers redundant was through 'internal retirement' (*neitui*). Beginning in 1992, older redundant workers who would reach the legal retirement age[4] within five to ten years were permitted to stop working but to retain a connection with their enterprise and receive a proportion of their former wage (depending on the industry and financial situation of the enterprise). However, they received no bonus or wage increase as internal retirees. After they became eligible for the state pension, they would then be subjected to a pension increase. Nevertheless, this was attractive for many workers because the work unit was long seen by them as a key source of security and they could be unwilling to cut ties.

A third mechanism for enterprises to cut back their workers was through lay-offs (*xiagang*). This included both those who were called in on a needs basis (referred to as *daigang,* literally 'waiting for a position') and those who were on unpaid leave and no longer working in the enterprise but remained affiliated to it. This latter situation was referred to using a range of terms such as 'on suspended pay but with position retained' (*tingxin liuzhi*) and 'neither party looks after each other' (*liangbuzhao*). Additionally, '*xiagang*' also referred to workers who entered an RSC between 1998 and 2001, and who, if they failed to find work within that period could then be registered as 'unemployed' and became entitled to state unemployment benefits for up to two years. Laid-off workers who were 'waiting for a position' or in an RSC were supposed to receive the basic livelihood allowance, but since the mid-1990s whether or not it was provided and to what extent it was provided varied according to the profitability of individual enterprises.

A fourth method through which enterprises cut back on their workforce was by 'buying out' their workers (*mai duan gong ling*). These workers were paid a single lump sum (which varied by industry and enterprise), at which point they ceased to have any formal connection with their *danwei* and had to settle their own pension arrangements. Their remuneration was not directly comparable with the remuneration for the other forms of redundancy. This practice was in effect only from 1997. People who were 'bought out' (like internal retirees) were formally distinguished from *xiagang* (laid-off) and thus omitted from official lay-off statistics. Finally, from 2002, workers from enterprises declared bankrupt have been eligible register as 'unemployed workers'. Previously, workers from bankrupt enterprises were transferred to an RSC set up by the specific industrial bureau and administered by their enterprise.

Of the people I interviewed, eighteen workers were internally retired, ten were laid off and seven were bought out. Their remuneration varied considerably, depending on their mode of redundancy, the financial state of their former enterprise and its type and industry. But they had one thing in common: they were all stripped of the bonuses attached to their basic wage, even though basic wages stagnated and bonuses became a key part of workers' income during the reform period. Therefore, bonuses formed a key part of wage disparity for those who were made redundant and the income gap between redundant workers and other groups of workers tended to widen.

Rising health-care costs further worsened the living situation of the redundant workers I interviewed. In the late 1990s, redundant workers were supposed to receive partial reimbursement of their medical expenses from their former work units but because many enterprises ran at a loss or were near closure, this was often unavailable. Although medical insurance reform began in Nanjing in 2001 (Gu 2000), it only covered citizens whose employer had consistently paid contributions to the government-organized local medical fund along with their own individual contributions taken from their wages at source. Given rapidly rising medical charges, a commonly expressed wish among redundant workers I interviewed was that they did not want to fall ill. One interviewee commented that a few of her former colleagues had committed suicide rather than go to hospital when they found out that they had a very serious illness (Interviewee No. 20).

Monthly payments given to internal retirees varied widely across different industries – from 135 to 650 yuan – whereas the remuneration for laid-off workers was fairly similar – between 190 and 300 yuan. Although internal retirement provided redundant workers a wage sometimes higher than the living allowance offered to laid-off workers, the money actually received was completely subject to the profit of individual enterprise. As one 45-year-old factory worker put it: 'some years, when the enterprise was doing well, we got our wages but some years, if profits were small, we didn't get our wages for several months' (Interviewee No. 12). With a few exceptions (those working in non-industrial work units) the remuneration for internal retirees was well below the average monthly income of Nanjing citizens: 135 and 650 yuan represented about 10 per cent and 47 per cent respectively of the average monthly income for 2002.[5] In particular, textile industry internal retirees who had retired in the early 1990s had no income increase at all and found ten years later that they received only about one-tenth of the average monthly income. With the exception of the chemical industry (see below), 'bought-out' workers were treated fairly equally across different industrial sectors: women who worked in machine manufacturing and 'light' industries, including textile and clothing reported buy-outs received at between 400 and 650 yuan per year of service in a lump sum payment.

90 *Jieyu Liu*

The type of work unit also played a very important role in differentiating workers' experience. In my sample, there were no redundant staff from administrative work units, and twenty-four women were made redundant from industrial enterprises. Zhang Qiujian, in her national study (1995–98), found that a large majority (86.5 per cent) of laid-off workers mainly came from industrial enterprises, a much higher proportion than those from non-industrial work units (13.2 per cent) and from the administrative work units (0.3 per cent) (Zhang 1999: 89). The interviewees' accounts did indicate, however, significant differences in remuneration for redundant workers between industrial and non-industrial enterprises. For example, a teacher in a kindergarten affiliated to a university (one kind of non-industrial work unit) reported that although her bonus was deducted, she was paid 100 per cent of her previous basic wage, worth 1,800 yuan per month in 2003. A female worker, previously working in a clothes-making factory (industrial work unit), who received 220 yuan per month as an internal retiree, was aware of such a disparity and commented: 'In the city, is there any non-industrial work unit (*shiye danwei*) that is not good? You know why everybody says "if you want work, look for a non-industrial work unit?" That's the reason' (Interviewee No. 15). However, women who worked in non-industrial work units were relatively fewer than those who worked in industrial enterprises in the mid-1990s: local statistics showed that 94,000 women worked in non-industrial work units in comparison with 495,000 women in industrial enterprises (Nanjing Bureau of Statistics 1994: 33), which meant that workers who benefited from the decent remuneration of non-industrial work unit were indeed a minority. More importantly, despite the small proportion of the workforce absorbed by the administrative work units in relation to the whole workforce in Nanjing (54,000 out of 1.4 million), local statistics indicate that the gender disparity within the administrative sector was significant: in comparison with men (76 per cent), women only made up 24 per cent (13,000) of those who worked in administrative work units and were least vulnerable to redundancy (Nanjing Bureau of Statistics 1994: 33). Thus institutional segregation by sex has contributed to women's greater disadvantage in economic restructuring.

There were also differences in experience among workers depending on industrial sector. My data show that textile factories in Nanjing were among the first enterprises in the city to be heavily hit (c.f. Sun and Liang 2000). Textile workers suffered the greatest financial losses. They were made redundant earlier, often as internal retirees in early 1990s before other forms of redundancy were in full practice, received the lowest remuneration, and benefited least from the social protection schemes that were installed several years after they had lost their jobs (c.f. Sun and Liang 2000). By contrast, chemical industries were relatively profitable in Nanjing. My data show that although several factories were required to merge together around 1997, redundant chemical workers were much better remunerated (e.g. bought-out workers were awarded 2,500 yuan per year of service). Due to China's socialist rhetoric of promoting gender equality before the large-scale reforms began, the overt wage discrimination for men and women performing similar work in one industry was constrained. However, my interviewees' accounts indicated the differences between wages in different sectors – 'light' industries such as textiles found much lower pay than 'heavy' industries such as machinery and chemicals – similar to the conclusion from other survey findings that the main source of wage inequality was the concentration of women workers in low-paying sectors of China's economy (see Maurer-Fazio et al. 1999). An interesting practice was found in retail, a heavily feminized sector where women accounted for over 80 per cent of workers in the 1990s. In 1992 the Nanjing Women's Federation praised this sector for having a large number of female workers but no redundancies. However, by the end of the 1990s, my data showed that the retail sector introduced a redundancy scheme that targeted older workers (mostly women, that is – even in this sector women were disproportionately among the redundant).

Reponses to redundancy

Redundancy was externally imposed upon these workers during the economic restructuring. Its involuntary nature can be seen in the documents on internal retirement policy in one Nanjing chemical plant. It notes that 'workers must submit an individual application' but later states that 'those who are qualified for internal retirement but have not submitted an application will be categorised as lay-offs in the next month'. The term 'application' makes it seem voluntary but actually it only offered a choice of form of redundancy for which a worker could opt.

Yet my interviewees were not passive victims. Several workers emphasized that their own action when faced with redundancy was to maximize their own interests. For example, one chemical worker (Interviewee No. 26) was insistent upon choosing internal retirement instead of taking a one-off redundancy payment at the age of 42. At that time all her relatives tried to persuade her to choose the buy-out option because they thought if she retired formally at 45,[6] she would only have to pay three more years of contribution to her pension scheme and then she would still have a lot of money left from the single lump sum payment. Four years later, aged 46, she gave me her reason why she did not opt for the buy-out scheme:

> At that time, work unit leaders read the documents [to us], [and said] that after we were bought off, those who had working histories with chemicals could still qualify for early retirement. So supposing I were bought out, it apparently looked favourable to me because I could retire formally in three years [so only three more years of pension contribution]. But I felt what if in 3 years time they didn't keep their promise to let me retire formally, I would still have to keep paying contribution to my pension scheme until the age of 50. Although the single one-off payment appeared

92 *Jieyu Liu*

so much money at the start, it could be spent very quickly and easily as well. So I felt it was not sensible to choose the buy-out option.

(Interviewee No. 26)

Even though later she did manage to retire formally at 45, she still considered that she had chosen what was best for her.

Another interviewee, a textiles worker, in 1998 when her factory was closed down, decided to take a one-off payment rather than enter the reemployment service centre run by the Nanjing Textile Bureau (Interviewee No. 18). According to Solinger, these Centres are 'supposed to distribute livelihood allowances to them, contribute pension, unemployment and medical insurance money for them, and help them obtain retraining and a new job, while paying for their welfare benefits' (2001: 677). Solinger called laid-off workers who entered the Centres 'the most fortunate among the furloughed' (2003: 70). However, many of the women I interviewed presented a different picture: their workmates who entered the Centre still had to look for jobs by themselves. The Centre had only been running for three years; if workers had failed to take jobs allocated to them or had failed to find work during this period, they would be cut off from their previous work unit permanently without any financial arrangement. Even if they were allocated work in another unit, if it had low profit margins, they would have the same risk of being cut off from their work unit without any reimbursement. One 40-year-old worker explained her worries to me: 'There was a reemployment service centre. It would allocate jobs to you. If you didn't take it, you would be automatically cut off from the work unit without any financial reimbursement' (Interviewee No 13). I asked her what the financial arrangements was after entering the Centre, to which she replied:

After you enter it, your former factory will pay a certain amount of money to the Centre. So you will get living expenses from the Centre. It is the same money [as that given to someone bought-out]. If any other factory accepts you, the money will be transferred to them. Otherwise, why would they want you? Now the centre had already been closed down.

(Interviewee No 13)

When asked whether any of her workmates had chosen that option, she answered:

Hardly any. Because the allocation of work wasn't like that in the pre-reform era, that is, after allocation you were there safely until retirement. Now, look, one workmate was allocated to another clothes-making factory. But after two years, that factory was closed down again. The type of your previous work unit also affected the type of the possible units that might accept you.

(Interviewee No. 13)

Life goes on 93

These stories reveal that the workers took many factors into consideration and tried hard to choose the best among the available options. Because of the increasing uncertainty and risk during this economic transformation, even in the enterprises making a good profit, workers opted for redundancy if the remuneration was satisfactory. One industrial worker (Interviewee No. 23) had worked previously in a factory whose profit was among the top ten in the city. Within the wider environment of 'reducing staff to increase efficiency', the factory started to adopt internal retirement in 2003. The conditions were very good: the wage which internal retirees got remained the same as before and they also received wage rises until formal retirement. In the first year of internal retirement, they could still get a 100 per cent bonus, then in the second year 95 per cent, in the third year, 90 per cent in the fourth year 40 per cent and in the fifth year 30 per cent. This policy was so favourable that many workers wanted it and the original eligible age was changed from 47 to 45 for women, and from 57 to 55 for men. She felt lucky to benefit (aged 46 when interviewed):

> About one hundred workers wanted to take internal retirement because people didn't know how long this factory leader would be in that position. This year, this policy is still in effect but who knows how many years this policy will last? What if next year this policy stops – workers would have to work very hard till their formal retirement age.
>
> (Interviewee No 23)

The desire to seize the chance afforded by the favourable policy also reflected workers' anxiety about their present situation and an unforeseeable future. Thus, holding on to any benefits they could get was for them the best way to defer any insecurity in the future.

Social support and networks

Workers tried hard to maximize their interests during the economic restructuring though their solutions also often reflected their lack of power and anxiety in pursuit of security. So after losing their jobs how did they cope with their everyday life and how were they situated in the social support system?

The work unit used to serve as a welfare unit and looked after its members from cradle to grave, like a socialist family. By contrast, the relationship between the redundant workers and their work unit was very different after redundancy. Although they were allowed to retain their work unit accommodation, they were deprived of all other welfare it provided. Most workers talked about this changing relationship with resentment or fury. For example, as one of the bought-out workers (Interviewee No. 18, aged 40) put it: 'the work unit treated us like discarded rotten meat'. Another internal retiree (Interviewee No. 25, aged 50) comparing her past contribution to the work

94 *Jieyu Liu*

unit with the current treatment from her work unit commented: 'Our work unit is pretty bad. With us, those who return home, they had no contact at all [to check whether we were alright, whether we were in need of anything]. After all, we'd been working very hard for our whole life there.'

The common view among the redundant workers I interviewed was that they had been 'abandoned' or 'ignored' by their former work unit and that they deserved continual support from their former work unit since they had spent so many years working hard for it. In recounting their unhappiness about this changing relationship, all the workers also indicated that they thought the former factory leaders should be blamed for mismanagement of the poorly performing work unit. They reported that their factory leaders did not suffer like the ordinary workers: they were transferred to other factories or government jobs. Thus, redundant workers were well aware of the inequalities and unfairness in the market reforms, yet they had to accept it as another event in their lives that they could do little about.

With the withdrawal of the work unit from the provision of welfare, the state in the face of massive redundancies began to develop new social security provisions. However, these new provisions provided for redundant workers differentially depending upon their mode of redundancy. As noted above, laid-off workers who had been transferred to the RSCs and issued a certificate of layoff (*xiagang zheng*) were considered to be best treated among redundant workers (Solinger 2003). Nevertheless, in reality the situation was more complex. In a 1998 national survey of laid-off workers, Li *et al.* (2001) found that only about 10 per cent benefited from this arrangement. Certainly, some of my interviewees were suspicious of provision by the Centres and did not take up the option of entering one. Only one had joined an RSC and was issued with a certificate of lay-off. She found a new job working as a hospital carer, however, through reading newspaper advertisements. But her certificate had been of use because the job prioritized workers who had a certificate of lay-off (Interviewee No. 17). In contrast, internal retirees and bought-outs were not officially qualified for state support and were excluded from the beneficial policies towards laid-off workers. For example, one 46-year-old internal retiree had to pay all the fees for her own reemployment training:

> Like us, if we go to any class, we aren't considered unemployed or laid-off, we are internal retirees. Wherever you go for work, there is no benefit for you. In some places, if you are unemployed, your tuition fee for lessons will be waived, but ours are not. You can't bring any certificate [to prove you as anything]. So under such conditions, both sides – the factory and the society–have nothing to do with you. We have no way out.
>
> (Interviewee No. 6)

There was a distinct contrast between this and the way the women I interviewed commented on provision by the state. Unlike their strongly felt sense of entitlement to welfare provision from their former work unit, they were uncertain or had doubts about what the state could and should provide. With the withdrawal of the work unit as a representative of the state, many workers felt uneasy about their new relationship with the 'abstract' state. Some of them preferred not to get involved or had little faith in state provision. For example, in Nanjing, an MLG allowance was issued to workers whose average household per capita income was less than 248 yuan per month, but none of the women interviewed had applied for this state benefit. They commented that they did not want to make a fuss by going through a complicated application for something that was still subject to judgement and decision by some state officials.[7]

Redundant workers were mostly cut off from the formal support system, but informal support was intensifying in the transition to a market economy. My interviewees had received moral support and assistance in searching for jobs from their wider family. Being given financial support was less common, partly because of the increasing impact of redundancies which meant that some interviewees' relatives too were losing jobs and had little money. The following are some examples of help provided by kin. One 54-year-old factory worker and her siblings, all of whom had been made redundant, gave each other emotional support. Another textile worker (aged 50) followed her brother-in-law's advice to buy a knitting machine so that she could combine caring for her daughter with earning money. Meanwhile, the women interviewees themselves also contributed their labour to sustain family networks. Indeed, some of them became unpaid domestic carers for the wider family.

In addition to support from their families, redundant workers also received emotional support from other redundant workers, some of whom were friends from their former workplaces and others, mainly neighbours in their husband's work unit,[8] with whom they had become acquainted as a result of their common experience of redundancy. Such companionship did not alter their circumstances, but it helped ease the loss derived from unemployment. However, the social space open to them was restricted and the gap between redundant workers and other groups of people tended to widen. For most of the interviewees, rejoining the work force was the priority.

Finding work

Most of the women workers needed to find work because the vast majority became redundant when their children were still in middle school or at university and so were faced with caring for ageing parents whilst also having to bring up children.[9] One laid-off worker, aged 38, used a metaphor to describe the pressure of supporting children's education: 'We are climbing the slope of children. We are in great need of money' (Interviewee No. 4).

Previous studies have found that social networks (*guanxi wang*) are vital to redundant workers finding work (Li *et al.* 2001; Zhao 2002).[10] By asking respondents about the methods they used to find jobs, the kinds of resources they gained from their personal networks, and the characteristics of the contacts they

96   *Jieyu Liu*

considered 'played the most important role', I examined how redundant workers used social networks, or 'connections', in finding their new jobs.

Most interviewees had found their first new job using informal methods – that is social networks rather than by applying for jobs through formal channels. Only one found her first job through a formal method by reading newspaper advertisements (Interviewee No. 17). It is clear that the workers' social networks were often very crucial to reemployment. As one factory worker succinctly put it, 'if you are laid off, it is easy [to find work] if you have someone to introduce you. It'll be very difficult if you have no-one to introduce you' (Interviewee No. 23).

Social networks are made up of one's social contacts (network members). I found three patterns emerging from the ways in which jobs were introduced through social networks. First, there was a relationship between the work status of contacts (manual or non-manual) and the types of jobs they led to. Eight interviewees had contacts who were only manual workers with no post or rank, consistent with Zhao's (2002) findings in Wuhan that redundant workers tended to have contacts in manual occupations. The jobs introduced by manual worker contacts were mostly cleaning, baby-sitting, and cooking meals for families or companies. By contrast, one mid-level cadre (Interviewee No. 27) and one professional (Interviewee No. 19) found full-time and stable jobs through the introduction of their social contacts, who were themselves professionals. My data indicate that the higher the position of the contact, the better the jobs that could be obtained; hence, the power of contacts directly affected the quality of accessible jobs. But the position of the contact is closely linked to the pre-redundancy status/rank of the person seeking work because people tend to develop social networks with people like themselves.

Manual workers mostly associated with manual workers while mid-level cadres and professionals had more opportunities to become acquainted with professional and managerial staff. As a result, the cadre and the professional's prior status advantage were maintained in the job search: a woman, formerly the director of her factory's trade union (Interviewee No. 27), was asked by the municipal trade-union leader whom she already knew to work for them as a full-time consultant after she retired. Another former female accountant (Interviewee No. 19) was working full-time for a private trade company to which she had been introduced by her neighbour,[11] the director of an accounting agency. Their new jobs also offered the potential of gaining additional high-quality social connections from which they might benefit in the future. But manual workers with poor social connections were trapped in a vicious circle of low-paid, unskilled, part time work providing only further poor social connections.

Second, gendered networks and the gender of the social contacts also differentially affected people's opportunities for finding new work. Women's social networks were mostly made up of women, consonant with gender segregation in the workplace, as is shown in other studies (e.g. Tartakovskaya and Ashwin 2004). And these gender-specific networks did them no favours.

Their lower position in the labour market affected the connections they could make for their contacts. In my study, jobs secured through women contacts tended to be irregular kinds of work in the informal labour market. By contrast, the job introductions made for men and women through male contacts were more likely to be full-time. This corroborates Lin's 1998 survey in eighteen Chinese cities, which found that men held a substantial advantage over women with respect to the embedded resources in social networks (2001: 109). Although two of my interviewees found work through men, all the rest relied upon their female contacts. My life-history interviews with them showed that the gendered surveillance of women's sexuality at the work unit put a constraint on their developing social networks with male colleagues and superiors. The golden rule for women to maintain a good reputation was to avoid close contact with men which accordingly confined themselves to gender-specific networks (see more on sexual control in the work unit in Liu 2007). In turn, due to women's poorer social resources in the network, gender discrimination was reproduced in job seeking because of these gender-specific networks.

Finally, there is a difference between women using their own social contacts and their husband's social contacts in finding a job. Five women who got jobs through their husband's contacts were more likely to be full-time and well paid. This distinction explains why women workers tend to 'marry up' to cadres or professionals who possess richer and wider social networks (Rofel 1999). A woman can draw on her husband's social networks; and a husband may also independently use his social contacts to find work for his wife. Thus, as Xu and Tan (2002) argue, marriage is a certain form of social capital for Chinese women. Conversely, a husband is less likely to draw upon his wife's social network, first because the resources embedded in women's networks are usually fewer than those in men's networks and second because it is culturally considered humiliating for a man to rely on his wife's contacts for social improvement.

Other constraints on finding work

In addition to the negative effects of their limited social networks upon their re-employment opportunities, interviewees described other hindrances to finding work. First, familial demands created hurdles to finding and keeping work because being redundant reinforced women's domestic roles. The women I interviewed not only had to look after their own family, but were also regarded as an unpaid reserve labour force by the wider family, which justified demands being made of them by their own and their husband's kin, even to the extent of obliging them to give up a hard-won job. For example, one factory worker (Interviewee No. 17) was called upon to act as a full-time carer to her granddaughters, which put an end to her newly found job after she was laid off. Our interview was held when the baby was having an afternoon nap, and during this time she was busy knitting a sweater for her granddaughter.

98 *Jieyu Liu*

Another factory worker (Interviewee No. 24) started selling homemade accessories near a university campus after she was retired internally at 47. She enjoyed this because her products were praised by many students. However, the illness of her husband's sister put paid to her enterprise. It seems that only if they become 'redundant' a second time from their familial work can women in their position control their time and do something they want to do. Other studies also show that being made redundant pushed women into full-time domesticity (see also Dong *et al.* 2005).

By contrast, being redundant did not trap men in domesticity. A woman worker (Interviewee No. 28, aged 46) survived a lay-off crisis at 42 because she had a very good relationship with her leader. Her husband was laid off and stayed at home. However, she still took charge of everything in the house: 'anything in the family called housework falls upon me'. Another factory worker's husband had left his job to run a taxi business, but that had failed and he had been unemployed for five years. Despite this, he did nothing to help her around the home, even though she had become reemployed (Interviewee No. 30). Thus, familial demands upon women meant that they continued to shoulder a 'double burden' even when their husband was without work.

Second, age also seemed to limit the types of work open to them, though women near 40 years of age sometimes found their way around discriminatory practices. For example, one factory worker (Interviewee No. 30) became a product promoter in a department store after she was laid off at 36, but a few years later, because of a crisis in the store, all promoters over 40 were fired. Through a friend's introduction, she was interviewed to be a saleswoman for another product. For this she dressed up to look smart and energetic, so the manager thought she was only in her 30s and thus accepted her. The expansion of the service sector in the economic restructuring was once praised for its potential to absorb a large proportion of women workers however only younger ones were more likely to benefit from it. As one woman worker (Interviewee 24, aged 50) put it, 'they [service industries] want younger faces but not us'.

With many constraints, women who were less qualified and/or had poorer social capital were ready to take whatever jobs came up. However, for their husbands who became redundant, dignity seemed to be a prominent issue in the process of getting reemployed. This suggests that men need to get a decent job to maintain their male esteem and pride. When one factory worker's husband failed in his taxi business, other reemployment opportunities were available to him because he had a wide social network as a result of having been a driver in his work unit.[12] However, according to his wife he was pernickety in choosing jobs and ended up staying at home for a total of five years. As his wife (Interviewee No. 30) put it:

> He loves his face [dignity] very much. He was introduced [by his friends] to a job working as a security guard in the Education Department of the Provincial Government. He only worked there for ten days and then quit.

Life goes on 99

He said, 'standing there just like a dog'. He is such a person. He can't get a high status job and he doesn't want to take a lowly job either.

However, men's attempts to get decent jobs seemed to be thwarted by the fierce competition in the labour market. In turn, this has served to justify factory leaders' decisions to prioritise women for redundancy in the work units, because men needed work to maintain their dignity as breadwinner in the family. For example, some social workers in the community committee directly told me that women should be laid off rather than men because men found it more difficult to obtain 'suitable' jobs.

No matter how many constraints there were, or what social networks they might draw upon, the majority of my women interviewees (26 out of 33) found some form of work. The most frequent types of work were cleaning, cooking, caring for children, invalids or the elderly, working in shops or selling on street; these forms of work generally involved part-time work, home-based working or self-employment and were mostly in the private sector. Accordingly, women who were engaged in such activities were exposed to unpleasant conditions: there was almost no formal regulation or protection for reemployed redundant workers. None of the women who worked in the private sector had signed a contract. Pay for part-time workers was not legally regulated: women who worked a varied number of hours a day might receive the same amount of money at the end of month. Women who became self-employed were no better off than private-sector employees. According to a Nanjing governmental initiative to encourage re-employment, laid-off workers were entitled to apply for allowances to assist their self-employment project. However, none of the self-employed women (internal retirees, lay-offs and bought-outs) I interviewed had benefited from that. Some workers bluntly commented: 'Do people really believe those state policies? Look at what the City Environment Management Committee officers [*chengguan*] have done to us! If the state really wants to help us, it should get rid of those committee officers first' (Interviewee No. 23). They reported many incidents where they were harassed by the City Environment Management Committee. For example, one factory worker (Interviewee No. 7, aged 37) began by selling flowers but gave it up within a month: 'Those people [from the Committee] are just like dogs. In the evening there is no way for you to sell in front of supermarkets. Those people come to catch you, throw your things away and smash them.'

A former factory worker (Interviewee No. 3, aged 46), currently a social worker, confirmed:

If you sell instant meals on the street, you must dare to take risks because those people [from the Committee] might confiscate your stuff. You must be feisty because when they come, you must be able to bamboozle and deal with them. Or they won't allow you to put your stall for a moment. ... Sometimes we also help them by pleading on their behalf:

100   *Jieyu Liu*

> they are already laid off, living a hard life or something like that. So then they give the confiscated things back. But it is also exhausting after these troubles. The workers pull your stall out in the morning but have to push it back before they come out to check.

The contradictory signals sent by the state further distanced redundant workers from the official support system. Most workers took the official initiatives more as rhetoric rather than a reality.

After they were made redundant, my interviewees hoped to get support from their former work unit. But unfortunately my data showed that the unit usually was not in a position to offer help. Given their sceptical attitude towards the state, most workers chose to rely on the informal support system made up of kinship and other social relationships. This self-reliance to some extent is also attributable to the self-motivational stance adopted in official discourse. For example, since the 1990s, the All China Women's Federation has promoted the 'four selves' – self-esteem (*zizun*), self-confidence (*zixin*), self-reliance (*zili*), and self-cultivation (*ziqiang*) in the work units. Other state organizations such as the All China Federation of Trade Unions have also carried out similar campaigns.

However, there are drawbacks to this official discourse because it has the danger of attributing social problems such as redundancy to the deficiencies of individuals (Wong 2002). Thus, in line with the official commentary and media discourse, my interviewees often blamed themselves for their situation: 'Workers after all don't have any skills. You have to carry on searching for menial work to do' (Interviewee No. 17). Similarly, rather than seek state support in protecting their rights in their newly gained jobs, redundant women workers were prepared to make compromises to keep their jobs:

> You are just a temporary worker, [so] who will take you seriously? Also there are so many people out there looking for jobs, aren't there? In the work unit, I could argue with them. But now you don't have a say. You must give up everything [face, dignity.] Otherwise, you just stay at home eating porridge.
>
> (Interviewee No. 2)

Furthermore, redundant workers' responses towards losing their jobs must be placed in the context of their specific life experiences. Most of them were of the Cultural Revolution generation, the first cohort born and growing up under CCP rule. These people had had their lives shaped by many major changes in state policies: the 1960–62 famine as a result of the disastrous Great Leap Forward, the Cultural Revolution in the 1960s and 1970s, the one-child policy introduced in the 1980s and the market-oriented economic restructuring which began in the 1990s. Over the course of these national projects, state propaganda called for citizens to make sacrifices for the devel-opment of China. For example, the official discourse justified redundancy as an inevitable consequence of China's inexorable transition to a market economy. The older generation had to be sacrificed because they had few qualifications and skills. Women workers in particular were called upon to return home to open up more job opportunities for men and young people (see Liu 2007). Therefore, all the women workers from the Cultural Revolution generation (20) perceived the experience of redundancy as another unpleasant sacrifice they had made for the development of the nation:

> Our generation has run into everything in our lifetime. When we should have received education, we didn't have the chance, and only graduated from primary school. When we started work only at 15, we worked in three-shift rotations, destroying our health. When we tried to study something, the three-shift rotation prevented us from it. Later when you could devote yourself at 40, the factory went down and you were laid off. Now you want to work, but nobody wants you. I feel our whole life has been too miserable.
>
> (Interviewee No. 10, a 50-year-old textile worker)

Conclusion

I have outlined the experiences of redundancy recounted in life-history interviews with women workers in Nanjing and identified the gendered consequences of China's economic restructuring. Confirming the existing literature on women and redundancy in China, my data show women disproportionately bearing the cost of economic restructuring. However, my Nanjing study has revealed the varieties of experiences of redundant workers. I show that redundant women workers' experiences are greatly stratified depending upon the nature of their work unit, specific industries, finances of individual enterprises, their prior work status and the mode of redundancy. In particular, I have drawn attention to the experiences of a particular group of women (older and less-educated), most of whom from the Cultural Revolution cohort, and shown that they perceived redundancy as another sacrifice for the development of China. In the past, despite the state's rhetoric of gender equality and the major efforts made to implement this, in reality, women workers were horizontally and vertically segregated at workplace and had limited access to resources and power in the work unit (see Liu 2007). Since the 1990s when the reforms began to take place on a large scale, women have been thrown out into the marketplace, and they now no longer have even the state rhetoric to protect their interests and are exposed directly to the sexist and ageist discrimination in the labour market.

By examining their lives after being made redundant, I show that the informal support system made up of kinship and other social relationships played an important role as work-unit support was withdrawn. Although they strongly felt entitled to welfare provision from their former work unit, they were uncertain or had doubts about the state provision and many felt uneasy about

102 *Jieyu Liu*

their new relationship with the 'abstract' state without the work unit as the representative. My study shows that redundant workers tended to resort to self-reliance rather than seek assistance from the new state welfare provisions, and that their self-reliance strategy reflected their lack of trust and confidence in the state. This finding is illuminating because Nanjing is financially better off in comparison to cities in the western part of China. The Nanjing government appears to also have relatively actively complied with the national policies in providing support for redundant workers. However, as I have shown, many redundant workers were either not qualified for the support catering specifically for 'layoffs' because of the failure of national policies to match up the reality of varieties of redundancies in place, or more interestingly, opted not to be part of the state efforts. This highlights the importance of social and human factors that affect the delivery of state policies in addition to the calculation of financial budgeting for welfare provisions.

Furthermore, the reliance upon informal support system also takes place in the context where personal networks become increasingly important in obtaining job opportunities in the market reforms. By examining the process of re-employment of redundant workers, I identified new empirical evidence on the gendered nature of networks and their impact on the workers' abilities to find new jobs. I suggest that due to their manual status and the gendered disadvantage in networking, these women workers' prior lower social position has been reproduced in the process of finding work and the gap between them and other groups of urban citizens tends to widen.

In light of these results, more comprehensive measures and their implementation are urgently called for. One of the necessities for many jobless workers is to find new work. I would propose the following. First, governmental measures should be consistent across different governmental sectors to show they are genuinely trying to facilitate reemployment. For example, the City Environment Management Committee should be tolerant of street vending. Second, sexist and ageist ideology in the Chinese labour market needs to be tackled. For women aged over 45, finding a regular job can be hard and most are confined to jobs such as cleaning, cooking and looking after children in the informal labour market. The age tolerance for men is slightly greater but they are excluded from jobs that are considered to be women's work and also face increasing competition from migrant workers. Furthermore, transparency should be introduced into the recruitment process to give a chance to those workers who do not possess great resources in their networks. The local government should fine the enterprises that do not implement the principle.

In sum, while acknowledging the important functions informal support systems play for redundant workers in Nanjing I have also shown that over-reliance upon one's own resources in getting support has the danger of furthering the existing stratification and gender inequalities. To tackle this, policymakers should make an effort to rebuild citizens' trust in the state and strike a balance between the informal support and the formal welfare system with the latter as the major actor. Given that many redundant workers are among the Cultural Revolution cohort whose life course has been affected by changing state policies, the state should take responsibility and compensate them for the lifetime of sacrifice and suffering they have endured.

Notes

1 Here, 'redundancy' refers to any situation in which workers lost their jobs for reasons beyond their control, which includes instances in which workers' ties to their workplace continue.
2 There were in fact three types of work units: industrial enterprises producing material commodities, non-industrial institutions providing non-material services and administrative institutions (Bian 1994). This chapter focuses upon the first type as most redundant workers were from industrial enterprises.
3 Lease is not a common form of restructuring outside China. It refers to the way that the capital of enterprises could be leased to individuals in return for rental income. This form is more associated with restructuring of small state enterprises.
4 The state retirement age for women is 50 for workers and 55 for cadres (*ganbu*) who are workplace superiors, but it is 60 for both male workers and cadres. Within the category of cadre, there are several hierarchical levels (see Liu 2007).
5 In Nanjing in 2002, the average monthly income was 1,257 yuan in industrial enterprises, 1,551 yuan in non-industrial institutions, and 2,023 yuan in administrative institutions (Nanjing Bureau of Statistics 2003: 33).
6 By state regulation, workers who had histories of working in a chemical environment for more than eight years qualified for formal retirement five years earlier than the age set for ordinary workers.
7 This programme was also ineffective among laid-off workers in the cities of Guangzhou and Wuhan (Leung and Wong 1999; Solinger 2002).
8 Both spouses often worked in different work units but mostly lived in the husband's work units (see more on gendered housing allocation in Liu 2007).
9 In China, generally income from both spouses is needed for the running of the household.
10 A survey of laid-off workers (*xiagang*) from four cities in 1997 found that connections had positive effects upon the chances of getting re-employed (Li *et al.* 2000: 96–97).
11 In the pre-reform period, work unit housing was allocated to workers taking into consideration their position. Thus, people with similar positions in the work unit were more likely to be allocated flats in the same building.
12 In the work unit during pre-reform era, driving was a powerful position because it involved driving for the leaders.

6 'If you can walk and eat, you don't go to hospital'

The quest for healthcare in rural Sichuan

Anna Lora-Wainwright

Aunt Li was only 57 when she died of a heart attack in April 2006. However sad, the news did not come to me as a surprise. Aunt Li had been my neighbour during the 15 months I spent living in a village in Langzhong municipality, north-east Sichuan (2004–5) and doing anthropological fieldwork on health and healthcare for rural Chinese. She and her husband were very enterprising farmers, who in 2004 raised six pigs and over 30 ducks. I had become close to her through trading tips on which doctors were both reliable and inexpensive – a treasured form of local knowledge and symbolic capital given the scant access to healthcare for Chinese villagers like Aunt Li. Aunt Li had long suffered with shortness of breath and tachycardia, but had been unwilling to make a trip to the city's hospital (a 15-minute journey by motorbike or one hour on foot) for check-ups and treatment. She was afraid the doctors might deceive her, and prescribe expensive treatment simply to increase their own revenue, a perception that is widespread among villagers.

When she heard I had acquired some good friends in the city's People's Hospital, Aunt Li had asked me to accompany her to a trustworthy practitioner to have a computerized tomography (CT) scan. The doctor strongly advised her to undergo in-patient treatment for two weeks, for a total of 2000 yuan. He explained that this would considerably improve what he saw as a very serious heart condition, although – he admitted – it would not cure her completely. She resolved to take some medicine, which was bought for her by one of the hospital's doctors through his own health insurance scheme. The doctor told her she would only live a few more months if she did not rest and take medication regularly. Aunt Li shrugged her shoulders and replied: 'hospital treatment is too expensive, and if I rest who is going to farm my land? My husband can't do it alone, he's not well either. If I have to die, I will just die' (10 July 2005). She took medication for a month following her check-up but refused to buy any more, claiming it was not working. She was adamant that she would not undergo in-patient treatment and that she would rather save the money for her two grandsons, who lived with her and received little financial support from their parents. Nine months later, after a long day of work transplanting rice, Aunt Li 'came home, lay on the bed saying she was unwell, and she just died' (Aunt Li's neighbour, 28 April 2006).

'If you can walk and eat, you don't go to hospital'   105

Under what circumstances did Aunt Li become convinced not only that treatment was unaffordable, but also that it was unreliable, inefficacious and therefore not worth investing in? This chapter examines these two aspects in turn – financial barriers to access and perceptions of efficacy – to trace the various factors influencing healthcare-seeking patterns. It illustrates how hospital treatment (and cancer surgery in particular) is understood in a Sichuan village affected by high cancer rates. After a brief background on the research setting, the paper presents an account of the developments of healthcare provision since the founding of the People's Republic (1949) at the national, provincial, municipal and village level. This elucidates the ongoing healthcare disparities between rural and urban and wealthy and poor regions both in terms of quality and quantity of care available and the clear structural obstacles villagers face in accessing extortionately expensive care. As cancer sufferer Uncle Wang stated, 'when we [farmers] get ill we can't even afford treatment, we're just left to die' (October 2004). This sentence was perhaps the one that recurred with the most frequency during my fieldwork. In this light, before the introduction of the new rural cooperative medical system (RCMS, a collective health insurance programme) in the area in 2006, the answer to the question why do farmers not seek hospital treatment for cancer may seem straightforwardly financial.

The second part of the chapter argues that, however important cost may be, the widespread failure to resort to surgery is not only a consequence of lack of funds, but also of how sufferers perceived treatment. With cancer recognized as one of the main killers locally, I take the example of the perceived inefficacy of cancer surgery and examine how it is produced and how it influences action. I suggest that the high cost of surgery, understood within the wider context of commodified healthcare, contributes to producing its perceived inefficacy. Although this may seem equivalent to a straightforward inability to access care because of its cost, there is a subtle but crucial difference. While the earlier part of the illustrates the financial obstacles to accessing care, here the focus turns on how *perceptions* of such costs produce particular understandings of care. I argue that perceptions of hospital care as premised on raising revenue for healthcare providers contribute to forming scepticism towards such care. The most obvious response to this context is a widespread unwillingness to resort to hospital treatment.

This understanding of hospital care as money-oriented intersects with social, cultural and historical dimensions in ways that reinforce perceptions of it as inefficacious. Medical anthropologists have proposed that a treatment's efficacy is not only due to its inherent properties, but is also dependent on its social, cultural and economic contexts.[1] Anita Hardon's work on self-care for common health problems in Manila highlights that mothers choose particular cold remedies for children because they are part of a shared symbolic system through which mothers are constituted as caring individuals. Treatments have 'economic efficacy' when the balance between cost and quality of care is adequate and the financial effort is seen to lead to a long-term and worthwhile

106   *Anna Lora-Wainwright*

outcome. They have social and cultural efficacy to the extent that they mark people's identities, they produce or contest family and social relations, they intimately affect their perceptions of themselves, and enable particular kinds of social and symbolic processes (Van Der Geest *et al.* 1996: 156–57; see also Crandon-Malamud 1991). Conversely, through close analysis of one case (that of Gandie) I show that the recent context of commodified care intersects with locals' past living conditions and social positions – including the sufferer's social standing, their gender, their position within the family and the community, their sense of duty and filial piety – to configure cancer surgery as socially, culturally and economically inefficacious.[2]

Against this backdrop, the looks at some early reactions to the implementation of RCMS, pondering the extent to which RCMS has made a difference to perceptions of medical care and patterns of accessing it. I will argue that despite recent reforms to make healthcare more accessible to farmers, healthcare providers are still perceived as putting profit before their patients' wellbeing. In response, villagers continue to avoid seeking hospital care, especially from practitioners who have not been recommended by family or friends. A sufferer's social identity and relationship with his or her family, as we shall see in Grandma Qing's example, further reinforce this reluctance to seek care. For as long as doctors are regarded as akin to businessmen, state efforts to improve access to hospitals will continue to be frustrated.

The research setting

This chapter is based on anthropological fieldwork undertaken from 2004 for an initial period of 15 months, with follow-up visits in 2006, 2007 and 2008. Participant observation was supplemented by semi-structured interviews with medical practitioners at the village and municipal level, with municipal Public Health Bureau staff, and with village and township officials. I also carried out a survey of attitudes to health, cancer and health-seeking behaviour in 30 local families. During fieldwork, I resided in Baoma village (a pseudonym), six kilometres from the municipality of Langzhong, and with a population of approximately 500. Most of my data are based on Baoma, and are substantiated by research in a number of other villages in rural Langzhong. Langzhong municipality is a hilly area in the north-east of the Sichuan basin, just over 300 kilometres from the provincial capital, Chengdu. The municipality is poor even by Sichuan's standards, with an average yearly per capita income of roughly 2,000 yuan according to 2004 municipal records (interview with Baoma village secretary, 29 July 2004). According to official township records, the standard per capita income in Baoma in 2003 was 2,300 yuan, which is average within the township. This estimate however is made artificially high by three extremely wealthy families (one in particular). According to villagers, families where wage labour was absent had an average income of roughly 1,500 yuan per year per family, mostly based on animal breeding. In 2004–5, wage labourers working in the town or in the city (as builders,

'If you can walk and eat, you don't go to hospital' 107

carpenters, restaurant or hotel attendants) earned between 15 and 30 yuan per day. Migrant labourers working away from home earned between 400 and over 1,000 yuan per month (that is, from 15 yuan to over 40 yuan per day), but did not necessarily send any remittances home, depending on whether they had savings after they covered their own living costs, and whether funds were needed at home, for instance to cover schooling and healthcare costs.

Baoma's village doctor, doctors in the municipal hospital, and municipal Public Health Bureau staff frequently referred to epidemiological research carried out in Langzhong in the 1980s, which had attributed high rates of stomach and oesophagus cancer in the locality to consumption of salt-preserved meat and vegetables. Unfortunately, my attempts to collect hard data on the local incidence of cancer in Langzhong were frustrated by the scarcity of such data and restrictions to accessing it (particularly for foreigners), when it is classified as 'internal' (*neibu*). Nevertheless, available epidemiological data for the neighbouring county of Cangxi – one of the sites for an ongoing study by Oxford University's Clinical Trial Service Unit on diet, life-style and mortality in China (Chen *et al.* 1990, 2006) – shows high rates of stomach and oesophagus cancer. While I do not have similar data on cancer in Langzhong, my research highlighted that doctors and local residents alike considered these types of cancer to be major local killers in the area. The deputy head of Langzhong's People's Hospital remarked that many patients who visit the hospital for a check-up are diagnosed with cancer, and that many of the serious surgical procedures carried out are cancer-related (interviews, April 2005). Baoma's village doctor could list over 30 village residents, including his own parents, who had died of cancer in the past 20 years. Long-term fieldwork substantiated their claims. I counted 11 cases of cancer from 2003 to 2007 among Baoma's 500 or so residents. As cancer had affected a significant number of locals, it was perceived to be usually incurable and as incurring great financial loss, and was often a topic of conversation. It provides a good case to investigate how local farmers experience healthcare provision and how they have responded first to commodification of healthcare during reform and more recently to the introduction of the new RCMS.

Healthcare provision in context

The national context

In a short piece written as part of *The Lancet* Series on Health System Reform in China, Zhe Dong and Michael Phillips (2008) divide 'the evolution of China's health-care system' into five phases, which are useful for making sense of the changes in healthcare since the communist takeover in 1949. During the early 'post-liberation' phase (1949–65) the government gradually took over the management of healthcare, started a number of public-health campaigns, and tackled healthcare provision through a hierarchical structure of resort with village (brigade) clinics at its base, township (commune)

108   *Anna Lora-Wainwright*

hospitals as the second step and county hospitals for more complex health problems. This structure was further reinforced during the second phase, the Cultural Revolution (1966–76), when village clinics were strengthened through barefoot doctors – farmers trained with city doctors (sometimes for as little as three months, others over a year) to offer primary healthcare at the village level. County hospitals also provided mobile medical teams which took turns to serve in the countryside (see Sidel and Sidel 1974; Lampton 1977).

Finance for rural health services during these two phases came from a combination of government funding, cash payments from patients and funds from RCMS, with higher levels (county level and above) receiving state funding and village health centres mostly relying on local contributions. Pre-reform RCMS has often been credited as providing coverage for all rural dwellers and producing exceptionally good results for a developing country, but their extent and evenness of provision are probably less comprehensive than is often thought (White 1998; Duckett 2010). A rural–urban divide in healthcare insurance emerged, as both areas relied on their respective structures of governance: rural communes and urban work units. On the one hand, greater government investment was devoted to cities resulting in more and better facilities, and urban dwellers received treatment free at the point of delivery (Duckett 2007a: 50). On the other, rural areas depended on a cooperative scheme that was 'self-funded and much less generous (ibid.: 51). This meant urban dwellers faced fewer financial and physical obstacles to accessing care than their rural counterparts. Ultimately, self-reliance was 'the mantra for "peasants" … during the Maoist period, just as it has continued to be during the post-Mao period' (White 1998: 483). Accordingly, accounts which indicate very high coverage by the late 1970s (90 per cent in some cases) are likely to be inflated (Duckett 2010). Whatever the coverage rate for RCMS in the late 1970s, coverage was less than 5 per cent by 1984 (Carrin *et al.* 1999; Feng *et al.* 1995).

Phase three of Dong and Phillips' chronology (2008) covers the time span of early reforms (1977–89) and is characterized by a general commodification of healthcare.[3] As a consequence of the transition to a market economy, the available healthcare options have multiplied; yet, prices have risen rapidly, insurance coverage (including RCMS) has declined, and user fees have been introduced or increased without an adequate exemption system for the poor. Urban dwellers, likewise, increasingly found they have to pay for their own care (Duckett 2007; Wang 2008). The radical decentralization of financial responsibility to the provinces has exacerbated disparities between regions and between urban and rural areas and meant that with less funding devoted to the lower levels of healthcare, village and township clinics have suffered from a shortage of staff and decline in quality of care (Tang and Bloom 2000).[4] As these levels of care are the most accessible to rural Chinese because they are cheaper and closer geographically, rural populations have suffered the most from the changes. In turn, as financing was gradually privatized, hospitals have increasingly relied on sophisticated medical technologies and expensive drugs for revenue (Fang 2008). This has entailed a huge barrier to accessing hospital care for all those who cannot afford its direct costs (notably medical care, tests, food and loss of earnings) and informal costs (such as under-the-table payments to hospital staff).[5] As a result, patterns of income inequality have become key determinants of health inequalities, and illnesses can precipitate a family into economic disaster. An 'interpersonal pattern of inequality in financial access to health care' has also become more pronounced (Duckett 2007a: 54). The booming informal sector provides an alternative to formal care, especially in the case of over-the-counter medicines, but has not been adequately regulated, posing problems of inappropriate drug consumption as well as the sale of fake drugs (Segall 2000). Although the Chinese government in the late 1980s made efforts to improve access to care in rural areas (Yu 1992), attempts to maintain or re-establish RCMS were limited.

Phase four, the late reform period (1990–2002), was characterized by some attempts to provide more community-based health services, though they were mostly unsuccessful. In the early 1990s the government launched an initial trial of different health insurance schemes in poor counties, beginning in 1994 (Carrin *et al.* 1997). 1997 saw a renewed effort to promote RCMS, on a voluntary basis and mainly based on individual investment, with little government input and flexibility to adapt to local conditions (Duckett 2010). These efforts however did not lead to implementation on a large scale. In 2000, China's healthcare system ranked 188th out of 191 World Health Organization (WHO) member nations in terms of its fairness of financing, outperforming only Brazil, Burma and Sierra Leone (WHO 2000: 152). Health inequalities and the gap between healthcare available to China's new wealthy and the deprivation characterizing the poor remained unchallenged (Reddy 2007). Dong and Phillips see the SARS epidemic in 2003 as the cause for the start of a fifth and most recent phase in the evolution of China's health system. SARS, they argue, highlighted the poor state of healthcare, its infrastructure and problems of access and spurred the necessary political will to reform the system, with central funding supporting the re-establishment of RCMS and a parallel programme for urban areas, aiming to achieve total coverage by 2020.[6]

Documents and official speeches throughout 2004 bear testimony to a further strengthening of RCMS (Duckett 2010). This support of RCMS was also evident in the Chinese government's latest five-year plan (2006–10), which stressed the importance of building a 'new socialist countryside', which promised to increase rural investment and improve social services. Among its aims was the resolution of the problem of healthcare provision through the implementation of RCMS, which was scheduled to cover all of China's vast countryside by the end of 2008.[7] The success of RCMS both locally and nationwide, however, has been mixed. Several studies have already identified some of the problems in its implementation.[8] In poorer areas there are few local resources to finance these schemes, and in sparsely populated or remote areas, the time invested and costs incurred by travel, accommodation and

110　*Anna Lora-Wainwright*

food while accessing healthcare may discourage people from seeking it. Sarah Cook's (2007) research on RCMS shows that while individual contributions stayed at 10 yuan, contributions from local and central government increased from 10 to 20 yuan each per person, raising the total funds per person from the original 30 yuan to 50 yuan. RCMS, however, cover costs for only certain conditions and reimbursements mechanisms are often complex, and only cover a proportion of these costs. In its pilot period, each county developed its own approach, and areas where only in-patient coverage was offered had significantly lower coverage rates than those where outpatient care was also offered. Cook (2007) argues that at current levels of funding, based on pilots until 2006, RCMS had limited impact and only against catastrophic illness. She concludes that the central state needs to play a stronger role in funding this scheme. Whatever its actual shape and use, a report on 27 November 2008 on the official site of the Centre for China Cooperative Medical Scheme (CCMS) states that the whole countryside is now covered by RCMS (CCMS 27 November 2008).

The local context: Sichuan province

Developments in healthcare provision in Sichuan since the founding of the People's Republic closely resemble those outlined for China as a whole. While RCMS was established in the late 1960s, it was dismantled by the early 1980s (Langzhong Public Health Bureau staff, April 2007). A 2006 report in the online government forum *China National Social Security* (CNSS 23 November 2006) on RCMS in Sichuan states that it was re-established in June 2003 and that in trial areas the participation rate is 78 per cent, up by 19.5 per cent from 2005. As in the trend described by Cook (2007), contributions per person also rose from 30 yuan originally to 45 yuan in 2006, including 10 yuan per person from farmers, 20 yuan per person from the central Finance Bureau and 15 yuan from province, municipality and county, including a contribution from the provincial Finance Bureau of nine yuan per person. In 2005 the provincial government gave 36 million yuan to 21 counties included in the trial, and in 2006 the figure rose to 236 million. With an increase in participating areas, in 2007 the province is expected to contribute 600 million yuan, which according to the CNSS report strains the financial capacity of an agricultural province like Sichuan (23 November 2008). In an attempt to ease these pressures in 2008 the central government's Finance Bureau contributed over 2.4 billion yuan to Sichuan's RCMS (Central government web portal 16 September 2008).[9] The same report in September 2008, states that all of Sichuan province and its 176 counties and all rural population is now covered (*ibid.*).

The local context: Langzhong municipality

Baoma's first barefoot doctor, Doctor Wang, recalled that there was very little if any biomedical treatment available until 1957 in the Langzhong area, and only in Langzhong city's hospital, formerly established by Christian missionaries from Britain. Baoma villagers were fortunate enough to have a renowned 'senior Chinese medicine doctor' (*laozhongyi*) based in the village, who provided Chinese medicine treatment. Doctor Wang started training in 1966 by attending short courses (over three months) in the municipal hospital and by serving as an apprentice for three years to the village's *laozhongyi*, who was also incorporated into the village health clinic. Between 1969 and 1975, Doctor Wang explained, each villager would contribute one yuan per year towards a village cooperative healthcare scheme. Resources however, he added, were scant. 'We had only 20 to 30 shots of penicillin, around 100 pills, and some Chinese medical herbs. Western medicine was too expensive so we were told to rely mainly on Chinese medicine. I tried to grow some medicinal plants but the climate is no good for that here. We were also told to use acupuncture but people didn't want to' (4 July 2005). Prescriptions cost five *fen* (five cents of a yuan) for villagers and two *jiao* (twenty cents) for outsiders and payments would go to the collective. The village health clinic was maintained until decollectivization (which started in 1980 and was complete in 1981), when the clinic was privatized and transferred to the barefoot doctor's own house and his title was changed from 'barefoot doctor' to 'village doctor'. The village's *laozhongyi* opted instead to open a clinic in Langzhong city, and earned so much money that he bought his son a house and renovated one for his daughter. This, according to Doctor Wang, was a reflection of how steeply the cost of healthcare escalated since the onset of economic reforms.

When I first settled in the Langzhong area in 2004, it became clear that – as in the rest of China – the gap in quantity and quality of healthcare between rural and urban areas was wide. Langzhong city offered a great proliferation of medical services, ranging from hospitals, clinics, and chemists to masseurs and street stalls selling a wide variety of local herbal and animal remedies (such as silk worms to cure rheumatisms). In contrast, at the village level, there were only two clinics: one along the public road at the hilltop, established by a young local trained in Chinese medicine (and basic biomedicine) in a distance education college, and one run by the former barefoot doctor. For minor illnesses, villagers consulted village level doctors. In some cases, they consulted doctors from nearby villages when they had connections to them, or when these doctors were recommended by neighbours or relatives.

For persistent and more serious ailments, villagers resorted to hospital care. Hospitals, however, and in particular the more sophisticated 'People's Hospital' in Langzhong city, were seen as places where farmers 'don't dare go in' (*bu gan jinqu*), or 'can't afford to go in' (*jinbuqi*). In 2004–5, the cost of a minor surgical operation amounted to around 3,000 yuan and a more serious one, of the kind required for oesophagus cancer, started at 6,000. Informal costs are also extortionate: financial 'gifts' (*hongbao*) of 500 yuan for minor and 1,000 for major operations were offered to doctors. To these costs should be added those of hospitalization preceding and following surgery, and of

112   *Anna Lora-Wainwright*

other medications. Considering that according to township statistics average annual income per capita in 2004 was 2,300 yuan, these costs usually entail spending all the family's savings and very often borrowing money. This provides a very concrete sense of the obstacles villagers faced when accessing care, and is an important element in discouraging villagers from resorting to hospital care, and particularly to surgery for cancer.

While no form of medical insurance was available to local farmers during my initial period of fieldwork, the first post-reform RCMS was introduced in Langzhong in December 2005 (two months after I left the area), as it was designated to be one of the trial sites in Sichuan (Langzhong Rural Healthcare Cooperative Management Centre 2005). The government contributed 30 yuan per person in 2006 and 40 yuan per person in 2007 (Langzhong municipal Health Bureau official, 4 April 2007), a figure consonant with Cook's findings (2007). Rates of reimbursement also increased: while in 2006 one could receive 30 per cent for municipal hospital care, 40 per cent for township and 50 per cent for village care, in 2007 these rates rose to 40, 50 and 60 per cent respectively.[10] According to official figures, in 2006 the RCMS joining rate in Langzhong was 81 per cent and in 2007 it went up to 90 per cent (Langzhong Administrative Service Centre, 4 January 2008). In early 2008, Langzhong's Mayor, Jiang Jianping, wrote in the Langzhong online news (4 January 2008) that coverage was 98 per cent, and exhorted an expansion of the scheme. A report published by Langzhong's Administrative Service Centre on the same date (4 January 2008) stated that in 2007 (until November) RCMS had reimbursed 190,000 people for out-patient treatment, amounting to over three million yuan, for an average of 16 yuan per person. 28,000 people receiving in-patient treatment were reimbursed over 17 million yuan, for an average of 613 per person. Sufferers seeking treatment in the city's hospitals had increased to such an extent that in 2007 the corridors of the People's Hospital were lined with provisional beds and by the end of 2008 a new hospital building was completed to cope with growing numbers of patients.

To illustrate RCMS's benefits, the report gives the example of a 53-year-old man diagnosed with a bladder tumour in 2006 who was advised by the hospital in the provincial capital, Chengdu to intervene promptly through chemotherapy. The total cost of treatment was 70,000 yuan. The patient is said to have received 10,100 yuan initially in 2006 and a further 11,360 yuan in April 2008. Attempting to cope with potential scepticism towards RCMS in 2007 those who joined but had not made use of the scheme were entitled to receive a free health check-up; 155,945 people did so, at a cost of almost 1.9 million yuan. From October 2007 a 'special method for reimbursing the medical costs of outpatient treatment for chronic illness' was formulated, ruling that malignant tumours, chronic kidney failure and 12 other illnesses could be treated through outpatient treatment in 1,382 designated clinics. The total budget available for reimbursing these treatments was 1.5 million yuan. The next section provides an ethnographic account of perceptions of care

'If you can walk and eat, you don't go to hospital'   113

before the new RCMS came into being. It illustrates the effect commodification of healthcare had on perceptions of it, and examines how experiences
and relationships also configured a rejection of cancer surgery as a strategic
and moral response.

Commodified health and its consequences

Perceptions of care at the municipal hospital and their effects on action

As we have seen, following healthcare reforms the cost of hospital care escalated to levels often unaffordable for those without insurance. Absolute cost
doubtlessly poses obstacles to accessing hospital treatment. But the reforms
have also had the effect of making hospitals and their practitioners more
profit-oriented, as they are required to generate much of their own revenue.
This in turn strengthens perceptions of doctors, and hospital practitioners in
particular, as money-grabbing and untrustworthy. Villagers' routine complaints about the cost of previously more affordable and widespread treatments – for instance, penicillin pills or cold remedies – indicate that objections
about the cost of healthcare are not simply due to an inability to afford it, but
are also attacks on the political economy that sustains it, and on the ideology
that legitimates it. It also shows that villagers' rejection of surgery for cancer
was not rooted in mistrust towards biomedicine. On the contrary, they are
often keen to resort to biomedical pills for flu symptoms, and to intravenous
injections of antibiotics if symptoms persist. They also argue that technolo-
gically sophisticated diagnostic tools and treatments are necessary for complex conditions.[11] What they do oppose is the profit principle underlying
diagnosis and treatment, which becomes all the more painfully obvious as
resort is made to care providers beyond the township, most notably the city's
hospitals. A perception that city dwellers typically have a salary and a pension, and are more likely to have health insurance (whether or not this is the
case is a separate issue) also exacerbates villagers' sense that they are not
entitled to the same quantity nor quality of care as their urban counterparts.[12]

According to Mark Nichter (2003: 265–326), in South Asia the commodification of healthcare has decontextualized healthcare issues from wider social
issues and engendered a false sense of security based on the assumption that
health can be achieved provided one pays for it. Similar processes of commodification have had very different effects in rural Langzhong. In Nichter's
account, people mostly follow the dominant rhetoric of a pill for every ill,
albeit with their cultural appropriations of what medicines do. This in turn
reduces their impetus to mobilize in favour of a better environment and
hygiene. In rural Langzhong, by contrast, villagers are highly critical of the
consumerist approach to healthcare, which has fostered a widespread distrust
of care outside one's social network, most typically hospital care. As a friend
working in the financial administration of the People's Hospital remarked,
'before, doctors served the people (*wei renmin fuwu*), now they serve the

114 *Anna Lora-Wainwright*

(people's) money (*wei renminbi fuwu*)' (1 July 2005).[13] While this may be an overstatement, and a romanticization of the past, it is telling of how hospital treatment and staff are perceived, and has crucial implications for patterns of resort and perceptions of efficacy.

It was well known and debated both within and outside the People's Hospital that doctors prescribed expensive treatments to gain profit. Villagers and doctors alike maintained that some practitioners prescribe expensive medications because they are bribed by the company producing them, and this created a widespread sense of scepticism and increased attention to avoid being deceived. In this context, sufferers adopt various strategies to identify adequate treatment and avoid being cheated into paying more than is necessary. For flu, for instance, doctors usually suggest a number of different pills and capsules to be taken together. Patients are in my experience very conversant with the cost of each of these pills, and often design their prescription with the doctor demanding, where possible, that the most expensive pills be replaced with less costly options. Another widespread strategy is to obtain a prescription from hospital and then consult a more trusted doctor or chemist to establish whether there are any cheaper alternatives without compromising too much on quality. At any rate, villagers commented to me that they would never buy medicine at the hospital, because the same or similar treatment is available at local pharmacies or from the village doctor for less money. Treatment at the city's hospital lacked economic efficacy since it was assumed to cost more without much (or any) improvement on the result.

These perceptions have two major consequences for sufferers' attitudes to efficacy and in turn for their practices. First, receiving treatment from a trusted practitioner – whether it be because the sufferer had connections with them, or because it had been suggested by neighbours – contributes to perceptions of a given treatment as efficacious. Local doctors, such as the village doctor, indeed draw much of their efficacy from being part of the local community, as I have discussed elsewhere (Lora-Wainwright 2005). Similarly, when the needed treatment is only available in hospital, the extent and quality of connections between hospital staff and the sufferer's family contribute crucially to perceptions of the quality of treatment and of the advice given. For instance, when I became close to some members of staff at the People's Hospital, some villagers (such as Aunt Li) sought me to serve as a reference point to have check-ups or find medicine with a positive balance between cost and quality. Local knowledge and neighbours' advice on which doctors had successfully treated particular problems and were reasonably priced, or, even better, neighbours who counted a doctor amongst their relatives, also served as a key resource for securing adequate treatment and producing perceptions of it as efficacious and value for money. In other words, practitioners one knows, or those associated with the positive experiences of others, accrue social efficacy. Trust in the practitioner then acts as a sort of placebo effect or 'meaning response', as Moerman (2002) termed it, thereby contributing to the clinical efficacy of treatment. Social efficacy does not, of course, imply that

'If you can walk and eat, you don't go to hospital' 115

trusted practitioners are seen as infallible. But it increases the likelihood that sufferers will be content with the result of treatment and with the balance between cost and quality, and that they will return to the same practitioner in the future.

Second, and conversely, hospital treatment such as cancer surgery is usually seen to be inefficacious (unless it is provided by a trusted practitioner) because it often lacks a network of connections perceived as necessary to ensure that practitioners will not cheat their patients. This treatment then lacks both social and economic efficacy. Indeed, sufferers and their families often suspect that doctors advise in favour of surgery simply because it is the most expensive course of treatment. By delaying diagnosis, lack of social and economic efficacy in turn increase the likelihood that surgery for cancer will be clinically ineffi-cacious. Combined with experiences amongst other villagers that cancer surgery is often ineffective in the long (and often short) term, their suspicion typically results in a rejection of surgical treatment. The high cost of care (including informal payments) and understanding of the revenue-seeking incentives of hospital practitioners therefore creates not only a structural obstacle to acces-sing treatment (as I outlined in the previous section) but also constitutes treat-ment as undesirable and practitioners as untrustworthy. By denying hospital treatment social and economic efficacy, high cost further persuades villagers to rule out the possibility of resorting to such care. The next section will look at some additional factors that motivate a rejection of hospital treatment. By highlighting the importance of social relations and identities involved in decision-making, it shows that economic reductionism is inadequate for understanding the complex negotiations surrounding illness and care.

Cancer surgery in rural Langzhong before the new RCMS

When a family member is diagnosed with cancer, the most important decision the family faces is whether to invest in surgery.[14] Ultimately, very few villagers decide to undergo surgery, and even fewer make a full recovery in its after-math. As I have already mentioned, the barefoot-turned-village doctor (Doctor Wang) could easily list over 30 villagers who had died of cancer in the past 20 years. Of all these cases only one, a 52 year-old woman, had surgery for oesophagus cancer and is still well (2008). Doctor Wang could only think of four more villagers affected by other types of cancer who opted for surgery. Two of them died within two years of the operation, while the remaining two were less fortunate. 40-year-old Uncle Song was diagnosed with bladder cancer in 2002 and died in the operating theatre. His family was poor by local stan-dards, and his only son, 14 years old and a good student when his father was diagnosed, discontinued his studies and migrated to Chengdu to work in a factory to finance his father's operation. His neighbour, Uncle Zhao, was diagnosed with oesophagus cancer in May 2006 at the age of 46. His family sold all their pigs and chickens and borrowed money from relatives so he could undergo surgery. He died the day following surgery. His case was seen as

116 *Anna Lora-Wainwright*

yet another example that surgery is not clinically efficacious and, crucially, reproduced surgery as socially, culturally and economically inefficacious.

In most cases I encountered in Baoma, the reasons given for avoiding surgery were, in the words of my respondents, that 'we found out too late (*faxian le tai wan le*)' or 'it's too expensive (*tai gui le*)'. Given the cost of surgery and its poor success rate, cancer-stricken villagers usually 'waited to die (*deng si*)', or killed themselves drinking pesticides. But while locals' emphasis on the cost of treatment is central to their perceptions of efficacy and (non)entitlement to care, I argue that the refusal of surgery cannot be explained only as a function of limited funds or of what Paul Farmer calls 'structural violence' (2003: 40). In fact in some cases sufferers and their families were able to afford hospital treatment by investing all of the family's resources or even by borrowing money. But they chose not to. Gandie's example will illustrate why this may be so.

Gandie was my host Dajie's father and he was about to turn 62 when he was diagnosed with oesophagus cancer in October 2004. With three sons and three daughters-in-law, four of whom had paid occupations in Langzhong city, and two migrant worker grandsons, Gandie's extended family had enough income to be able to afford surgery. As opposed to most other villagers who were diagnosed late with cancer and did not have an operation, his family was advised that surgery did present some hope for recovery. However, Gandie still refused to undergo surgical treatment. A number of factors affected Gandie and his family's perceptions of cancer and of what constituted an efficacious treatment: his identity as a 'strong' man; his and his children's filial piety; his experiences as a former village cadre; experiences of past shortage; limited access to hospital treatment in the past and in the present; and the current context of commodified healthcare. I will examine each of these aspects to shed light on how Gandie's rejection of surgery both relies on and articulates family relations and attitudes to the past and the present. These factors, I argue, were central to shaping the course of action Gandie and his family took in response to cancer.

Gandie's family and neighbours regarded him as a very healthy man, and his cancer came to all as an unexpected shock. Still a very able worker, his family felt that at 62 Gandie was neither 'old' nor weak. Gandie's confidence in his own strength probably delayed his admission that he was suffering and in turn delayed his visit to the municipal hospital for a check-up. Initially at least, his family thought he was healthy enough to overcome cancer; he simply needed to stop getting angry and anxious. This contributed to persuading them not to reveal the diagnosis to Gandie.[15] The expectation that a strong man would be in a good position to fight off cancer paradoxically worked to his disadvantage. By the time Gandie realized he had cancer, he had been in pain at least two months, and had a clear sense of the deteriorating state of his body. This experience may have contributed to his perception of his cancer as already too advanced to be curable, and to the conviction that surgery would not have long-term effects.

'*If you can walk and eat, you don't go to hospital*' 117

Once Gandie became aware of his cancer, his family promptly suggested surgery. He alone was opposed to it. Gandie's children's insistence that he undergo surgery and take medication was an embodiment of their filial piety (*xiao*), their affection and respect for him.[16] The ability to care adequately for their father would have legitimated their social position and materialized their care and concern. In this sense, surgery had social and cultural efficacy – it enabled particular family relations and was in tune with the widespread cultural value of filial piety. Conversely, being unable to relieve his pain exacerbated their sense of unfulfilled care towards Gandie, which became stronger as the cancer aggravated. Towards the final stages, his youngest son complained: 'This illness has no filial sons' (*zhe ge bing meiyou xiao zi*) (2 February 2005). This resonates with the widespread proverb 'long illnesses do not have filial sons' (*jiu bing wu xiao zi*) (Dong 2001: 166). Long illnesses such as cancer confronted Gandie's offspring with the insurmountable challenge of caring adequately for their father and sparing him from suffering. The inability to succeed on these accounts constituted for them a lack of filial responsibility.

If feelings of affection and responsibility for their father motivated Gandie's children to insist he undergo surgery, Gandie's own filial piety committed him against it. According to Confucian doctrine and traditional customs (*chuantong xiguan*), explained Ganma and Dajie, surgery would violate the entirety of the body given to him by his parents and in turn express lack of respect towards them (see Anon., *Xiaojing* 1975: 2–3). This constitutes surgery as unfilial and therefore inappropriate. This ideology, at the same time, provided a culturally legitimate rationale for not seeking expensive treatment, and thereby alleviated Gandie's family's moral obligation to care for him by putting forward an alternative morality. As such, surgery lacked cultural efficacy. Examining a case of someone who refused treatment for TB on the basis that it was not compatible with her body, Nichter suggested that 'cultural concepts are used by the poor to cope with hard choices' (2002: 92). According to Nichter's model, it would follow that Gandie resorted to Confucian doctrine in an almost utilitarian way, with the explicit aim of justifying lack of treatment. In so far as Nichter explains resort to cultural concepts as produced by its socio-economic settings, his approach is valid. I would, however, stress the more dialectical relationship between culture and socio-economic conditions and the role of culture in producing social inequalities. Culture is not only a product of these conditions, but also serves to articulate them. Indeed, Gandie's decision to avoid surgery produced and embodied his responsibility (*zeren*) for the care of the 'wider self' of his family (*jia*), including all three sons, two daughters and their families, who would have contributed money towards the operation. It highlighted the contestability of what constitutes 'filial responsibility', moral behaviour and family boundaries. This lack of both cultural and social efficacy reinforced Gandie's determination to avoid surgery.

Gandie's past role as a village-level cadre in the late 1960s and 1970s further reinforced his sense of responsibility for the wider good. Having managed

118   *Anna Lora-Wainwright*

the financial affairs of his village unit until 1981, Gandie had long-term experience of administering public resources. He was praised by his neighbours as a good cadre who looked out for the needs of the local community and invested wisely in farming equipment for his 'production team'. During the Cultural Revolution he volunteered to host a rusticated worker for over a year, and treated him like 'one of the family', ensuring he was given the best food on their table (Gandie, 1 November 2004). He was repeatedly invited to become village party secretary, but refused to do so. He explained to me this would have been too troublesome, and would have involved giving and taking bribes, something he stated he had never done and was not prepared to do. Gandie's commitment to his community earned him the respect of his neighbours and a certain social standing. His social position within the family and the local community predisposed him to endure pain for longer without drawing attention to himself, which in turn proved detrimental. Transposing his past experience of managing limited funds for the public good to the present, Gandie was unwilling to require a large investment towards his individual wellbeing. He argued that it would be pointless to waste funds on something with short-term effects like an operation, but rather more desirable to invest in the long-term future of his family members.

Gandie's socio-economic conditions in the past further disposed him against surgery. His experiences of food shortage, austerity and hard work taught Gandie to put the good of the family before the good of the self, and made him unwilling to invest a large amount of money on himself. Even though the poverty Gandie endured in the past was no longer characteristic of his life, his experience shaped his sense of non-entitlement, which was retained even when economic conditions changed. Equally, his past experience of healthcare had a significant impact on his current attitudes to it. As we have seen, during the Mao period (1949–76) rural healthcare was organized as a three-tier system, and therefore county hospitals would only be resorted to in cases that could not be tackled by lower levels. Although cancer surgery would indeed be such a case, a more general sense of limited experience of healthcare as a whole, and county hospital care in particular, denied it social and economic efficacy. If surgery retained a level of social and cultural efficacy in that it would have embodied Gandie's offspring care for their father, his social identities – as a healthy man, a filial son, the head of the family, a former official and a farmer who experienced chronic shortage – denied it efficacy on all accounts: social, cultural and economic. The current setting – commodified healthcare and the ensuing distrust of doctors and hospitals as outlined above – only reinforced the likelihood of rejection of cancer surgery.

The New Rural Cooperative Medical Scheme – potential for change?

Aware of the rising rural discontent caused by the absence of a functioning welfare system, and of the potential threats this posed to national stability, the Chinese government has taken steps to provide more equitable access to healthcare for the rural population through a new Rural Cooperative Medical Scheme (RCMS). Its implementation in Baoma, however, shows that the success of such structural changes is far from secured. There, staff shortages in the township and village government produced some clear structural challenges to implementing the new RCMS. Together with the village head and the village doctor, the village secretary was responsible for informing locals about how RCMS worked, and is accountable for local joining rates. Yet, the village school, from which new policies were broadcast through the village tannoy system until 2005, was closed and sold to a local family in 2006. Though the village secretary retained use of a small upstairs room where the tannoy system was operated, the system was broken until 2007, leaving the village secretary with little means to introduce RCMS and urge locals to join them. His only option was visiting villagers at home, but most are out during the day (either in the fields or commuting to the city for construction and other menial work), which according to him hinders his chances of implementing policies, including RCMS. Indeed, in their first year of running in the Langzhong area (2006), joining rates were higher amongst residents of village units closer to the houses of the village secretary, village head, and village doctor, who also share the same surname (fieldwork, July 2006). This physical and kinship proximity to the village cadres and the village doctor ensures better access to some villagers and fosters higher levels of trust, which might explain the discrepancy in joining rates.

During my initial research on RCMS in July 2006, Baoma villagers felt that the scheme was a swindle (*pian ren de*) and fake (*jia de*), no different from all the other fees officials imposed on the local population to extort money without offering any real benefit. Since RCMS was initially perceived to be administered by the village secretary, experiences with other fees, which fomented mistrust and resentment towards him, extended such mistrust to the RCMS. A few examples illustrate this. The central government introduced a law to lift the agricultural tax and all arbitrary levies on farmers as of 2003. Yet some farmers in Langzhong continued to be charged until 2005. Although part of the amounts required was allegedly levies overdue from previous years, it fuelled perceptions that local officials were pocketing the money. During my research in 2006, locals were still not convinced that levies had actually been lifted. By my following research visit in April 2007, with most people not having paid any levies in the past year, locals seemed increasingly convinced that central government policies were being implemented. Yet discontent was still fierce since compensation for a reforestation project (*tuigen huanlin*) had not been offered to farmers.[17] The village secretary claimed he used these funds to cover the water tax and costs of building the local road. But farmers complained they had been given no transparent account of how much money had been invested in these activities. These experiences added to scepticism towards RCMS, especially when it was seen to be the village secretary's responsibility.

120   *Anna Lora-Wainwright*

The scepticism of RCMS I encountered in July 2006 had largely abated by the following fieldtrip in March 2007, giving way to increased trust in the scheme. One reason for this growth of faith may be that locals had had positive experiences of using RCMS. The ability to use payments to the new RCMS as credit to purchase medicine from the village doctor had contributed to convincing locals that these schemes were beneficial (*bu de chi kui*, literally, 'you do not have to suffer losses'). The fact that those who had treatment as in-patients appeared to have received the amount promised as reimbursement had also been instrumental in establishing trust in the healthcare schemes amongst locals. Roughly one-third (nine out of 30) of villagers interviewed in depth in March 2007 stressed that one of the most positive aspects of the new RCMS was that whereas the Maoist rural cooperative medical system was a 'village matter' (that is, administered in the village, based on village funds and mostly only offering village-level care) the new system offered assistance for hospital treatment. Moreover, they argued, the new RCMS was mostly funded by the central government and was not controlled by village or township officials, which meant these officials had little opportunity to squeeze money out of the schemes for themselves. The partial disassociation of RCMS from local officials therefore contributed to their efficacy. The same interviewees also added that unwillingness of some villagers to join the schemes was most likely attributed to a lack of understanding of precisely this aspect.

Joining rates alone, however, do not prove that RCMS actually helps farmers in any significant way or that it is changing their perception of hospital practitioners. Even though by 2007 most villagers had joined RCMS, they were not satisfied that the scheme offered enough reimbursement, and complained that it was limited to inpatient services and did not include crucial out-patient or preventive healthcare. The introduction of coverage for out-patient treatment starting in 2008 (Langzhong Administrative Service Centre, 4 January 2008) may change these attitudes, but more research is needed to establish the extent to which it will do so. In March–April 2007 the predominant feeling in rural Langzhong was, as Cook (2007) pointed out, that RCMS had so far done little to raise farmers' sense of entitlement to hospital care and to dispel perceptions that medical treatment was unaffordable and expenses were liable to rise uncontrollably. Villagers felt that RCMS could diminish the cost of treatment, but did not completely eliminate the problem: medical care remained extremely expensive. As a 23-year-old villager (23 March 2007) put it:

> ... even 60 per cent [the current rate of reimbursement for village clinic treatment] is not enough. Surgery for cancer costs 6,000 yuan, it still leaves thousands for the family to pay, [and] farmers still cannot afford it. And it excludes the cost of medication at home. Doctors are corrupt, they prescribe the most expensive medicine, and inflate prices. If the government could control this and keep the prices low, they would not need to invest in RCMS.

'If you can walk and eat, you don't go to hospital' 121

This quote begins to highlight how the fierce scepticism towards hospital treatment is a major obstacle to RCMS functioning and benefiting farmers. A 60-year-old woman, for instance, claimed that one could only be reimbursed through RCMS if he or she had contacts (*shuren*) in the hospital. Grandma Qing, in her early 70s, refused to have surgery for glaucoma, even when it was offered at half price, because she felt that the cost would escalate uncontrollably. When I explained that municipal hospital staff had assured me the operation would only cost 200 yuan she replied sarcastically: 'And you believe *them*, do you?' She then added 'one eye is enough, I'm old and there is no point spending so much money on me' (16 March 2007). She explained that her son was renting a room in Langzhong city to support her grandson through his final year of high school. Work in Langzhong was poorly paid, and her daughter-in-law's earnings (from work in a Shenzhen factory) were barely enough to cover their living costs and her grandson's school fees. Like Gandie, Grandma Qing denied herself treatment to save funds for the family as a whole and by doing so showed her care to the rest of the family. As far as she was concerned, treatment for glaucoma lacked efficacy economically (costs might escalate), socially and culturally (caring for her family was more important than caring for her health). Although both Grandma Qing and her neighbour had joined RCMS, their perception of hospital practitioners remained that they 'cheat/extort your money' (*pian ni de qian*). Many interviewees stated that one goes to hospital only when he or she absolutely has to: 'if you can walk and eat, you don't go to hospital.' Despite the recent structural changes in welfare provision, mistrust of hospitals remains rife.

Conclusion

This chapter shows that the commodification of healthcare has established not only structural barriers to it for the poorest but also a widespread scepticism towards the medical profession and its for-profit practice, which in turn results in a general unwillingness to resort to formal medical care, and to hospitals in particular. Ruiping Fan (2006) has argued for the need to shed collectivist and egalitarian commitments and recognize (and accept) the profit motive in providing healthcare as ethical and in tune with 'the new economic realities of China' (*ibid.*: 541). This is in stark contrast not only to a wide literature promoting health equality (see, for instance, Farmer 2003; Nichter and Nichter 2003; Anand *et al.* 2004), which Fan may deem culturally and socially unfitting for contemporary China, but to how villagers themselves understand healthcare.

Locals' scepticism towards hospital care and marketized medicine is not founded on a timeless and abstract ideal of a healthcare system fully funded and able to cure all ills, but measured against two idealized parameters: the Maoist RCMS and urban insurance schemes. During my fieldwork in 2004–5,

122 *Anna Lora-Wainwright*

before the introduction of the new RCMS, villagers often compared their current predicament with insurance coverage under Mao. The wife of cancer-sufferer Uncle Wang explained: 'in the past, if you went to the hospital but had no money to pay, they would still treat you, but now they only let you in if you have money' (September 2004). Rather than being accurate portrayals of Maoist RCMS, these accounts served to critique lack of insurance cover and the market orientation of medical treatment in the present. Similarly, villagers contrasted their situation with that of their urban counterparts who, they thought, were covered by more comprehensive insurance schemes. Although this is no longer necessarily true, their perception is rooted in a long-standing gap in welfare provision for rural and urban dwellers (Duckett 2007) and in widespread feelings of dissatisfaction about the rural–urban gap in incomes and lifestyles. Though there is evidence that villagers have recently re-envisioned their memories of Maoist RCMS in favour of the new version, these schemes have not done much to undermine a sense of inequality compared to their urban counterparts.

Using the example of Gandie, this chapter has examined the complex processes through which surgery is constituted as lacking efficacy and their influence of health-seeking practices. Gandie rejected surgery because by doing so he reproduced his social identity and his relationship with his family, and thereby expressed a particular (dis)engagement with the commodification of healthcare. Indeed, Gandie's rejection of surgery may be seen as a moral response to crisis, based on parameters (such as morality but also filial responsibility) formed historically, which to some extent persisted beyond their conditions of production, but which were also newly activated by the socio-economic conditions of reform. Self-abnegation functioned to reproduce Gandie's sense of responsibility and care towards his family. Conversely, their insistence he undergo surgery embodied their care and concern for him. Perceptions of the present society as corrupt, and of hospitals as money-oriented powerfully informed Gandie's attitude. Yet rather than take his judgement at face value, as evidence that corruption is an ineluctable fact, I regard it as a social fact, which carries the important social effect of producing new ways to deal with corruption and constituting alternative moral worlds. For instance, perceived immorality reproduces a sense that social networks are vital to guarantee fair treatment, and vice versa, their presence produces a given treatment as fair, reliable and efficacious. Sufferers' active engagement in the diagnosis and healing process – by cross-checking hospital prescriptions with more trusted practitioners, purchasing medications in local clinics, and avoiding treatment they regard as expensive yet ineffective – is also a moral response to the commodification of health-care, in as far as they strive to reproduce a moral universe in the face of market challenges.

The relatively high incidence of cancer in the area of Langzhong no doubt influences responses to illness and affects attitudes towards seeking treatment and trust in its efficacy. In particular, stomach and oesophagus cancer, the two types of cancer with highest incidence locally, are notoriously difficult to detect, and when the sufferer begins to feel unwell cancer is usually already at an advanced stage. Likelihood of late diagnosis is also increased by villagers' hesitation and delay in visiting the city hospital (the nearest place where cancer can be diagnosed) for a check-up. Late diagnosis in turn sharply decreases the likelihood of success of any intervention. When the rare villager invests in surgery and dies in the process or shortly after, this only reinforces perceptions that cancer cannot be cured, that surgery is pointless and that doctors only advise in favour of it with revenue in mind (given cost is so high and success rate is so poor). The cost incurred is reduced by RCMS reimbursements, but remains steep. Local incidence of cancer makes findings in Langzhong difficult to generalize for the whole of Sichuan, let alone China. The processes by which villagers assess the efficacy of hospital treatment and views of commodified healthcare are likely, however, to be similar to those experienced by other rural dwellers weighting the pros and cons of expensive healthcare. Attention to the intricacies of individual cases, as I have done for Gandie, also highlights the pitfalls of sweeping analyses of the impacts of policy on people as if these effects were homogenous. In each case, rather, decision-making has complex contexts. In Gandie's case at least, while pure cost is certainly a consideration, attributing lack of treatment simply to poverty would be an oversight. Rather, perceptions of cost, its social and cultural connotations, and the social relations it enables or denies are just as important to constituting cancer surgery as socially, culturally and economically inefficacious and thereby motivating a rejection of it.

New perceptions do not form overnight. Changes in healthcare policy aimed at offering more affordable treatment, such as the introduction of new RCMS, are frustrated by lasting perceptions that healthcare remains a commodity and that doctors act with financial interests in mind. Locals will require a new set of experiences of local policies and their executors to be convinced that what they invest in healthcare cooperatives will indeed benefit them. In a similar fashion, less suspicion towards medical practitioners and the medical establishment as a whole is fundamental to ensuring that when illness strikes, sufferers do not deny themselves treatment, as Aunt Li, Grandma Qing and Gandie did. This can only be fostered by creating a perception of medical institutions and its practitioners as not only market-driven, but also available to those with fewer means. The new RCMSs are beginning to go some way to meet this challenge, but there is so far little evidence that attitudes to hospitals and medical practitioners and practices of health-seeking have changed significantly. The schemes would produce better results if they could be extended beyond in-patient treatment (the service which is least likely to be sought by farmers) to other expensive medications for chronic problems treated at home. This was the type of treatment that those like Aunt Li would be more inclined to resort to. The road to more accessible and equitable healthcare is long and winding.

124   *Anna Lora-Wainwright*

Acknowledgements

This research was supported by the Arts and Humanities Research Council, The Leverhulme Trust, the Universities' China Committee in London, and the Contemporary China Study Programme (Oxford University). My deepest thanks go to the friends and informants in China who made my research not only possible, but also thoroughly enjoyable and memorable. In order to protect them, personal names and place names (except for Langzhong) have been changed. Reflecting the Chinese custom I adopted during fieldwork, I use surnames followed by kinship terms according to generation in relation to me (for instance 'Aunt' for women of my mother's generation). The man I refer to as Gandie, or 'dry father', was my host's father. Having been 'adopted' into the family, I followed his case closely until well after he died of cancer in February 2005.

Notes

1 See Crandon-Malamud (1991); Etkin (1988); Etkin and Tan (1994); Kamat (2009) Moerman (2002); Van Der Geest *et al.* (1996); Waldram (2000); Whyte (1997) and Whyte *et al.* (2002).
2 This is not meant to suggest that socio-culturally situated attitudes act as a nocebo effect (cf. Moerman 2002), making cancer surgery clinically inefficacious in my fieldsite. Rather, by producing a perception of cancer surgery as inefficacious, such attitudes discourage cancer sufferers from resorting to surgery at all.
3 Useful recent overviews of these processes include Bloom *et al.* (2008) and Fang (2008). See also *The Lancet Series on Health Systems reform in China* (online 20/10/2008) www.thelancet.com/series/health-system-reform-in-china (accessed 3 November 2008). For a recent full-length volume in Chinese on healthcare reforms see Gu *et al.* (2006).
4 For an insightful account of healthcare financing see Duckett (2007a).
5 See Hu *et al.* (2008) and Tang *et al.* (2008) for a recent analysis of healthcare inequity.
6 Signs of change were however present already in 2002 (see Central Party Committee and State Council 19 October 2002; Duckett 2010).
7 See the official website for RCMS: ccms.org.cn (accessed March 2007).
8 The literature on these issues is wide, and growing fast. See Cook (2007), Dummer and Cook (2007) and Sun *et al.* (2008).
9 On problems and countermeasures faced by health insurance systems in Western rural areas see Wang and Chen (2005). Li and Zhang (2005) examine problems and countermeasures in Sichuan's new RCMS pilot implementation areas.
10 Rates of reimbursement grow for lower-level care because these are less expensive (and therefore more sustainably reimbursed) and to discourage patients from using higher-level care unless they need to do so (Langzhong municipal Health Bureau official, 4 April 2007).
11 On understandings of biomedicine adapted to non-Western locales see Kamat (2009) and Kleinman (1995).
12 Migrant workers are of course an obvious exception, as they usually have no stable pay, pension entitlements or health insurance schemes. See Xiang (2007) on migrants' health.
13 This is a play on words, juxtaposing the Maoist phrase 'serve the people' (*wei renmin fuwu*) and the official term for China's currency, 'the people's currency' (*renminbi*).

'*If you can walk and eat, you don't go to hospital*' 125

14 This is not to imply that access to care is only defined in terms of access to bio-medical treatment, or surgery, nor to unproblematically reproduce the hegemony of biomedicine as the only efficacious treatment. Changes in diet, self-cultivation practices (see Farquhar 2002) and Chinese medical treatments are employed for general health maintenance and for chronic conditions. However, cancer is perceived to require fast intervention, making surgery the only treatment seen to have the potential to cure cancer. This is in tune with widespread stereotypes that Chinese medicine is adequate for chronic illnesses (and villagers did resort to Chinese medicine to treat rheumatism and chronic stomach conditions) but biomedicine is more efficacious in treating acute conditions. See Scheid (2002: 107–33) on how these stereotypes do not always inform action in a straightforward way.

15 Local cancer aetiologies which related it to negative emotions may partly explain patterns of non-disclosure, which in turn may have disposed Gandie against treatment (see Lora-Wainwright, n.d.: Chapters 2 and 3). Here I focus on the range of other aspects which contributed to creating a perception of surgery as inefficacious and motivating its rejection.

16 On filiality see the volumes edited by Chan and Tan (2004) and Ikels (2004). See also Anon., *The Classic of Filial Piety* (*Xiaojing*, 1975).

17 Following a state-wide reforestation policy, local farmers were instructed to plant fruit trees, and a total of 400 mu (1 mu = 667 m^2) was planted with peach and apricots trees in 2001. According to national-level laws, the local government was required to provide farmers who took part in the scheme with 150 kg of grains per mu and with 20 yuan worth of chemicals per year per person for the first 5 years (confirmed by informal conversation with host family, 25 January 2005). On this policy and its reception see for instance Leonard and Flower (2006).

7 Regional disparities and educational inequalities

City responses and coping strategies

Ka Ho Mok and Yu Cheung Wong

In the last two decades, China's education system has been transformed by privatization and marketization. In the Maoist era (1949–78) the state was responsible for financing and providing education. Now, in the post-Mao era, individuals and families have to bear an increasing share of the costs, a burden for many. These changes have intensified educational inequalities and regional disparities between the developed areas on the east coast and the less developed areas of the inland and western provinces. What has further intensified educational inequalities is closely related to the policy of decentralizing the administration and financing education in the last few decades. Together with the consequences of privatizing and marketizing education, this has meant that Chinese residents today encounter a 'new mountain' in the heavy financial burden of education.

Moreover, these burdens are unevenly distributed – as recognized in very recent policies. As local governments bear a considerable share of the financial responsibility for providing education, poorer households in low-income regions have suffered lower levels of investment and thus inferior input into public education. On top of this are the growing costs of extracurricular activities, many of which are unaffordable to the poor.

The growing inequalities in the provision of education, in addition to increasing costs, have attracted public criticism and the central government's abiding concern about social unrest has forced it to revisit their strategies concerning educational development. Since 2006 attempts have been made to reverse some of the negative effects of its earlier market-oriented and decentralizing policies.

Within the social, economic and political contexts, this chapter examines how China's education system has been transformed by the pro-competition and market-oriented reform measures that were implemented from the mid-1980s to 2005. Several sources of data are used. These include intensive secondary data analysis and fieldwork observations, and the findings generated from a household survey conducted in eight different cities in China regarding people's perceived educational hardship.[1] Two cities are used for comparison purposes because they presented the greatest contrast in terms of economic development and income levels, namely Beijing, the national capital, and

Regional disparities and educational inequalities 127

Lanzhou, the provincial capital of Gansu, one of the poorest provinces in China. We give special attention to the lower-income households to examine how they are being affected by this trend of changing education policy. Although this chapter discusses mainly the inequalities in urban areas across different income regions in China and its impact to urban households, the disparities between urban and rural areas and hardship experienced by the rural households are no less serious. In this chapter, we will also address certain aspects of the urban-rural divide in education resources and opportunities.

Policy context: China's transitional economy and educational restructuring

Since the late 1970s, the modernization drive, the economic reforms and opening up to the outside world have transformed the highly centralized planned economy into a market oriented and more dynamic one. Adherence to market principles and practices has affected not only the economic sphere but also the way social welfare and social policy are managed. Unlike the Maoist era when citizens in urban China generally had access to social welfare via their employing work units, the policy of decentralization and marketization adopted to the reform of the social policy domain significantly reduced state provision and financing in social services and welfare provision (Leung 1994; Guan 2001). In order to cut the welfare burden and promote the economic efficiency of the state sector, social policy provision, social security and social protection experienced significant restructuring. One of the main consequences of that restructuring was that Chinese citizens had increasingly to pay for major social services such as health, education and housing (Wong and Flynn 2001; Wong *et al.* 2004), as they no longer enjoyed a welfare 'iron rice bowl' (Cook 2002). Hence, it has been common to hear complaints from Chinese citizens about the 'three new mountains'[2] the state expects them to climb: in education, health and housing (Zhu 2005; Mok *et al.* 2010).

The new socialist market economy rendered the old way of 'centralized governance' inappropriate (Yang 2002). Acknowledging that over-centralization and stringent rules would kill the initiative and enthusiasm of local educational institutions, the Chinese Communist Party (CCP) called for resolute steps to streamline administration and devolve power to units at lower levels to allow them more flexibility to run education. As early as 1985, the CCP issued the 'Decision of the Central Committee of the Chinese Communist Party of China on the Reform of the Educational System', which marked the beginning of a process of educational reform and gradually aligned the educational system with the newly emerging market economy. This and other documents called for the devolution of power to lower levels of government and a reduction in the rigid governmental controls over schools (CCCCP 1985). From then onwards the state started to diversify educational services, allowing and encouraging the non-state sector to establish and run educational institutions. Meanwhile, the state deliberately devolved responsibility and power to local governments, local communities and other non-state actors by providing the necessary framework for educational development (Hawkins 2000; Ngok and Chan 2003). The 'Outline for Reform and Development of Education in China', issued in 1993, restated the reduction of centralization and government control in general as the long-term goals of reform (CCCCP 1993). The government reduced its role to macro-management through legislation, allocation of funding, planning, provision of information, policy guidance and essential administration (CCCCP 1993). The retreat of the central government provided space for local governments as well as non-state actors to take more responsibility for the provision, financing and regulation of education. This permitted non-government bodies to provide education in the formal educational sector, thereby leading to the emergence of *minban* (people-run) schools.

In the mid-1980s, as the state retreated from its monopolistic role in educational provision, the reform of the educational structure resulted in a mix of private and public consumption (Cheng 1995). With the emergence of self-financing students and non-state education providers (including both private and foreign) the education system experienced diversification, marketization, privatization, commodification and decentralization (Borevskaya 2003; Mok and Ngok 2008b; Mok 2009). To meet the challenges of a rapidly changing socio-economic environment brought about by the rise of the knowledge-based economy, the Chinese government recognized that depending upon state provision alone would not satisfy the strong demand for education. In these circumstances, the proliferation of education providers and the diversification of funding mechanisms became increasingly common (Chen and Li 2002; Ngok and Kwong 2003). Despite the ideological debates over the distinction between the private and public provision of education, the post-Mao leaders pragmatically allowed non-state sectors, including the private sector, to provide education (Yang 1997; Mok 2000). Nevertheless, because local governments have to shoulder the heavy burden of financing local education, as well as a host of other local social services, there is also the issue about the extent to which central policies are being fully implemented in the face of a shortage of revenues at lower tier governments (Mountfield and Wong 2005; Duckett and Hussain 2008). For example, when the central government requires schools to waive tuition and miscellaneous fees up to junior secondary schools, some schools have instead asked parents to enrol their children in 'summer tuition classes', or simply to make donations to the school. Increasing spending in education through parental contributions is not uncommon in China despite the fact that the central government has tried to discourage schools and colleges from charging tuition fees. The popularity in private tutoring and interest classes clearly suggests the growing importance of 'privateness' in education (as manifested by funding sources and multiple providers other than public/state ones) (Mok 2009). In order to capitalize on market forces, many educational institutions became active in establishing

Regional disparities and educational inequalities 129

collaborations with other sectors of the economy, both public and private, as well as with overseas institutions. Having briefly reviewed the background to the rise of the neo-liberal approach to providing education, we will now examine the effects of introducing privatization and marketization to a previously state-owned and state-controlled system.

Central features of the privatization and marketization of education[3]

The privatization and marketization of education in China has been associated with three major transforming features. First, fee-charging became increasingly prevalent, the development of which made the role of individuals and families more important in financing education. Second, the same processes diversified education providers. Third, educational services became further commodified and commercialized because parents were keen to send their children to after-school interest and tutorial classes.

The adoption of the fee-charging principle and growing individual contributions

In the early 1980s, Deng Xiaoping, the late leader of the CCP, stated that the Chinese government would commit to increasing its investment in educational development to around 4 per cent of GDP. Since then, even though the Chinese economy experienced significant and consistent growth of an average annual rate of 9–10 per cent, the total allocation of government funds for education remained low. By 1995, only 2.4 per cent of GDP was allocated to the education sector, although there were slight increases in 1999 (to 2.8 per cent) and 2002 (3.2 per cent). But public financing for education declined again in 2005, with only around 2.8 per cent of GDP allocated to education (see Table 7.1). More recently in 2006, the State Council of the People's Republic of China (PRC) openly recognized that insufficient government funding had been allocated to education. In connection with this, the 11th Five Year Plan (2006–10) called on governments at all levels to make the development of education a strategic priority and 'to commit to a public education system that can be accessed by all' (cited in Li 2007: 1).

Despite its prosperous coastal regions, China is still a low-income developing country and its vast population puts its GNP per capita among the 24 poorest countries in the world. Providing schooling and education for its huge population is a monumental task especially for the poorer hinterland provinces. While considerable progress has been made in addressing inequality issues since the 1950s, educational investment as a percentage of GDP in China has historically been low even up until recent years (Table 7.1). Despite the fact that during the past three decades the Chinese government made several public announcements stating that it would increase state funding for education, public expenditure on education still remains low even by the

130 Ka Ho Mok and Yu Cheung Wong

standards of developing countries such as Thailand, Malaysia, India and the Philippines (see Table 7.2). Unlike most countries in the world, China has not enshrined in law the percentage of GDP that should be spent on education.

Table 7.1 China's public education expenditure as a percentage of GDP (unit: billion yuan)

Year	Goss Domestic Product	Government Appropriation for Education	Percentage (%)
1992	2,663.8	72.9	2.74
1995	5,847.8	141.2	2.41
1999	8,206.8	228.7	2.79
2000	8,946.8	256.3	2.86
2001	9,731.5	305.7	3.14
2002	10,517.2	349.1	3.32
2003	11,739.0	385.1	3.28
2004	15,987.8	446.6	2.79
2005	18,321.7	516.1	2.82
2006	21,192.4	634.8	3.00
2007	25,730.6	828.0	3.22

Source: NBSC 2005, 2009 (the latest figures available were from 2007)
Note: government appropriation for education includes the expenditure of central and local governments on education

Table 7.2 International comparison of public education expenditure as a percentage of GDP, 2003

Country	Education Expenditure as a Percentage of GDP	Government Expenditure on Education as a Percentage of GDP
Developed countries		
United States	7.5	5.7
United Kingdom	6.1	5.4
France	6.3	5.9
Germany	5.3	4.7
Japan	4.8	3.7
South Korea	7.5	4.6
Australia	5.8	4.8
New Zealand	6.8	6.8
Israel	8.5	7.0
Developing countries		
Thailand	6.8	5.0
Malaysia	8.1	8.1
India	4.8	3.4
Philippines	5.2	3.1
China (2005)	*4.6*	*2.8*

Sources: MOE 2006; OECD 2006

Regional disparities and educational inequalities   131

In early 2003, the Ministry of Education, on the basis of the doctrines of the 16th National People's Congress (NPC) of the Chinese Communist Party (CCP),[4] organized scholars from various specialties to formulate a large research report on education. The report was to establish a road-map that would change China from being a nation with a large population to a nation with a well-educated population (Yang 2005). The report considered modern education not only as the 'engine' and 'accelerator' of economic development but also as the 'stabilizer' and 'balancer' of Chinese society (Yang 2005). It also acknowledged that there would be insufficient human capital to develop the economy if education expenditure did not occupy a larger percentage of GDP. In response to such research findings, the central government began to increase its funding to education, even though it is yet to match existing educational demand.

With reductions in the share of state financing for education since the 1980s, local governments and education institutions had attempted to increase their student intake and tuition fees in order to generate additional revenues for educational development and to improve teachers' incomes. Some local education bureaus and individual schools and higher education institutions have charged unreasonable fees. According to the annual audit exercise in 2004, the National Auditing Department discovered that a significant number of government education bureaus and departments across the country were involved in cases of corruption, overcharging and excessive borrowing from banks. That same year, the Ministry of Education also found that 18 public universities had overcharged students by a total of 8,680,000 yuan. In 2003, one university in Beijing over-charged students by 1,866,000 yuan, and violated state regulations by receiving students' 'donations', totalling 1,035,000 yuan. The Ministry also discovered that about one-sixth of the new students admitted to this university had made 'special donations' (from 20,000 to 100,000 yuan) to the institution (Chen 2005). Similar problems can be easily found in other localities. For instance, the Hunan Bureau of Education discovered about 3.45 million yuan in fees from over-charging after completing an audit of 5,108 education-related programmes (Yang 2005).

Many such reported cases suggest Chinese citizens have to bear very high school and university fees. Despite the fact that the State Council decided in the autumn of 2008 that tuition fees and miscellaneous fees were to be waived for students in the cities (the fee waiver was introduced to rural schools in 2006) up to junior secondary education, it has been widely reported that public schools continue to charge different kinds of fees hence creating an additional financial burden on parents. For example, in a recent report published by *China Daily* regarding the closure of a *minban* (people-run) school in Beijing, students interviewed told the press that they would prefer to return to their home province instead of going to a state school in Beijing, as had been arranged by the local Bureau of Education. When asked about the reasons for refusing the offer, the interviewees sadly admitted that they could not afford to pay the excessive fees charged by the state school (*China Daily*, 26 August 2006: 5).

132 *Ka Ho Mok and Yu Cheung Wong*

State financial support has retreated significantly from the higher education sector. One source suggests that it declined from 93.5 per cent to 50 per cent between 1990 and 2002, respectively (Chen 2006). The diffusion of financial responsibility for social services from the state to society has been signalled by governmental encouragement of the use of a mixed economy of welfare based on 'multiple-channel' (*duoqudao*) and 'multi-method' (*duofangfa*) approaches to the provision of educational services during the 'primary state of socialism' (*shehui zhuyi chuji jieduan*) (Mok 1996).

Furthermore, the introduction of a 'fee-paying' principle significantly affected higher education financing in China. As university students were made to pay tuition fees the 'user-pays' principle became the foundation for funding Chinese higher education. According to a recent report, the tuition fees in higher education increased 24-fold, jumping from an average annual tuition of 200 yuan per student in 1986 to about 7,000 yuan in 2006 (Wang 2007), although some families may pay up to 8,000 yuan (*People's Daily*, 5 March 2007). Such an amount represents around 35 years of income for ordinary peasants in rural China. Other sources also report rising private expenditure on education, suggesting parents and families are paying more for their children's education (Dai 2005; Zhu 2005; Li 2007). The 2006 yearbook compiled by the Chinese Academy of Social Sciences reported that spending on education ranked sixth on a list of serious public concerns by Chinese citizens, with school bills gobbling up more than 10 per cent of the average household budget (Anon., *Bluebook of Chinese Society* 2007).

Moreover, a growing number of families in urban China, who strongly believe that a degree from a university in the West could bring their children a brighter future, have tried very hard to save money to send their children to study abroad. According to the Chinese Service Centre for Scholarly Exchange of the Ministry of Education, more than 100,000 students have chosen to study overseas since 2002 although they have to pay higher tuition and living expenses. Because so many more young people now hold a university degree, university graduates in China experience difficulty in finding employment. Therefore, pursuing higher degrees overseas has become increasingly popular with the intention of differentiating themselves in a highly competitive labour market. As statistics released by the Chinese Service Centre for Scholarly Exchange show, 71.3 per cent of graduates returning from studying overseas found jobs within six months, while 32.7 per cent of them secured employment in foreign companies. Noticing these positive figures, many Chinese parents have become eager to send their children to study abroad, even though this means enduring hardship in securing sufficient money to pay for their children's education (*China Daily*, 28 February 2007: 20). The above observations make it clear that pursuing education is deeply embedded in Chinese traditions and culture; implementing such values causes tremendous financial and psychological pressures for many families (particularly in rural China) (Cummings 1996).

Regional disparities and educational inequalities 133

Proliferating education providers and the rise of the private (minban) sector

Another prominent change resulting from the privatization and marketization of education is the growing prominence of privatization in China's education system at various educational levels. The emergence of the private (*minban*) sector in China's education system has given rise to a hybrid of public and private provision. In addition to those schools run by non-state sectors and actors, public schools in China have also undergone a process of privatization and marketization, by which these public education institutions are no longer entirely public in nature but are classified as *guoyou minban* (state-owned and people-run) (Mok 2005: 224–25). *Guoyou minban* schools remain under government ownership but the proportion of finance from the private (non-state) sector is increased mainly through tuition fees. The establishment of *guoyou minban* schools started in 1993 in Shanghai, and was widely adopted throughout the country thereafter. This policy of transformation (*zhuanzhi*) provided a higher degree of autonomy regarding school management, especially in terms of personnel and finance. Under the new management framework, school teachers no longer enjoy the 'iron rice bowl' and could be dismissed if they underperformed. The other side of the coin is that these schools can offer financial incentives to reward the high-performing teaching staff (Shanghai Research Institute of Educational Sciences 2005).

In the higher education sector, *guoyou minban* institutions are referred to as second-tier colleges, and are usually extensions of public (national) universities. Similarly, these colleges are run as 'self-financing' entities and operated in terms of 'market' principles. Conventional *minban* schools and colleges are perceived by the education authorities as lacking 'self-discipline' and posing management difficulties. These kinds of publicly-owned but privately-run institutions have been established largely as a means to achieve the policy objective of expanding enrolment rates (Mok and Ngok 2008b; Lin 2004; Lin *et al.* 2005; Shi *et al.* 2005; Shanghai Research Institute of Educational Sciences 2005).

However, the ideological debates over the private–public distinction in education remain an unresolved issue in the development of *minban* education. For instance, because the *guoyou minban* charge fees they also generate revenue, necessary in the context of reductions in central funding. But many find the for-profit nature of the *guoyou minban* institutions distasteful, even unacceptable. Despite ideological debates, *minban* education has become a trend in China, particularly with the increase in the number of 'quasi *minban*' institutions. In 1998, there were around 50,000 private (*minban*) education institutions at various levels, recruiting around 10.66 million students. With the support of government initiatives in 2004 the number of solely private (*minban*) education institutions reached over 70,000, which recruited 17.69 million students (*China Education Yearbook* 1999; 2005). More recent statistics show that over 1,000 public schools had applied for this 'privatized' status that same year meaning they became *guoyou minban* (Lin and Chen 2004: 46). By 2005, there were 344 second-tier colleges throughout China, enrolling

134 *Ka Ho Mok and Yu Cheung Wong*

540,000 undergraduate students (Chen and Yu 2005: 167). These figures indicate that China's higher education sector has become far more diversified, due to the proliferation of providers, diversification of financing and marketization of education. All of this takes place against the backdrop of the government's decentralization policies.

But despite the fact that the privatization of higher education has created more learning opportunities for Chinese citizens, these transformations along the lines of neo-liberalism have resulted in educational inequalities, regional disparities and social injustice. Despite the fact that most schools, colleges and universities are still publicly run in China, the public and private distinction in education has become increasingly blurred when more and more families are paying fees. In both public and private education institutional fee-charging is prevalent not only in higher education, but also in primary and secondary schools, thus undermining the educational chances of students with limited financial means.

The commercialization of education in meeting pressing educational demands

Another major feature related to the privatization and marketization of education occurs at the primary and secondary levels of education. Specifically, parents' desire to provide their children with the best education despite the overwhelming financial burden favours the growing commercialization of after-school children's learning activities. The case of Catherine Zhang, a Shanghai resident, illustrates this point. She admitted her daughter to an early-education centre, which cost her about 10,000 yuan per year, and planned to spend about half of her salary to send her daughter to a 'good kindergarten'. According to a survey conducted by the Shanghai Municipal Women's Federation in 2005, expenditure on education constituted 25 per cent of the household income of those families with a child 18 years old or younger (*Xinhua*, 30 Nov. 2005). In addition, a survey conducted in 2004 by the People's Bank of China showed that children's education, followed by housing and retirement, was the main purpose of household savings. This situation is quite different from that of developed countries such as the USA and Canada, because parents in China seem more willing to cut down on other expenses in order to save more for their children's education (*China Daily*, 28 May 2007). Presumably they see this as an investment in the family's future.

Parents' perception of the importance of education facilitated the emergence of after-school education, which has become an important indicator of the commercialization of China's education. In order to prepare their children for the competitive globalizing world, Chinese parents consider learning English to be very important for the future of their children. Government population policies permit couples in urban areas to have only one child. Naturally, the parents invest all their hopes, expectations and, inevitably, money to ensure a brighter future for their son or daughter. Believing that the

Regional disparities and educational inequalities 135

mastery of English and a good career go hand in hand, a growing number of parents want to send their children to private tutoring classes or private English schools. A case that illustrates the rising demand for English tutoring in China is that of *English First*, a part of the EF Education conglomerate (a private corporation running English courses worldwide), which has expanded rapidly in China. In 2006, EF had 79 schools in 54 Chinese cities and had a target of having 200 schools across China by 2008. The company provides English language training to people across different social groups, including school children, teenagers and adults. Judging from the employment package that EF offers to its English teachers, with an annual salary starting at US $17,500 after tax (a huge sum in Chinese terms), one can easily imagine how much this corporation can generate. Realizing that Asian and Chinese parents have deeply embedded beliefs in the high value of education, EF has captured the expanding market in China by opening more private tutoring and English courses to meet the rapidly growing demand (English First China 2007; English First Worldwide 2007).

In addition to academic performance, Chinese parents are increasingly concerned about their children being able to master a wide variety of skills. Equipping their children with special skills has become a popular trend in China, especially when these artistic or athletic skills can count as part of their entrance examination scores, thereby giving them a better chance of getting into a prestigious university. The experience of Xiao Di, a grade-two pupil in a primary school in Beijing, who attends after-school classes in music, mathematics, English, piano and dance from Friday evening to Sunday, is not uncommon among children of her age. According to a survey conducted by the market research company Horizonkey, 52 per cent of children under the age of 12 in China attend extracurricular classes at the weekends, while 62 per cent of children aged 10 to 12 take additional classes such as English, maths, music, art, dance and martial arts. Furthermore, numerous competitions are seen as important stepping stones in getting established in a successful career. A success story in a neighbourhood can push other parents to become even more eager to send their children to after-school classes. As a consequence, many parents in China are prepared to pay additional costs in order to send their children to the class that produces prize winners. They also want to hire the best high-school teachers to give private tutoring to their children especially before the university entrance examinations (*China Daily*, 27 March 2004; 5 June 2007). It is against this backdrop of parents' growing concerns about children's education that an education market is evolving.

Consequences of the privatization and marketization of education

A new mountain of educational hardship: urban residents' responses

In 2004, a study with a representative sample of 2,823 households was undertaken in 8 cities in China. It was jointly conducted by the School of

136   Ka Ho Mok and Yu Cheung Wong

Social Development and Public Policy in Beijing Normal University and the Minimum Livelihood Guarantee Department of the Ministry of Civil Affairs. The head of all surveyed households had to have local residency status,[5] and was the person responsible for providing information about their household. In addition, the study also collected data about a total of 8940 individuals living in these households. Two cities were selected here to contrast the impact of the changes in the Chinese education system on households at different levels of socio-economic development. The cities selected were Beijing, China's capital city, which has a high level of socio-economic development, and Lanzhou, the provincial capital of Gansu, an interior province with one of the highest poverty rates. According to the data provided by the National Bureau of Statistics of China, there were 11.8 million local residents (excluding those without a local urban *hukou*) in Beijing in 2007, and only 3.1 million in Lanzhou. The gross regional output of Beijing was 68.9 billion versus 5.67 billion yuan in Lanzhou. The population of Beijing was around four times that of Lanzhou but the gross output was 12 times bigger.

The data of the 2004 household study indicated that the average household income in Beijing was 38,406 yuan while that in Lanzhou was 14,138 yuan. Both of them had a high standard deviation in household income indicating that large income disparities existed. The ratio of standard deviation to the mean value in Beijing was 0.92 and 0.71 in Lanzhou, indicating that Beijing had a higher income gap (Table 7.3). Lanzhou had a higher proportion of young people. Those aged below 15 constituted 15 per cent of Lanzhou's population, compared to 7.3 percent in Beijing (Table 7.3).

Because of the income disparity between the two cities, Beijing had a much bigger capacity to invest in education than Lanzhou. Table 7.4 indicates that in 2008, the student–teacher ratio in Beijing was lower than in Lanzhou and than the national average. Although a lower student–teacher ratio does not automatically equate with better educational outcomes, this shows the disparities of education resources available to students in the two cities.

Table 7.3 Characteristics of the survey sample

	Beijing		Lanzhou	
Age distribution	*Number*	*%*	*Number*	*%*
Under 15	160	7.3	137	15.0
15–24	313	14.3	120	13.1
25–59	1,214	55.4	492	53.8
60 or above	506	23.1	165	18.1
Total	2,193	100.0	914	100.0
	Mean	*Std. Deviation*	*Mean*	*Std. Deviation*
Household income (unit: yuan)	38,406	35,480	14,138	10,055
Total no. of households	716		299	

Regional disparities and educational inequalities   137

Table 7.4 Primary and secondary school staffing and student enrolment, Beijing and Lanzhou, 2008

		No. of schools		Student enrolment ('000 persons)	No. of full-time teachers ('000 persons)	Student–teacher ratio
Primary	National	300,854		103,315.1	5,621.9	18.4
	Beijing	1,202		659.5	48.7	13.5
	Lanzhou	786		234.6	14.1	16.6
Secondary		Junior	Senior			
	National	57,701	15,206	80,504.4	4,944.5	16.3
	Beijing	349	325	544.3	49.9	10.9
	Lanzhou	224		248.8	13.4	18.5

Source: Compiled by authors from China Statistical Year Book 2009 and Gansu Statistical Year Book 2009
Note: * figures include only regular schools (evening school/adult schools are excluded)

Table 7.5 presents the percentage of spending on children's education among households in the two cities. In Lanzhou, given the lower household income, education expenditure constituted a larger percentage of household's income than in Beijing. The variation as measured by the standard deviation of the percentage of household expenditure in education was also larger in Beijing than in Lanzhou. The figures indicated that for Lanzhou households with children studying at the post-secondary level, average household spending on education equalled half of the household income.

Households with low-income levels (defined as having less than half of the median income for their household size in their respective city) had fewer education resources available for their children. In this study 18.5 per cent of the households were identified as low-income households. We investigated how these low-income households differed from the others in the provision of additional education resources to their children. Table 7.5 presents the differences in the participation rates in tuition and training during out-of-school hours. In Beijing, 78 per cent of the non-low-income households with school-aged children sent them to out-of-school-hours tuition classes at their school or another social organization, while only 40 per cent of the low-income households did so. In Lanzhou, a much smaller percentage of households was able to afford after-school classes, and the difference in the percentage between low-income households and other households in sending their children to these tuition classes was greater than in Beijing. A smaller percentage of households in both cities sent their children to physical training or interest classes after school, while an even smaller percentage did so when the activity required paid private tuition at home (Table 7.6). The pattern in terms of the differences across the two cities and between low-income households and others was the same throughout. In Lanzhou, none of the households could afford to have paid private tuition at home for their children.

138 Ka Ho Mok and Yu Cheung Wong

Table 7.5 Share of household spending on education in the previous year (unit: %)

With children studying in	Beijing		Lanzhou	
	Mean	Std. Deviation	Mean	Std. Deviation
Basic education only	14.7	16.4	20.1	17.7
Post-secondary[a]	25.5	19.8	50.8	20.3

Note: [a] also includes those households with children studying in both basic and post-secondary education. The number of these households was very small because of the current one-child policy

Table 7.6 Families reporting after-school tuition and activities (primary and secondary education students) (unit: %)

	Beijing		Lanzhou	
	Others	Low income	Others	Low income
Tuition class at school or other social organizations	78.3	40.0	40.4	15.2
Physical training or interest class	45.8	30.0	27.4	6.5
Paid private tuition at home	26.5	10.0	11.6	0.0

In the study, respondents were also asked about the difficulties they experienced in financing the education of their children. Three statements: 'Cannot afford child care/tuition/school's miscellaneous fees', 'Cannot afford children's after school learning fees' and 'Cannot afford children's toys and/or physical exercise fees' were presented to the respondents and they were asked to indicate their situation on a four-point scale, with 1 representing 'never', 2 'sometimes', 3 'frequently' and 4 'always'.[6] Over 90 per cent of non low-income households in Beijing with a child in school reported that they never had difficulty in meeting these three items. A smaller percentage amongst the low-income households in Beijing also mentioned never having had difficulty meeting such needs, though 10 per cent of this latter group mentioned that they sometimes did face difficulties meetings those three items. The situation in Lanzhou was much worse. Among the non low-income households around three-quarters mentioned having no problems paying those fees; but close to 20 per cent mentioned experiencing difficulties meeting those fees. More than half of the low-income households reported that, apart from the tuition fees that were covered by the government, they had difficulties in paying the after-school fees for their children. A quarter of them also said they always had difficulties paying for toys and physical exercise class fees (Table 7.7).

Non-low-income households in Beijing with children pursuing post-secondary education experienced few difficulties in meeting tuition fees and related educational expenditure. The difficulties for the low-income households with a child in post-secondary education were more obvious. The

Table 7.7 Hardship related to education for households with children studying in primary or secondary school

Cannot afford	Beijing				Lanzhou			
	Others		Low income		Others		Low income	
	No.	%	No.	%	No.	%	No.	%
Child care/tuition/school misc. fees								
Never	81	96.4	7	87.5	70	75.3	19	59.4
Sometimes	2	2.4	1	12.5	16	17.2	10	31.2
Frequently	1	1.2	0	0.0	3	3.2	2	6.2
Always	0	0.0	0	0.0	4	4.3	1	3.1
After school learning fees								
Never	81	96.4	6	75.0	64	74.4	10	47.6
Sometimes	2	2.4	1	12.5	16	18.6	4	19.0
Frequently	0	0.0	0	0.0	5	5.8	5	23.8
Always	1	1.2	1	12.5	1	1.2	2	9.5
Toys, physical exercise fees								
Never	75	91.5	7	77.8	62	72.9	8	34.8
Sometimes	5	6.1	1	11.1	17	20.0	5	21.7
Frequently	1	1.2	0	0.0	4	4.7	4	17.4
Always	1	1.2	1	11.1	2	2.4	6	26.1

situation amongst Lanzhou's low-income households was the most precarious, with a large percentage of households reporting difficulty meeting these expenditures frequently or always. However, since the number of low-income households that had children studying in post-secondary education in the sample was small, caution has to be taken when interpreting these results (Table 7.8).

The overall picture of the heavy financial burden of children's education was also echoed in the subjective experience of the households. The findings about the educational hardship experienced by those interviewed in the two selected cities clearly showed the growing influence of neo-liberal and market-driven approaches to financing education. With the growing prevalence of neo-liberalism in the provision of education, it is probable that this burden and consequent hardship will increased in the future. Our comparative study of Beijing and Lanzhou clearly shows how educational disparities and inequalities are intensified when access to better educational opportunities is reliant upon people's financial abilities. Given the fact that the policy of decentralization adopted to transform educational development in China has already widened the gap between the capacities of the local governments to invest in education, the above survey data clearly remind us of the combined disadvantageous positions of the urban poor households in less well-off cities in terms of getting education opportunities for their children to succeed in the future. The findings also point to the importance of awareness and sensitivity to within country (as well as between countries) differences in socio-economic, historical and cultural contexts in which education services are delivered.

140 *Ka Ho Mok and Yu Cheung Wong*

Table 7.8 Hardship related to education for households with children studying in post-secondary education

Cannot afford	Beijing				Lanzhou			
	Others		Low income		Others		Low income	
	No.	%	No.	%	No.	%	No.	%
Child care/ tuition/school misc. fees								
Never	52	96.3	3	42.9	15	71.4	3	33.3
Sometimes	1	1.9	3	42.9	4	19.0	3	33.3
Frequently	1	1.9	0	0.0	1	4.8	2	22.2
Always	0	0.0	1	14.3	1	4.8	1	11.1
Children after school learning fees								
Never	52	100.0	4	50.0	13	92.9	1	11.1
Sometimes	0	0.0	3	37.5	1	7.1	3	33.3
Frequently	0	0.0	0	0.0	0	0.0	4	44.4
Always	0	0.0	1	12.5	0	0.0	1	11.1
Toys, physical exercise fees								
Never	46	97.9	2	40.0	15	93.8	2	22.2
Sometimes	0	0.0	2	40.0	0	0.0	5	55.6
Frequently	1	2.1	1	20.0	1	6.2	1	11.1
Always	0	0.0	0	0.0	0	0.0	1	11.1

The widening regional and urban–rural divide

Why do these regional and rural–urban disparities exist? It is a direct result of policies that the central government adopted deliberately concentrating on the development of the coastal rather than the inland provinces, as well as favouring cities over the countryside. According to official statistics, 214,913 million yuan were allocated to the coastal regions,[7] constituting 55.8 per cent of the total government budget for education. Regarding non-governmental financial resources,[8] 36,361 million yuan were generated in the region, representing about 67.2 per cent of total expenditure on education. However, the population of the coastal region constitutes only 41.4 per cent of the total population (MOE 2004). Another important indicator showing inter-province inequity is the number of students per 100,000 inhabitants. The national average was 1,420 students studying in higher education but in Beijing alone the figure was 6,204 in 2003, and as low as 985 in Anhui in the same year. Comparing the percentage of students studying in higher education in three relatively wealthy Chinese cities (Beijing, Shanghai and Tianjin) with three relatively poor provinces (Guizhou, Guangxi and Gansu), we find the average ratio of the three wealthy cities is 4.6 per cent but that of the three poor provinces is only 0.9 per cent. The total non-governmental financial resources of the three wealthy cities grew to 3.45 billion yuan in 2003 (from 312 million yuan in 1993) (MOE 1994: 88–89) but was only 800 million yuan in the three poor provinces in 2003 (see Table 7.9) (MOE 2004).

Regional disparities and educational inequalities   141

Table 7.9 Non-state educational grants in selected regions, 2003 (unit: million yuan)

Region	Social organizations and individual	Donation and fund raising	Total
National	25,901	10,459	36,360
Eastern			
Beijing	624	522	1,146
Tianjin	477	21	498
Shanghai	1,315	491	1,806
Jiangsu	2,204	229	2,433
Western/Central			
Gansu	186	57	243
Anhui	452	241	693
Guangxi	251	97	348
Guizhou	150	58	208

Source: MOE 2004: 68–69

Statistics from 2006 show that the disparities between wealthy and poor regions were still present (see Table 7.10). In the more prosperous regions, specifically in Beijing and Shanghai, there is a greater concentration of higher education institutions. The entrance requirement into these universities, i.e. the score of national university entrance examination (*gaokao*), is lower for the local students than the national average. For places with a higher proportion of students studying in higher education, the per capita total education funds, and government appropriation for education (which includes a significant amount that is not provided directly by the central government but financed from lower tiers of the administrative hierarchy and from revenue generation) was higher. However, given the same proportion of students studying in higher-education institutions, the per capita educational funds as well as government appropriations were obviously higher in the more prosperous regions.

The 'East-Central-West strategy'[9] favours east China over the western regions in the allocation of development funds. As a result, the disparity between the rich areas and the poor regions is further intensified, especially when evaluating the growing inequality in terms of revenue available for education. Worsening educational inequality has inevitably resulted in social, economic and political repercussions, leading to a 'vicious circle' of reduced economic development in poor regions because of lower educational levels. Putting the current developments of private (*minban*) education together with intensified regional disparities, it is clear that the people living in the eastern coastal areas of China have disproportionately experienced the success of economic growth in the last two decades and many of them are willing and have the financial ability to pay for overseas education.

142　Ka Ho Mok and Yu Cheung Wong

Table 7.10　Education funds per student across regions, 2006

	Population (millions)	No. of students per 100,000	% of students in higher education*	Total educational funds** per Student (unit: yuan)	Government appropriation for education per student (unit: yuan)
National	1,314	1,9617	9.26	3806	2462
Eastern					
Beijing***	15.81	16,620	41.5	12,842	9,675
Shanghai	18.15	14,153	29.7	14,432	10,313
Jiangsu	75.50	18,729	12.3	4,841	2,793
Zhejiang	49.80	18,952	11.2	6,691	3,826
Fujian	35.58	20,232	8.2	3,850	2,500
Shandong	93.09	17,891	10.1	3,285	2,094
Guangdong	93.04	23,737	6.7	3,919	2,395
Western/Central					
Chongqing	28.08	20,815	9.2	2,877	1,843
Guizhou	37.57	23,371	3.9	1,765	1,353
Tibet	2.81	19,760	5.1	4,987	4,744
Jiangxi	43.39	21,058	10.0	2,423	1,290
Gansu	26.06	23,155	6.2	2,190	1,698
Qinghai	5.48	19,070	4.9	3,579	3,169
Ningxia	6.04	23,272	6.5	2,837	2,241

Sources: table compiled by authors from NBSC 2007: Tables 4-4 and 21–35; NBSC 2008: Tables 20–36
Notes: * institutions of higher education include regular institutions of higher education and institutions of higher education for adults; ** total educational funds include all sources of funds such as government appropriation, private funds, fee-charging, and donations, etc.; *** includes also the 'floating' population, who originate from rural areas and stay in the host cities but do not have city residency status

With reference to the above educational funding figures, it is obvious that the economic reforms and developments of the last 30 years have significantly improved the livelihood of those living in the coastal areas. Nonetheless, the same social and economic transformations have also intensified the coastal-inland disparity. This has resulted in a concentration of educational opportunities in the socio-economically prosperous regions of the eastern coastal area. Regarding urban–rural disparities, the most recent *China Human Development Report* (2008) indicates that the gap between the rich and poor in China has been widening. In 2006, the per capita disposable income of the richest 10 per cent of families was 8.96 times more than that of the poorest 10 per cent among urban residents. Commenting on this urban–rural income gap, the United Nations reported that China has perhaps the highest income disparity in the world (UNDP 2008). Between 2000 and 2006, the urban–rural income gap widened from 2.79 to 1 in 2000 to 3.33 to 1 in 2007. Recent studies have suggested that educational inequalities are larger at the higher levels (Qian and Smyth 2005; Rong and Shi 2001). Given that there are no universities in rural China, rural students are eligible to apply for admissions to urban universities nationwide (Zhong 2006). However, as shown in a 2003 study carried out in Guangdong province, rural students are often considered inferior to those from urban areas (Wang 2005). Another study from Guangdong also showed that students from urban areas in Guangdong occupied 72.2 per cent and 89.9 per cent of places in the key universities led by central ministries and *minban* vocational colleges respectively, even though there was a relatively even allocation of places in other public universities and vocational colleges (see Table 7.11) (Wang 2005a: 11).

Yang (2007) also examined educational opportunities between urban and rural China, and argued that disparities in educational funding and provision between urban areas and the rural hinterland had been a persistent problem since the foundation of the People's Republic of China in 1949 (Yang 2007). Like other developing countries that are influenced by the global trends towards privatization, marketization and commodification of education, China's adoption of neoliberal policies has created problems of access to education. Concerns over social justice have emerged as Chinese society experiences growing social stratification and inequality (Cheng 2006; Luke and Ismail 2007).

China has now to confront the intensification of educational inequality that has occurred despite economic growth and educational expansion; the implementation of education reforms with a neoliberal approach has inevitably led to 'differential impacts upon different groups' as Mak (2007) has described in other Asian societies. The economic reforms since the late 1970s undoubtedly gave rise to the new, wealthier middle class in China (Lui 2005; So 2005). Recent consumption studies have once more confirmed that as incomes rise, spending patterns change. It is projected that urban spending on recreation and education will grow by 9.5 per cent annually during the next two decades, making it one of the largest consumption categories in urban areas and making China one of the fastest-growing recreation and education markets in the world (Farrell *et al.* 2006: 66–67).

Table 7.11 Allocations of places of study in Guangdong, 2003 (unit: %)

	Overall	Key universities led by central ministries	Normal public universities	Public vocational colleges	Minban vocational colleges
Students from urban areas	60.7	72.2	50.6	48.0	89.9
Students from rural areas	39.3	28.8	49.4	52.0	10.1

Source: Wang 2005

Despite the fact that some urban families are willing to pay additional costs to enrich their children's education, many of them have raised concerns about the increasing financial burden this presents. If wealthier families can 'feel the pinch' then one can imagine how many citizens in rural China who find themselves socially and economically marginalized have responded to growing educational disparities (Khan and Riskin 2005; Keng 2006) while simultaneously facing the prospect of poor schooling or, in some cases, no schooling at all (Murphy 2004). Another point that deserves particular attention is a strong tendency to favour boys over girls in education, even though national policy has repeatedly emphasized equality of opportunity for boys and girls. Particularly in rural areas, where the one child policy has been implemented with more flexibility allowing for families whose first born child is a girl to have a second child, many families experiencing financial difficulties choose to educate their sons over their daughters. This reflects both the deeply rooted traditional preference for sons in China, still prevalent in rural areas, as well as the more pragmatic reasons that sons are expected to financially support their elderly parents, and that employers tend to favour males over females (Tilky 2008).

In addition to the educational inequality directly experienced by females in China, there is a growing number of migrant workers whose children have not been provided similar educational opportunities compared to those of their urban counterparts. According to He and Li's (2007) survey related to migrant workers' expectations for their children's education, a total of 6,343 rural migrant households in nine cities in China indicated that 84 per cent of interviewed parents considered the educational problems of their children as one of their biggest concerns. Another study conducted by Nankai University in 2006 and 2007 in seven cities, including Shanghai, Shenyang, Tianjin, Kunming, Guangzhou, Yibin and Weihai, showed that out of a total of 3,024 sampled rural migrant workers, 87.8 per cent expected their children to achieve an educational level of a bachelor's degree or above; 6.9 per cent expected them to achieve a technical high school degree; 5.3 per cent a college or associated degree; 4.3 per cent a high school degree; while only 1.6 per cent expected their children only to complete junior middle school (Nankai University Research Group 2007). In order to boost the educational attainment of the children, migrant workers have to make hard choices given limited resources and the limited state assistance that they receive.

While being denied full citizenship rights by the government, there are institutional barriers for migrant children to enter public schools, which in most cases only accept children with an urban household registration or *hukou*. Private migrant schools are one of the only feasible options for rural migrant workers' children living in the city. For example, in Beijing as of 2002 there were more than 200 private schools established for migrant children, most of them located in districts densely populated by migrants like Chaoyang, Haidian and Xicheng. The largest school had more than 3,000 students enrolled, while the smallest one had less than 10 students. Li Sumei, headmaster of the Xingzhi Migrant Children's School conceived that ' ... it is unfeasible to eradicate all private migrant children's schools since state-funded schools have no capacity to admit such a large number of migrant children' (*China Daily*, 15 August 2002). Table 7.12 clearly shows the big difference in the tuition fees charged by urban public schools and private migrant schools.

The fee levels shown in Table 7.12 clearly illustrate the heavy financial burden faced by parents to meet the pressing education demand of their children. According to statistics from the Beijing city government, in 2000, there were about 75,000 primary and 11,000 junior secondary school students paying 'transient study fees' (placement fees), constituting 78.2 and 98.1 per cent of the cohort of the overall floating children (Feng 2003: 38). The charging of various kinds of extra fees is seen as a compensation for the limited resources allocated by local states. It is reported that it costs the government about 700 yuan to support a child in primary school, and 1,250 yuan to keep one in junior high school (Tsang and Ding 2003 cited in Kwong 2004: 1077). Based upon the above observations, it is clear that migrant workers' children are developing into a socially disadvantaged group because they have been denied with equal service and welfare entitlements when compared to those children born in urban areas. Although migrant workers' children are citizens under the same red flag, their citizenship rights are not equally recognized and protected (Mok *et al.* 2010a).

Discussion and conclusion

The comparison between Beijing and Lanzhou indicates that inequality between wealthy and poor cities comes in several forms. First, households in

Table 7.12 Annual school fees for migrant children in the Fengtai, Haidian, and Chaoyang district of Beijing, 2002

School and fee type (in yuan)	Grade level					
	1	2	3	4	5	6
Urban public school						
School fee (*Xue Fei*)	759	490	728	510	454	443
Placement fee (*Jie Du Fei*)	926	1,581	1,798	1,842	1,420	1,503
Sponsor fee (*Zan Zhu Fei*)	3,635	2,583	4,062	2,412	2,000	825
Miscellaneous fee (*Za Fei*)	467	423	917	809	433	650
Total fees	4,422	3,764	3,563	5,252	3,774	6,156
Monthly fees (Total fees/12)	369	314	297	438	315	513
Number of respondents	15	13	12	17	7	5
Migrant-sponsored school						
School fee (*Xue Fei*)	930	1,040	771	830	1,400	1,400
Monthly fees (total fees/12)	78	87	64	69	117	117
Number of respondents	20	5	9	4	2	2

Source: MCE (2000), cited in Chen and Liang (2007: 122)
Note: The two rows of 'monthly fee' are calculated by the author

poorer regions have to spend a larger proportion of their household income on education. This is particularly true for households with children in post-secondary education. Second, in wealthier cities, a higher proportion of parents will send their children to tuition classes and after-school activities. Children in these cities tend to enjoy better educational resources and thus stand a better chance of getting into more prestigious institutions of higher education. Finally, a larger proportion of parents in poor cities suffer from education-related hardship. This is more so among parents with children studying in post-secondary education. Inevitably, low-income households suffer more from the increasing costs of education. Given the current financing mode of public education the capacity of poorer cities to invest in public education trails behind the richer ones; as a result, low-income households in poorer cities in fact have to spend a higher proportion of their income and endure more hardship, and yet receive lower input in education resources from the state.

Our research found that the commodification of education has not only taken place in higher education but is also prevalent in secondary and primary education, mainly in the form of after-school tuitions and other learning activities, even though in 2008 the central government promised to make compulsory education free for all students up to junior secondary education. Hence, Chinese people continue to complain about experiencing education hardship as a result of this marketization and commodification of education, at the same time that they criticize the government for reducing its role in the finance and provision of education, allowing education to become increasingly privatized. The immediate result is that those who can afford it have better education resources and experiences, and most likely will also have better education outcome as well. Since 2006, popular dissatisfaction has led the Chinese government to review its policies in regards to education governance by attempting to reverse those trends and bring the 'welfare' back into education provision and financing (Painter and Mok 2008). The following section discusses some of the major strategies adopted by the Chinese government in order to promote social equality in education.

The central government, realizing that educational inequalities have intensified, has recognized the importance of providing basic education to all its citizens. As a result of this, primary schools have attracted more state funding than higher education. Thanks to this increase in state funding for primary education, the net enrolment rate for primary school children grew to 99 per cent in 2005, while the gross enrolment rate in junior secondary school reached 95 per cent (China Education and Research Network 2006). The central government has also allocated extra resources to create more educational opportunities in rural areas during the 10th Five Year Plan (2001–5).[10] In late 2005, the State Council decided to further reform the funding system of school education in rural areas, with the nine-year compulsory education funded through general public finances (China Education and Research Network 2006).

Regional disparities and educational inequalities 147

During the Fifth Plenary Session of the 16th Central Committee of the CCP, the Chinese government further promulgated a strengthening and rejuvenation strategy through science and education, which clearly gives higher priority to education when compared to other policy areas in the 11th Five Year Plan (2006–10). Among the various tasks outlined, the consolidation of nine-year compulsory education in rural areas has been given high priority with the implementation of the 'Two Basics' project to universalize nine-year compulsory education and to eradicate illiteracy among young and middle-aged groups in the western part of China. In 2006, in order to release peasants from the heavy burden of educational expenses, the government decided to waive all tuition and miscellaneous fees of rural students in western China. The same policy was introduced to the central and eastern parts of the country in 2007 (China Education and Research Network 2006). In his government report in 2007, Premier Wen Jiabao announced an educational investment plan that committed a total of 85.85 billion yuan from the central budget to education, a 41.7 per cent increase over the previous year. In order to uphold the principles of educational equality and equity, part of the funding will be used to support children from poor families to guarantee their access to education. In addition, the government will continue to provide free textbooks for students from low socio-economic backgrounds, and living allowances for those in boarding schools. If these proposed policies are successfully implemented, about 150 million households with school-age children in rural areas will benefit (*People's Daily*, 5 March 2007).

In 1999 the government introduced the national student loan scheme in eight major cities, including Beijing and Shanghai and then extended the scheme to the rest of the country in 2004 (*People's Daily*, 5 March 2007). This was in recognition of the increasing financial difficulties faced by students in paying for higher education. The loan scheme, with a maximum annual loan of 6,000 yuan per person, mainly offers financial help to students who are offered places at public universities. In addition, the government also provides various grants to students with financial difficulties. For example, the National Scholarship grants an annual amount of 4,000 yuan to support outstanding students, while the National Grant Scheme provides a monthly subsidy of 150 yuan to students from poor families. The government launched a 'Green Path System', which guarantees that students do not lose their offers of admission because of financial difficulties (China Higher Education Student Information 2007). Premier Wen Jiabao announced further increases in government expenditure for grants and loans for university students from 1.8 billion yuan in 2006 to 9.5 in 2007, and up to 20 billion yuan in 2008 (*Mingpao*, 5 March 2007). He also announced that all students from poor families wanting to study in normal universities and colleges (teacher training) under the Ministry of Education would have their tuition fees waived, in order to attract more students into education while in turn building up the pool of qualified teachers in the less developed parts of China (*Mingpao*, 5 March 2007).

148   *Ka Ho Mok and Yu Cheung Wong*

'People-oriented development' and 'harmonious society' have become increasingly popular slogans shaping the political discourse in China. According to Ngok (2005), this is because the present political regime is more aware of the importance of the well-being of the people, especially devising new policy measures in helping socially disadvantaged groups. When choosing policy instruments, more attention has been given to address the fundamental interests of the overwhelming majority of the country's people and to minimize the gap between rich and poor. However, while the state is intensifying the funding for poverty relief and helping disadvantaged social groups, a 'self-dependence spirit' has also been emphasized by Chinese leaders (*People's Daily*, 12 February 2005). Yet the government recognizes that market forces cannot address social justice and social equality issues, and thus the emphasis on developing people-oriented social policy and social protection strategies has the aim of rectifying market failures in social provision. In 2006, both President Hu and Premier Wen chaired high-level meetings in the Communist Party's Politburo to stress the importance of education and call for a shift from the market-driven approach to a more welfare-based education system (Yang cited in Li 2007). In these meetings, senior leaders called on governments at all levels to make the development of education a strategic priority and to commit to a public education system that can be accessed by all. In order to achieve such policy objectives, the Ministry of Education has started to develop new mechanisms to calculate college costs and cap university tuition fees.

After collecting views from different social groups, coupled with various forms of public consultations, the State Council issued an 'Outline for Education Reforms' in early 2010 to engage with the wider policy community and the public in debating the proposed measures in promoting quality education in China. One of the major strategic directions is to increase the GDP share in support of educational development, with particularly emphasis being placed upon enhancing the educational opportunities of socially disadvantaged groups (State Council 2010). In this regard, Chinese authorities have established policies aiming to strike a balance between market efficiency and social equality; the efficacy of these policies is yet to be tested but it will be dependent on how they are implemented in different localities. As the OECD observed 'the shortage of revenues at the lower tiers and especially in poor regions constitutes a bottleneck to national policy implementation in the sectors of social security, basic education and health' (OECD 2005: 34). Ideally, this implies the development of an appropriate regulatory framework to govern the market in social policy without slowing down overall economic growth and to curb the rampant corruption among local cadres. The question remains as to whether or not China's increasingly globalized economy will be able to promote better social protection for the Chinese people. The irony is that a 'People's Republic' founded on the principles of communism is looking to its dominant role in global capitalism to fund its 'new' people-oriented strategies. Furthermore, whether or not the Chinese government is able to

Regional disparities and educational inequalities 149

achieve its policy goals of promoting social cohesion and educational equality through the adoption of the new measures outlined above will depend heavily upon both the policy design imposed by the central government and the political will and implementation capacity of local governments in realizing those policy goals.

Acknowledgements

The authors want to thank the participants of the *Provincial China Workshop 2008* held at Nankai University, Tianjin China from 27–30 October 2008 for their useful comments on this chapter. Particular thanks to the editors and reviewers of this volume for providing insightful comments to improve the chapter.

Notes

1 Part of the material reported in this article is based on a household survey of the Research Institute of Social Development and Public Policy, Beijing Normal University. The authors want to thank the Institute for providing assistance in data collection and analysis during the writing process of this paper.
2 The 'three old-mountains' before the communist revolution were capitalism, feudalism, and colonial occupation.
3 When discussing the privatization and marketization of education in China, there are two related processes, i.e. commercialization and commodification, that have significantly affected educational financing and provision in China. By 'commercialization' of education, we mean education is now treated as a type of commercial/business activity, whereby profit and financial incentives become more important; while 'commodification' of education refers to the situation where education is priced and students pay various kinds of fees in order to receive education and related services. These two processes are not entirely separate but have become increasingly popular in the context of the privatization and marketization of education in China (see, for example: Neubauer 2008; Chan *et al.* 2008).
4 The doctrines refer to the 'Three Represents' ideology formally written into the Party Constitution during the 16th NPC. The Three Represents ideology says that the CCP represents 1) advanced social production forces, 2) the progressive course of China's advanced culture and 3) the fundamental interests of the majority. The Three Represents ideology indicates that the CCP, under the impetus of the former party general secretary Jiang Zemin, tried to move from its preoccupation with Marxist-Leninist-Maoist doctrines to embrace economic development, educational/cultural advancement, and more pragmatic political objectives.
5 China still practises a very strict residential status classification system (the *hukou* system). Residents are classified into rural or urban residents usually according to the characteristics of their place of birth. Change of residential status is difficult for people with a rural *hukou* wanting to become urban residents. Even among urban residents, without a local *hukou*, migrants from another city are usually not entitled to local social benefits.
6 The original questions in Chinese were 1) '*jiaobuqi zinu rutou feilxuezafei*', 2) '*jiaobqi zinu de guowai jiaoyu feiyong*'and 3) '*maibuqi haizi de wanju, yundong yongping deng*'.
7 Coastal region here includes Beijing, Tianjin, Hebei, Liaoning, Shanghai, Jiangsu, Zhejiang, Zhejiang, Fujian, Shandong, Guangdong, Guangxi and Hainan.

8 Non-government financial resources here refer to input from social organizations and individuals, and donations in general.
9 In the beginning of the reform era in the early 1980s, the overall economic development strategy was to develop the eastern coastal area first and gradually extend it to the central and western region.
10 For instance, it initiated a series of projects such as the State's Compulsory Education Project in Poverty-Stricken Areas; the Project for the Reconstruction of Dilapidated School Buildings in Rural Primary and Secondary Schools; and the Project for Making Breakthroughs in Universalizing Compulsory Education and Eradicating Illiteracy among middle and young-age groups in Western China to speed up the delayed development of education.

8 Life considerations and the housing of rural to urban migrants

The case of Taiyuan

Bingqin Li and Mark Duda

The pressure of rural to urban migration on Chinese cities' ability to accommodate the extra population has increased rapidly since economic reform began. The urban system that was based upon strict population control policies nationwide helped to keep the pressure down in the early stage of reform. The opening up of urban labour markets to migrant workers in the late 1990s added to the pressure. Urban authorities, especially those in the large cities, have often complained that rural to urban migration has pushed the capacity of urban infrastructure and administration to the limit (Seeborg *et al.* 2000).

One of the major challenges to the host cities is housing provision. Before the 1980s the housing system in Chinese cities was a public one. Most urban families were able to secure public rental housing either through their employers or local housing bureaux. Tenants only paid symbolic amounts for rent. During the economic reform period, especially in the 1990s, the housing system became increasingly privatized. However, private houses were unaffordable to many urban residents (Li and Gong 2003). People who had already obtained housing in the central planning era were able to continue to occupy public housing by either renting cheaply or buying private houses with the help of heavy subsidies. They were also able to pass the houses on to their children. Low affordability in the market therefore has been partly disguised by the legacy of the old housing system. On the supply side, private developers were mostly keen to provide for better off urban middle and high income groups. There has been little interest in providing houses for the low-income groups (Liang and Yuan 2008).

As a result, anyone who had not worked for the public sector in the past and who did not have a parent with housing to rely on would struggle in the private housing market. To address this problem in 1995 the Central Government started the 'Anju Project', replaced in 1998 by the 'Comfortable Housing Scheme' (*jingjishiyong fang*), in which people whose income fell below a certain threshold could receive a subsidy when buying housing. State funding for the Anju Project was to be provided by municipal governments.

At the same time, employers were supposed to contribute to a Housing Provident Fund together with employees to help them save money in order to buy housing. Despite the fact that the housing system reform still has various problems; reforms have helped more people to own houses.

Housing benefits have until recently been highly localized, however, in that only registered local residents have been able to enjoy those benefits (Li 2005: 145–68). Some cities (for example, Beijing in 2003 and Chongqing in 2006) nevertheless have gradually removed restrictions for people from other cities to buy subsidized housing. Furthermore, in 2007 entitlement to subsidized homeownership and employer-backed saving schemes was made available to people of rural origin (Ruan 2007).

For many years after the economic reforms began, because the government did not officially endorse the right of rural to urban migrants to work and live in the city, there was no housing policy to accommodate the increasing number of migrant workers. The lack of formal housing supply for migrant workers has been considered a serious issue. Insufficient housing can directly or indirectly cause serious problems for cities, such as the development of slums and ghettos (Seeborg et al. 2000; Gu and Shen 2003; Wu 2004a), which suffer from poor housing quality (Wu 2002; Ma 2004), poor basic services and higher crime rates (Chan 1998; Zhang and Song 2003).

There are various ways to respond to the challenges. The most frequently used practice by local governments was demolishing urban squats, so that urban ghettos or 'urban villages' did not become an eyesore (Zhang 2002; Zhang et al. 2003). The hope was to force migrant workers to rent or buy houses properly in the private market. However, this approach did not solve the problem. Migrants often simply returned to the demolished areas and reclaimed the squatted housing simply because they had no real alternatives (Zhang 2001). This led to the realization that so long as existing urban housing markets were inaccessible to the migrant population, the battles between urban authorities and migrant squatters over illegal settlements would never end.

Two other types of approaches have offered solutions to the problem. The first approach comes from the perspective of citizens' rights. It traces the sources of housing inequality, focusing on the unequal access to urban housing benefits that migrants have suffered. The sources of this inequality are in line with the other social inequalities that migrants suffer in many different aspects of urban life (Solinger 1999, 2004; Li, B. 2006). This approach also attributes housing inequality to the discriminatory Household Registration System (often referred to as 'hukou'). The hukou is considered to be an institutional factor that has systematically led to the disadvantages suffered by rural to urban migrants. It is therefore seen as important to remove the Household Registration System and allow migrants to enjoy urban housing benefits as other urban citizens (Huang 2003; Wu 2004b). However, this line of research does not really address the fact that the majority of rural to urban migrants are only newcomers or transient migrants to cities. Many do not

Life considerations and the housing of rural to urban migrants 153

have the time and job security to accumulate a sufficient amount of money to buy a house in the city like other urban residents. The key question then is: if the Household Registration System were removed, would the housing conditions of rural to urban migrants improve?

The second approach focuses on increasing targeted supply. In some cities, local governments have started to offer dormitory-style cheap rental housing. The idea was to provide houses specifically for migrant workers. As a result, flats or dormitories were built in the peri-urban areas and a symbolic amount of rent was charged (Li *et al.* 2007). This strategy creates a separate housing sector for migrants without making major changes to the existing housing system. However, these houses have often turned out to be unpopular among migrant workers, mainly because they were usually not close to their work place. Unlike employer-provided houses or urban villages, which were often close to work and (in the case of the former) mainly free of charge, living in the state-provided cheap rental houses meant that migrant workers had to travel for quite a long time to work every day. This could be a particularly troublesome issue in large cities and where employers were located mainly in the city centre. What is more, the dormitories are mainly flats with shared rooms, and are thus not suitable for families (Li, L. 2006). As a result, migrants have not been eager to move into these state provided dormitories and have preferred to stay where they are even if the housing conditions are poor (Xiao 2006).

Thus solutions to migrant housing problems to date have focused on the institution that is considered to be the cause of inequality and on housing supply. Although tackling housing inequality in urban China is crucial, it is important to note that the sources of housing inequality may not be the same as the causes of migrants' poor housing conditions. Supply-side policies assume that migrant workers should live in 'adequate houses' of a certain standard, hence the interventionist campaign for providing cheap rental housing. But so far, there has been no detailed research into the housing demands of migrant workers, and thus we do not yet know what is considered to be adequate housing by migrant workers. Probably, this is the reason why earlier state provision schemes did not necessarily lead to good results.

In this chapter we try to understand the housing demand of migrant workers and show what they can realistically afford given their income and current life priorities. We seek to answer two questions. First, what types of housing are rural-to-urban migrants living in? Second, how did they end up living in their current housing? We use data collected in mid-2007 in Taiyuan, the capital city of Shanxi Province, for the analysis. Since the survey was carried out when the local government had not yet intervened in the housing provision for migrant workers in this city, Taiyuan can function as a case that offers insights into the housing outcomes of migrant workers when state intervention was not present. Studying a city without state intervention prevents the picture from being confused by such intervention.

154 *Bingqin Li and Mark Duda*

Housing choices in rapidly urbanizing cities – previous studies

The association between migrant labourers and inadequate housing has been documented in many parts of the world (Handelman 1975; Lowry 1990; Raffaelli 1997; Harpham 1994; Mitlin 2001; Fobil and Atuguba 2004; Kim and Gottdiener 2004; Huchzermeyer 2008), many of which may not have a Household Registration System like China's. Moreover, some studies have looked at migrants' housing choices in cities that, like China's, are actively urbanizing. Gilbert and Ward (1982) studied 13 low-income migrants' settlements in three Latin American cities finding that residential patterns resulted from constraints imposed upon land and housing markets rather than reflecting migrant choices. In Bucaramanga, Colombia, Edwards (1983) found that the changing structure of the housing market, rather than lifestyle triggers, led to residential moves among low-income households, including migrants. Arimah (1997) studied tenure choice in Ibadan, Nigeria finding that, in addition to standard economic and life-cycle characteristics such as income and number of children, length of stay in the city and access to land through ethnic ties influenced housing choice. Da Piedade Morais and de Oliveira Cruz (2007) looked at tenure choice in Brazil, finding that after controlling for other factors, being a recent migrant reduces the likelihood of owner tenure.

In China, a number of studies show the relationship between the state, housing market and migrant housing mobility within cities. They find that mobility can be caused by state-initiated demolition of urban villages (Yu 2005) or through regeneration of dilapidated neighbourhoods (Wu 2006). However, few studies have focused on the choices made by migrants themselves. We anticipate that in China, the housing outcomes of a rural to urban migrant are the results of various considerations in the life of rural to urban migrants. It is difficult to tell whether it is simply because under the current circumstances, they do not have much choice or if they voluntarily decide to spend the least possible on housing.

The Taiyuan research

This chapter is based on a survey with 805 interviewees during May and July 2007 in Taiyuan, the capital city of Shanxi Province. The built-up town area of the city is 6,988 square kilometres. The population in that town area of Taiyuan that year was 2.3 million. The most quoted number of rural to urban migrants working and living in Taiyuan is over 300,000 people (Li 2006). Including urban and suburban areas, the city is subdivided into six districts: Yingze, Xinghualing, Wanbolin, Xiaodian, Jiancaoping and Jinyuan. Our survey took place in the urban parts of these districts.

Taiyuan is a business and industrial city, known for its heavy industries. The economy is heavily dependent on natural resources. The main industries are coal production and chemicals. Unlike in many coastal cities, light industries are not well developed in Taiyuan. In the past twenty years or so the demand for natural resources in China has grown dramatically as China was turned into the workshop of the world, and Taiyuan has benefited tremendously from this process. Shanxi has become the centre for coal production in China and exports large quantities of coal to the world. As the city becomes richer, the service sector booms and has become a key attraction for rural to urban migrants.

Taiyuan was not an early starter in terms of state intervention in the housing for rural to urban migrants. Migrant workers mainly obtain accommodation from their employers and the private rental market. Not until late 2007 did the local authorities try to impose some formal requirement in regards to housing for employers that hire large numbers of migrant workers. These employers were subsequently required to build more permanent dormitories for their employees. The government also intended to transform some of the dilapidated neighbourhoods into migrant workers' accommodation. There were also plans to grant migrant workers access to the housing provident fund. However, at the time of this survey, there was no government policy that targeted rural to urban migrants.

The survey was carried out by a team of twenty interviewers, in the form of a structured schedule combining open and closed-ended questions. The sample included 805 rural to urban migrants. Unlike urban residents, who are all registered with city residents' committees (*jumin weiyuanhui*), rural to urban migrants were not comprehensively registered and so there was no full record of all migrants across the city. There was therefore no pre-existing sample frame for surveying housing for rural to urban migrants.

Instead, our sample is stratified based on migrant occupation categories. Reliable data on the occupational distribution of rural-urban migrants was found in a report published by the Rural Household Survey Team of the National Statistics Bureau (2005), which provides information on the employment structure of rural to urban migrants living in the central provinces of China. Sample percentages in our survey were matched to the major job categories (e.g. manufacturing, construction, service and catering, and transportation) in the report and we sought out respondents at their workplaces. By covering the range of variation in migrant occupations the sample is assured of capturing the range of housing types occupied by the majority of rural migrants. Stratifying by job type also helped us identify variation in housing choice since there is often a linkage between job category and residence type (Wu 2004b). For instance, construction workers almost always live in employer-provided housing on site, but this is rare for domestic workers. We also tried to maximize the representativeness of our sample by drawing from workplaces across all of the city's six urban districts.

Our sampling strategy is an effective response to a situation that presents substantial methodological challenges for those seeking to use statistical methods. Nonetheless, it is important to acknowledge some potential problems associated with our approach. First, because our interviewers identified

156 *Bingqin Li and Mark Duda*

many respondents on the street outside their workplaces, or as they moved through the city (in the case of street vendors, garbage collectors), there was little possibility to do follow-up visits to improve the response rate if the initial contact was unsatisfactory. Interviewers instead identified and interviewed replacement interviewees from the same sub-district and employment category if the initial interviewee declined to participate or could not be located. The sample is therefore biased toward those willing to be interviewed. Interviewees were given a small gift in exchange for participation.

Unwillingness to participate was least problematic among self-employed individuals and most challenging among workers in more formal employment. Not only could members of this group (e.g. factory workers) not be reached during working hours but in some cases employers tried to forbid interviewees from giving interviews. It is possible that this is another source of bias as potential interviewees working in the least desirable conditions might be more likely to be excluded from the sample (though it is not clear what impact this might have on characteristics of housing units in the sample). In any case, we attempted to minimize this problem by having interviewers wait outside factories at the end of each working day and conducting interviews after work outside the workplace itself.

Table 8.1 shows the distribution of migrant employment by industrial sector in our sample and in the report of the China Rural Survey Team. Catering and construction were the two largest groups, each accounting for about 20 per cent of the total migrant population. Manufacturing was the third largest sector that rural to urban migrants worked in. In Taiyuan, the service sector was the largest employer of migrant workers. Although Taiyuan is known for its heavy industries, apart from coal mines, other heavy industries are dependent on skilled labourers with at least high school education. However, rural to urban migrants are often not qualified for these jobs. Therefore, manufacturing-sector employment for migrant workers was less important in Taiyuan than in many coastal cities that had more active light industries.

Table 8.1 Migrant employment distribution by industrial sector

	Taiyuan sample composition		Rural survey team
	Frequency	*Percentage*	*Percentage*
Manufacturing	145	18.0	*18*
Restaurant/hotel	162	20.1	*20*
Wholesale/retailing	125	15.5	*15*
Construction	162	20.1	*20*
Domestic and other services	130	16.2	*18*
Street vending	49	6.1	*5*
Recycling	32	4.0	*4*
Total	805	100	*100*

Note: data in the column of Rural survey team has been re-categorized to fit into the categories listed in the left column

Is there a migrant 'housing problem'?

Before we start analysing the housing conditions of migrant workers, it is important to look at whether there is a 'housing problem' as perceived by migrant workers themselves. In the existing literature the concept of adequate housing is mostly defined by researchers or international organizations, such as the UN-HABITAT (May *et al.* 2000). Considering that migrant workers come from rural China, where living standards are on average much lower than in the cities, inadequate housing that might be problematic for urban citizens may not be as problematic for migrant workers. This is potentially one of the reasons behind rural migrant workers' willingness to live in poorer quality housing. We therefore need to first examine whether migrant workers really feel that there is a housing problem. In this section, we first examine the overall housing conditions of the respondents and then examine whether they find those conditions problematic.

As shown in Table 8.2, among our respondents the average rent paid by a single person was about 170 yuan per month in mid-2007. For a family, it was 290 yuan per month. The average living space was six square metres per person. About half of the people were living in a space of less than three square metres per person.

In terms of housing quality, the respondents were asked to report on any housing problems they experienced. The main problems reported included: 1) environmental problems, such as dampness (27.3 per cent), cold in winter (18.2 per cent), and noise (11.6 per cent); and 2) lack of facilities, such as no heating (8.1 per cent), no interior tap water (31.4 per cent), no interior toilet (49.6 per cent), no kitchen (63.4 per cent), and no shower facilities (89.2 per cent). Most respondents (86.1 per cent) lived in a permanent structure, but 32.6 per cent lived on the job site. A small number of people's accommodation was also used for other purposes (10.1 per cent). The majority (78.7 per cent) lived in inner city areas and about 20 per cent lived in suburban areas. 91.1 per cent spent less than half an hour to travel to work everyday.

We built a quality indicator based on the housing problems reported by respondents. Considering the lifestyle of most rural to urban migrants whose employers offered food and shower facilities, we only include five key problems in the quality index. They are marked with an asterisk [*] in Table 8.2, and each of these characteristics earned a single point if it was considered to be problematic by the respondents. The maximum index score is five for the worst housing and zero the minimum for the least problematic. We grouped the scores into four classes 'severe'/'significant'/'some'/'none' as indicated in the table. About one third of respondents fell into the category of 'none'; 42 per cent belonged to 'some'; and one fourth was in the 'severe' group.

A large proportion of the respondents reported living in houses with some major quality problems. But did it matter that they live in such poor housing conditions? After all, housing satisfaction is subjective. If people are happy about their housing conditions, should they not be left alone? To check this

158 *Bingqin Li and Mark Duda*

Table 8.2 Housing characteristics

	Median	Mean	[min, max]
Monthly rent paid			
Single people	100	168.8	[15, 2000]
Families	200	288.8	[30, 1500]
Living space (sq. m. per capita)	3	5.8	[3, 120]
Location	*Count*	*Per cent*	*Cumulative*
Inner city	633	78.7	78.7
Inner suburb	157	19.5	98.2
Outer suburb	15	1.8	100
Commuting time (one way)			
Live on site	262	32.6	32.6
< ½ hour	471	58.5	91.1
½–1hour	58	7.2	98.3
1–1½ hours	11	1.4	99.6
> 1½ hours	3	0.4	100.0
Housing problems			
Cold in winter	146	18.2	
Damp	220	27.3	
very damp and unhealthy	31	3.9	
somewhat damp but not unbearable	189	23.5	
Very noisy/noise disturbs sleep	93	11.6	
*No interior toilet	399	49.6	
*No interior tap water	253	31.4	
Not heated	65	8.1	
No kitchen (private or shared)	510	63.4	
No shower	716	89.2	
*Building also used for other purposes	81	10.1	
*Structure is temporary	112	13.1	
Quality indicator			
No problem	249	30.9	30.9
Some problems (1 problem)	341	42.4	73.3
Significant problems (2 problems)	143	17.8	91.1
Severe problems (3–5 problems)	72	8.9	100

Note: * items that are used to calculate the quality indicator.

we asked the question: 'Are you satisfied with your current housing?' The answers were ranked from 1 to 5 with '1' being 'very dissatisfied' and '5' being 'very satisfied.' A cross-tabulation of housing satisfaction by quality shows that (Table 8.3) housing satisfaction/dissatisfaction is correlated with the number of housing problems. A quarter of the respondents lived in housing with severe or significant problems and were unhappy about their housing conditions. About 16 per cent of the respondents living in housing with some problems were dissatisfied. This means that people were aware of the problems

Life considerations and the housing of rural to urban migrants 159

and were indeed less happy about housing with more problems. However, what made them end up in their current housing? Was poor housing merely the result of their low income?

Given the housing problems and the situation of poor quality housing, we use Table 8.4 to find out whether quality and household income are related. There is no obvious connection between the two variables. People coming from all different income groups can all live in very poor quality housing. The survey found that 60 per cent of the people living in the poorest quality housing earned less than 1,200 yuan per month, and a relatively smaller proportion of people earning more than 2,000 yuan lived in housing with severe problems. The pattern becomes undetectable when we look at better quality housing. The share of people living in houses with 'no problems' is the highest. Among those facing severe problems, the highest earners have the smallest share but are only slightly ahead of the lowest earners. The people who were most likely to suffer from poor housing conditions were the lower-middle-income group.

These findings suggest that there were indeed problems with migrant workers' housing. The first is that poor quality housing was not rare. Some

Table 8.3 Satisfaction by quality

Indicator	Severe problems (%)	Significant problems (%)	Some problem (%)	No problem (%)	Total (%)	Total (#)
Very dissatisfied	9.8	5.2	1.2	1.0	30	24
Dissatisfied	15.7	10.3	15.5	6.0	10.9	88
No strong opinion	36.3	35.5	24.0	16.0	24.8	199
Satisfied	18.6	23.3	29.3	36.2	29.4	236
Very satisfied	19.6	25.8	30.1	40.9	32.0	257
Total (%)	*100*	*100*	*100*	*100*	*100*	*804*
Total (count)	*102*	*155*	*246*	*301*	*804*	

Note: Pearson chi2 (12) = 85.8054 Pr = 0.000

Table 8.4 Housing quality and income

All respondents	Per cent					
	Severe problems	Significant problems	Some problems	No problems	Total	Number
< 800	8.8	21.4	25.3	44.5	100.0	182
800 to 1,200	21.6	19.1	26.6	32.7	100.0	199
1,200 to 2,000	14.3	19.2	37.9	28.6	100.0	182
> 2,000	7.0	18.2	32.2	42.6	100.0	242
Total	12.7	19.4	30.6	37.4	100.0	805
Number	102	156	246	301	805	

160 *Bingqin Li and Mark Duda*

houses did not even have any of the basic facilities that are usually considered necessary for a decent life. The second is that people do indeed feel very unhappy when they do not live in good quality housing. The explanation for this could be that housing was too expensive and people were not able to afford better housing. However, we can also see that when people earned more money, their housing conditions were not necessarily better. This indicates that there must be other factors behind these housing outcomes.

Life considerations and housing outcomes of migrant workers

In this section, we look at the factors that may affect migrants' housing outcomes. When migrants come to the cities, either employers provide dormitories for them, or they acquire housing privately (through the market, friends or relatives). Some people need to pay rent; others do not. We constructed two logistic models. The first model looks at what kinds of people lived in employer provided housing. The second examines what kinds of people were more likely to pay rent. The independent variables used in the models included variables that can reflect life considerations, such as convenience to work, saving money, convenience for family life and expected migration plans. The reasons behind the use of these variables are as follows.

Most migrant workers are drawn into cities because of the rural–urban income gap. Also, because newcomers do not have much savings, they count on monthly or even daily cash flow in the city to cover their living costs. Therefore, a job that can offer income is the top priority in the life of most rural to urban migrants. Newcomers may not have the money to rent privately. Usually, they either stay temporarily with their fellow villagers or county-men until they find a job (Pahl 1966; Tacoli 1998). Alternatively, they may accept a job that offers housing even before they come to the city (Knight *et al.* 1999). For those who are already working in cities, living close to work is crucial (Abu-Lughod 1961; Yang *et al.* 2005).

Although migrant workers earn money in the city, their families may remain in the village. This is often a deliberate decision adopted by migrants and their families (Agesa and Kim 2001). The person working in the town sends remittances back home to support the family, and saves for the future (Rempel and Lobdell 1978; Taylor and Wyatt 1996), hoping they will return to the village after earning some money (Gmelch 1980; Wu and Zhou 1996). As a result, they may prefer to save as much as possible when they are working in the city, not spend money on better quality housing.

When the family of a migrant worker joins him/her in the same city, the issues that they need to take care of change accordingly. Convenience for work is not the only priority when trying to look for accommodation. They also have to find accommodation that is convenient for family life (Duda and Li 2008). For example, single people might be more likely to live in shared rooms, whereas couples need more privacy. If a child joins the couple, they need to make plans to adjust to the extra person, for example arranging

Life considerations and the housing of rural to urban migrants   161

schooling or childcare and extra space at home (Brockerhoff 1990; Li and Zahniser 2002).

Migrants, especially those coming from rural areas, do not necessarily enjoy job stability, moving between jobs in different parts of the city or in different cities. When urban life is not suitable for them, they may abandon urban life temporarily or even permanently. Whether a person feels he or she can stay at the destination for a relatively long period also affects their likelihood of buying a house or their willingness to spend more money on housing (Costello 1987).

On top of all these aspects, we also included socio-economic factors and household structure into our analysis. Educational level, for example, might be related to the type of job a worker does and in turn have an effect on their income. Gender may also play a role in the sector that a person ends up in, especially when he/she first comes to the city. For example, a woman is more likely to do manual jobs in the manufacturing sector, whereas a man is more likely to work in construction. Different sectors may have different norms in organizing housing provision, affecting housing outcomes (Wu 2002). Some household characteristics, such as size and marriage status, can also be used to analyse family concerns when people make housing decisions. On these understandings, we included the following variables in the analysis.

Model variables and descriptive statistics

Socio-demographic characteristics and household structure

About two-thirds of the respondents were men, while the average age of respondents was 31.9 years. The youngest person was 17 years old and the oldest 72. Most respondents were under the age of 40, and about half were under the age of 30. The education profile shows that 22 per cent of the respondents had completed only primary school education, while 66.2 per cent had completed secondary school or equivalent education. Less than 12 per cent had high-school or equivalent education. Most of the interviewees (61.9 per cent) were married, while 218 respondents had brought their children with them to Taiyuan. Among those 218 respondents, 158 had school-age children. The average household size was 1.89. The mean household income was 1,554 yuan per month and the median was 1,200 yuan.

Employment

We used two employment characteristics: employer type and industry sector. For the former, we capture five categories that we collapsed into three: state/collective[1] (13.8 per cent), private (48.8 per cent) and self-employed/no employer (37.3 per cent). In terms of industry sector, our sampling included eight industry groups. We later merged the sectors of similar types, and the eight original sectors were turned into four broad classifications. The purpose of

162 *Bingqin Li and Mark Duda*

doing so is to avoid small numbers in some groups (such as garbage collector) that would make the results impossible to interpret, given the relatively small sample size. The four categories are manufacturing (18 per cent), construction (20.1 per cent), services (51.8 per cent) and street business (10.1 per cent).[2]

Migration and mobility

Most migrants had left their villages relatively recently (the median time as migrants was five years) and some people had stayed in other places before they came to Taiyuan (median time in Taiyuan was three years). Those who wanted to settle down in Taiyuan permanently are quite different from those who did not want to stay permanently. Most of the respondents who decided to settle down in Taiyuan (73 per cent) did not have land in the village any more, whereas people who wanted to go back still held land in the villages. On average, people who wanted to stay in Taiyuan permanently had already lived there for an average of 6.6 years. In contrast, the rest of respondents had only stayed in Taiyuan for an average of 3.7 years. A larger proportion (37 per cent) of those respondents who wanted to settle down permanently (vs. 14 per cent of those who did not want to settle in Taiyuan) also managed to come with their partners. The people who wanted to stay earned a higher income (1,894 yuan) than did the people who did not want to stay (1,196 yuan). Most respondents (80.6 per cent) had been able to visit their home villages at least once in the preceding year, and 43.3 per cent had made two or more visits home during that same period. More than 60 per cent sent monthly remittances home.

Housing providers and rental payment

38 per cent of respondents lived in employer provided accommodation; the rest had found housing from other sources, mainly private-market renting, while a small number of people lived temporarily with their friends and relatives. Overall, the majority (61.5 per cent) paid rent while the rest did not (see Table 8.5).

Logistic regressions on providers and rent payment

The first logistic model is about what kinds of migrants lived in employer provided housing. The second is who paid rent and who got free housing. The independent variables are sorted according to the life considerations discussed in the last section. In order to see whether income matters in people's housing decisions, we included household income as an independent variable.

As shown in Table 8.6, older respondents were less likely to live in employer-provided houses and more likely to pay rent. Having a partner in Taiyuan and living with a spouse also reduced the odds of living in employer provided housing, but increased the odds of paying rent. If a couple were both

Table 8.5 Descriptive statistics for the models

Socio-demographic characteristics and household structure	Count	Mean	[min, max]
Age	805	31.9	[17, 72]
Age by group	*Count*	*Percent*	*Cumulative*
< = 20	134	16.7	16.7
20–30	278	34.5	51.2
30–40	231	28.7	79.9
40–50	119	14.8	94.7
50–60	34	4.2	98.9
> 60	9	1.2	100.0
	805		
Gender			
Male	530	65.8	65.8
Female	275	34.2	100.0
	803		
Education			
No formal Education	34	4.2	4.2
Primary	143	17.8	22.0
Secondary	520	64.8	86.8
Vocational school	11	1.4	88.2
High school	93	11.6	99.8
Polytechnic	2	0.3	100.0
	805		
Marital status			
Married	498	61.9	61.9
Unmarried	307	39.1	100.0
	503		
Partner living together in Taiyuan			
No	194	38.6	38.6
Yes	309	61.4	100.0
Workin partner in Taiyuan(including singles)			
No	563	69.9	69.9
Yes	242	30.1	100.0
	743		
Children studying in Taiyuan			
No	585	78.7	78.7
Yes	159	21.3	100.0
Income	*Monthly (yuan)*	*min*	*max*
Household income, median	1200	100	20000
Household income, mean	1554		
(std. dev.)	(1446)		
Employment	*Count*	*Per cent*	*Cumulative*
	805		
Employer type			
State/collective	111	13.8	13.8
Private	393	48.8	62.6
Self employed/no employer	300	37.3	100

(continued on next page)

164 *Bingqin Li and Mark Duda*

Table 8.5 (continued)

Socio-demographic characteristics and household structure	Count	Mean	[min, max]
	805		
Industry			
Manufacturing	145	18.0	18.0
Construction	162	20.1	38.1
Services	417	51.8	90.0
Street	81	10.1	100
Migration			
		Min	*Max*
Years as migrant			
Median	5	0.1	30.3
Mean	6.4 (5.8)		
Years in Taiyuan			
Median	3	0.1	28
Mean			
Plan to settle permanently in Taiyuan	804		
Yes	239	29.7	29.7
No	565	70.3	100
Send remittances			
Yes	503	62.5	62.5
No	302	37.5	100.0
Housing Provider	803		
Employer	305	38.0	38.0
Non employer	498	62.0	100.0
Rent	805		
Pay rent	495	61.5	61.5
Free	310	38.5	100

working, they were more likely to live in employer provided housing and not paying rent, although they might live separately. Respondents who were single were more likely to take up housing provided by employers than were couples.

Migration plans could also affect housing outcomes. The longer a person lived in Taiyuan, the less likely he or she lived in employer-provided housing and the more likely that he or she lived in rented accommodation. Intention to settle down in Taiyuan indeed mattered.

Employment sector also affected migrant housing decisions. Relative to working in manufacturing, working in construction reduced the odds of paying rent. Manufacturers were also less likely to provide housing to employees than construction companies. Working in the service or street business sectors decreased the odds of employer provided housing, and significantly increased the odds of paying rent. Working in the state sector means that a person was more likely to be housed by the employer and less

Table 8.6 Housing choice logistic regression results

	Housing Provider (1 = employer; 0 = market)			Pay rent or not (1 = yes)		
	coefficient	*odds ratio*		*coefficient*	*odds ratio*	
Socio-demographic						
Gender (1 = male)	-0.21	0.82		0.45	1.57	**
Age	-0.23	0.80	***	0.23	1.26	***
Age squared	0.00	1.00	***	0.00	1.00	***
Education (ref: primary or less)						
Secondary school	0.16	1.18		-0.15	0.86	
High Sch./Vocational/Polytechnic	-0.06	0.95		0.06	1.07	
Household structure						
Marriage status (1 = married/cohabit)	-0.11	0.89		0.59	1.81	*
Partner in Taiyuan (1 = yes)	-3.67	0.03	***	3.34	28.24	***
Child studying in Taiyuan (1 = yes)	0.50	1.66		0.07	1.07	
Working partner in Taiyuan (1 = yes)	2.61	13.53	**	-2.17	0.11	**
Migration						
Plan to settle in Taiyuan permanently (1 = yes)	-0.23	0.79		0.59	1.81	**
Years as a migrant	0.08	1.08	***	-0.05	0.95	**
Years in Taiyuan	-0.12	0.89	***	0.09	1.09	**
Send remittances (1 = yes)	-0.26	0.77		0.29	1.33	
Employment						
Working for the state sector (1 = yes)	0.61	1.85	**	-0.49	0.61	**
Industry sector (construction omitted)						
Manufacturing industry	-0.52	0.60	*	0.99	2.70	***
Service industry	-1.73	0.18	***	2.04	7.71	***
Street vendors	-4.29	0.01	***	4.01	54.95	***

(continued on next page)

Table 8.6 (continued)

	Housing Provider (1 = employer; 0 = market)			Pay rent or not (1 = yes)	
	coefficient	odds ratio		coefficient	odds ratio
Income					
Household income	0.00	1.00		0.00	1.00
Household income sq	0.00	1.00		0.00	1.00
Constant	6.38		***	-6.66	***
Log likelihood	-323.78			-340.67	
LR chi square /degrees of freedom	385.81	19		382.11	19
Pseudo R2	0.373			0.359	
N	772			798	

Note: */**/*** denote significance at 0.10/0.05/0.01 levels

Life considerations and the housing of rural to urban migrants 167

likely to pay rent. Interestingly, the impact of income was very small. This means that as income increased the extra money was not spent on improving housing, but was most probably saved.

Housing decisions from a subjective perspective

We also asked direct questions regarding migrants' considerations when they decided to accept their current housing arrangement. Table 8.7 shows their answers. The respondents reported three main reasons for their decision to live in the current housing at the time of the interview, as well as three problems they suffered from living in that accommodation. The numbers reported in Table 8.7 are weighted totals, as the interviewees ranked the answers by importance. To reflect the varying level of importance, the most important concern received three points and the third got one point. The results suggest that the top concern was convenience of travel to work. Price ranked second. Proximity to social networks came third. Social networks are in general considered to be helpful for sharing useful information on how to survive in the city. Safety, family life and children's schooling were also raised as factors. Facilities, indicating the importance of housing quality, were at the bottom of the list.

However, what made people unhappy about their current housing was mainly quality related factors such as size and facilities or lack thereof. These findings also confirmed our argument that people prioritize convenience to work and family life over quality. However, when these considerations were taken into account, respondents became helpless regarding their housing conditions, and had to tolerate poor housing quality. The answers did not touch upon future migration plans, but they might be internalized by the choice of rental payment.

Conclusion

It is probably true that the housing difficulties and dissatisfaction faced by rural to urban migrants can be a result of having no alternatives in the housing market, and that thus migrant workers had to live in poor quality

Table 8.7 Standard for housing choice

Why choose current house ($1 \times 3 + 2 \times 2 + 3 \times 1$)		Dislike current house ($1 \times 3 + 2 \times 2 + 3 \times 1$)	
1. Convenient for work	1881	1. Crowdedness/size	965
2. Cheap	649	2. Poor facilities	851
3. Close to relatives and friends	325	3. Rentals	324
4. Safety	269	4. Inconvenient for family life	91
5. Convenient for family	184	5. Inconvenient for work	56
6. Convenient for school	182		
7. Convenient facilities	135		

housing. If this is the only explanation for their housing problems, we would anticipate that when migrants earn a higher income or when housing is provided free of charge they would be prepared to improve their housing conditions. Yet, cheap rental housing provided by the state in other parts of the country turned out to be unpopular among migrant workers (Duda *et al.* 2008). Our survey results also show that income did not strongly co-relate to housing quality when other factors are controlled.

Then it is important to know how other factors have lead to the outcomes of the current migrant housing circumstances. Our findings suggest that if housing is in a location that is convenient to work, can accommodate a family when necessary and would allow migrant workers to travel whenever they need to, and – on top of these – if it is also cheap, then it will be attractive to migrants even if the quality is poor.

These findings have some important implications. It helps to argue for the state to play a role in the housing for low-income migrants, and to suggest how the interventions might work better. When migrant workers' goal is to save money or live closer to work, they may not be interested in spending more money to live in more comfortable houses. On the contrary, many of them would decide to spend as little as possible on housing even if they can afford better housing. However, this does not mean that they actually enjoy living in poor quality housing. They suffer both physically and psychologically, but the sufferings are a sacrifice for the future and for the family. In this sense, even if the Household Registration System were removed and migrants could gain full access to the urban housing market, this would not necessarily automatically lead to better housing results for migrant workers.

From a societal perspective, this is also a typical case of a private decision that does not take into account the social benefits and costs of their actions. This means that when migrant workers decide to live in poor quality housing, they have not considered the potential impacts this might have on the host community. These impacts can be negative, such as a deteriorating living environment in terms of hygiene, poorer safety or even greater health problems. Their consumption decisions are only based on balancing private costs and benefits. Therefore, there needs to be some external support or incentives to push the spending on housing up to a higher level so that the social costs can be minimized. To achieve this some demand side policies are potentially worth considering.

We suggest that migrants who are more established want to settle down in the city and are able to afford better housing. The recent policies aimed at improving access to urban home ownership, higher end private rental markets, saving schemes and relevant benefits can be useful for those migrants. But for those who are more likely to move to other places in the future, private rental of low cost and minimum quality requirements might be a more relevant solution. At the same time, it may also be useful to encourage migrants to consider settling down in the city permanently as a realistic goal for the future. This can be achieved through reduced formal discrimination

Life considerations and the housing of rural to urban migrants 169

such as differential treatment based on Household Registration status. What is also important is to help rural migrants understand the long-term health effects of poor housing. Given that in rural areas houses are self-built with a one-off investment, it might be difficult for migrant workers to adapt to the idea of having to spend a significant amount of their monthly income on rented housing on a regular basis.

On the supply side, there is a need to encourage provision of better quality but low-cost housing through the market. This works both for employer-provided housing and for private housing. Efforts to improve migrant housing quality might be best targeted through regulation or investment in employer-provided housing. Minimally, this would have the advantage of improving the majority of housing units occupied by low-income and relatively newer migrants. Further efforts to encourage more organized service provision and upgrading of poor quality housing in the dilapidated urban neighbourhoods might provide cheaper alternatives to migrant workers. On the whole, low-income housing for migrants and the urban poor has the potential to be streamlined.

Our data indicate that the failed state interventions in other parts of the country might be equally unsuccessful in Taiyuan because of the life priorities of migrant workers. What is more, given that Taiyuan's migrants are highly concentrated in the service sector, where the role of employer provision is not as strong as in manufacture-based cities, more effective encouragement of private rental housing could prove to be a useful solution.

In the two years previous to our survey, Taiyuan's government had started to transform some old neighbourhoods, which were unpopular with locals, into cheap rental housing for migrant workers. This policy, if fully implemented, is in line with our research findings, which indicate the need to provide housing within the city rather than in suburban areas, a solution that has proven to be uneconomical in other cities. Trying to take into account the needs of low-income migrant workers, not only focusing on housing difficulties, but also on accessibility to an urban life and employment would be a more realistic and user-friendly solution to migrant worker's housing needs.[3] Transforming existing public housing into cheap rental housing partially answers the problem of long commuting times and costs associated with publicly provided dormitories in peri-urban areas, and because this housing was originally designed for family use, it can be potentially cheaper to provide and be more popular.

However, the importance of state-provided cheap rental housing should not be over-emphasized, mainly because provision of this type of housing would only work under the premise that migrants will continue to increase in number and put pressure on the urban housing sector. There is, however, the risk that external factors – such as an economic downturn – might cause migrants to return to their villages or to move out of the city on a large scale, after which state-provided cheap houses might not be absorbed by the urban housing market and become vacant (Li 2007). In this sense, cultivating the

170 *Bingqin Li and Mark Duda*

roles of employers and the market as the main providers can also be a relevant solution.

It is also important to highlight that the demolition of existing housing stock in urban areas is mostly driven by increased land prices and by the interests of businesses to take over good locations. Therefore, houses of relatively lower quality in the inner-city areas are unavoidably targets of real estate developers. The municipal government has to balance the potentially growing business interests in these areas and the intention to satisfy the housing needs of migrant workers. In this sense, the outcome of this policy is very difficult to predict.

Acknowledgements

This study was funded by a grant from the Suntory and Toyota International Centres for Economics and Related Disciplines (STICERD) at LSE and builds directly upon our earlier works funded by the Lincoln Institute of Land Policy in the United States.

Notes

1 These are employers from the public sector, state-owned enterprises and collectively owned enterprises.
2 'Services' combines wholesale/retail, restaurant and domestic services. 'Street business' combines recycling, street vending and other. Manufacturing and construction are unadjusted.
3 It is unclear whether the policies were a result of learning from the lessons from other cities as there had been a number of widely publicized policies or suggestions based on the experience of other cities regarding the failure of government direct provision.

9 Older people and the (un)caring state in 'China's Manhattan'

Anna Boermel

A promotional brochure published by the Beijing Municipal Working committee on Ageing and the Beijing Association on Ageing in April 2002 dedicated a whole page to a photo montage (BSLGWB 2002: 21) showing an older, grey-haired woman and a white-haired man, happily gazing into the distance. Both are carefully coiffed and formally dressed, she in a patterned Chinese dress and he in a dark grey suit, white shirt and red tie. In the background a number of tall and shiny modern buildings, all located in central Beijing, are visible. The flyover with cars passing underneath reinforces the impression of technological progress; a temple with its orange-brown roofs is hardly noticeable behind the man's back. This image suggests that rapid economic growth and profound spatial changes have benefited older people in Beijing.

Most of the commercial high-rises visible in the photo montage are located in the Jianguomenwai ('Jianwai' for short) area in Chaoyang District in East Beijing. Jianwai covers 4.4 km between the eastern Second Ring Road in the west, the western Dawang Road in the east, Guanghua Road in the north and Tonghui River in the south. The numerous (and well-known) commercial buildings (including CITIC, SCITECH, the Jianguo Hotel, the China World Trade Centre, the new Silk Market and Jianwai Soho) bear witness to the rapid economic development the area has undergone since the onset of the reform era in the late 1970s. In the last decade this process has been intensified. The pursuit of a specific vision of modernity has turned Jianwai into an exceptionally vibrant, economically thriving hub which attracts Chinese and foreign business elites and is littered with an ever-growing number of new and shiny high-rises in all shapes, sizes and styles.[1] Jianwai is now widely considered to be one of the most prosperous areas in China; a beacon of enormous commercial success and proof of China's ability to compete internationally. Local officials proudly refer to their area as 'China's Manhattan' and compare it not only to its namesake in New York but also to La Défense in Paris. Owing to the fact that numerous multi-national and high-end Chinese companies have their China headquarters in Jianwai and thus pay taxes locally, the area is of fiscal importance to China's economic development. These companies provide employment for tens of thousands of white-collar workers as well as for thousands of service-sector staff.

In Chinese governmental circles the Jianwai officials enjoy a very good reputation for their resourcefulness. The constant stream of visitors they

172 *Anna Boermel*

receive, foreign and Chinese alike, testifies to the fact that they excel at forging links with the outside world and other commercial hubs in urban China. Their reputation not only stems from the fact that Jianwai is the epitome of a pathway to rapid economic development which is viewed as highly desirable by China's urban planners, but is also attributable to the respect they have gained nationwide for their innovative contributions to the debate about and implementation of local government reform.

These two factors, the privileged economic situation of the area and the capacity of local officials to efficiently put into practice policies developed at the central level, and devise novel strategies to deal with challenging issues, make Jianwai a prime location for an examination of the claim that urban Chinese modernity, marked by the creation of material wealth, profound socioeconomic and spatial changes, is conducive to improving well-being in old age.

In the past decade the growing awareness in Chinese official circles of the changing demographic make-up of the population, combined with the problems faced by state and collectively owned enterprises in meeting their pension liabilities, and more recently, intensifying concerns about social inequity, have given renewed impetus to the reform of the welfare system for older people. Changes in the pension system and the delivery of social services at the local level attest to these governmental efforts.

Drawing on qualitative data gathered in Jianwai between 2003 and 2010, this chapter examines the provision of social services for older people in Jianwai, a prosperous area with a higher than average proportion of older residents. I argue that despite recent improvements in service delivery, the privileged economic status of the area has brought only a few benefits to the majority of its older residents. I attribute this outcome to three factors. First, the pursuit of a specific vision of modernity has turned land into prime real estate affordable only to a tiny financial elite and has led to the forced relocation of long-term residents, many of whom are close to or past the age of retirement. This intense wealth-creation strategy has undermined other policy goals, such as the development of old-age work, and threatened the livelihood of older people who used to and, to some extent, still reside in areas earmarked for re-development in Jianwai. Second, the in-built hierarchy of the welfare system for older people, which provides preferential access to services not according to need but based on the socio-political status the elderly person has been given by the bureaucracy, has led to an extremely uneven distribution of social services. Last, the limited availability of funds for 'old-age work' at the community (*shequ*) level poses severe problems given the multitude of functions that have recently been assigned to this administrative tier.

The ethnographic data presented here was collected in the course of a larger research project, which investigates changing governmental and societal discourses and practices concerning 'old age' as well as experiences of 'old age' in urban China at the turn of the century. While living in Jianwai between April 2003 and October 2004, and again from July to December 2005, I conducted twenty months of multi-sited field research in Beijing. In

Older people and the (un)caring state 173

Jianwai I focused my research on how the local government developed responses to the 'problem of old age' and studied residents' responses to these efforts. To this end I interviewed officials at the street office (_jiedao banshichu_) and community (_shequ_) levels, observed (and often participated in) the full range of activities on offer for older people and had informal conversations with many older residents, male and female, retired workers and cadres, in public and private spaces. While I interacted most frequently with officials and residents in the community in which I lived, I regularly visited one other community and occasionally took part in activities organized in some of the other Jianwai communities.[2] Between 2008 and 2010 I conducted another eleven weeks of field research in Jianwai. I (re-)interviewed community and street office officials and older people, many of whom I had first met in 2004, and observed activities at a new centre for old people.

The chapter is divided into two main parts. Part one provides a brief overview of reforms in the pension system and the delivery of social services in urban areas. The second and main part of the chapter focuses on the provision and consumption of social services for older people in Jianwai. The chapter ends with a conclusion which, drawing on this case study, assesses the impact of urban Chinese modernity on older people's lives.

Policy innovation at the central level: the case of pensions

Debates about the reform of the pension system within the Chinese bureaucracy have already received some academic attention (Davis 1988; Shan 1995; Raymo and Xie 2000; Zhuang 2002; Béland and Yu 2004; Frazier 2004). Suffice it to say that after a period of intense insecurity caused by the delay in or non-payment of pensions in the 1990s,[3] the pension system was increasingly regulated and standardized in the late 1990s and early 2000s. While the central government defines the spending targets, the actual delivery of pensions is the responsibility of the cities (Wong 2007: 20).

Retirement benefits for the current generation of older people in China not only depend on the number of years they have worked (_gongling_), the last salary they received, or their age at the point of retirement.[4] Also taken into account are their contribution to the revolutionary cause (if any), their employment status and their place of residence (urban or rural) prior to retirement. In very general terms, urban pensioners who are deemed to have made special contributions to the Chinese revolution and retirees who used to work for government agencies and public institutions receive relatively higher pensions and enjoy privileged access to good social services; permanent urban residents who have retired from work in state-owned or collectively owned enterprises are entitled to a pension and some social services; while older people without urban residential status (_hukou_) only very rarely get a pension and have very little – if any – access to social services.

In urban areas a uniform basic old-age insurance system, which covers all the employees of different types of enterprises, was introduced in 1997. To

174 Anna Boermel

ensure that basic pensions would be paid in full and on time the government promoted the delivery of pensions by social service institutions. At the end of 2003 social service institutions paid the basic pensions of all enterprise retirees (White Paper 2004: 3, 7). Pensions for retired staff members of government agencies and public institutions are paid either by central government or by their former employers at the rate stipulated by the state (White Paper 2006).

Social services delivery at the community level

The Chinese government has developed a vision of a social service system for older people that is 'based on family care for the aged, and supported by community services and supplemented by institutional services for seniors' (White Paper 2006). This tri-partite plan is the outcome of financial considerations, the official perception that older people prefer to stay in their own living space for as long as possible and the fact that fewer children are available to take care of older people. The development of social services at the community level is therefore a key component of the plan. To be able to make sense of welfare delivery at the local level, one must pay attention to the recent reforms of local government structure (Derleth and Koldyk 2002; Kojima and Kokubun 2002; Bray 2005, 2006; Wong and Poon 2005). Urban communities (*shequ*) were set up from the late 1990s onwards to address social problems which emerged in the aftermath of the restructuring of collective- and state-owned enterprises. These 'communities' do not refer to local collectivities that have grown over time, nor are they voluntary associations or communities of interest (Wong and Poon 2005: 413). Instead, they were formed by merging former 'residents' committees' (*jumin weiyuanhui*). In theory they are independent of the government but in practice they usually constitute the lowest administrative level and are often used to implement policy. There has been pressure on the communities to take care of people who were marginalized in the process of reform, such as retired workers who no longer have any links with their enterprises (Wong and Poon 2005: 414).

In order to improve the local infrastructure and thus facilitate the delivery of social services to older people at the community level, the three-year Starlight (*Xingguang*) Project was launched by the Ministry of Civil Affairs in 2001. The overall investment of this scheme totalled 13.4 billion yuan, the largest amount spent on older people since 1949. The funds came from various sources, notably the Ministry of Civil Affairs, provincial departments of civil affairs, and, crucially, social welfare lotteries (*China Daily*, 6 November 2003; *China Daily*, 18 January 2006; White Paper 2006).

Policy implementation at the local level: urban modernity and its discontent in 'China's Manhattan'

Jianwai is now viewed as a 'business district (*shangwu qu*)' but this has not always been the case. Until well into the 1990s, factories were the main

Older people and the (un)caring state 175

employers there. In the last decade, most of them were either shut down because they were not competitive in the new economic climate or were moved into suburban areas. The land they occupied has been made available for the development of high-end commercial and residential properties.

The local government's 2005 brochure, entitled 'Harmonious Jianwai', describes the area in the following way:

> The area is riddled with three contradictions: Both sides of the main roads are lined with high-end buildings, office high-rises, trade towers, hiding behind them the old residential areas and one-story buildings waiting to be torn down. Newly established private companies co-exist with old state-owned enterprises that face problems. The white-collar, high-income employees co-exist with laid-off and unemployed people. These contradictions create an increasingly complex situation in this area.
>
> (Jianwai Street Office 2005).

What the local officials refer to as a 'complex situation' means in practice that the area is undergoing profound structural changes – not only with regard to its architecture but also in relation to the local residents (approximately 50,000 people, roughly 20 per cent of whom are aged 60 or over).

Plans for demolition had been hanging over the head of all communities in Jianwai like the Sword of Damocles ever since the State Council approved plans for the development of a Central Business District (CBD) in Beijing in 1993. Jianwai, it was decided, was to be at the core of the CBD (Chaoyang District Government n.d.). The partial demolition and rebuilding of the area to suit the (perceived) needs of local and international business elites was the logical result of this plan. The desire to complete many high-profile building projects before the Olympic Games lent the restructuring plans an added sense of urgency.

The impact of these plans could be felt in all of the (then) six communities in Jianwai. The community in which I lived was no exception. It had been set up in 2000 as a result of the community reform by merging nine residents' committees, five based on (former) work units (a newspaper, a ministry, two factories and a department store) and four geographic ones. The types of housing present in the community ranged from well-maintained gated five-story apartment complexes with a little garden in front (ministry), several blocks of flats, partly gated, in a good state (newspaper), run-down blocks of apartments, four to ten storeys (factories and department store) and a few newly erected blocks of flats. The residents were as diverse as the housing they lived in, ranging from highly successful entrepreneurs and top civil servants to unemployed and poor people and many retirees. In 2004 4,200 people had their permanent residence registered in the community; approximately 30 per cent of them were aged 60 or over.

In addition to the wide range of housing, and a number of commercial and office buildings, the community also boasted a few kiosks, a supermarket

176   *Anna Boermel*

and several shops and stalls, all at ground level, an inexpensive daily farmers' market, more than a dozen snack shops and restaurants, several schools and kindergartens, a number of open spaces for socializing, a well-maintained park about ten minutes on foot away and excellent public transport links (several bus lines and an underground stop). Basic healthcare was available locally[5] and the district hospital only a ten-minute bus ride away. The area was what Charlotte Ikels (2004: 341) calls 'elder-friendly', i.e. close to parks, clinics and hospitals, and in its 'physical aspects ... minimiz[ing] the impacts of impairments and maximiz[ing] the capacity for independent living. Even if one can scarcely see or walk, it is still possible in most cases to procure one's daily necessities, slowly perhaps, but nevertheless unaided as one need not negotiate heavy traffic'. I often saw an older woman, probably in her late seventies, who suffered from a spinal deformity that forced her to walk bent over, do her daily shopping at the farmers' market and the nearby stalls; she walked very slowly but managed to take care of herself. While the vast majority of the older people I knew in the community were not suffering from such debilitating conditions, they also valued the easy access to shops and public transport. Many of the older residents had first moved to the area when the work units they had joined as young adults had allocated housing to them.

At the beginning of my fieldwork in 2003, the local residents I talked to were only aware of the overall plans for the development of the CBD but did not know if and how they would be personally affected by the demolition plans. Very little information was made available to them. This led to endless rumours and a mixture of denial, anxiety, frustration, desperation and anger.

After a delay of a number of months caused by the outbreak of SARS in the spring, the demolition threat became more real and tangible in the summer of 2003. First, the local supermarket shut down and was subsequently demolished, then a number of restaurants closed, the community office was moved to another (temporary) site and rumours began to circulate that the dreaded demolition notices would be put up on the buildings soon.

It was an extremely tense time for the local residents, many of whom faced real hardship in finding a new place to live because of the extremely high cost of accommodation in Beijing, their inability to secure a loan for a new house due to their low incomes or age, their desire not to move too far away from amenities and the lack of any official support in finding a new place of residence. Unsurprisingly, the threat of demolition was the main topic of conversation in the community. Early on in my fieldwork, many of the older residents I spoke to brushed the topic aside and tried to reassure themselves and everyone within earshot that they would not be affected, that somehow the threat would vanish. When I left the community in September 2004, there was a strong sense of foreboding. By the time I returned in July 2005, many of the people I had known before had moved away, even some of those who had refused (publicly) to consider this possibility a year earlier. When I attended activities in the community, fewer people were present. Many of those who were still around belonged to the poorest group, who could not afford to make a down payment on another flat without first getting compensation from the developers.

While many residents were becoming increasingly anxious about the future of the buildings they lived in, the community officials moved into their new office, located in a state-of-the-art residential complex that had been built a stone's throw away from their old office. The contrast was astounding. The old office had been housed in a temporary building, essentially one large room with rows of desks, right next to a few particularly shabby houses, only 50 metres away from the space used by older people for their morning exercises. The spatial proximity to residents translated into frequent contact between them and community officials. Local residents would drop into the community office without appointments when they needed help with an issue. In stark contrast, the new office was located on the second floor of a brand-new luxurious apartment complex, complete with a newly paved road, sculpted garden and security guards, which now towers over the entire neighbourhood and houses the newly rich and wealthy foreigners. It was hard to imagine that older people would approach community officials in the same way they had done before. The location of the new office suggested that the local state had benefited from the re-structuring of the community and had in the process reconceived its target group.

'Old age work' at the grassroots: self-reliance or care?

Which social services were on offer to older residents then? From around 2003 onwards, in line with central and city policies, more attention was paid to issues related to old age in Jianwai. Local officials, both at the street office and community level, reported that they had been instructed to improve the quality of services for older people. The development and delivery of services, however, was not entrusted to professionals. Instead the responsibility for enhancing services was firmly placed on the community – with minimal financial support and limited training opportunities. Funding, as I will show below, was only available for occasional activities. The street office organized a compulsory training session for all community officials in 2004 which I attended. A professor with expertise in social policy and aging issues gave a lecture that provided an overview of recent demographic changes. Afterwards all participants had to complete a written exercise which was reviewed by the officials based at the street office. Further training opportunities were very rare but community officials would be told about the services offered by their colleagues in other Jianwai communities in regular meetings at the street office. In the absence of in-depth training and sufficient funding, the quality of services in the local community depended to a large extent on the resourcefulness of individual officials working at the community level.

At the insistence of the street office old-age associations were set up in all of the six communities. In the spring of 2004 I attended the lacklustre event at

178 *Anna Boermel*

which the old-age association in the community I lived in was established. It was a decidedly top-down affair. Community and street office officials gave short speeches, a few older volunteers who had been handpicked by local officials were voted into the association's committee, the rules were read out and a photo was taken. Both the officials and the residents appeared to have only a perfunctory interest in the association. I heard later that there had been a few more meetings, but the association definitely did not become an active force of change in the community.

When, in late 2003, I asked the heads (*shequ zhuren*)[6] of the two Jianwai communities I focused my research on about old-age work in the communities they were responsible for, they told me the following:

COMMUNITY LEADER 1: The government now pays more attention to old-age work; population ageing is intensifying. We are setting up old-age associations.
AB: What is the role of the community (*shequ*) in providing services to older people?
COMMUNITY LEADER 2: To provide a location (*tigong changsuo*) and a little bit of other help.
COMMUNITY LEADER 1: If old people have a project which they would like to pursue, they can apply (*baoming*), then we check the project and if it's approved, we can offer them a place.
COMMUNITY LEADER 2: Old people sort out things by themselves (*ziji anpai*). They do things on their own.

This hands-off approach to old-age work was demonstrated to me in February 2004 on my first official research visit to the second Jianwai community I studied. The Jianwai propaganda official who had organized this event in collaboration with officials working for the community had not asked me whom I wanted to meet nor had he explained to me what was going to happen in the course of the afternoon. Based on my reading of the official publications, which suggested that urban communities had received funds to improve their facilities for older people through the Starlight Project, I expected that I would be shown around the new facilities. As it turned out, no facilities were on the local officials' list of 'must see' things. They first took the Jianwai official, the photographer[7] and me to the home of an older couple who shared a very modest one-bedroom flat with their daughter and grandson. On the way to their flat, the gregarious female officials pointed to a number of wooden sculptures in the courtyard. The older person we were about to meet, they explained to me, was a gifted sculptor. His intricate sculptures all depicted scenes of hardship from pre-revolutionary China, often accompanied by poems reinforcing the message that life had much improved after the founding of the People's Republic of China.

After having visited his apartment, the community officials took us to an unheated community office in a simple one-storey building where they introduced us to a woman in her early seventies. It appeared that she had been selected because she was good at handicraft; her speciality was small crocheted depictions of animals which she put into colourful frames. Next on the programme was a woman in her late sixties who, in my presence, cut the hair of a woman in her eighties. Her voluntary work, in the spirit of Lei Feng, was highly praised by the community officials; they were clearly very proud of her and all the other active older people to whom they had introduced me. In the early evening they took us to a newly designed public space by the roadside which, we were told, was often used by local residents, most of them past retirement age, for disco-dance practice. The all-female group of residents, most of them wearing identical dark-pink tracksuits, clearly enjoyed the rigorous exercise and were, it seemed, oblivious to the sub-zero temperatures and the heavy rush-hour traffic rushing past a few metres away. The contribution of the community officials to this activity consisted of providing moveable loudspeakers.

When the photographer and I returned to the community the following morning, the older residents' exercise group, about two dozen people in total, most of whom were women, performed several exercise routines to a very high standard. They were allowed to use the public space just outside the (gated) community area only very early in the morning; from about 8.30 a.m. onwards it was reserved for the cars of the employees of the blue-chip companies resident in the high-rise block towering over this public space. On Sundays, a Chinese opera troupe run by older people was allowed to use one of the community's offices for music practice.

In the community in which I lived the same facilitating and supervisory approach to old-age work resulted in officials asking older residents they knew well if they were interested in running activities on a voluntary basis. These 'teachers' were given permission to hold their classes either in the open, in public spaces such as the pavement or a little enclosed space in the middle of the community, or in run-down rooms that did not have access to sanitary facilities. These rooms were usually locked and on several occasions the local officials who had the keys were not around to open the rooms on time.

Between March and October 2004 I participated in most of the classes. A knitting class offered by a retired woman in her late 50s was attended by between three and seven women, aged between 45 and 75. The atmosphere was very welcoming, friendly and supportive. While exchanging knitting tips and producing bags and slippers, the women also discussed their worries and fears about the impending demolition process. Another handicraft group, run by a female volunteer in her mid-60s, focused on making collages. I went along to the meeting once, only the teacher and one retired woman were present; the group ceased to meet soon after. *Taijiquan* and *taijishan* exercise sessions, taught in rotation by a female and male teacher most mornings on the pavement outside one of the apartment blocks, attracted between five and 20 women, ranging in age between their mid-40s to late 70s. Many of the participants worked very hard to master the exercises; some practised between meetings and were able to perform difficult routines.

180   *Anna Boermel*

Occasionally the community official in charge of cultural matters, herself retired, ran choir and music sessions; between three and 20 people, mostly women, showed up to these classes. One activity that local officials organized was a Chinese painting class, which was taught by an experienced and very well-respected female teacher who lived locally. The first two sessions in the late summer of 2004 that I attended attracted a crowd of about 15 highly motivated women. They were very grateful for this additional activity. This was the only class that incurred a very small charge (a few yuan per session). There had been some debate about charging participants for this activity; the officials were uncomfortable with fees as they strongly believed that all activities should be free of charge. They argued that exceptionally a small charge was necessary as the teacher only had limited time on her hands due to (paid) teaching obligations elsewhere.

All of these activities attracted no more than 40 people, mostly women. Those who took part seemed thoroughly to enjoy the classes and the sociability they engendered; several of the women told me enthusiastically that the activities on offer gave them an opportunity to socialize with other residents, who they had not known before, and to learn something new. With the exception of the wife of a retired high-ranking official at the ministry, who attended every meeting of the knitting class, all of the other participants were of lower socio-economic status and ranged in age from their mid-40s to early 70s.

This separation, which resulted from the boundaries of socio-political status, was not surprising to local officials; after all, the ministry ran a completely separate activity programme for its retirees. On my only visit to the building, which housed the ministry's old-age cadre centre, the facilities looked far superior to those available to ordinary older residents in the community. The ministry employed one full-time staff member, a man in his 40s, to run the centre. While the building was almost empty at the time of my visit, the blackboard listed numerous events. On leaving the centre, one of the community officials, the wife of a retired employee of the ministry, who had accompanied me to support my (unsuccessful) request to do research at the centre, remarked pointedly: 'The policies are biased (*zhengce qingke*), some people get a better deal.' Apart from having access to superior facilities and being able to take classes that were of a higher standard, the activities on offer were also different. The community official told me that in addition to classes held at the centre, guided trips to popular tourist destinations were organized for the ministry's retirees. The cash-starved local community was unable to offer such opportunities to the retired workers it was responsible for.

The only activity that attracted substantial interest among a wider range of older people was the monthly health lectures that the community officials organized in 2003 and 2004. Between 15 and 60 people attended each lecture; a sizeable number of them came from the ministry's blocks of flats. The speakers for these lectures were recruited from local hospitals and health-care centres and talked about medical issues pertinent to older people from both biomedical and traditional medical perspectives. They lectured on topics such

Older people and the (un)caring state   181

as high blood pressure, coronary heart disease, old-age diabetes and a healthy lifestyle in old age. Community officials paid the speakers between 100 and 200 yuan per talk but did not charge residents for attending.

Generally speaking, interest in the community activities was very low; no more than one hundred older residents ever took part in any of the activities on offer. A clear gender bias was noticeable – the vast majority of the participants were women. This issue was raised repeatedly by the community officials (also predominantly female) who encouraged the women to bring their husbands and male neighbours along – without much success. Older men were clearly not averse to socializing in the community; I often saw small groups of them playing cards or other games.

Why did so few residents take part in the community's activities? It is, of course, beyond doubt that many older people, in urban China as elsewhere in the world, have no desire to engage in any group activity whatsoever. While this was acknowledged by community officials and residents alike, when I asked them to explain the prevailing lack of interest, they also pointed to a number of other factors, all specific to the situation of the community.

The party secretary of the community blamed the redevelopment of the neighbourhood for the low degree of interest. Many older people, she noted, were preoccupied with more pressing issues such as finding a new place to live, had already left the community or were about to move away. When I asked two other community officials why so few residents took part in the activities, their initial responses attributed this outcome to factors that were beyond their control, notably education and socialization. 'They have a low educational level. Especially the people who are over 70, many of them have only finished primary school, they "don't move". Many of them grew up in the "feudal society", they don't come out. They just enjoy playing mah-jong.' Time, they argued, was another factor. 'The old people don't have time; many of them take care of their grandchildren.' In a more relaxed atmosphere, away from their offices, they pointed to other factors: infrastructural and budgetary constraints and the heavy workload imposed on them by the street office. The places available for exercise, in particular the pavement in front of one row of houses, one said, was unsuitable for older people's physical exercise; it was too narrow, the neighbours had complained about the sound of the loudspeaker used and everyone could observe those who were exercising. The limited funding available for older people's activities, the other community official complained, did not allow them to organize events popular with local residents, such as a sports competition (*yundonghui*), which they had once organized free of charge but could not repeat due to the cost.

The older people I spoke to gave rather different explanations for their non-participation. Most claimed to have been unaware of the events due to lack of publicity. It was indeed very difficult to find out about when and where the activities would take place. Some events would be advertised on handwritten notices, which were pasted on one of the local notice boards, usually at very short notice. Details about the group meetings were passed on orally between

182   Anna Boermel

participants or, on request, by local officials. One grown-up daughter brought her widowed mother along to one knitting group meeting after having been told about the existence of this group by officials in the community office where she had gone to ask which services were available. Some residents became aware of the activities because they walked past the spaces in which they were held. This applied primarily to the *taijiquan* and *taijishan* activities and, to a lesser extent, the knitting group.

In addition to not knowing about community events, several of the older residents I talked to told me that they found the activities on offer uninteresting.[8] Some of them preferred to meet new people outside their neighbourhood, for instance by going to the splendid park nearby which, especially in the morning, was always heaving with older people who were exercising, socializing or just enjoying a walk.

Over the entire course of my fieldwork between 2003 and 2005 the local community leaders were not able to solve the problem of low interest in activities, which appeared to be – at least in part – the result of not consulting residents. Very little effort, it seemed to me, was made to find out what older residents required, let alone to design and deliver services according to their needs and interests. When I raised this issue with officials working at the street office, they offered two explanations. In response to my questions as to why no sustained efforts had been made to find out what older people expected of the community, and what kind of services or activities they would like to be on offer, one of them gave this candid answer: 'If we ask them, they will tell us what they want. But since we can't afford to offer them what they want, what's the point of asking?' Two other officials working at the street office acknowledged the problem but stressed that older people could no longer be forced to do things. If they chose not to attend, they insisted, there was nothing the local government could do about it. By ascribing older people's non-participation in activities to their lack of education, time and comprehension and by arguing that older people could not be forced to take part, local officials absolved themselves from the responsibility to provide attractive services to residents.

This lack of mutual interest and comprehension became particularly obvious in mid-August 2004 when the Jianwai street office circulated a notice to all retirees in the area. The notice informed them that 'the social insurance section of the Jianwai street office and the labour insurance work stations to the community' would take over responsibility for retired residents whose previous point of contact for social services had been the enterprise they had worked for. In order to enable the social insurance section to do its work well, and in compliance with a requirement from Beijing City and Chaoyang District, the notice also stated that all residents who had retired from work in an enterprise (*qiye tuixiu renyuan*) were to attend a registration event. The reason given for this week-long registration exercise was to collect quantitative data about every individual with the purpose of producing a computer file, and to issue a 'Beijing City, enterprise retiree, socialization management service

Older people and the (un)caring state 183

contact card'. The laminated card, similar in size to a credit card, listed contact numbers on the front and services available to card holders and another dedicated phone number on the back. These services included, amongst others, providing information about social insurance policies, organizing cultural and physical activities for retirees, delivering pension payments to the homes of older people in need and providing medical advice. As if in anticipation of a limited reaction to this announcement, the notice concluded by saying that 'this work is closely linked to individual benefits', and, in bold print, requested retirees to spread the word and take this exercise seriously.

Halfway through the registration process in late August 2004, I spent an afternoon observing the exercise in the community I lived in. It quickly became clear that only a small proportion of the older people who had been expected had registered by this point. Over the course of the afternoon only a few more people arrived, passed on the information required of them (including details about their health) and were given a card. The middle-aged official in charge of this exercise emphasized that the sole aim of the data collection was to make access to social services easier for retired people. When she explained to me why so few older people had acted on the notice, her tone of voice betrayed a mix of frustration with and sympathy for older people:

> Older people do not want to register because they do not understand the logic (*daoli*) of doing it. For 30 to 50 years, they dealt with their work unit; it always paid their salaries and was very reliable. In the CBD [Central Business District] many of the factories have been closed and many buildings and houses have been demolished. Now all of this, apart from the payment of their pensions, is handled by the street office which they don't trust. It's basically a question of how educated they are; there are definitely differences between them in their ability to understand all of this. Our data is out of date; we only have access to the old work unit files. The people don't understand that it's better for the community to have their information up-to-date, including their phone number. In the past we knew where everyone lived but now a lot of people have already moved away, to the East and the West, in all directions. Many people disagree with the demolition. Some want to escape from official attention; they only transfer their residence status (*hukou*) at the local police station but do not reveal where exactly they live.

What emerges from her account is the intensity of the distance between older residents and the local state which appeared to be, at least in part, a result of the break-down of the earlier implicit social contract between the collective (work unit) and (older) people, which had been premised on the exchange of loyalty and hard work for care. In urban China until the late 1990s, the most important reference point was not an abstract 'social state' but the work unit. The transfer of care from work unit to local state, a purely technical matter in

184 *Anna Boermel*

the eyes of the official quoted above, was clearly not a smooth process for older people. Given that the local state in Jianwai did not deliver substantial social services, but even threatened the livelihood of older residents by demolishing their homes, their reluctance to submit themselves to the state's data-collecting processes is easy to understand.

In the absence of substantial social services on offer, other than maybe the improved health-care station, whom did older residents rely on for support (if they needed any)?[9] As a result of the government's (re)definition of its role in the provision of old age care, the ultimate responsibility for the care of older people in Jianwai, and indeed in all other areas in Beijing, lay with older people and their families. The Beijing government welcomed, and indeed supported, the development of a market for such services in Beijing but the vast majority of older residents I met in the course of my research did not (yet) need to, would not or could not afford to use any commercial services. In the community where I lived, I knew two families who in 2004–5 employed live-in maids from the countryside. A few others occasionally paid migrant women (by the hour) to help them cook and clean their apartments. While tight budgets would have made it difficult for many older people to afford any services, they were also not widely advertised. Many of the children of older people living alone or with a partner would help if necessary but many were not able to do so on a daily basis. In this context, self-reliance and mutual support played the most important role.

Elsewhere (Boermel 2008) I have shown that older people's self-organized collective activities have rapidly increased in Beijing, particularly in the last decade, which has seen the greatest upheaval in welfare-service provision for non-privileged older people since the onset of the reform era. These activities comprise, for example, exercise, singing and music performances in Beijing's large parks, folk-dance performances (*niu yangge*) at street corners after sunset and early morning trips across Beijing to climb the Fragrant Mountains. Older people reported that they mainly participated in such activities to improve their physical and mental well-being. Taking part, I was repeatedly told by men and women, helped them improve their immunity to illnesses, thus decreasing health-care spending, and made them feel at ease because they were surrounded by people who had had similar experiences in life.

'Protecting people's livelihood': substantial change or variation on a theme?

When I returned to Beijing in the autumn of 2008, the physical changes in the community I had previously lived in were not as radical as the local residents and officials had predicted when I left the community at the end of 2005. Several older commercial buildings and a number of small stalls and shops had given way to shiny new office towers and glittering commercial spaces. A few more apartment blocks, belonging to a newspaper and a factory, had been torn down. All of the ministry's apartment blocks were still intact. Some of the most run-down houses had been painted on the outside, apparently just before the Olympics, the farmers' market had become bigger and some new inexpensive restaurants had been set up. The small gardens outside the apartments were no longer taken care of, there were fewer groups of residents having a chat at street corners and fewer older people could be seen moving about the neighbourhood.

When I interviewed community officials[10] in November 2008, they ascribed the slowing down of the re-structuring process to the high cost now incurred to move people against their will. The compensation payments per square metre, between 8,000 to 12,000 yuan in 2004–5, had skyrocketed to 12,000–25,000 yuan, making it difficult for developers to raise funds, especially in view of falling prices for real estate. They did, however, believe that the area was still in limbo and that the CBD restructuring progress had always been predicted to take about 20 years and thus would not be complete until 2013. They pointed out that the façade of decelerated physical change covered up the fact that many local residents who could afford to, usually reluctantly, had bought new apartments elsewhere while renting out their flats to businesspeople and traders. This applied, in particular, to the ministry's apartment blocks, the best of all the old buildings in the community.[11] This trend had first become visible in 2005 but had intensified in the intervening years, a clear sign that many (older) residents no longer expected to have a future in the community. Even though they had moved, many had failed to change their registration to their new community, thus depriving community officials of up-to-date data about the residential structure. Instead of intensifying their data-collection efforts, they were nonchalant about the residents' refusal to comply and blamed their non-cooperation on the fact that they continued to feel a strong sense of belonging to the community. The officials also pointed out that the ministry had finally decided to build a new compound for all its employees living in the Jianwai apartments elsewhere in Beijing. In 2003–5 this solution had been ruled and been met with protest and disappointment by numerous retired civil servants who felt that the ministry should not expose them to these vicissitudes but instead act as their guardian.

Given these profound changes, and the less than bright outlook for the majority of the community's long-term (older) residents, I was surprised to learn that old-age work had been improved since 2005: questionnaires had been sent out to residents to find out which services older residents or their families would welcome; the Jianwai street office had built a state-of-the-art activity and regeneration centre for older people in the community; and an official had been appointed to oversee the community's old-age work.

Communication between community officials and older residents (or their families) appeared to have improved somewhat; a questionnaire, which in 2007 had been distributed in the community to find out from local residents which services for older people they required, had been filled in and returned by hundreds of households. According to the enthusiastic community official in charge of old-age work, many families expressed concerns about older people not being able to cook for themselves and urged the community to find a solution to this problem. Other complaints focused on the difficulty of buying things locally, the fact that only very few places were available for entertainment and that seeing a good doctor locally was difficult. The community leadership took the complaints seriously. The party secretary succeeded in negotiating a contract with a local restaurant to provide a buffet lunch for older residents. She persuaded them to offer lighter and softer food popular with older people. For 8 yuan (12 yuan for non-retirees) they could choose from eight dishes, two cold, six hot, rice or noodles, and soup. The canteen was located on the second floor of a new commercial building, in a light rectangular room with about twenty tables. When I had lunch there in December 2008, the food was freshly cooked and of similar quality to that offered in mid-range restaurants in Beijing; the well-dressed young waiters and waitresses were polite and friendly. Only roughly a fifth of the guests, mostly single men, were of retirement age; the majority were young white-collar workers. The community official explained to me that in winter many older people did not feel comfortable leaving their houses. To make the business viable for the restaurant during this time, she said, the community leadership had decided to allow younger people to eat there too, at least for the time being. She also suggested that there had been complaints that the canteen was on the second floor in a building without a lift, which prevented a number of older people (arguably the most needy) from eating there. The community leadership had tried very hard to find alternative premises, she recounted, but due to the extremely high rents charged in the CBD, it had proved impossible to find an affordable and suitable space at ground level.

Had it not been for the fact that the building housing the 'Industry and Commerce Office' (*gongshangsuo*) under the control of the Jianwai street office had become vacant following the re-location of that government outfit to a brand new office building in another community, the exorbitant cost of real estate in the area would have prevented the new activity and regeneration centre for old people from being built. The centre represents a quantum leap in social service provision at the community level. A street office operation, it opened in August 2008 and was the first of its kind in the whole of Chaoyang. The extensive and thus very costly redevelopment of the building was co-financed by the Jianwai street office, Chaoyang district and by donations from local enterprises. The aim of the centre is to provide cultural activities and opportunities for regeneration after a period of illness, and day-care for older people who can no longer stay at home on their own.

The light and spacious building was designed with older people's needs in mind. The manager of the community told me that street office officials had decided to set up such a centre after having toured social welfare facilities in Shanghai in early 2008. At the core of the ground-level building is a multi-function room, with rooms designed for the use of smaller groups of people leading off it. Adjacent to this large open space is the day-care area consisting of several rooms with two beds each, a regeneration area with exercise equipment, a bathroom and toilet adapted for the use of disabled people, a kitchen, dining area and office space. While activities were free, the cost of day-care was 300 yuan per month and food was charged at 10 yuan a day. The manager is a highly motivated street office employee who has extensive experience in enterprise management and is a keen sportswoman with good contacts to local exercise groups. In addition, a cook and a few 'volunteers' worked at the centre, none of whom had received any training in old-age care or physiotherapy. Even though the centre was supposed to provide services to all older Jianwai residents, it was primarily used by a small group of women and, to a lesser extent men, who are aged 55 and over and lived in the surrounding community. The fact that it is at the ground level makes it a better venue for activities than the activity space the community has access to in the basement of the luxurious apartment complex. Older people from other communities, I was told, rarely attended as they find travelling back and forth too cumbersome. The activities on offer were similar to those that were offered by the community in 2004–5: knitting, handicraft and painting. The teachers were still not paid for their work. The centre manager was in favour of paying them and expressed her willingness to widen the scope of activities to attract more users, including retirees from the ministry, two of whom were attending the centre's day-care when I visited.

In late 2008 I learned that non-privileged pensioners had also benefited from the improved services. Ms Hu, a retired worker in her late 60s, who had been living in one of the apartments built in the community by her factory for several decades, was particularly enthusiastic about these changes. I had first met (and become close to) her in 2004 when she acted as one of the *taijiquan* teachers and regularly participated in most community activities. Together with her husband, son, daughter-in-law and granddaughter she has been living in a run-down apartment consisting of two small rooms, a very simple kitchen and bathroom. Her husband, who in 2004 had spent his days alternately listening to the radio at home and meeting friends in the nearby park, had subsequently fallen ill and spent a long time in hospital. On his release he needed a lot of care and attention which Ms Hu, who also shouldered the responsibility for the after-school care of her granddaughter and for cooking dinner for the entire family, was unable to provide. She applied for and was given a place for her husband at the day-care centre. He had lunch there and was able to do some simple exercise under the watchful eyes of the centre staff. When I visited the centre on two separate occasions in November 2008, he sat forlorn on the bed in one of the sparsely furnished small rooms leading off the care area. Ms Hu regularly ate at the canteen, sometimes with her granddaughter, and occasionally bought fresh dumplings there that she served her family for dinner. I saw her three times in the autumn of 2008; every time she emphasized how grateful she was for the improvement of social services in the community. She still felt threatened by the relocation, especially given the recent improvements in service provision.

188   *Anna Boermel*

The street office and community officials I interviewed were proud of having been able to improve social services for older people. They linked their work to the central government's new discourse on 'people's livelihood' (*minsheng*). This term had not been part of the vocabulary of local officials in Beijing between 2003 and 2005; it only appears to have entered official discourse after Hu Jintao's speech at the 17th Party Congress in 2007. Hu had stressed that social development was entwined with people's well-being and that social security was an important guarantee of social stability (Hu 2007).[12] Several community officials suggested that the new Beijing card for retirees was a clear example of the strengthened emphasis on improving the lives of older people. Since 1 January 2009 it gives permanent Beijing residents over the age of 65 free use of buses and free entry to parks. By the end of November 2008 between 700 and 800 of the 1000 or so older residents who were (still) registered in the community had applied for the card, which suggests that older people are interested in using services that are tailored to their needs.

Given the significant improvement of services for some older people in the community and the dedication and resourcefulness of local officials that I had witnessed in 2008, I was surprised to learn on visits to the community in November – December 2009 and March – April 2010 that services had worsened since my last visit in late 2008. The canteen Ms Hu had regularly attended had been closed down and very few older people appeared to use the Centre – which had, as a large colourful sign outside indicated, re-adjusted its target group. No longer solely dedicated to older people, its new mission was now to provide a 'warm home' (*wenxin jiayuan*) for disabled people. The only notable group activity that was organized at the Centre during my four-week stay in 2009 was a get-together for disabled people to celebrate the UN International Day of Persons with Disabilities in early December. About 50 disabled Jianwai residents of all ages attended and most of them appeared to enjoy the lively games and competitions that the Centre manager and a community in charge of work for disabled people who was given her own office in the Centre had organized.

Over the course of long conversations with local officials, at the community and street office level, and with several older residents I learned that this re-designation was the outcome of new city-wide regulations that stipulated that disabled people were offered better services. In view of the fact that the street office had already invested a lot of money into building the Centre, which some officials felt was underused, the decision was made to re-focus the target group. As a result, the duties of the manager of the Centre were broadened and her salary is now no longer paid by the street office but by the China Disabled Persons' Federation. As a result most of the activities that she now organizes are aimed at handicapped people. Old-age work was, she mused, probably better done not by a centre run by the street office but by the communities as that is where older people live. When I visited again in the spring of 2010, the Centre was livelier than in the autumn, primarily because the volunteer-run community exercise groups for older women were busy practising their routines for their performances at the upcoming annual Jianwai Culture Festival.

Ms Hu, who had fully endorsed the Centre's services in 2008, complained bitterly about the change of direction. Like most of the other older people who had benefited from the Centre's affordable day-care service, her husband was no longer cared for at the Centre but now lived in a small, affordable nursing home on the outskirts of the city that she had reluctantly moved him to. While the Centre manager attributed this decline in service provision to the former users' failing health and, in two cases, their having left the area for good, Ms Hu was convinced that the problem was not the users but the local officials' reluctance to recruit new users. When the Centre terminated the service of picking up older people at their homes in the morning and taking them home in the evening, thus providing much needed relief to their families, interest in the service declined. In March 2010 the only older woman who was still attending the Centre on a daily basis was the mother of a son who lived around the corner from the Centre and was thus able to take her there before work and pick her up in the evening.

Ms Hu was also very unhappy about the closure of the canteen. It was also a source of regret for local officials, a few of whom attributed this failure to older residents. They had, an official complained, rarely attended. Some, they suggested, had paid for only one meal but secretly taken food home for their partners or families in spite of the low cost. Another official emphasized that an irreversible conflict was to blame for the failure of the canteen. While many older residents, on an average pension of about 2000 yuan, regarded eight yuan for a single meal as too expensive, the company that had been contracted to provide this service failed to make a profit. Like several of her colleagues she felt that the 'state can offer something but if local residents will make use of it is quite another matter'.

While local officials may in the past have accepted the status quo, these days new policy guidelines emphasizing the importance of old-age work and pressure from the street office to come up with new solutions means that officials in several communities were busy sorting out alternative arrangements for 'older people lunch tables' by negotiating contracts with successful local restaurants who were offered tax breaks in exchange for keeping prices for older people's lunches low. After our last meeting at her modest apartment Ms Hu walked me to the main road. On the way we passed the community's new 'older people's lunch table', a small room with a large round table, a stone's throw away from one of the best restaurants in the area that had been persuaded by the community officials to provide a lunch buffet for older residents at the cost of 10 yuan per meal. Ms Hu, who has resigned herself to having to leave the community as soon as the development company has raised the funds to compensate her and her neighbours, for one was very excited by the prospect of eating lunch there in the new future.

Conclusion

Empirical evidence from a very prosperous area in central Beijing with an above-average proportion of older residents challenges the suggestion that urban Chinese modernity marked by the creation of material wealth, and profound socio-economic and spatial changes, enhances well-being in old age. In Jianwai the relentless pursuit of this specific vision of modernity has led to unfettered economic development with negative consequences for older people. Zygmunt Bauman (2004: 30) has argued that 'modernity is a condition of compulsive, and addictive, designing. Where there is design, there is waste.' Waste, in Bauman's terms, does not refer to unwanted material but people. He (*ibid*: 5) opines that 'the production of ... wasted humans (the 'excessive' and 'redundant' ... those who ... were not allowed to stay) is an inevitable outcome of modernization, and an inescapable side-effect of *order-building* ... and of *economic progress*' (his emphasis). In Jianwai, the production of a new socio-economic order designed by the Chinese government to be attractive to international and Chinese investors has turned land into prime real estate affordable only to a small elite, and shoved people – perceived as being unproductive and undesirable – out of sight. Instead of benefiting long-term residents, the enormous wealth has been created at great social cost to them. Many of those who have been marginalized in the process of restructuring are close to or past the age of retirement and thus in a particularly vulnerable position as losing access to good healthcare facilities, public transport and social networks established over many years is much harder to deal with for older than for younger people.

As Murphy and Fong (2006: 3) remind us, 'marginality is always relative'. The support and care provided by the ministry was far superior to the services available to non-privileged older people at the community level. The ministry's retirees clearly had a greater sense of entitlement than ordinary pensioners whose primary reference point, the work unit, had ceased to exist. It was therefore more difficult for them to address their grievances. Frazier (2004: 97), confirming Hurst and O'Brien's (2002: 360) observation that 'pensions appear to be considered a truly sacred right in the eyes of both workers and the state', attributes protests by pensioners in Chinese cities to 'the fact that pension reform often threatens to undermine an implicit social contract between the state and a specific, usually loyal group of beneficiaries'. While retirees aired their pension grievances collectively in public, often vociferously, dissatisfaction with the delivery of social services at the community level in Jianwai was by some older residents expressed through lack of co-operation.

At any rate social services provided by the state play a very small part in the lives of the overwhelming majority of older people. Some of those who have been thrown back on their own resources to cope with these profound changes described in this chapter have creatively set up new support structures by organizing joint activities, thus defying stereotypes of passivity and dependency (Boermel 2008).

Shue and Wong (2007a: 11) have argued that social inequality and suffering in the reform era were not only caused by structural deficiencies but also by official discourses that have stressed competition and individual responsibility. If the recently changed discourse which now stresses the importance of 'people's livelihood' is combined with substantial measures to alleviate the suffering of those affected by rapid economic growth at the planning stage and not as an afterthought, and with better communication between providers and consumers of social services, more older people may, in time, happily gaze into the future.

Acknowledgements

The research process for this chapter was funded by grants from the Economic and Social Science Research Council, the Urban China Research Network, the Beijing office of the British Council, the British Federation of Women Graduates, the Chiang Ching-kuo Foundation, the Mellon Foundation, the Davis Fund (Institute for Chinese Studies, Oxford), the George Hogg Memorial Fund and the Pollard Fund (Wadham College, Oxford) and the Bagby Fund (Institute of Social and Cultural Anthropology, Oxford). Frank Pieke's guidance over many years has been invaluable. For thoughtful comments on drafts of this chapter I am grateful to the workshop participants, Jane Duckett, Beatriz Carrillo, Karen Fisher, Istvan Praet, Brigitte Steger, Barak Kushner and an anonymous reviewer. During my field research I had the privilege of being a visiting scholar at the Institute of Sociology at the Chinese Academy of Social Sciences. Li Hanlin and Xia Chuanling deserve special thanks for their backing of my fieldwork in Jianwai and for many inspiring conversations. I thank the Jianwai street office team for supporting my long-term research in the area; they have been exemplary hosts. The kind good humour, warmth and trust of the community officials and residents made working with them and living in their midst a very enjoyable experience.

Notes

1 The pursuit of this type of modernity is by no means limited to Jianwai. On the contrary, it has, to a greater or lesser extent, affected most Chinese cities. Based on her study of these profound spatial changes in the city of Kunming in southwestern China, Li Zhang (2006) convincingly argues that the combination of a sense of 'lateness' and a 'pro-growth' coalition between local governments and real-estate developers has shaped urban re-development.
2 In 2004 six communities (*shequ*) belonged to the Jianwai street office (*jiedao banshichu*). By 2008 two more had been created by splitting two of the original six communities into two.
3 Retirees were often outspoken in their critique of the government and would not shy away from taking to the streets to complain about their plight (Hurst and O'Brien 2002). Most of these protests appear to have taken place in the north-east which suffered major economic decline in the 1990s, leading to cash flow difficulties for the many large SOEs in the region.

192 *Anna Boermel*

4 Men are allowed to retire at 60, female cadres at 55 and female workers at 50. There is an ongoing debate in Chinese academic and policy-making circles about postponing the age of retirement which has stayed constant despite increased longevity. In practice non-voluntary early retirement is not uncommon.
5 The small health-care station was redecorated and enlarged in 2004, thus giving (older) residents the opportunity to access health-care locally.
6 In Jianwai most of the leading community (*shequ*) officials are middle-aged and have been working for the Jianwai administration only since the establishment of the communities, i.e. since about 2000. While many live quite close to their place of work, very few are long-term residents of the communities they work in and thus are not part of any local networks. The officials working at the street office tend to be younger and better qualified (many have university degrees) than those at the community level. They have also had to pass exams and are on the civil-servant career track which guarantees higher incomes and more job security than an appointment at the community level.
7 A photo-journalist of the Beijing Evening News (*Beijing Wanbao*), the daily newspaper with the highest circulation in Beijing, who happened to be in Jianwai on that day to cover a different story, decided to come along and subsequently published a one-page article about my research.
8 In their study of a community in Guangzhou, Wong and Poon (2005) similarly observed that activities were poorly advertised and for the most part poorly attended. Health talks, however, were popular.
9 Even though I visited five institutions offering residential care for older people which ranged from a very modest care home to brand-new, exclusive 'old age'-villages on the outskirts of the city, I will refrain from discussing the issue of institutional care here for the simple reason that Jianwai did not have a single care home at the time of my research and none of the older people whose acquaintance I made in Jianwai or elsewhere in Beijing had to confront this issue while I was conducting research.
10 By 2008 about half of the community officials I had known before had either been moved to other communities or retired from office. The new staff members were all under the age of 40 and better qualified (one even had a degree in social work).
11 Buying a new apartment elsewhere while renting out their apartments in the community was a strategy only a few of the better-off older residents who had resigned themselves to having to ultimately leave the area resorted to. In view of the then seemingly imminent demolition of their homes, they regarded this as the only way of productively dealing with the uncertainty of the situation, not as a profit-making strategy.
12 The Hu-Wen administration had first indicated this change of direction by emphasizing the importance of balanced, people-centred development at the 16th Party Congress in 2002 (Wong 2007: 13).

10 Support for the social participation of children and young people with disability in China

A Jiangxi county case study

Karen R. Fisher, Xiaoyuan Shang and Jiawen Xie

Children and young people with disability in provincial China struggle to share the same citizenship rights to social participation as other children in their communities. Social interaction can be a positive aspect of a child's quality of life and, more instrumentally, can affect their likely experiences in later adult life. However, little research has focused on the social experiences of children with disability in China or on which social institutions facilitate positive social experiences.

This research redresses this gap by analysing the experiences of children and young people with hearing and speech impairments in a poor Jiangxi county to examine the impact on three dimensions of social participation – communication, social relationships and interest representation. It analyses the effect of the mix of social institutions as conceptualized in an ecological approach. The social institutions that are relevant to the research are the family, school, informal community groups and government organizations.

A key children's right is to social participation in the child's social context. We analyse experience of that right using an ecological approach to social institutions likely to facilitate or hinder fulfilment of the rights. We apply that analysis to children with hearing and speech impairments because of the significance of the link between a lack of social support for other forms of communication and poor experiences of social participation. We chose a poor county because it is a rural community with few resources, representing an extreme social setting for the fulfilment of child disability rights. The ecological model of childhood enables us to analyse which social institutions support their social participation in this local context; to what degree does that rely on the agency of the child and their family; and what are the implications for social policy change in provincial China? It finds that exciting local connections between institutions are emerging as families, informal groups and young people themselves take initiative to build social relations. It informs directions for social policy change to support these efforts to improve the fulfilment of the rights of children and young people with disability.

194   *Karen R. Fisher, Xiaoyuan Shang and Jiawen Xie*

Government systems to support children with disability and their families are only available in the most developed areas in China. Many less developed areas in China cannot afford such provisions (Chen and Chen 2008). How does this situation in less developed areas affect children's rights to social participation? Research about the effects of informal and formal social institutions on the social participation of children with disability in China is very limited. The purpose of the study is to understand the experiences of these children with disability in the local context of their families and community to inform social policy change and support their rights as citizens of China.

The chapter is structured as follows. In the next section, we introduce the policy context of social support in China, the theoretical framework for examining the rights of children with disability and the local Jiangxi county context. After explaining the methodology, we present the findings about the child and family circumstances, and social participation in the three dimensions of communication, social relationships and interest representation. We discuss the implications of these findings for the local social welfare mix in terms of the relevant social institutions: the family, school, community groups and government organizations in the conclusion of the chapter.

Chinese policy context, research framework and fieldwork site

According to the Second China National Sample Survey on Disability (SCNSSD), China has over five million children with disability under 16 years of age (CDPF 2007). They are over-represented in measures of vulnerability and disadvantage (Johnson *et al.* 1998; OSCNSSD and IPS 2008). The current child disability support system in China was developed before China's transition to a market economy, and remains based on the premise that the primary source of protection for children with disability is the family (Shang 2002; Shang *et al.* 2005; CDPF 2008a). But rapid social, economic and demographic changes are having significant impacts on all aspects of childhood, including the values and material circumstances of children, and on the informal system of social support for children. This has severely reduced the capacity of family and kinship networks to support children with disability, who are most affected by these changes (Johnson *et al.* 1998; Shang and Wu 2003; Shang 2008). Moreover, China does not have a western-style social welfare system – free public health care did not extend to children in rural areas when the investigation was conducted and local schools do not receive enough resources for additional support needs (Mcloughlin *et al.* 2005; Chen and Chen 2008). Poor local resources accentuate this deprivation in the social welfare mix.

The research framework for this article is based on the UN human rights model of child rights (Funder 1996; Quinn and Degener 2002; UNICEF 2005; UNCRC 2005; UNCRPD 2007). This model upholds the principle that children with disability 'should enjoy a full and decent life, in conditions which ensure dignity, promote self-reliance and facilitate the child's active

Support for children and young people with disability 195

participation in the community' (UNCRC 2006b). In a rights framework, meeting the support needs of children with disability is required to fulfil their rights as children (UNCRPD 2007). Nationally, China adopts a rights framework in children's and disability law (CDPF 2008a). It is a signatory to the UN Convention on the Rights of the Child and the more recent UN Convention on the Rights of Persons with Disabilities 2007.

The China Disabled Persons Federation (CDPF) is the national government body responsible for disability policy.[1] If the person with disability does not have family members, income and housing, the Ministry of Civil Affairs is also responsible. Provincial, county and local DPF and Civil Affairs departments are responsible for local administration of disability policy and local governments fund provision, which therefore varies across China according to the local resources, capacity and priorities.[2] The primary disability policy is the Law of the People's Republic of China on the Protection of Disabled Persons 2008, which amended the 1990 policy. It is a general goal statement of government commitment to disability rights and government responsibilities.

Preliminary research on child disability in China indicates that as in other countries, there are gaps between government commitment and children's experiences of policies. Children consequently do not receive sufficient support to fulfil their rights (Shang 2001). In 2005 and 2006, the United Nations Committee on the Rights of the Child formally raised concerns about child rights in China, the vulnerability of children with disability and the limited information available about these issues (UNCRC 2006a, 2006b). In light of increased international and Chinese concerns about child disability policy (Miles 2000; Ali *et al.* 2001; Kohrman 2005), it is timely to investigate experiences of formal and informal social support for fulfilling children's disability rights, especially at a local level.

A key aspect of children's rights is social participation in the social contexts in which they live – family, schools, neighbourhood and community. It is particularly relevant to children with disability who are at risk of exclusionary practices that prevent their equal participation. In many respects, social participation can reflect the cumulative experiences of other core rights to care and protection, economic security and development (Dean 2007). In the context of childhood, analysis of the right to social participation should include attention to age-specific experiences of social networks and activities within the family, neighbourhood and community with peers and adults, including communication, social relationships and interest representation. Child disability can also affect the social participation of other family members.

In this study, we focus on the mix of social institutions that might affect child social participation and the changes as the children age. While we examine the rights of children, we focus on children within the context of their families and other social institutions (Case 2000; Baker and Donelly 2001; Tudball *et al.* 2002; Banks 2003; Jenks 2005; Kelly 2005;). This follows the ecological approach to childhood, which recognizes the social context of development (Bronfenbrenner 1979; Dowling and Dolan 2001). We extend

196 *Karen R. Fisher, Xiaoyuan Shang and Jiawen Xie*

application of this approach to analysing experiences of rights and outcomes and how the social institutions in a child's life contribute to or negate experiences of the social participation. We adopt a recent application of the ecological model which identifies key social institutions as spheres of influence (Irwin *et al.* 2007). Most relevant to this research are the social institutions of family, school, community groups and government organizations. The model conceptualizes these informal and formal social institutions in the broader national and international context, described in this background section.

We focus on the experiences of children with hearing and speech impairments. Hearing and speech impairment can change how children and young people communicate with other people, a key dimension of social participation. Approximately 570,000 children in China have hearing and speech impairments (CDPF 2007). Unless people adapt the ways they communicate to these children's needs, the children can be excluded from the social opportunities expected for other children, such as school and play. In addition, because these children may communicate with each other in different ways, their social interaction attracts public attention.

The research location is County H (de-identified), in northeast Jiangxi Province, adjacent to Zhejiang, Fujian and Anhui Provinces. It is less than 250 km from the provincial capital Nanchang and less than 650 km from Shanghai. The county is small, 655 square kilometres in size; with six sub-townships, two townships and one subdistrict office. Its population is 212,300 – including 172,000 agricultural and 40,300 non-agricultural people (Bureau of Statistics of County H 2007). The county has been on the list of national 'poverty counties' since 2001 – 10,120 people are living in poverty and 23,000 people have low income. The per capita net income of rural households in the county was 2,598 *yuan* in 2006, which was only 70 per cent of the national average that year (3,587 *yuan*) (Bureau of Statistics of County H 2008).

According to the SCNSSD, people with disability are 6.39 per cent of Jiangxi Province population (CPDF 2007). On that basis extrapolating from the provincial data, approximately 13,570 people with disability are likely to live in the case study county, including 3,288 people with hearing and speech impairments (24.23 per cent) and 69 children with hearing and speech impairments (11.78 per cent of all children with disability).

The context for the research is therefore one of a poorer county, close to wealthier large cities on the east coast. This is likely to affect the welfare mix in terms of availability of support for the rights of children with disability to social participation in the local community. For example, poor families could be expected to remain in the county that has less support for children with disability and wealthier families could be expected to try to access support that might be available in the nearby localities. As with any research in China, caution should be taken generalizing beyond the specific location.

Methodology

The research involved qualitative research using a case-study approach. Case studies offer an opportunity to intensely observe, record and analyse data relating to the social relationships in a relevant research site (Miles and Huberman 1994; Stake 2000; Yin 2003). From this experience, the data can be analysed for patterns of action to address the research question. More generally, the analysis can also inform exploration of the case or theory (Lijphart 1971). A limitation of the approach is that when only one or a small number of case studies are examined there is no capacity for comparative investigation, so the ability to generalize beyond the case study is restricted (Yin 2003: 10). This chapter addresses this limitation by using the case study subject as the focus for other related qualitative data collection at the same research site, explained below.

We analysed the life history of a child with disability via semi-structured observation about the living environment of his family and in-depth interviews. The sampling method for the in-depth interviews was snowballing and opportunistic sampling, by interviewing several families of children with disability at first, then including more families and other people from their social networks.

We examined the life history of a deaf child named Hengheng (not his real name), who is now in his late teenage years. The family was selected through convenient sampling. One of the authors visited the Disabled Persons Federation in the county and randomly selected a few families with children with different impairments from the list of people with disability in the county. Hengheng's family was the only one selected that has a child with hearing and speaking impairment. Other families interviewed have children with different impairments. The researcher interviewed Hengheng, his family members and other people connected with his life. The social institutions include families, peers and informal and formal organizations (Ah Ying Salon, an informal community group and the local Disabled Persons Federation – DPF).

The researcher also conducted observation, conversations and in-depth interviews with other people with disability who gather at the Ah Ying hair salon. Ah Ying Salon is an informal community group of people with hearing and speech impairments in the county. It is not an incorporated NGO (*minban feiqiye*) or a government organized 'community' organization (*shequ*) and the people who meet there do not work in the salon. Interviews with people who use sign language only were assisted by a hearing member of Ah Ying Salon with their consent. We also conducted repeat interviews with the staff of local DPF and examined the relationship between DPF and the informal community group, and local people, such as neighbours, doctors and other people who know these people with hearing and speaking impairments. Fieldwork was conducted from June 2007 to March 2008.

The data were analysed with the intention of developing a comprehensive picture of social participation of children with hearing and speech impairments

198 *Karen R. Fisher, Xiaoyuan Shang and Jiawen Xie*

and their families, strategies and difficulties they experienced and the social support they received. The information from different interviews and observations were critically analysed against the rights framework, from the perspective of Hengheng's social participation. A life history and perspective of the child's experiences and each of the social institutions with which he had contact was developed from the repeat interviews and observation data.

The findings about the opportunities for social participation are presented chronologically because of likely changes due to children's ages. The types of social participation are divided into communication, social relationships and interest representation. The roles of social institutions that might affect each of these dimensions of social participation are analysed. In this analysis, the social institutions in which children and young people interact and communicate include family, peers, community groups and government organizations, reflective of the ecological approach described above.

Child and family circumstances

Our analysis started with the life history of Hengheng, who was aged 16–17 years at the time of the fieldwork (he was born in 1990). He has hearing and speech impairments. His family has five members. Hengheng's father is a carpenter with junior middle school education background and his mother is an illiterate housewife. Hengheng also has an older brother and sister who work in Guangdong and Zhejiang respectively. They both left school after graduating from junior middle school. The income source of the family is from the father and older sister. The family has lived in a 40m^2 unit – an old, single storey unit that is attached to many other small units that are in very poor condition – for the past 20 years, partly because of the family-borne economic costs of supporting a child with disability.

Hengheng was found to have a hearing impairment when he was age three, probably from a severe fever when he was one year old. After identifying the hearing impairment, his family actively sought treatment. In urban China, state-backed basic social health insurance does not provide for dependants and so families bear almost all the medical costs of their children's needs. As a result, for low-income families such as Hengheng's, medical expenses can be a heavy economic responsibility. The family went to hospitals in Nanchang and Shanghai many times for examinations and treatments for Hengheng, costing them 20,000–30,000 *yuan* (3–5 times an average annual rural salary in Jiangxi). When they found that one of Hengheng's ears had retained 30 per cent hearing, they spent over 3,000 *yuan* on an imported hearing aid. The doctor said that with this much hearing, if Hengheng received good education, he could learn to speak to hearing people. The family did not receive any support and benefits from the government or organizations in the process of diagnosis, treatment and therapy.

Hengheng's parents love him very much. They not only care for him in daily life but also place great emphasis on helping him master the means to communicate with hearing people. Hengheng is the youngest in the family and disabled so his parents said they spoil him often. If they have a difference of opinion with Hengheng, it normally results in the parents giving up. They said Hengheng can usually make decisions for himself. Because of this, the parents said they had difficulty disciplining him.

Schools were also an important social institution in Hengheng's childhood for meeting peers and teachers. After he temporarily left school the first time at the age of 15, he met other people with hearing and speech impairments and adults in the community and in informal and formal organizations with common interests, work or support. The effect of these social institutions – family, schools, community and organizations – in each dimension of participation (communication, relationships and interest representation) are analysed below.

Communication

The first dimension of social participation analysed is communication. When he was very young, Hengheng used only body language and gestures to communicate with his family. Because he could not speak to anybody before he received education at the special schools, he did not have contact with peers or have any friends during that time. Hengheng's brother said that Hengheng played simple games with him and their sister when he was little. He was quiet, shy and stayed alone.

As he grew up, he wanted more sophisticated means of communication. Hengheng and his parents soon had difficulties communicating with each other, causing frustration between them all. His family did not have the knowledge, means or education to learn sign language themselves. Instead, they did their best to invest in Hengheng's education, with the expectation that he would learn skills to communicate with people who can hear. His family could not communicate well with him until he learned to read and write at school. Neither could he talk with his family by writing unless they were with each other during school holidays. Hengheng's mother, who is unable to read, cannot communicate with him directly. The only way the family can talk with Hengheng now is through writing but his mother cannot read or write. Observation during the research found that the family does not actually communicate a lot with paper and pen, Hengheng's written language structure is only suitable for relatively simple concepts. Similarly, the investigator – one of the authors – was only able to communicate simple ideas in written form.

Hengheng's entry into education was delayed. Most children start school aged 6 or 7 years old in his community. Like many other children with disability he was not welcomed to attend his local mainstream school because they did not have the skills and resources to support his communication needs. When he was aged 10 years old, his parents took him to Jingdezhen Special Education School, which is in another city, 250 km away from H county, hoping he would recover his speaking skills with the help of this school. Jingdezhen Special Education School was famous for its qualified teachers and high teaching quality. Hengheng's development, education and social skills improved there.

When he was 13 years of age his father heard about a new special education school in Shangrao City, 45 km from his home. Because of its impressive new buildings, geographic convenience and low tuition fees, Hengheng and his father reached agreement to transfer him to this school. However, soon after the transfer, Hengheng's father found the school did not have classes in lip reading and speech training because of its limited finances. In addition, this school did not offer education after grade five, which meant Hengheng would need to transfer again to attend grade six. At the new school, Hengheng's academic development did not improve and he stopped speaking. He chose to leave the second school when he was 15 years old so that he could work. He returned to the first school when he was 16 years to finish grade five. He did not want to complete any further schooling.

Hengheng's father thinks that although the family is not wealthy, they have offered their son the best education they could afford. His father wished Hengheng would finish junior high middle school (grade 6–9, usually for children aged 13–16 years, though Hengheng started school education three years later than normal children), but Hengheng does not want to return to school at such a late age. At this stage of his life, what the parents want is assistance from the government, such as training with professional skills, allocating them into state-owned enterprises with safe, stable work posts and fringe welfare benefits.

In his first school, training included teaching speaking skills to children with some hearing capacity or teaching sign language to children without any hearing capacity. In the second school, no speaking was taught. In school, he learned basic sign language, reading, writing and computer skills. He is able to use sign language to communicate with other deaf children, young people and adults who use sign language. He also uses the internet to connect with friends and his sister. These capabilities have helped Hengheng to develop a social life outside the family, in his school, with peers and in the community. He has had less opportunity to develop his speaking capability and currently cannot speak.

Among the ten people with disability associated with Ah Ying Salon, seven, like Hengheng, received formal special education in Nanchang, Jingdezhen and Zhejiang. The other three people are illiterate. Among the seven people with formal education, only two finished junior middle school education (grade 9). They have paid employment washing cars and as handicraftsmen in a steelyard. The other five people with education only graduated from primary school. The majority of people who meet at Ah Ying Salon have stable jobs and incomes, irrespective of their education. Seven of them have their own business (haircutting, a steelyard and car washing). Others work in welfare enterprises that employ a large number of people with disability (Shang 2000) with lower income.

Because of the differences in their formal education, members of Ah Ying Salon informally teach each other through gatherings and chatting. They share new skills or improve their proficiency in formal sign language. In this way, Hengheng improved his command of sign language and corrected errors acquired through formal education. The hearing interpreter at Ah Ying Salon has similarly developed his signing skills from starting with simple sign language and progressing through learning with the Ah Ying Salon members to reach a higher level of sign language.

The family retold stories about how their communication difficulties had caused them great stress and placed Hengheng in vulnerable situations about which they were unaware and where they were at a loss about how to assist him. First, Hengheng's father told us a story about how helpless he felt when, in 2007 New Year, Hengheng had a three-day break from school and was due to come home. Hengheng was 16 years old and had asked his tutor to telephone his father and tell him that he would be home by the end of the day. But the parents waited until midnight and still he had not returned. To get back to H County from Jingdezhen city, Hengheng had to change trains. His father wondered whether Hengheng might have missed the second train. It was bitterly cold and Hengheng did not have extra money. The parents spent a sleepless night. At about four the next afternoon, Hengheng finally turned up, but with a very upset look on his face. He refused to have dinner. His father, who had been worrying for a whole night, was enraged by his behaviour and told Hengheng to get out if he insisted on not having dinner. To his great disbelief, Hengheng left the house immediately. His father followed him for several hundred metres and stopped him by pulling his clothes. The father told us he felt extremely helpless because he did not know how to make himself understood by his child. They remained in this stalemate for half an hour. They finally calmed down and the father suggested to Hengheng that they should go home and talk by writing everything down. Only through this process did the father find out that Hengheng had not attended classes for two months; the tutor did not care about him; and that his teacher was on leave and the surrogate teacher did not offer a special class for him. Hengheng's father said that he still does not know what happened to Hengheng that night.

They also told a second story about another time when Hengheng suddenly left home when he was 15 years old. In July 2006 Hengheng's father returned home and found Hengheng was not at home. He thought Hengheng was just playing outside, and he did not care about this too much until he found a piece of paper on the bed: 'Dear papa and mama, I am so bored at home! I wanna find a job and earn some money. Please do not worry, I will return.' Seeing this, Hengheng's parents were very afraid. They went to the railway and bus stations to look for their son. They also contacted the school and his classmates. They spent every day in a state of anxiety after Hengheng left home, especially when they saw reported on the TV news some crimes where handicapped people were forced to do illegal things. After about 20 days,

Hengheng's older sister, who was working in Zhejiang, received a strange phone call; there was no sound on the other side of the line. The same number soon called again but still no-one spoke. She guessed it might be Hengheng. Hengheng's father reported the case to the police, but because the phone call was from Hubei Province the case required cooperation with the Hubei Police and was hard to solve. Finally, three months later, by the time Hengheng's parents had become extremely pessimistic, Hengheng returned home. According to the parents, he arrived home at 10 at night, with lots of packages in his hands. He brought back his salary (1000 *yuan*, equivalent to an annual rural salary) and he bought his father cigarettes and his mother fruit. Hengheng told his father later that he had been with a middle-aged man from H County, who also had a hearing and speech impairment. They earned 800 *yuan* per month in Zhejiang Province by selling handicraft articles. Since then, he has gone away to work three times. In June 2007 at 16 years, Hengheng suddenly said he would like to return to school at Jingdezhen. His father asked why but Hengheng would not say. The school very reluctantly accepted him back but isolated him from the other students in his living arrangements so that he would not influence them. His father was very angry about this discrimination and of course Hengheng resented the conditions.

During the interview, Hengheng's father continuously expressed his anxiety about communicating with Hengheng. He thinks he cannot communicate with his child, and most of the time he does not know what is going on in his son's mind. And together with the child's determination, he cannot give his son any instruction using his experience. His father is afraid that once Hengheng leaves home, he might be vulnerable to abuse or exploitation by other people.

Hengheng not only receives love and care from his famil; he also loves them and tries to contribute to the family. Through his experience of working in Zhejiang, Hengheng has greater confidence about his ability to contribute to his family and care for himself. When he returned he brought gifts for his parents. He said he is now saving to reconstruct the family home and to prepare for marriage.

Social relationships

The second dimension of social participation is relationships. Hengheng's parents and siblings are not deaf and they know no sign language at all. This limits his social interaction with them. Hengheng's need for social participation increased with his age. He sought other meaningful relationships with people outside the family, as other children do as they grow older. In Hengheng's case the need was more urgent since he needed to find people who could use sign language. Once Hengheng started school, he was able to seek opportunities for social interaction with people who shared his communication skills, initially through the school communities and then through informal disability groups. Beside friends at school, Hengheng also made new deaf friends from the local community.

Students in the special education schools that he attended all have hearing and speech impairments. When Hengheng was at school, he could communicate with teachers and students, and established his social relationships with them. He made many new friends in both schools. His father said that Hengheng used to visit his classmates by himself in holidays and his friends also went to his home to play with him. Most of his friends are deaf children who use the same language, share common interests and face similar difficulties in their daily lives. After he left school he kept up these relationships by meeting people in person and over the internet. Other adults interviewed also said that some informal or illegal organizations recruit children with disability through the special schools. Hengheng also likes to use the internet. He makes friends and chats with them online. Internet and texting are the main ways he communicates with this sister to whom he is closest in the family.

When Hengheng was 15 years old he met a deaf handicraftsman named Ying, Hengheng's family do not know how they met. The DPF director reflected that often initially coincidental meetings between people with similar impairments lead to longer-term social connections. Through his friendship with Ying, Hengheng found another group of peers in Ah Ying Salon, which became an important place for Hengheng to develop his social connections in the local community.

More than ten people with hearing impairments often come to the hair salon. Their average age is over thirty. In addition, two teenagers come, including Hengheng. The salon was opened in May 2007. The owner, Ah Ying, is a local deaf person aged 32 years old. His wife, who came from Jingdezhen, also has a hearing impairment.

Before the salon opened, local deaf people had already formed a small group. This informal group was originally founded by three couples with hearing and speech impairments in the county town. Their families were relatively rich in H County and were able to afford formal special education for them. As they grew up, their families also supported them to learn crafts and to start their own businesses. Since they had stable shops and had more contact with various people in the community, they became well known. As they were the same age and all communicated through sign language, they became good friends. They responded to the needs of the growing number of people with hearing and speech impairments in the county town, attracting more and more friends. Developing as a rolling snowball, the organization became bigger and bigger, including members without disability.

After the salon opened, this group used it as a place for activities. They gathered in the salon every day to chat and play card games and *mahjong*. The interviews, conversations and observation data showed that the primary function of this organization is that it provides a public space for people with hearing and speech impairments to know and communicate with each other.

Hengheng's father said that after meeting Ying and the other members of Ah Ying Salon Hengheng has grown to know many other people with hearing and speech impairments. Since then Hengheng has become more outgoing. In the past he used to mainly watch TV at home, but now he goes out to see his friends at every opportunity and often comes back home late at night. Hengheng told us that he likes to go there because the people often discuss news and tell stories, which he loves. The research process confirmed his positive approach to Ah Ying. So that he could be interviewed, Hengheng's father brought Hengheng home from the salon, but after only half an hour, Hengheng was in a hurry to return. He was so eager to be with his friends because only in this community could he understand others and express himself adequately.

Another function of the salon, described further in the next section, is that its members support each other. According to the members and comments from neighbours, a doctor and the DPF director, if one person has a problem, others offer their help to try to solve it. For example, a doctor at the county hospital mentioned that if a person with hearing and speech impairments comes to the hospital, other members of Ah Ying Salon would accompany this person. One who can write is in charge of communicating with the doctor, while the others help to take care of the sick person, pay for the fees and manage the medicine. The doctor also mentioned that they are very warm-hearted to each other and the hospital staff is always impressed whenever they visit. The mutual help also includes introducing work opportunities to each other when one member gets some information. The DPF director mentioned that a similar organization in the county set up by people with physical impairments has about 40 members.

Interest representation

The third dimension of social participation we analysed was interest representation. When he was young Hengheng's interests were represented by his family. They sought out a diagnosis, treatment and therapy; and education choices and suitable schools. Without a political voice, government support or information, their only choices were attempting to select appropriate, affordable services available through the market. In Hengheng's case this was restricted by his parents' own education; balancing the limited family resources among all the family members; and the lack of exposure to information about the options to best meet the needs of children with disability. Hengheng's parents made a large financial investment in these choices, thinking that it might maximize his skills to interact with people who can hear. His parents and siblings have provided significant support and representation for Hengheng during his childhood.

In addition, his parents had a limited capacity to understand Hengheng's wishes and preferences because they could not fully communicate with him. For example, when Hengheng was mistreated in his second school, he could not tell them the whole story. Because of this, his parents could not articulate or support his rights in the school context effectively. Although his father complained to the school about the treatment he received there, he did not

Support for children and young people with disability   205

have sufficient power to protect Hengheng's rights. Once Hengheng returned to school after a period working, the school would not take him back in case he had a negative influence on the other students. Our data collection did not extend to interviewing staff from the schools, therefore we cannot comment on the role of schools in expressing or protecting the interests of children with disability.

The formal government organization for people with disability in the county is the Disabled Persons Federation, at the local government level. Its major functions are representation, service and administration of disability-policy implementation. Their responsibility is to represent the common interests of people with disability and safeguard their legal rights and interests; develop support and activities to serve people with disability directly; take charge of partial administrative functions with official commission to develop and manage the government affairs of people with disability (CDPF 2008b; for a critical review see Kohrman 2005).

Some people with disability register with the DPF as disabled. In our study county, they generally only registered if they wanted assistance such as tax benefits, a licence to attend a special school, or a fee subsidy when compulsory education schools charged fees in the past. The DPF does not provide assistance such as support to families or training such as sign language to children or family members. They charge people for equipment.

As the local government organization officially responsible to the State Council the DPF has stable funds from public finances and can charge a tax penalty to businesses that do not employ the required proportion of people with disability (1.5–2 per cent of employees). This resource base contrasts with that of informal groups. The DPF is also potentially a channel for enabling people with disability to participate in government decision-making as well as having responsibility for administering policies relating to people with disability (including disability NGOs) on behalf of the government (CDPF 2008b). However, informal groups are a necessary bridge to reach people with disability when the DPF wants to gather information about the interests of people with disability. The county DPF director admitted to us that it is difficult for the DPF to work without the informal groups. The people with disability and their families we interviewed spoke about how the formal government organization and informal groups mutually support and complement each other's functions.

The DPF relies on Ah Ying Salon to communicate with its members. Because it does not have anyone with hearing and speech impairments, the county DPF often asks two core people from Ah Ying Salon for help when it needs to contact people with hearing and speech impairments or provide information to them. The DPF director said that if it needed to inform them of something or hold an event, the DPF would ask Ah Ying Salon to assist. Another more formal function of the Ah Ying Salon has been to gather and express the common interests of its members. The local DPF director reported that usually when a person with disability comes to the DPF for help, if they had not joined an organization they would come by themselves or with one or two relatives. In contrast, people with hearing and speech impediments in the county worked collectively. He gave the example of one occasion on which the DPF office was filled by seven or eight deaf people who came in support of someone who wanted to consult about the application for the Minimum Livelihood Guarantee [MLG] benefits (see Solinger's and Hammond's chapters in this volume).

In order to enhance the cooperation between Ah Ying Salon and the DPF, the DPF validated the status of the core members of the informal group by inviting them as representatives of people with disability in the county to attend a Civic People with Disability Congress at the county and city levels. Compared to the other members of the Ah Ying Salon, these two representatives have a higher level of education, fluent writing skills and sign language for communication with both people with and without hearing and speech impairments.

Ah Ying, as an informal group is independent from the DPF, was spontaneously formed, and operates without government assistance. On the other hand, it also cooperates with the DPF. From the perspective of members of the informal group, it is impossible for people with hearing and speech impairments to have a politically effective voice without the DPF. With help from the DPF, people with hearing and speech impairments have been able to use formal channels to express their interests or affect decisions. This has also been to the benefit of the DPF, which has been able to establish contact with people with disability and to be able to represent their interests locally and politically. According to the director of the DPF, without the informal groups the DPF would not have the means to make contact with people with disability. He said this would weaken its capacity to function as a representative of the interests of people with disability. As an official organization, the DPF is required to provide a communication platform and aids for people with disability, but it cannot do this without the assistance of organizations set up by people with disability.

However, the support from the DPF to informal groups is very limited. For example, in 2004, another physical disability organization asked the DPF for support to register as an NGO, but their request was rejected. Without that support, the government regulations prevent it from gaining legal status and its opportunities for further action, such as receiving funding, are therefore restricted. Ah Ying does not intend to register as an NGO because it functions primarily as a social group.

These examples of cooperation illustrate how the people with disability in H county use both informal and formal channels to articulate their interests. Both the formal government organizations and informal community groups play important roles representing the interests of people with disability; through working with the DPF the informal groups have more access to relevant information. The case also illustrates how the interest representation by the informal community group is limited: it is difficult for an informal group to become formally recognized or supported financially or organizationally by the DPF.

Implications for the local social welfare mix

Our study shows that children and young people with hearing and speech impairments in a poor rural county experience opportunities for social participation through communication, social relationships and interest representation within each of the expected social institutions. In Hengheng's case, the key institutions were his family, school friends and schools during his childhood years; and the informal community group of people with disability during his teenage years. In contrast, the formal local government disability organization in the county had less direct impact on his participation, as discussed below.

The examples showed that it was Hengheng's family who organized and paid for his access to special schools where he met other children who use the same communication skills as him during his childhood. He was not able to attend the tuition free local government school because it did not have the resources or skills to support children with disability. As he reached teenage years, it was through his own social interactions that he found other young people and adults with hearing impairments in his own community. Through these contacts he found a vibrant social network that gives him access to socializing, discussion, support and communication to access the hearing community, further informal training about communication skills for people with hearing and speech impairments, and information about job opportunities. These opportunities are not available through the DPF, the formal local government disability organization in the county, which relies on informal groups to support and communicate with people with disability.

In the remainder of this section we discuss how the implications for social policy changes to fulfil the rights of children with disability to social participation relate to support for social institutions at these four levels in the ecological approach – family, school, informal community groups and government. Families like Hengheng's currently bear the full cost of medical diagnosis and treatment, therapy and special education of children with disability (Shang and Wu 2003). If they cannot afford the support, the child does not have access. In a poor rural context, if they can bear the cost, the whole family is likely to be economically disadvantaged by the extra expenses. Families in a rural community also do not have access to information about what support might best meet the social needs of their child. Hengheng's family, for example, did not have information about communication skills that would help him within the hearing and non-hearing communities, learning sign language themselves or writing skills for his mother so she could communicate with him directly. Such reliance on the family in early years can risk abuse and neglect in the home (Shang *et al.* 2008). If other family members are not people with disability, they often only have information to consider the needs of children with disability from the perspective of people without disability. Other needs of some children with disability may be neglected, such as sign-language education by parents and schools. One advantage of this rural context was that, unlike city families, Hengheng's family situation was probably eased by having three children, with the benefit that the older children financially contributed to the cost of supporting Hengheng's education. Family-planning rules allow exceptions to the one-child policy in some rural communities.

The second social institution supporting children's participation is school. Rural mainstream schools do not have resources, teachers or skills to support children with disability within the local community. The impact for children like Hengheng is that they face the risk of missing out on local connections with children in a school environment; they might attend school but without additional assistance their education and social outcomes suffer, including bullying and abuse (Shang *et al.* 2008); their entry into school can be delayed; they do not have formal support to develop communication skills unless their family can afford to send them to specialist schools; and at worst, they do not attend any formal education. Alternatively, their family might have the information, commitment and resources to access special schools outside the community. While this helps provide social contact with children with similar impairments, education and communication skills development, it dislocates the children from their family, local community and other children without disability. The quality of the education also relies on the resources of the school, as illustrated by Hengheng's experience in the second school, which did not teach speaking skills.

The third set of social institutions is the community and local informal groups. As children grow older they might acquire agency to find these themselves, as in Hengheng's case, or presumably some families or other social contacts introduce children and young people directly. This introduction would require both that the families have information about them and that they understand the benefit to their child about contact and support from other people with disability. While the informal group in this community provides direct benefits for social participation in all three dimensions (communication, relationships and interest representation), it is entirely self-organized. It is not supported by the local government with formal recognition of the groups or resources to facilitate the activities that complement local government functions. These groups which were established by people with disability themselves to meet their participation needs play an important and irreplaceable role in fulfilling the participation rights of people with disability, including children and young people. However, the informal groups lack government resources support, funding and formal channels to express the interests of their members. They may not exist in all communities or localities.

The fourth social institutions are formal government organizations. The local government organization, the DPF, relies on informal groups to fulfil its formal functions of contact with the disability community. This county DPF,

Support for children and young people with disability 209

like others (Kohrman 2005), neither employs people with the necessary communication skills nor organizes the support to facilitate social participation of people with disability itself. But the DPF has official responsibilities, channels to government, and stable financial and administrative resources. The cooperation between the local formal government organizations and informal groups is beneficial to both levels to fulfil their own missions and serve the interests of people with disability. While they cooperate well in this county, development into sustainable support for children and young people with disability is hampered by the rigidity of structural support. Partly this reflects a central policy limitation on the regulation of NGOs. But even within that regulatory framework, the DPF seems to lack the will to formalize established community groups into incorporated NGOs. In this instance, the DPF does not seem to have moved even the first steps towards contracting social support to NGOs or the market.

We expect that the local context of a poor, rural county accentuated our findings about the limits to the ability of each of the four sets of social institutions to address the rights of children with disability. The poverty of information, resources, business activity and qualified professionals no doubt partly explains the inability of the families, schools, community and local government to understand, support and engage with the citizenship rights of these children. For example, the mother's poor literacy; the schools' lack of specialist support for children with additional needs; the lack of resource support for informal groups; and the absence of direct financial, information or other support to children with disability from the responsible local government agency. None of the people we interviewed in the course of the research referred to concepts of rights or entitlements. At most, they indirectly spoke of the injustice of the lack of access to opportunities compared to other people without disability, such as education, training and jobs.

In summary, the implications of our findings for local social policy change are that there is a need to increase direct government engagement with people with disability and to fund or provide information, support, resources and formal structures to assist children and young people with disability, their families, communities, schools, local informal and formal nongovernment organizations. Tangible steps would be access to government supported diagnosis, treatment and therapy; information, teachers, training and resources in mainstream and specialist schools; and processes to register and support the development of local nongovernment organizations. In this way local social policy would support a sustainable social welfare mix that maximizes support for children's rights from each of the social institutions with which children with disability have contact.

By understanding family experiences of child disability and informing local social policy development, the findings make an important contribution to furthering the rights of children in China and improving the wellbeing of families and children with disability. The research provides vital information to support the efforts of the Chinese local government and nongovernment organizations to establish effective child-disability policy. The findings also provide a basis for further research, such as evaluating models of support policies in China; comparing them with those in other countries to identify models of best practice; and analysing disability experiences in the Chinese context. They offer new insights into policy and add to theories of children's rights in the context of the relationships between parents and children, and between local government, the family and civil society within East Asian welfare regimes.

Acknowledgements

The research was funded by the Australian Research Council and supported by the University of New South Wales, Beijing Normal University and Rights To Play. Thanks to Robyn Edwards and the workshop participants for useful comments on the draft.

Notes

1 CDPF official status is as a non-government organization but its functions include government policy and funding responsibilities that would not be associated with a non-government organization in other countries (Kohrman 2005).
2 Most income for a local DPF comes from tax penalties to businesses that do not employ the required quota of people with disability. This varies by location according to the degree of business activity. Counties with less business activity have fewer resources for disability policy implementation.

11 Global discourses, national policies, local outcomes
Reflections on China's welfare reforms

Sarah Cook

On 6 April 2009, the Chinese government announced a massive expansion of its health-care provisions with the aim of providing basic health care to the whole population by 2020. This announcement represents a further step by the Chinese state to help its less advantaged citizens climb the 'three mountains' of health, education and housing. Just as the architects of Britain's post-war welfare state sought to tackle the 'Five Giants' (of want, ignorance, disease, squalor and idleness), the current Chinese leadership aims to address problems of poverty and insecurity through the extension of social protection – particularly basic health care, education, and income or other social transfers – to assist low-income citizens in meeting their basic needs. Some of these efforts have been documented in this volume, and highlight the challenges of delivering welfare in a country of such great size and diversity, and in the midst of rapid social and economic change.

The chapters in this book illustrate, from various 'local' perspectives, the variation in welfare needs, resources and provisions, among different 'localities' and between different social and demographic groups. Building on the preceding accounts of local diversity, these concluding remarks take a more macro look at the process of change at the national level, and beyond that to the regional and global context, to identify possible trends and trajectories, and to suggest the significance of China's social policy developments in a comparative perspective. The chapter asks what these snapshots of the changing mix of welfare needs, provisions and outcomes tell us about the trajectory of China's evolving welfare reforms and, within this, about central–local relations. How have the national, regional and even global contexts shaped local outcomes? Is there an overarching narrative or logic that can help us understand China's welfare changes over recent decades, and what might drive future directions, towards what ends?

Constructing a national picture of social welfare provision from the 'bottom up' or through local experiences provides valuable insights into the needs of citizens, the relevance of provision and the role of different actors, as well as processes of changing state–citizen or provider–beneficiary relations, and the creation of subject identities such as 'welfare recipient' or citizen with entitlements and rights. Such insights can inform policy formulation and implementation, leading to improvements in welfare systems and delivery mechanisms. At the same time, this 'bottom-up' approach can also lead to the depiction of a fragmented patchwork of interventions, poorly financed, often inadequate to meet identified needs and possibly inappropriate to local circumstances, in which the basic needs and entitlements of some groups go unmet. It tends to highlight gaps and tensions rather than achievements and progress. The observed problems (as noted in a number of the papers) are readily attributed by different stakeholders or observers to a range of factors: misinterpretation of the problem; state failure in policy design; lack of political will; insufficient financial resources; weak administrative and technical capacity; implementation failures; non-compliant or insensitive local bureaucrats; fraudulent claimants or welfare scroungers.

Another narrative can be found, however, less prominently in this volume but nonetheless visibly emerging through some of the analyses as well as in a growing literature on welfare reform in China. This alternative narrative describes successes, as well as the inevitable setbacks, as the Chinese state – from the centre to its grassroots – finds its way at unprecedented speed through uncharted territory of economic transition and welfare restructuring. The story involves the transformation of a poor, internationally isolated rural country over a period of thirty years to become the world's third largest economy, and one of the most globally integrated, built by a workforce that is, on average, relatively healthy and educated. The government has delivered a massive reduction in poverty, with rising incomes and living standards for the majority. It has restructured the economy towards capitalism, with the many benefits that market-driven growth can deliver.

This positive narrative of reform and modernization is not necessarily complacent about the limits and constraints on China's development, and recognizes the new problems that have arisen in this transition process. Few discussions of China's economic successes fail to mention the concomitant rise in inequality along a number of dimensions. Many point to a range of social issues where the deficits and failures have emerged prominently: among migrants, those dispossessed of land, or discriminated against due to HIV-AIDS or other infectious diseases; the environmental degradation that has accompanied growth; and the failure of institutional provision in areas such as health and education. We see evidence (documented in some of the papers) of a breakdown in trust as government fails to deliver and as representatives of the local state embrace new agendas of modernization and the market, their clients no longer the poor, elderly and disabled but rather the new property owners, entrepreneurs and elites; and where courts or formal institutions are seen to favour the interests of officials and the wealthy against the protection of the vulnerable.

At the same time, in the more positive narrative of reform, emphasis is placed on the state's capacity to respond to problems as they emerge and to deliver outcomes when it has the will to do so. The efforts of the state to construct systems designed to deliver greater security to its citizens are recognized, even

Global discourses, national policies, local outcomes 213

though these are not yet fully realized in implementation. Initiatives such as the establishment of a national income support programme (the Minimum Livelihood Guarantee, or *dibao*), the expansion of health provisions, the funding of basic education, and new labour and other laws to protect workers support this story, despite insufficient resources, weak governance and implementation, and uneven outcomes. Thus, behind the everyday failures to meet individual needs at the local level, described in some of the preceding chapters, we also see a state presiding over the restructuring of welfare provisions on an unprecedented scale, and at a relatively early stage (at least as measured by per capita incomes) in the nation's economic development.

How should we reconcile or make sense of these divergent narratives? Do we see moves towards the establishment of a welfare system with the potential to deliver services to and protect all of its citizens, or do we see increasingly entrenched forms of marginalization and exclusion created as much by state failures in policy and provisioning as by the expansion of the market? How should we analyse and explain the different 'states' of welfare that seem to be emerging across and within localities and groups? The remainder of this concluding chapter explores dimensions of these questions: the variation across time and place; institutional processes such as fiscal decentralization that shape local outcomes; and the discourses at international and national levels that shape policies and influence the motivations of the state and other actors to deliver expanded welfare provisions. It then returns to the issue of local variation, illustrated in the volume particularly by papers on *dibao,* in an effort to reconcile the macro and micro narratives.

A changing welfare geography: needs and provision in transition

These alternative narratives and possibilities obviously need to be understood in the context of rapid change and transition – processes which eliminate some inequalities and exclusions among localities and groups, exacerbate others, while also creating new ones. Each of the papers in this volume illustrates a specific moment in place and time, all of which are part of a complex trajectory of changing needs, provisions and discourses about reform. Only by placing these moments in their wider context can we assess whether the failures of provision are systemic or transitional; whether they are part of an effort to find a new welfare settlement or social contract, the fall out from the collapse of the old one, or the recognition of persistent, but formerly overlooked and neglected, dimensions of exclusion.

Unquestionably, as stated in the introduction to this volume, China's welfare mix or social policy provisions bear little resemblance to those existing at the start of the reform period three decades ago and are outcomes of both the pre-reform system and its subsequent evolution (see also Cook 2002). China's transformation from a planned economy to one where market forces largely determine distribution destroyed the social contract associated with the urban iron rice bowl and collective rural welfare provisions. In its place, a new

214   *Sarah Cook*

relationship between state and subject/citizen has emerged, based largely on an individual's ability to participate in and share the benefits of a growing economy. In Deng's China and beyond, increased incomes were expected to deliver benefits previously provided through a system of state distribution, while the party-state also derived legitimacy through the shared benefits of economic growth.

Prior to reform, the integration of economic production and social reproduction meant that minimum security (for consumption, employment, shelter, health and education) was provided collectively. After 1978, economic growth was prioritized at the expense of social and redistributive objectives. State withdrawal from functions of social reproduction undermined existing institutional arrangements of security, while creating new forms of insecurity. The residual social assistance mechanisms covering those with no other means of support – the rural 'Five Guarantee' (*wubao*) households and urban 'Three Nos' (*sanwu*) programmes – were unable to cope with growing numbers of people left without jobs or livelihoods by transition. Nor were there any mechanisms to support the working poor, rural or urban, against the creeping commercialization and rising costs of health and education. The critical functions of any social security system – to provide guarantees against contingencies; support for social reproduction; and an acceptable degree of equality through redistribution – were no longer being adequately performed by the state. The role of safety net of last resort returned to the family which had few coping mechanisms suited to the new economy.

The process of transition from plan to market has been inextricably interlinked with processes of structural and demographic change – held back by the Maoist system, curtailed in the early years of reform but then unleashed at unprecedented pace. These multiple transitions, of health, aging and family structures, have reconfigured the social landscape, including the institutions and networks of social reproduction. Even if the emerging problems of welfare commercialization had been recognized sooner, it is unlikely the system could have adapted sufficiently rapidly to these complex changing needs of a transitional economy and society – one with increasing wealth and demands, and an increasingly mobile and aging population. Reforms have had both to reduce benefits to a previously protected population (laid-off workers, elderly in work units) as well as expand support to the more vulnerable. Many of the papers in this volume (those by Jieyu Liu, Dorothy Solinger, Daniel Hammond and Anna Boermel) are concerned with the former; others (those by Anna Lora-Wainwright and Karen Fisher, Xiaoyuan Shang and Jiawen Xie, Bingqin Li and Mark Duda) are about the failure of expansion to meet the needs of the excluded (elderly rural cancer sufferers, the disabled, rural migrants in cities).

Faced with this dual challenge, the state has made substantial efforts at reform. Since the late 1990s, new social protection programmes, described in previous chapters, have proliferated. These include the well-documented expansion of pension, health-care and unemployment benefits funded through

Global discourses, national policies, local outcomes 215

employer and employee contributions; the expansion of the urban basic medical scheme to cover all workers and dependents; the non-contributory Minimum Livelihood Guarantee (*dibao*) programme and the rural cooperative medical system (see Solinger, Hammond and Lora-Wainwright on *dibao* and RCMS). Less well-documented are a medical assistance programme to support the poorest with the high costs of care; programmes of support for heating and housing costs (see Li and Duda); and a range of locally implemented transfer and poverty alleviation programmes.

These efforts, particularly since 2002–3 under the leadership of Hu Jintao and Wen Jiabao, to adopt new welfare provisions suited to a market economy are undeniably uneven in their outcomes. However, much of the local variation observed in this volume is not necessarily new. The egalitarian Maoist system, while delivering some degree of security, redistribution and support for social reproduction, also hid huge inequalities, between rural and urban areas and between localities, with equality of poverty often being the main outcome in the poorest localities. Despite limited local autonomy and similar institutional arrangements, location and local resource inequality translated into unequal outcomes and shared inequalities across communes or collectives. While there was some degree of security from certain kinds of contingencies, the system also created its own risks through exposure to policy-generated and politically motivated insecurity. The inter-'local' or regional variation in economic and human development outcomes have in many cases been intensified by reforms as structural inequalities associated with location and resource endowments are exacerbated by rapid development in some regions and a weakness of redistributive mechanisms. But intra-regional/locale inequalities have also increased sharply, with idiosyncratic shocks (ill-health, loss of employment) affecting individuals and households, while predictable events – reproduction and aging – once again strain the resources of over-stretched families. The outcomes are new forms of marginalization, poverty in relatively wealthy regions and cities, and deeper 'horizontal' inequalities between groups in society differentially placed to benefit from reforms, for example along lines of ethnicity, disability, age or gender. Overall, then, a more complex geography of welfare has emerged, with strong regional or local features cross-cut by change along other dimensions such as community and family structures, social networks, gender roles and aging.

Decentralization, local governance and welfare provision

The capacity to respond to this more complex welfare geography through public action depends to a large extent on the capacity, resources and incentives of the local state – those officials who are closest to the people in need, and in theory best able to identify and deliver appropriate services. Throughout the developing world, a trend towards decentralization of responsibilities and resources to local government was promoted over the past decade or more, as a mechanism for responsive and effective governance and service

216 *Sarah Cook*

delivery. While the literature argues for the benefits of devolving responsibility for provision closest to demand, experience also shows that outcomes are varied, and depend on a range of institutional conditions, financing arrangements, capacity and incentives.

In China, divergent local outcomes reflect to a large extent variation in local-level institutional and governance arrangements that evolved during the reform years. The devolution of responsibilities accompanied by fiscal decentralization meant that local governments were tasked with a growing burden of unfunded mandates, including those related to the provision of public goods and social services (see, for example, Shue and Wong, 2007a). The incentives of local governments to increase revenues and promote local economic growth came at the cost of investments in 'non-productive' activities such as social services, public health or basic education. The inevitable outcome was declining public or collective welfare provisions (including health and education) and the effective privatization of these services (especially in rural areas), leading to high user fees and increasing impoverishment of the vulnerable. Only from the late 1990s, when the state stepped in to recentralize fiscal revenues, abolish unauthorized fees and increase resources from central revenues to cover some costs, has there been a renewed focus on the extension of basic services.

As Xinping Guan and Bing Xu argue in this volume, of all elements in the central–local relationship the fiscal relationship is the most important. As the state shifted responsibility down the system, the role of the central government became increasingly constrained to a policy making and guidance role backed up by regulatory, enforcement and monitoring mechanisms. The limited capacity of the state to regulate, along with weak compliance mechanisms (especially with respect to financing arrangements), translates into limited institutional capacity to achieve state objectives from above. Equally, without greater space for citizen engagement or expression of demands, there are few effective mechanisms of monitoring and compliance from below. The local state in many cases is caught between systemic incentives to generate local economic growth and increase revenues in order to deliver services, and a declining capacity to raise and retain such revenues. Public service units (*shiye danwei*) – the quasi-government bodies such as schools and hospitals which are the actual providers of services – are similarly caught between their public service mandates and a revenue generating role, which in turn gives them some degree of autonomy from state regulation (World Bank 2008).

Given this pattern of central–local relationships, it is not surprising to see local variation in outcomes mapping on to geographic variation in economic development, as described in some of the papers presented above. Those areas with weakest resource raising capacities are those with greatest need (in terms for example of poverty, ill-health and low incomes). These deficits also translate into weak human resource and other administrative capacities for government and service delivery. Without an effective system for fiscal redistribution and greater central government responsibility for welfare provisions

Global discourses, national policies, local outcomes 217

in poor regions, such inequalities of outcome will persist. More central government financing, as is currently being invested in social protection programmes, is part of the solution: however, as Christine Wong (2007) has argued, without more substantial reform of the fiscal system it is unlikely that the resources will reach the appropriate levels and be effectively used.

Even within localities, resource allocations are determined by a complex set of political and administrative relations. Government departments responsible for most welfare expenditures – particularly the Civil Affairs system – tend to be relatively weak given that they have limited capacity for revenue generation. Their incentives are to develop programmes that can attract resources from the government, while also ensuring that their mandates, and the potential beneficiaries of their programmes, are contained within manageable bounds. This creates the kind of local variations in approaches to implementation described for example in the case of *dibao*, between Wuhan and Lanzhou (Solinger) and Dalian (Hammond). Access of local officials to resources beyond the locality – in Beijing or even from international organizations, as Hammond describes for Dalian – may generate additional support for innovation, but may also exacerbate inequalities between localities.

With limited resources, local governments may seek to devolve responsibilities still further – to 'society' or social organizations (*shehui tuanti*) or other non-government organizations. The expansion of the mix of welfare providers through a process of 'socialization' (*shehuihua*) is part of the story of the commercialization of previously socially provided goods such as care of the elderly, children or the disabled. It has largely been driven by state withdrawal and a response to gaps in provision rather than a deliberate redistribution of roles and responsibilities. At the same time, local governments also have incentives to limit their responsibilities through exclusions – easily enforceable in the case of migrants without local residence registration (see Li and Duda). The outcomes are thus patchy and uneven, often depending on local resource availability and thus reinforcing pre-existing inequalities.

Discourses of welfare reform: national debates and global context

Given the weakness of fiscal and administrative controls and incentives from centre to locality, what other mechanisms shape the directions of welfare change? Within China, widely used slogans set the discourse and broad goals for reform – to achieve a 'well-off' (*xiaokang*) and 'harmonious' (*hexie*) society, through people-centred (*yiren weiben*) development. Global debates and discourses also play a role in defining policy directions and outcomes at national and local levels.

China's liberalization and integration into the global economy coincided with significant change in the global discourse around welfare systems. The reform process started as western countries were questioning the Keynesian foundations of liberal welfare states and cutting back on welfare provisions, supported by a neo-liberal ideology which emphasized the supremacy of

218   *Sarah Cook*

markets and a minimal role for government. According to Christopher Pierson, 'The political consensus for a managed economy and state welfare' characteristic of the post-war years was breaking down; public opinion 'moved from support for collective solutions to problems of social need to a preference for market provision to satisfy individual welfare demands' and away from universalist, rights-based welfare towards a more residualist, needs-governed system of public relief (Pierson 1998: 150). In developing countries, already limited welfare spending was also being cut during this period, driven by fiscal crisis and through conditionalities imposed by the international financial institutions as part of stabilization or structural adjustment packages.

In this ideological climate, China started receiving advice and assistance from international agencies (notably the World Bank), and observing welfare reforms in other countries, as it sought ways to reform its own overstretched pensions, health care, housing and other social welfare programmes. While China pursued its own reform path and made distinctive policy choices, there were many channels for influence, and models of private-sector reforms in areas of health and pensions were seriously explored. The Dalian case illustrates a more limited local-level project impact of such channels.

While at times the outcomes point to a state that embraced neo-liberalism (Ka Ho Mok and Yu Cheung Wong in this volume), in reality China moved less intentionally in this direction than is sometimes suggested. China's emphasis on growth and a greater reliance on markets resonated with the dominant international ideology which in turn may have helped to justify market-led reforms, including the neglect of welfare provisions. For some in the international community, China's reform path could even be held up as a model of successful neo-liberal reforms in practice. However, the processes of decollectivization, decentralization and the shrinking role of the state had consequences that were not entirely foreseen. The outcomes were less the result of ideological choice than a set of pragmatic responses and experimentation through a period of rapid change. Conversely, the Chinese state has also resisted privatization and a reduction of its role in many areas of the economy. While there are certainly Chinese proponents of more radical privatization, there are equally strong countervailing arguments for a stronger state role and growing concerns about equality and social justice. The withdrawal of the state has been highly variable, and is now most apparent in areas which affect the livelihoods and security of the most vulnerable, as opposed to those supporting wealth creation or benefiting the wealthy.

As China negotiates its reform path within this international context, it has developed its own distinctive discourses to justify its policies – from market socialism to the harmonious society. The most enduring concern of the leadership has been the maintenance of stability in its on-going pursuit of reform and development. It has shown a responsiveness to innovations that work, allowing space for variation in policy implementation suited to local conditions but reining back reforms when stability appears threatened. In the case

Global discourses, national policies, local outcomes 219

of welfare reform, this translates into a series of policy responses to needs as they arise – addressing the grievances of laid-off workers, responding to growing unemployment and to the serious exclusions of a largely privatized health system, and expanding welfare provisions to migrant workers. When the core goals of the reform process are perceived to be threatened, as by some of the exclusions described in this volume, the central government shows a capacity to respond. In its response, it draws on discourses and slogans, such as those of the well-off and harmonious society, to create a sense of policy coherence from the centre to localities within which a range of specific policies, implementation strategies and outcomes are possible.

From this perspective, how do we assess the state's motives for welfare reform and thus possible future directions? Throughout the chapters in this volume, various interpretations are ascribed to the motivations of state or other actors at different levels in the system. The state at times is seen as driven by a privatizing reform agenda (in education or housing); at others by a concern with social control (in managing the threat of unrest). In the workshop where these papers were discussed, the attainment of social justice and more equitable outcomes was also viewed by some as a primary motivation. Different actors in the system also have diverse motives: from alleviating poverty and providing security to reducing expenditures, minimizing targeted 'recipients' and preventing welfare dependence. From the perspective of local officials or grass root bureaucrats, various motivations are attributed to those receiving welfare: from the real needs of the 'deserving' to the welfare scroungers.

Implicit in these interpretations are different understandings of what the central or local state can or should provide and fund, to whom, and debates about the best route to get there. In some cases we see evidence of resource constraints or administrative bottlenecks but an effort at the progressive realization of welfare entitlements for those in need or towards more universal forms of provision. In others, the interpretation suggests a state adopting minimalist provisions necessary to buy off short-term unrest and maintain its legitimacy. Whereas the progressive expansion of provisions may lead to the strengthening of a new social contract between state and citizens, and clarity about what the state will provide under different circumstances, the latter approach of 'fire-fighting' or managing short-term risks may lead to a continued struggle for legitimacy, growing distrust and the absence of a new social contract.

Social policy systems have taken shape across the world in the context of highly varied economic conditions and political regimes. Social contracts equally have emerged in different contexts, determining how much the state and citizens are prepared to pay through taxation or other mechanisms, for what type and level of protection and services, and towards what shared vision of society. Unions and collective organizing, political negotiation or cooption, populist regimes and social movements have all been instrumental in determining different welfare regimes and outcomes. In the Chinese case, the logic of welfare reform may be more akin to that found in the East Asian

220 Sarah Cook

developmental welfare states, where under authoritarian regimes, welfare programmes have been used in support of economic development goals, and by extension the maintenance of state legitimacy, with beneficiaries being determined by state objectives rather than on the basis of greatest need (Kwon 2005; Cook and Kwon 2008).

China's evolving welfare mix: local reform in practice

Returning to the local variation described in this volume, the above chapters suggest an evolving welfare mix in terms of financing and provision – state, market, civil society and households – as well as needs and outcomes. The variation in this mix is driven by economic conditions and systemic issues such as the weaknesses in the fiscal system and the failure of redistributive mechanisms; as well as by local political economies which determine how local governments interpret and implement policies, and their willingness to innovate. These dimensions of variation emerge clearly in the studies of China's major social assistance programme – *dibao*. A range of views on this programme are presented in the chapters providing an opportunity to explore whether collectively they shed further light on welfare reform. For example, is the apparent failure to meet even the minimal needs of vulnerable people in Wuhan an aberration arising from local implementation failures or the norm? Is it a step in the process of expanding provisions to become more generous and inclusive, or does it reflect entrenched resistance to such expansion? Can such provisions lead to new forms of citizenship and the crafting of a new social contract? Or is it instead a further step in the breakdown in trust between people and institutions of local governance?

Dibao is an important programme to understand in all its complexity: for the Chinese state it marked a significant conceptual departure from previous welfare programmes targeted at specific identifiable groups and from poverty programmes that focused almost exclusively on the rural poor. It recognized that a growing population of working poor would need assistance over the longer term, not merely as a transitional mechanism during state enterprise restructuring. The expansion of *dibao* illustrates a method that the Chinese state frequently adopts for piloting new programmes and rolling out new policies: one of local innovation and experimentation, with selected cases scaled up from local pilots to a national model, and rolled out nationwide with increasing state resource allocations. Guan and Xu describe the central elements of the policy process, using the development of *dibao* to illustrate key facets of central–local relations. Other chapters (Solinger, Hammond) also sketch the general process but focus specifically on local flexibility and variation in implementation. Whereas Wuhan provided one of the early pilots that informed the nationwide expansion, the case of the wealthy coastal city of Dalian illustrates the challenges of taking programmes to scale given diverse financing, technical and administrative capacity. Motivated, according to Hammond, to improve the system both by supporting those eligible and

Global discourses, national policies, local outcomes   221

excluding those perceived to be 'fraudulent', Dalian was able to raise additional resources and policy sponsors to test alternative mechanisms for implementation. The outcome, however, is a model that has not been widely replicated, and may not be financially sustainable even in the local context. Given the conditions and resource constraints described in Wuhan and Lanzhou, it is hard to envisage the more resource-intensive Dalian model being scaled up.

The capacity of this emerging welfare system to deliver basic security, fairness and justice are also addressed in these papers. Solinger, for example, discusses whether the system can provide 'fairness' as well as whether it protects against contingencies (loss of job, lack of income). On both accounts, it seems to fare poorly particularly in Wuhan, although the evaluations from beneficiaries do provide some positive accounts of the importance of even minimal benefits at the individual level. The notion of justice or fairness also permeates other discussions of local welfare programmes and outcomes: the sense of loss (comparison with a previous state) or unfair treatment (in comparison with others) is seen among welfare recipients and the elderly in urban areas. Among migrants, or villagers in poor, rural areas, these normative judgements are weaker: apparently these groups have limited expectations of the state or even the community or household to provide health care or other forms of support in the event of contingencies.

The studies of *dibao* illustrate clearly the different interpretations possible around programmes and their implementation. Local officials see mainly 'fraudulent' claimants and make little effort to explain the programmes; claimants see a stingy state, are unable to understand a complex and largely opaque system, and lack understanding of what is a legitimate claim; certain groups – women or the elderly, for example – feel particularly excluded. On the other hand, as Liu (in this volume) describes in the case of laid-off workers in Nanjing, individuals approach the system rationally, attempting to use it to support their livelihoods given the available information and constraints. Expectations about the programmes or the behaviour of local officials can thus create or reinforce negative stereotypes and further the breakdown in trust between citizens and local institutions of the state; or they may act as a mechanism – when implemented well – to promote a positive image of the state and rebuild trust in institutions. New discourses or images of the state as provider can be created to justify in some cases a loss of welfare provisions: Liu describes how the language of benefits and the welfare system – maternity leave, early retirement – creates an image of the benevolent state dealing with difficult circumstances, in turn creating a new discourse around gender roles and relations and the family unit. Boermel describes how the state reconceived its target group in the process of modernity away from the needy or aging and towards the new elite, thus alienating its former clientele. Over time, however, the local neighbourhood committee adapted and became more responsive to the changing needs of the elderly in the community.

Thus we return to a narrative at the local level that presents evidence of fragmentation, gaps and implementation failures. This needs to be placed

222 *Sarah Cook*

together with a more positive picture of changes taking place both at the policy level as well as at the grassroots, with new forms of mobilization, provision and organizing emerging as groups seek ways to engage with the top-down framework. Opportunities are being created and used to organize and make claims locally on resources. Fisher, Shang and Xie provide a description, on the one hand, of the extremely limited provisions available to those with disabilities; but, on the other hand, of local organizing of support networks and a growing capacity to make claims. Similarly in Boermel's story, evidence over time suggests changing attitudes, adaptation of the local cadres responsible for the elderly, greater awareness of their needs and continued room for change and influence.

Conclusion

China is embarking on a significant new phase in constructing its welfare regime. The current global economic crisis provides a significant moment to reflect on this process, and particularly on the challenges facing countries like China that have grown rapidly but find themselves exposed to global economic volatility. The role of China's welfare system in protecting its poor and vulnerable during times of crisis is being tested. Social policies also provide an instrument for the government to assist in the economic restructuring that is needed as a response to this crisis. Like its neighbouring East Asian developmental states (particularly South Korea and Taiwan) a decade ago, China now needs to adapt its social policies to lay the foundations for sustainable and inclusive growth, based on stronger domestic demand and greater socio-economic security for the majority of its population.

The challenges facing the leadership in this task are reflected in the analyses presented above. While the crisis may open up new policy space to promote further welfare reform and a more redistributive policy agenda, it also creates further divergence of interests among differentially affected regions and localities; between different levels of government and between different sectors and bureaucracies. Such variation will highlight again the limited capacity of the central state to ensure fiscal resource flows to where they are most needed, and to monitor and enforce policy implementation at the local level. While these systemic challenges will remain obstacles to the smooth implementation of welfare reforms that address the needs of the most vulnerable, nonetheless China has the resources and capacity – and at this point probably the political motivation – to expand welfare provisions and to integrate more redistributive social policies into its dominant economic reform agenda. This would be not only – or even principally – a means to protect its poorest people, but will be an essential mechanism for supporting economic restructuring and rebuilding the social contract necessary for achieving a harmonious society.

Bibliography

Abu-Lughod, J. (1961) 'Migrant adjustment to city life: The Egyptian case', *American Journal of Sociology*, 67: 22–32.

Adams, Jennifer and Hannum, Emily (2005) 'Children's social welfare in China, 1989–97: Access to health insurance and education', *The China Quarterly*, 181 (March): 100–121.

Agesa, R. U. and Kim, S. (2001) 'Rural to urban migration as a household decision: evidence from Kenya', *Review of Development Economics*, 5: 60–75.

Ali, Z., Fazil, Q., Bywaters, P., Wallace, L. and Singh, G. (2001) 'Disability, ethnicity and childhood: A critical review of research', *Disability & Society*, 16 (7): 949–68.

Anagnost, A. (2004) 'The corporeal politics of quality (*Suzhi*)', *Public Culture*, 16 (2): 189–208.

Anand, Sudhir, Peter, Fabienne and Sen, Amartya (2004) *Public Health, Ethics and Equity*, Oxford: Oxford University Press.

Anon. (1975) *Xiaojing* (Classic on Filial Piety) Chinese–English Edition, trans. M. Makra, ed. P. Sih, New York: St. John's University Press.

—— (1999) 'Chengshi jumin zuidi shenghuo baozhang tiaoli' (Regulations on the urban residents' minimum livelihood guarantee), *Zhongguo minzheng* (China Civil Affairs), 11: 16–17.

—— (1999). *China Education Yearbook 1998*, Beijing: People's Press.

—— (1999), 'Xiao ziliao: Quanguo gechengshi juimin zuidi shenghuo baozhang biaojun' (Small material: Nationwide various cities' residents' minimum livelihood guarantee norms), *Shehui* (Society), 6: 26.

—— (2005). *China Education Yearbook 2004*, Beijing: People's Press.

—— (2007). *Bluebook of Chinese Society*, Beijing: Social Sciences Academic Press.

—— (2008) *Yiju Zhongguo Dalian Jigou*. Online. Available HTTP: www.dl.home.sina.com.cn (accessed 1 March 2009).

Anson, O. and Sun, S. (2005) *Healthcare in Rural China: Lessons from Hebei Province*, London: Ashgate.

Appleton, Simon, Knight, John, Song, Lina and Xia, Qingjie Xia (2002) 'Labour retrenchment in China: determinants and consequences', *China Economic Review*, 13 (2/3): 252–75.

Arimah, B. C. (1997) 'The determinants of housing tenure choice in Ibadan, Nigeria', *Urban Studies*, 34: 105–24.

Arksey, H. and Glendinning, C. (2007) 'Informal welfare', in M. Powell (ed.) *Understanding the Mixed Economy of Welfare*, Bristol: Policy Press.

224   Bibliography

Baker, K. and Donelly, M. (2001) 'The social experiences of children with disability and the influence of environment: a framework for intervention', *Disability & Society*, 16 (1): 71–85.

Banks, M.E. (2003) 'Disability in the family: a life span perspective', *Cultural Diversity & Ethnic Minority Psychology*, 9 (4): 367–84.

Bauman, Z. (2004) *Wasted Lives: Modernity and its Outcasts*, Cambridge: Polity Press.

Baumgartner, F. and Jones, B. (1993) *Agendas and Instability in American Politics*, Chicago: University of Chicago Press.

Béland, Daniel and Yu, Ka Man (2004) 'A long financial march: pension reform in China', *Journal of Social Policy*, 33 (2): 267–88.

Beresford, Peter and Croft, Suzy (1983) 'Welfare pluralism: the new face of Fabianism', *Critical Social Policy,* (3): 19–39.

Bian, Yanjie (1994) *Work and Inequality in Urban China*, Albany: State University of New York.

Blekesaune, Morten (2006) 'Economic conditions and public attitudes towards welfare state policies', Institute for Social and Economic Research Working Paper, University of Essex.

Bloom, Gerald and Fang, Jing (2003) 'China's rural health system in changing institutional context', *IDS Working Paper* 194, Institute of Development Studies, Brighton.

Bloom, G. and Tang, S. (2004) *Health Care Transition in Urban China*, London: Ashgate.

Bloom, G., Kanjilal, B. and Peters, D. (2008) 'Regulating health care markets in China and India', *Health Affairs*, 27 (4): 952–63.

Blumenthal, David and Hsiao, William C. (2005) 'Privatisation and its discontents: the evolving chinese health care system', *New England Journal of Medicine*, 353 (11): 1165–69.

Boermel, A. (2008) '"No wasting" and "empty nesters": "Old Age" in Beijing', in R. Goodman and S. Harper (eds) *Ageing in Asia*, Abingdon: Routledge: 28–45.

Borevskaya, N. (2003) 'The private sector in the Chinese educational system: Problem and prospects', *Far Eastern Affairs*, 31 (4): 89–107.

Bourdieu, P. (1977) *Outline of a Theory of Practice*, Cambridge: Cambridge University Press.

—— (1990) *The Logic of Practice*, Cambridge: Polity Press.

Bray, D. (2005) *Social Space and Governance in Urban China: The Danwei System from Origin to Urban Reform*, Stanford: Stanford University Press.

—— (2006) 'Building "Community': new strategies of governance in urban China', *Economy and Society*, 35 (4): 530–49.

Brockerhoff, M. (1990) 'Rural-to-urban migration and child survival in Senegal', *Demography*, 27: 601–16.

Bronfenbrenner, U. (1979) *The Ecology of Human Development*, Cambridge: Harvard University Press.

BSLGWB – Office of the Beijing City Old Age Working Committee (2002) *Beijing Laoling Shiye: Jianjie* (Beijing's Undertaking for the Aged. A Brief Introduction), Beijing: Beijing shi laoling xiehui.

Bureau of Statistics of County H (2007) *Statistical Yearbook of County H, Jiangxi*, unpublished.

—— (2008) *Overview of Socioeconomic Development of County H*, Jiangxi Province 2007, unpublished.

Cai, Y. (2006) *State and Laid-off Workers in Reform China: The silence and collective action of the retrenched*, London: Routledge.

Bibliography 225

Carrillo, Beatriz (2008) 'From coal black to hospital white: The new welfare entrepreneurs and the pursuit for a "cleaner' status"', in David S. G. Goodman (ed.) *The New Rich in China: Future rulers, present lives*, London: Routledge: 99–111.

—— (2011) S*mall Town China: Rural Migrants and Social Inclusion*, London: Routledge.

Carrin, G. *et al.* (1997) 'Reforming the Rural Cooperative Medical System in China: A summary of Initial Experience', *IDS Bulletin*, 28 (1): 92–98.

—— (1999) 'The reform of the rural cooperative medical system in the People's Republic of China: interim experience in 14 pilot counties', *Social Science & Medicine* 48: 961–72.

Case, S. (2000) 'Refocusing on the parent: What are the social issues of concern for parents of disabled children?', *Disability & Society*, 15 (2): 271–92.

Central Committee of the Chinese Communist Party [CCCCP] (1985) 'The decision of the Central Committee of the Communist Party of China on the reform of educational structure', Beijing: People's Press.

—— (1993) 'The programme for educational reform and development in China', *Zhonghua Renmin Gongheguo Guowuyuan Gongbao*, 2: 58–66.

Central Party Committee and State Council (19 October 2002) '*Guanyu jin yi bu jiaqiang nongcun weisheng gongzuo de jueding*' (Decision on further strengthening rural health work). Online. Available HTTP: www.moh.gov.cn (accessed 1 February 2004).

Chan, A. and Tan, S. (eds) (2004) *Filial Piety in Chinese Thought and History*, London: Routledge.

Chan, C.K., Ngok, K.L. and Phillips, David (2008) *Social Policy in China: Development and Well-being*, Bristol: Policy Press.

Chan, K.W. (1998) 'Recent migration in mainland China: impact and policy issues', *Journal of Population Studies*, 19: 33–52.

Chang, Kai (1998) 'A survey and investigation of unemployment and reemployment of female employees in state-owned enterprises', *Chinese Sociology and Anthropology*, 30 (2):28–51.

Chaoyang District Government (n.d.) 'Beijing CBD' (Beijing's Central Business District). Online. Available HTTP: www.bjchy.gov.cn/chaoyang/mein/bjcbdmein/index.htm (accessed 17 August 2005).

Chen, B. and Li, G. (2002) 'Minban gaodeng jiaoyu ziketiqu yanjiu baogao' (The research report on people-run higher education), in B. Chen and G. Li (eds) *Minban Jiaoyu de Gaige yu Fazhan* (Minban Reform and Development of People-run Education), Beijing: Jiaoyu kexue chubanshe.

Chen, C.G and Yu, Q.Y. (2005) *Zoujin dazhonghua: 21 shijichu Guangzhou shi gaodeng jiaoyu fazhan yanjiu* (Towards Massification: Research on Guangzhou's Higher Education Development in Early 21st Century), Guangzhou: Jinan daxue chubanshe.

Chen, J., Campbell, C., Li, J. and Peto, R. (1990) *Diet, Lifestyle and Mortality in China*, Oxford: Oxford University Press.

Chen, J., Liu, B., Pan Wenharn, W., Campbell, C., Peto, R., Boreham, J., Parpia, B. Cassano, P. and Chen, Z. (2006) *Mortality, Biochemistry, Diet and Lifestyle in Rural China*, Oxford: Oxford University Press.

Chen, Mengjuan, Zhou, Tao, Yan, Yiping and Wu, Wei (2000) '*Nanjing zhigong xiagang fenliu yu zai jiuye de zouxiang he duice*' (Trends and policies for laid-off workers and their reemployment in Nanjing), *Nanjing Shexui kexue* (Social Sciences in Nanjing), 3.

Chen, Shaohua and Ravallion, Martin (2008) 'China is Poorer than We Thought, But No Less Successful in the Fight against Poverty', World Bank Policy Research Working Paper (No. 4621), Washington, DC.

226 *Bibliography*

Chen, Yiu Por and Liang, Zai (2007) 'Educational attainment of migrant children', in Emily Hannum and Albert Park (eds.) *Education and Reform in China*, New York: Routledge: 117–32.

Chen, X. (2006) 'High-risk enterprises: Will universities go bankrupt?'. Online. Available HTTP: www.dajun.com.cn/daxuepc.htm.

Chen, X.M. and Chen, Y.A. (2008) *The Status Analysis and Strategies Study of Children with Disability in China*, Beijing: Huaxia Press.

Chen, Y. (2005) 'Behind millions of donations', *China Youth News*, 30 June 2005.

Cheng, E. (2006) 'China: Capitalist restoration worsens inequality', *Green Left Weekly*, 12 April 2006: 1–4.

Cheng, K.M. (1995) 'Education – decentralisation and the market', in L. Wong and S. MacPherson (eds) *Social Change and Social Policy in Contemporary China*, Avebury: Aldershot: 70–87.

China Cooperative Medical Scheme [CCMS] (2008) 'Yin Li fubuzhang shicha weishengbu xinxing nongcun hezuo yiliao yanjiu zhongxin' (Vice Secretary Yin Li surveys the Ministry of Health's New Rural Cooperative Medical Scheme Research Centre). Online. Available HTTP: www.ccms.org.cn/third-xwxx.asp?id=226 (accessed 28 November 2008).

—— (2007) Online. Available HTTP: ccms.org.cn (accessed 4 July 2007)

China Daily (2002) '*Minban* education', 15 August.

—— (2003) 'Elderly project starts new stage', 6 November. Online. Available HTTP: app1.chinadaily.com.cn/chinagate/focus/relief/news/i002/20030611old.html (accessed 14 January 2009)

—— (2004) 'Minban education in China', 27 March.

—— (2006) 'Welfare lottery just the ticket for charities', 18 January. Online. Available HTTP: china.org.cn/english/Life/155549.htm (accessed 14 January 2009).

—— (2006) 'Citizens responses to high school fees', 26 August.

—— (2007) 'Heave financial burden of school fees', 28 February.

—— (2007) 'Household consumption trends in China', 28 May.

China Disabled Persons Federation (CDPF) (2007) *A Handbook of Main Data from the Second National Sampling Survey on Disability (2006–2007)*, Beijing: Huaxia Press.

—— (2008a) *Law of the People's Republic of China on the Protection of Persons with Disabilities*. Online. Available HTTP: www.cdpf.org.cn/english/law/content/2008–04/10/content_84949.htm (accessed 15 August 2008).

—— (2008b) *Main functions*. Online. Available HTTP: www.cdpf.org.cn/zyzn/node_5042.htm (accessed 19 June 2008).

China Education and Research Network (2006) 'The educational development during the 10th 5-Year Plan'. Online. Available HTTP: www.edu.cn/news_1461/20060228/t20060228_164200. shtml.

China Higher Education Student Information (2007). Online. Available HTTP: www.chsi.com.cn.

China National Social Security [CNSS] (*Zhongguo Shehui Baozhang*) (23 Nov. 2006) 'Sichuan "xinnonghe" zai wanshan zhong qianxing' (Sichuan's new rural cooperative healthcare progresses toward perfection). Online. Available HTTP: www.cnss.cn/yjpt/ztbd/200611/t20061123_108478.html (accessed 28 Nov. 2008).

Chinese Government web portal (2008) (*Zhongyang zhengfu menhu wangzhan*) (16 Sept. 2008) '*Zhongyang caizheng jinnian xiada Sichuan xin nong he buzhu zijin 241933 wan*' (This year the ministry of finance gives Sichuan's new rural cooperative

Bibliography 227

healthcare a subsidy of 2,419,330,000). Online. Available HTTP: www.gov.cn/gzdt/2008–9/16/content_1096947.htm (accessed 12 November 2008).

Chow, Nelson and Xu, Yuebin (2001) *Socialist Welfare in a Market Economy: Social Security Reforms in Guangzhou, China*, Aldershot: Ashgate.

Shi renmin zhengfu guanyu yinfa (2004) 'The Method of Implementation for Wuhan's Urban Residents Minimum Livelihood Guarantee and Wuhan City's (Experimental) Method for the Rural Residents' Minimum Livelihood Guarantee', City People's Government Circular Wuhan, no. 63 (issued 10 October 2004).

Clarke, H. (2006) 'Preventing social exclusion of disabled children and their families: literature review', paper produced for the National Evaluation of the Children's Fund, Institute of Applied Social Studies University of Birmingham, Research Report RR782.

Cook, Sarah (2002) 'From Rice Bowl to Safety Net: Insecurity and Social Protection during China's Transition', *Development Policy Review*, 20 (5): 615–35.

—— (2007) 'Putting health back in China's development', *China Perspectives*, 3: 100–08.

Cook, S. and Jolly S. (2000) *Unemployment, Poverty and Gender in Urban China: Perceptions and Experiences of Laid Off Workers in Three Chinese Cities* [IDS Research Report 50], Brighton: Institute of Development Studies.

Cook, Sarah and Kwon, Huck-Ju (2008) 'Revisiting welfare developmentalism: Economic reforms and trajectories of social policy in East Asia', *La Rivista delle Politiche Sociali* (Italian Journal of Social Policy), no. 1 (January/March) (in Italian and English).

Costello, M. A. (1987) 'Slums and squatter areas an entrepot for rural–urban migrants in a less developed society', *Social Forces*, 66: 427–45.

County Committee, Chinese Communist Party, the People's Government, H County, (2008) S*ituation of H County*. Online. Available HTTP: www.hfzc.com.cn (accessed 25 January 2008).

Crandon-Malamud, L. 1991 *From the Fat of Our Souls. Social Change, Political Process, and Medical Pluralism in Bolivia*, Berkeley: California University Press.

Cummings, W. (1996) 'Asian values, education and development', *Compare*, 26 (3): 287–304.

da Piedade Morais, M. and de Oliveira Cruz, B. (2007) *Housing Demand, Tenure Choice and Housing*: Institute de Pesquisa Economica Aplicada.

Dai, J.L. (2005) 'Resident's life: Moving towards the society of overall well-to-do level', in B. Ren (ed.) *2005 Blue book of Zhejiang*, Hangzhou: Hangzhou chubanshe.

Dalian Bureau of Statistics Online (2009). Online. Available: HTTP: www.stats.dl.gov.cn (accessed 1 March 2009).

Dalian Government Online (2003). Online. Available: HTTP: 2003.dl.gov.cn (accessed 9 June 2008).

Dalian CAB (1999) 'Gouzhu siwei yiti baozhang moushi tigao chengshi jumin zuidi shenghuo baozhang shuiping' (Construct a four-in-one security model toraise urban resident minimum livelihood guarantee level), in MCA Department of Disaster and Social Assistance (ed.), *Chengshi jumin zuidi shenghuo baozhang zhidu wenjian zike huibian* (Urban Resident Minimum Livelihood Guarantee System Document Collection), Beijing: 233–42.

Dalian CAB Online (2008) '*Dalian shi gongong fuwushe – hou fuli shidai pinkun quntide shehui jiuzhu he shehui zhichi wangge*' (Dalian City Community Public Service Agency – Final Period Poverty Gap Welfare, Social Relief and Social Support Network). Online. Available HTTP: zyzx.mca.gov.cn (accessed 17 November 2008).

Dalian CAB and SPRC CASS (2002) '*2002 dibao yu shequ gonggong fuwu she gongzuo peixun jiaocai: zuidi shenghuo baozhang & shequ gonggong fuwu she*' (2002

228 Bibliography

Minimum Livelihood Guarantee and Community Public Service Agency Training Materials: Minimum Livelihood Guarantee and Community Public Service Agency), Dalian: Dalian Civil Affairs Bureau.

Dalian Municipal Government (1999), '*Dalian shi chengzhen jumin zuidi shenghuo baozhang banfa*' (Dazhengfa [1999] No 23) (Dalian City Urban Resident Minimum Livelihood Guarantee Methods), in Dalian CAB & SPRC CASS (eds) *2002 Dibao yu shequ gonggong fuwu she gongzuo peixun jiaocai: zuidi shenghuo baozhang & shequ gonggong fuwu she*, Dalian: Dalian Civil Affairs Bureau.

Davis, D. (1988) 'Unequal chances, unequal outcomes: pension reform and urban inequality', *The China Quarterly*, no. 114: 223–42.

Dean, H. (2007) 'Social policy and human rights: rethinking the engagement', *Social Policy & Society*, 7 (1): 1–12.

Derleth, J. and Koldyk, D. (2002) 'Community development and political reform in urban China', *China Development Brief*, 1 October. Online. Available HTTP: www.chinadevelopmentbrief.com/node/159 (accessed 1 March 2007).

Derleth, J. and Koldyk, D. (2004) 'The *Shequ* experiment: grassroots political reform in urban China', *Journal of Contemporary China*, 13 (41): 747–77.

Di shi'erci quanguo minzheng huiyi zai jing juxing (12th National Civil Affairs Conference) (2006) '*Wen Jiabao: Yongxin liaojie sheqing menyi; bangzhu qunzhong paiyou jienan*' (Wen Jiabao: Be attentive and understand social conditions and popular sentiments, help the masses to get rid of worries and overcome difficulties). Online. Available HTTP: china.com.cn/city/txt/2006–11/28/content_420827.htm.

Ding L. (1999) 'From unit welfare to social security – recording the emergence of Chinese urban residents' minimum livelihood guarantee system' (*Cong danwei fuli dao shehui baozhang-ji zhongguo chengshi jumin zuidi shenghuo baozhang zhidu de dansheng*), *China Civil Affairs* (*Zhongguo minzheng*), 11: 6–7.

Dixon, John (1981) *The Chinese Welfare System, 1949–1979*, New York: Praeger.

Dong, X. (2001) *Little Dictionary of Proverbs*, Chengdu: Sichuan Phrasebook Publishing.

Dong, Xiao-Yuan (2003) 'China's urban labour market adjustment: a literature review', East Asia Human Development Sector Unit, World Bank.

Dong, Xiao-Yuan, Yang, Jianchun, Du, Fenglian and Ding, Sai (2005) 'Women's employment and public-sector restructuring: the case of Urban China', in Grace Lee and Malcolm Warner (eds) *Unemployment in China: Economy, Resources, and Labour Markets*, London and New York: Routledge: 87–107.

Dong, Z. and Phillips, M. (2008) 'Evolution of China's health-care system', *The Lancet*, 372 (9651): 1715–16.

Dowling, M. and Dolan, L. (2001) 'Families with children with disabilities – inequalities and the social model', *Disability & Society*, 16 (1): 21–25.

Duckett, Jane (2002) 'State self-earned income and welfare provision in China', *Provincial China*, 7 (1):1–19.

—— (2003) 'China's social security reform and the comparative politics of market transition', *Journal of Communist Studies and Transition Politics*, 19 (1): 80–101.

—— (2007a) 'Local governance, health financing, and changing patterns of inequality in access to healthcare', in Vivienne Shue and Christine Wong (eds) *Paying for Progress: Public Finance, Human Welfare and Changing Patterns of Inequality*, London: Routledge: 46–68.

—— (2007b) 'NGOs and Health Policy in China', paper presented at the British Inter-University China Centre Conference, University of Oxford.

—— (2010) *The Chinese State's Retreat from Health: Policy and the Politics of Retrenchment*, London: Routledge.

Duckett, J. and Hussain, A. (2005) 'Developing Unemployment Insurance and Employment Services', Policy Brief for the Sino-British China Unemployment Insurance Project, Beijing.

—— (2008) 'Tackling unemployment in China: state capacity and governance issues', *Pacific Review*, 21 (2): 211–29.

Duda, M. and Li, B. (2008) 'Housing inequality in Chinese cities how important is Hukou?' *Land Lines*, 20 (1): 14–19.

Duda, M., Li, Bingqin and Peng, Huamin (2008) 'Household Strategies and Migrant Housing Quality in Tianjin', in I. Nielsen and R. Smyth (eds) *Migration and Social Protection in China*, Oxford: World Scientific: 184–204.

Dummer, Trevor J.B. and Cook, Ian G. (2007) 'Exploring China's rural health crisis: Processes and policy implications', *Health Policy*, 83 (1): 1–16.

Editorial Committee of Annals of H County (1992) *Annals of H County*, Hangzhou: Zhejiang People's Press.

Edwards, M. (1983) 'Residential mobility in a changing housing market: the case of Bucaramanga, Colombia', *Urban Studies*, 20: 131–45.

English First China (2007). Online. Available HTTP: www.ef.com.cn (accessed on 14 June 2007).

English First Worldwide (2007). Online. Available HTTP: www.englishfirst.com (accessed 14 June 2007).

Esping-Andersen, Gøsta (1990) *The Three Worlds of Welfare Capitalism*, Cambridge: Polity Press.

Etkin, N. (1988) 'Cultural Constructions of Efficacy', in S. Van Der Geest and S. Whyte (eds) *The Context of Medicines in Developing Countries: Studies in Pharmaceutical Anthropology*, Dordrecht: Kluwer.

Etkin, N. and Tan, M. (eds) (1994) *Medicines: Meanings and Contexts*, Quezon City, Philippines: Health Action Information Network.

Evers, Adalbert (1995) 'Part of the welfare mix: The third sector as an intermediate area', *Voluntas: International Journal of Voluntary and Nonprofit Organisations,* 6 (2): 159–82.

Fan, Ruiping (2006) 'Towards a Confucian virtue bioethics: reframing Chinese medical ethics in a market economy', *Theoretical Medicine and Bioethics*, 27 (6): 541–66.

Fang, Jing (2008) 'The Chinese health care regulatory institutions in an era of transition', *Social Science and Medicine*, 66 (4): 952–62.

Farquhar, J. (2002) *Appetites. Food and Sex in Post-Socialist China*, London: Duke University Press.

Farmer, Paul (2003) *Pathologies of Power: Health, human rights and the new war on the poor.* Berkeley: University of California Press.

Farrell, D., Gersch, U.A. and Stephenson, E. (2006) 'The value of China's emerging middle class', *The McKinsey Quarterly*, Special Edition.

Feng, L. (2003) 'How far are the floating children in the cities from the compulsory nine-year schooling? The value analysis of schools for the children of casual laborers' (in Chinese), *Theory and Practice of Education*, 23(5): 38–42.

Feng L., Bao S. and Chen M. (2002) 'Liaoning shebao gaige chongguan' (Liaoning's social security reform's important period), *Liaowang,* 11: 26–27.

Feng, Xueshan, Tang, Shenglan, Gerald Bloom, Malcolm Segall, and Gu Xingyuan (1995) 'Cooperative medical schemes in contemporary rural China', *Social Science*

230 *Bibliography*

& *Medicine*. Special Issue on 'Aspects of the Medical Care System in the People's Republic of China' 41(8): 1111–18.

Fitoussi, Jean-Paul and Saraceno, Francisco (2008) 'The intergenerational content of social spending: Health care and sustainable growth in China', OFCE Working Paper No. 2008–27.

Fobil, J. N. and Atuguba, R. A. (2004) 'Ghana: migration and the African urban complex', in T. Falola and S. J. Salm (eds) *Globalization and Urbanization in Africa*, Trenton, NJ: Africa World Press: 249–70.

Frazier, Mark L. (2004) 'China's pension reform and its discontents', *China Journal*, 51: 97–114.

Froissart, Chloe (2003) 'The hazards of the right to an education. a study of the schooling of migrant worker children in Chengdu', *China Perspectives*, 48 (July–August).

Funder, K. (ed.) (1996) *Citizen Child: Australian Law and Children's Rights*, Melbourne: Australian Institute of Family Studies.

Gammeltoft, T. (2007) 'Prenatal diagnosis in postwar vietnam. power, subjectivity and citizenship', *American Anthropologist*, 109 (1): 153–63.

Gansusheng renmin zhengfu bangongting (2002), 'Guanyu zhuanfa "Gansusheng chengshi jumin zuidi shenghuo baozhang banfa" de tongzhi' ('Notice Concerning transmitting "Gansu Province urban residents' minimum livelihood guarantee method"'), *Caikuai yanjiu* (Finance and Accounting Research), 5: 58–60.

Gao, Jun, Tang, Shenglan, Tollhurst, Rachel and Rao, Keqin (2001) 'Changing access to health services in urban China: implications for equity', *Health Policy and Planning*, 16 (3): 302–12.

Ge, D. (2001a) 'Community public service agency development investigation report' (Shequ gonggong fuwu she fazhan diaocha baogao), in SPRC CASS (ed.) (2003) *Zhongguo shehui baozhang zhidu zaizao – Dalian xiangmu pinggu cailiao*, Beijing: CASS: 35–41.

—— (2001b) 'Dalian shequ gonggong fuwu she wenjuan diaocha shuju baogao' (Dalian CPSA statistical investigation report), in SPRC CASS (ed.) (2003) *Zhongguo shehui baozhang zhidu zaizao – Dalian xiangmu pinggu cailiao*, Beijing: CASS: 20–33.

Ge, D. and Yang, T. (2003) 'Why Community Public Service Agency Can Develop Rapidly', in Yang Tuan (ed.) *Social Policy in China*, Beijing: SPRC CASS: 241–75.

Gelissen, John (2002) *Worlds of Welfare, Worlds of Consent? Public opinion on the welfare state*, Leiden: Brill.

Geva-May, Iris and Maslove, Allan (2000) 'What prompts health care policy change? on political power contests and reform of health care systems (the case of Canada and Israel)', *Journal of Health Politics, Policy and Law*, 25 (4): 717–41.

Gilbert, A. G. and Ward, P. M. (1982) 'Residential Movement among the Poor: The Constraints on Housing Choice in Latin American Cities', *Transactions of the Institute of British Geographers*, 7: 129–49.

Giles, John, Park, Albert and Zhang, J.W. (2005) 'What is China's true unemployment rate?', *China Economic Review*, 16 (2): 149–70.

Giles, John, Park, Albert and Cai, Fang (2006) 'How has economic restructuring affected China's urban workers?', *The China Quarterly*, no. 185: 61–95.

Gmelch, G. (1980) 'Return migration', *Annual Reviews in Anthropology*, 9: 135–59.

Gong, Ting (2002) 'Women's unemployment, re-employment, and self-employment in China's economic restructuring', in Esther Ngan-Ling Chow (ed.) *Transforming Gender and Development in East Asia*, New York and London: Routledge: 125–39.

Bibliography 231

Goodman, David S.G. (2000) 'The localism of local leadership: cadres in reform Shanxi', *The China Quarterly*, no. 172: 837–62.

—— (2001) 'The interdependence of state and society: the political sociology of local leadership', in C.M. Chao and B. J. Dickson (eds), *Remaking the Chinese State: Strategies, Society and Security*, London: Routledge.

—— (2002) 'Structuring local identity: nation, province and county', *The China Quarterly*, no. 172: 837–62.

——(ed.) (2008) *The New Rich in China: Future rulers, present lives*, London: Routledge.

Gu, C. and Shen, J. (2003) 'Transformation of urban socio-spatial structure in socialist market economies: the case of Beijing', *Habitat International*, 27: 107–22.

Gu, Edward X. (1999) 'From permanent employment to massive layoffs: the political economy of 'transitional unemployment" in urban China (1993–98)', *Economy and Society*, 28 (2): 281–99.

—— (2000) 'Massive layoffs and the transformation of employment relations in urban China', *Labour, Capital and Society*, 33 (1): 46–74.

—— (2001) 'Beyond the property rights approach: Welfare policy and the reform of state-owned enterprises in China', *Development and Change*, 32 (1):129–50.

Gu, T., Gao, M. and Yao, Y. (2006) *Zhenduan yu chufang. Zhimian zhongguo yiliao tishi gaige* (China's Health Care Reforms: A Pathological Analysis), Beijing: Social Science Academic Press.

Gu, Zhaonong (2000) 'The issue of medical insurance reform schedules in Nanjing (Nanjing jiben yiliao baoxian zhidu gaige fang'an chutai)', *People's Newspaper* (*Renmin ribao*), 18 December.

Guan, Xinping (1995) 'Poverty and antipoverty programs in rural China since the mid-1980s', *Social Policy & Administration*, 29 (3): 204–27.

—— (2000) 'China's social policy: reform and development in the context of marketisation and globalisation', *Social Policy and Administration*, 34 (1): 115–30.

—— (2001) 'China's social policy in the context of globalisation', in Social Policy Research Centre, Hong Kong Polytechnic University (ed.) *Repositioning of the State: Challenges and Experiences of Social Policy in the Asia Pacific Region*, Hong Kong: Joint Publishing Co. Ltd.

—— (2003) 'Dangqian Zhongguo chengshi pingkun wenti ji fanpinkun zhengce' (Current urban poverty and anti-poverty policies in China), *Jiangsu Journal of Social Sciences*, 2: 108–15.

Handelman, H. (1975) 'The political mobilization of urban squatter settlements: Santiago's recent experience and its implications for urban research', *Latin American Research Review*, 10: 35–72.

Harpham, T. (1994) 'Cities and health in the Third World', in D. R. Phillips and Y. Verhasselt (eds) *Health and Development*, London: Routledge: 111–21.

Hawkins, J.N. (2000) 'Centralisation, decentralisation, recentralisation: Educational reform in China', *Journal of Educational Administration*, 38 (5): 442–54.

He, L., and Li, B. (2007) 'Policy analysis of migrant children in China', *Population Research*, 31 (2): 73–82.

Hindle, D. (2000) 'China in transition: the new health insurance scheme for the urban employed', *Australian Health Review*, 23 (3): 122–31.

Hong, Zhaohui (2002) 'Lun shehui zuanli de "pinkun" – zhongguo chengshi pinkun wenti de genyuan yu zhili lujing' [Poverty of social rights: Dilemmas of urban poverty in China], *Xiandai zhongguo yanjiu* [Modern China Studies], 79 (4): 9–10.

232 Bibliography

Hou, Xiaohui and Coyne, Joseph (2008) 'The emergence of proprietary medical facilities in China', *Health Policy*, 88 (1): 141–51.

Howell, Jude (2003) 'New directions in civil society: organisation around marginal interests', in J. Howell (ed.) *Governance in China*, Oxford: Rowman & Littlefield.

Hu, J. (2007) *Report Given at the 17th Party Congress*. Online. Available HTTP: news. xinhuanet.com/english/2007–10/24/content_6938749_7.htm (accessed 20 January 2009).

Hu, Shanlian, Tang, Shenglan, Liu, Yuanli, Zhao, Yuxin, Escobar, Maria-Luisa and de Ferrati, David (2008) 'Reform of how health care is paid for in China: challenges and opportunities', *The Lancet*, 372 (9652): 1846–53.

Huang, Y. (2003) 'Renters' housing behaviour in transitional urban China', *Housing Studies,* 18: 103–26.

Huchzermeyer, M. (2008) 'Slum upgrading in nairobi within the housing and basic services market: a housing rights concern', *Journal of Asian and African Studies*, 43: 19–39.

Hung, Eva P. W. and Chiu, Stephan W. K. (2003) 'The lost generation: life course dynamics and Xiagang in China', *Modern China*, 29 (2): 204–36.

Hurst, W. and O'Brien, K. (2002) 'China's contentious pensioners', *The China Quarterly*, 170: 345–60.

Hussain, Athar (2007) 'Setting up an integrated social security system', *China Perspectives*, no. 3: 92–98.

Hussain, Athar *et al.* (2002) 'Urban poverty in the PRC', Asian Development Bank Project No. TAR: PRC 33448.

Ikels, C. (2004) 'The impact of housing policy on China's urban elderly', *Urban Anthropology*, 33 (2–4): 321–55.

—— (ed.) (2004) *Filial Piety: Practice and discourse in contemporary East Asia*, Stanford: Stanford University Press.

Information Office of the State Council of the People's Republic of China (2004) 'China's Social Security and Its Policy'. Online. Available HTTP: www.china.org.cn/ e-white/20040907/index.htm (accessed 20 September 2004).

Irwin, L.G., Siddiqi, A. and Hertzman, C. (2007) *Early Child Development: A Powerful Equalizer*, Commission on the Social Determinants of Health, World Health Organisation.

Jenks, E.B. (2005) 'Explaining disability: parents' stories of raising children with visual impairments in a sighted world', *Journal of Contemporary Ethnography*, 34 (2): 143–69.

Jianwai Street Office (2005) *Harmonious Jianwai* (Hexie Jianwai), Beijing.

Jiang, J. (2008) 'Yi shiqida jingshen wei zhizhen – nuli tuidong langzhong jingji shehui you hao you kuai fazhan' ('Following the spirit of the seventeenth People's Congress – striving to promote better and faster social and economic development in Langzhong'), *Langzhong online news*, 4 January. Online. Available HTTP: www.lzgc. com/htm/a6/2008/1–4/zpcb30516879.asp (accessed 28 November 2008).

Johnson, K., Huang, B., and Wang, L. (1998) 'Infant abandonment and adoption in China', Population and Development Review, 24 (3): 469–510.

Kahn, Joseph (2005) 'China worries about economic surge that skips the poor', *New York Times*, 4 March. Online) Available: www.nytimes.com/2005/03/04/international/ asia/04china.html (accessed 4 March 2005).

Kamat, Vinay 2009 'Cultural interpretations of the efficacy and side effects of antimalarials in Tanzania'. *Anthropology and Medicine*, 16(3): 293–305.

Kelly, S. (2005) '"A different light": examining impairment through parent narratives of childhood disability', *Journal of Contemporary Ethnography*, 34 (2): 180–205.

Keng, C.W. (2006) 'China's unbalanced economic growth', *Journal of Contemporary China*, 15 (46): 183–214.

Khan, Azizur Rahman and Riskin, Carl (1998) 'Income and Inequality in China', *The China Quarterly*, no. 164: 221–53.

—— (2005) 'China's Household Income and Its Distribution, 1995–2002', *The China Quarterly*, no. 182: 356–84.

Khan, Azizur Rahman, Griffin, Keith and Riskin, Carl (2001) 'Income distribution in urban China during the period of economic reform and globalisation', in C. Riskin, R. Zhao and S. Li. (eds) *China's Retreat from Equality: income distribution and economic transition*, Armonk, NY: M.E. Sharpe.

Khan, Azizur Rahman, Griffin, Keith, Riskin, Carl and Zhao, Renwei (1992) 'Household income and its distribution in China', *The China Quarterly*, no. 132: 1029–61.

Kim, C. and Gottdiener, M. (2004) 'Urban Problems in global perspective', in G. Ritzer (ed.) *Handbook of Social Problems: A Comparative International Perspective*, Sage Publications: 172–92.

Kingdon, J. (1984) *Agendas, Alternatives and Public Policies*, Boston: Little Brown.

Kleinman, Arthur 1995 *Writing at the Margins: Discourse between Anthropology and Medicine*. Berkeley: University of California Press.

Knight, J., Song, Lina and Jia, Huabin (1999) 'Chinese rural migrants in urban enterprises: three perspectives', *Journal of Development Studies*, 35 (3): 73–104.

Kohrman, M. (2005) *Bodies of Difference Experiences of Disability and Institutional Advocacy in the Making of Modern China*, Berkeley: University of California Press.

Kojima, K. and R. Kokubun (2002) 'The "*Shequ* construction" programme and the Chinese Communist Party', *Copenhagen Journal of Asian Studies*, 16: 86–105.

Kwon, Huck-Ju (ed.) (2005) *Transforming the developmental welfare state in East Asia*, London: Unrisd/Palgrave.

Kwong, Julia (1996) 'The new educational mandate in China: running schools running businesses', *International Journal of Educational Development*, 16 (2): 185–94.

—— (2004) 'Educating migrant children: negotiations between state and civil society', *The China Quarterly*, no. 180: 1073–88.

Lampton, D. (1977) *The Politics of Medicine in China: the Policy Process 1949–1977*, Folkestone: Dawson.

Lancet, The (2008) 'Series on Health Systems reform in China'. Online. Available HTTP: www.thelancet.com/series/health-system-reform-in-china (accessed 25 November 2008).

Langzhong Administrative Service Centre (2008) '*Langzhong: qingli gouzhu xinxing nongcun hezuo yiliao shehui baozhang tixi*' (Langzhong: building the new rural healthcare cooperative social security system'), 4 January. Online, Available HTTP: www.lzzw.gov.cn:81/q_detail.asp?id=100005599&lm_id=1002; also published on Southwest economics network (*xibu jingji wang*) www.swbd.cn/zhuankan/ShowArticle. asp?ArticleID=8899 (accessed 28 November 2008).

Langzhong Rural Healthcare Cooperative Management Centre (2005) '*Tigao renshi, jiaqiang lingdao, jingxin zuzhi, qieshi zhua hao xinxing nongcun hezuo yiliao shidian gongzuo*' (Increasing knowledge, strengthening leadership, meticulous structuring and realistic grasping of the new form of rural cooperative healthcare pilot project work), speech by the vice-mayor at the training session for the municipal RCMS, 2 December.

Lee, Ching Kwan (2005) 'Livelihood struggles and market reform: (un)marking Chinese labour after state socialism', *Occasional Paper 2*, United Nations Research Institute for Social Development.

234 Bibliography

Lee, Grace O.M., and Warner, Malcolm (2004) 'The Shanghai re-employment model: from local experimentation to nation-wide labour market policy', *The China Quarterly*, no. 177: 174–89.

Lee, P.N.S. (1993) 'Reforming the social security system in China', in S. S. Nagel and M. K. Mills (eds) *Public Policy in China*, Westport, CN: Greenwood Press.

Leonard, P. and Flower, J. (2006) 'Ecological engineering on the West China frontier: socialism as development policy, local practice and contested ideology', unpublished paper.

Leung, Joe C.B. (1994) 'Dismantling the "Iron Rice Bowl": welfare reforms in the People's Republic of China', *Journal of Social Policy*, 23 (3): 341–61.

Leung, Joe C.B., and Wong, Hilda S.W. (1999) 'The emergence of a community-based social assistance programme in urban China', *Social Policy and Administration*, 33 (1): 39–54.

Li, Bingqin (2005) 'Urban housing privatisation: redefining the responsibilities of the state, employers and individuals', in S. Green and Shaojia G. L. (eds) *Exit the Dragon? Privatization and State Control in China*, London: Chatham House and Blackwell Publishing: 145–68.

—— (2006) 'Floating population or urban citizens? Status, social provision and circumstances of rural-urban migrants in China', *Social Policy & Administration*, 40: 174–95.

—— (2007) 'The transformation of cities and establishing flexible housing system in large cities' (*Chengshi bianqian he jianli lingguo de dachengshi zhufang tixi*), *International Economic Review* (*Guoji jingji pinglun*), 5: 26–30.

Li, B. and Gong, S. (2003) *Urban Social Inequalities and Wage, Housing and Pension Reforms in China*, Asian Program Working Paper Series, No. 3, London: Royal Institute of International Affairs at Chatham House.

Li, B., Duda, M. and Peng, H. (2007) *Low-Cost Urban Housing Markets: Serving the Needs of Low-Wage, Rural–Urban Migrants?* Final Report for Lincoln Institute of Land Policy, grant #: CMD111506.

Li, H. (1998) 'By levels take responsibility for conscientiously guaranteeing – Guangdong's Donghuang City's way of implementing urban and rural residents' minimal livelihood guarantee system', *Zhongguo minzheng*, 1 (no page numbers).

Li, H. and Zahniser, S. (2002) 'The determinants of temporary rural-to-urban migration in China', *Urban Studies*, 39 (12): 2219–35.

Li, J. (2006) 'Dragon City opens its arms to welcome new Taiyuan people', (*longcheng changkai huaibao yingjie xintaiyuan ren*), *Shanxi Commercial News*, 14 December, 2006.

Li, L. (2006) 'Changsha nongmingong lianzufang weihe zaoyu jiti lengluo' ('Why the cheap rental houses for migrant workers in Changsha were unpopular'), *People's Daily*, 5 September.

Li, Peiling, Zhang, Yi and Zhao, Yandong (2000) *Jiuye yu zhidu bianqian: liangge teshu qunti de qiuzhi guocheng* (Employment and Institutional Change: Job Searches of Two Special Groups), Hangzhou: Zhejiang renmin chubanshe.

Li, Qiang, Hu, Junsheng and Hong, Dayong (2001) *Shiye xiagang wenti duibi yanjiu* (A Comparative Study of Unemployment and Layoffs), Beijing: Tsinghua University Press.

Li, R. (2007) 'Casualties of the rush to profit from schooling', *South China Morning Post*, 27 January.

Li, S. and Zhang, Y. (2005) 'Sichuan sheng xinxing nongcun hezuo yiliao shidian zhong de wenti yu duice' (Problems and countermeasures for new rural cooperative

Bibliography 235

medical institution of sichuan province), *Chongqing gongshang daxue xue bao, xibu luntan* (Journal of Chongqing Technology and Business University, West Forum), 15 (4): 49–51.

Liang, X. and Yuan, Y. (2008) 'Woguo chengshi zhufang gongying tizhi xuanze de lilun he zhengce yanjiu' (Study on the theory and policy about urban housing – supplying system in our country), *Chengshi* (Cities), 1: 26–30.

Lieberthal, K. G. (1992) 'Introduction: The "fragmented authoritarianism" model and its limitations', in K. G. Lieberthal and D. M. Lampton (eds) *Bureaucracy, Politics, and Decision Making in Post-Mao China*, Berkeley: University of California Press: 1–30.

—— (1995) *Governing China: From Revolution Through Reform*, New York: Norton.

Lieberthal, K. and Oksenberg, M. (1988) *Policy Making in China: Leaders, Structures, and Processes*, Princeton: Princeton University Press.

Lijphart, A. (1971) 'Comparative politics and the comparative method', *American Political Science Review*, 65 (3): 682–93.

Lin, J. (2004) 'China: private trends', *International Higher Education*, 36: 17–18.

Lin, J., Zhang, Y., Gao, L. and Liu, Y. (2005) 'Trust, ownership, and autonomy: Challenges facing private higher education in China', *The China Review*, 5 (1): 61–82.

Lin, Nan (2001) *Social Capital: A Theory of Social Structure and Action*, Cambridge: Cambridge University Press.

Lin, Songle (1995) 'Guanyu xingbie jiaose de jici zhenglun' (Several debates on Gender Roles), *Sociology Studies*, 1: 106–8.

Lin, T. and Chen, Y. (2004) 'The plights and outlets of public primary school and middle school in the course of institution changing', *Forum on Contemporary Education*, 5: 45–49.

Lin, Zhifen (2004) 'Regional disparities in social security in china and transfer payments', *The Chinese Economy*, 16 (3): 59–73.

Lindelow, Magnus and Wagstaff, Adam (2005) 'Health shocks in China: Are the poor and uninsured less protected?', World Bank Policy Research Working Paper 3740 (Oct.), Washington, DC.

Liu, Dezhong and Niu, Bianxiu (2000) 'Zhongguo de hangye xingbie geli yu nüxing jiuye' (Chinese occupational segregation and women's employment)', *Journal of Women's Studies*, 4: 18–20.

Liu, Houjun, Zeng, Xiangdong and Zhang, Erzheng (2002) *Nanjing chengshi zonghe jingzhengli yanjiu* (The study of comprehensive competitive capacity of Nanjing city), Nanjing: South-Eastern China University Press.

Liu, Jieyu (2007) *Gender and Work in Urban China: Women Workers of the Unlucky Generation*, London: Routledge.

Liu, Jing (2002) 'Guanzhu chengshi dishouru qunti: Wuhanshi qiaokouqu chengshi jumin zuidi shenghuo baozhang gongzuo toushi' (Pay close attention to urban low-income masses: Wuhan's Qiaokou district's urban residents' minimum livelihood guarantee work perspective), *Hubei Caishui* (Hubei Finance and Taxes), 2: 4–5.

Liu, Jing and Deng, Jingyuan (2005) 'Gaishan woguo shiye xianzhuang de fangshi' (Measures to improve the current unemployed situation in China), *Statistics and Decisions* (Tongji yu Juece), 21.

Liui, T.L. (2005) 'Bringing class back in', *Critical Asian Studies*, 37 (3): 473–80.

Liu, Y. (2002) 'Reforming China's urban health insurance system', *Health Policy*, 60 (2): 133–50.

Liu, Yuanli, Rao, Keqin and Hu, Shanlian (2002) *People's Republic of China: Toward Establishing A Rural Health Protection System*, Manila: Asian Development Bank.

236   Bibliography

Liu, Zuo (2004) '"From profit to tax" in state enterprises and its historic significance' (*guoying qiye ligaishui ji qi lishi yiyi*), *Taxation Research Journal*, 10: 27–33.

Lora-Wainwright, A. (2005) 'Valorising local resources: barefoot doctors and bone manipulation in rural Langzhong, Sichuan province, PRC', *Asian Medicine: Tradition and Modernity*, 1 (2): 470–89

—— (n.d.) 'Fighting for breath: cancer and social change in a Sichuan village', (unpublished manuscript).

Lowry, I. S. (1990) 'World urbanization in perspective', *Population and Development Review*, 16: 148–76.

Luke, A. and Ismail, M. (2007) 'Introduction: Reframing urban education in the Asia Pacific', in A. Luke and M. Ismail (eds) *Handbook of Urban Education*, London: Routledge.

Ma, L. J. C. (2004) 'Economic reforms, urban spatial restructuring, and planning in China', *Progress in Planning*, 61: 237–60.

Mak, G. (2007) 'Women in Asian education and society: Whose gains in whose perspectives?', in A. Luke and M. Ismail (eds) *Handbook of Urban Education*, London: Routledge.

Mann, Kirk (2008) 'Remembering and rethinking the social divisions of welfare: 50 years on', *Journal of Social Policy*, 38 (1): 1–18.

Mao, Zedong (1977) 'Lun shi da guanxi' (On the Ten Major Relationships), in *Mao Zedong xuanjii wu juan* (The Collected Works of Mao Zedong, vol. 5), Renmin chubanshe: 267–88.

Maurer-Fazio, Margaret, Rawski, Thomas G. and Zhang, Wei (1999) 'Inequality in the rewards for holding up half the sky: gender wage gaps in china's urban labour market, 1988–94', *The China Journal*, 41: 55–88.

May, R. *et al.* (2000) 'UN habitat indicators database: evaluation as a source of the status of urban development problems and programs', *Cities*, 17: 237–44.

Mcloughlin, C.S., Zhou, Z. and Clark, E. (2005) 'Reflections on the development and status of contemporary special education services in China', *Psychology in Schools*, 42 (3): 273–83.

Meng, J. and Tan Z. (1996) '*Wuhan chengshi zuidi shenghuo baozhang zhidu de sige tedian*' (Four characteristics of Wuhan city's minimum livelihood guarantee system), *Zhongguo minzheng*, 7: 19.

Meng, Qingyue, Liu, Xingzhu and Shi, Junshi (2000) 'Comparing the services and quality of private and public clinics in rural China', *Health Policy and Planning*, 15 (4): 349–56.

Meng, Xianfan (1995) *Zhongguo gaige dachaozhong de nüxing* (Chinese Women in the Reforms), Beijing: Zhongguo shehui kexue chubanshe.

Miles, M. (2000) 'Disability on a different model: glimpses of an Asian heritage', *Disability & Society*, 15 (4): 603–18.

Miles, M. and Huberman, A. (1994) *Qualitative Data Analysis: An expanded sourcebook*, 2nd edn, Beverley Hills: Sage Publications.

Mingpao (2007) 'Premier pledges to invest more into education', 5 March.

Ministry of Civil Affairs [MCA] (2000) M*inzheng shiye fazhan tongji baogao, 2000* (Statistical Report on the Development of Civil Affairs Work, 2000). Online. Available HTTP: cws.mca.gov.cn/article/tjbg/200801/20080100009395.shtml (accessed 20 August 2008).

—— (2001) *Minzheng zhiye fazhan tongji baogao, 2001* (Statistical Report on the Development of Civil Affairs Work, 2001). Online. Available HTTP: cws.mca.gov. cn/article/tjbg/200801/20080100009394.shtml (accessed 20 August 2008).

Bibliography 237

—— (2002) *Minzheng shiye fazhan tongji baogao, 2002* (Statistical Report on the Development of Civil Affairs Work, 2002). Online. Available HTTP: cws.mca.gov.cn/article/tjbg/200801/20080100009382.shtml (accessed 10 December 2008).

—— (2004) *Minzheng shiye fazhan tongji baogao, 2004* (Statistical Report on the Development of Civil Affairs Work, 2004). Online. Available HTTP: cws.mca.gov.cn/article/tjbg/200801/20080100009393.shtml (accessed 1 March 2009).

Ministry of Education [MOE] (1994) *China Educational Finance Statistical Yearbook 1994*, Beijing: Zhongguo Tongji Chubanshe.

—— (2004) *China Educational Finance Statistical Yearbook 2004*, Beijing: Zhongguo tongji chubanshe.

—— (2006) *Statistics of Education*, Beijing: Ministry of Education, People's Republic of China.

Mitlin, D. (2001) 'Housing and urban poverty: a consideration of the criteria of affordability, diversity and inclusion', *Housing Studies*, 16: 509–22.

Moerman, D. (2002) *Meaning, Medicine and the 'Placebo Effect'*, Cambridge: Cambridge University Press.

Mok, K.H. (1996) 'Marketisation and decentralisation: Development of education and paradigm shift in social policy', *Hong Kong Public Administration*, 5 (1): 35–56.

—— (2000) 'Marketizing higher education in post-Mao China', *International Journal of Educational Development*, 20: 109–26.

—— (2001) 'Education policy reform', in L. Wong and N. Flynn (eds) *The Market in Chinese Social Policy*, Basingstoke: Palgrave.

—— (2005) 'Riding over socialism and global capitalism: Changing education governance and social policy paradigms in post-Mao China', *Comparative Education*, 41 (2): 217–42.

—— (2009) 'The growing importance of the privateness in education: Challenges for higher education governance in China', *Compare*, 39 (1): 35–49.

Mok, K.H. and Ngok, K.L. (2008a) 'Bringing the welfare back in: Bridging the gap between public finance and social policy formulation in China', paper presented at the 5th International Conference of East Asian Social Policy Network, National Taiwan University, 3–4 November.

—— (2008b) 'One country, diverse systems: Politics of educational decentralisation and challenges for the regulatory state in post-Mao China', *China Review*, 8 (2): 169–99.

Mok, K., Wong, L. and Lee, G.O.M. (2002) 'The challenges of global capitalism: unemployment and state workers' reactions and responses in post-reform China', *International Journal of Human Resource Management*, 13 (3): 399–415.

Mok, K. H., Wong, Y. C., Walker, R. and Zhang, X. L. (2010) 'Embracing the market: Examining the consequences for education, housing, and health in Chinese societies', in K. H. Mok and Y. W. Ku. (eds) *Social Cohesion in Greater China: Challenges for Social Policy and Governance*, Hackensack, NJ: World Scientific.

Mountfield, E. and Wong, C. (2005) 'Public expenditure on the frontline: Toward effective management by subnational governments', in World Bank (ed.) *East Asia Decentralizes: Making Local Government Work*, Washington, DC: World Bank: 85–106.

Murphy, Rachel (2004) 'Turning peasants into modern Chinese citizens: 'Population Quality' Discourse, Demographic Transition and Primary Education', *The China Quarterly*, no. 177: 1–20.

Murphy, R. and Fong, V. (2006) 'Introduction: Chinese experiences of citizenship at the margins', in V. Fong and R. Murphy (eds) *Chinese Citizenship. Views from the Margins,* London: Routledge: 1–8.

238   Bibliography

Nanjing Bureau of Statistics (1994) *Nanjing Statistical Yearbook 1994*, Beijing: China Statistical Press.

——(2003) *Nanjing Statistical Yearbook 2003*, Beijing: China Statistical Press.

National Bureau of Statistics of China [NBSC] (1999) *China Statistical Yearbook 1999*, Beijing: China Statistical Press.

—— (2005) *China Statistical Yearbook 2005*, Beijing: China Statistical Press.

—— (2007) *China Statistical Yearbook 2007*, Beijing: China Statistical Press.

—— (2008) *China City Statistical Yearbook 2008*, Beijing: China Statistical Press.

Nanjing Government (1999), Shizhengfu guanyu zhixing 'Nanjing shi chengzhen qiye zhigong yanglao baoxian shishi yijian' de buchong tongzhi (Municipal government Supplementary Notice concerning Implementing Nanjing municipal urban enterprise employee Old Age Insurance;) Online. Available HTTP: www.njqh.gov.cn/articleinfo.php?infoid=913 (accessed August 2004).

NBSC (2009) *China Statistical Yearbook 2009*, Beijing: China Statistical Press.

Neubauer, D. (2008) 'The historical transformation of public good', *Journal of Asian Public Policy*, 1 (2): 127–38.

Ngok, K.L. (2005) 'Redefining development in China: Towards a new policy paradigm for the new century?', paper presented at International Conference on Changing Governance and Public Policy paradigms: Asian Perspectives, Zhongshan University, Guangzhou, November.

Ngok, K.L. and Chan, K.K.D. (2003) 'Towards centralisation and decentralisation in educational development in China: The case of Shanghai', in K.H. Mok (ed.) *Centralisation and Decentralisation: Educational Reforms and Changing Governance in Chinese Societies*, Hong Kong: Comparative Education Research Centre, University of Hong Kong.

Ngok, K.L. and Kwong, J. (2003) 'Globalisation and educational restructuring in China', in K.H. Mok and A. Welch (eds) *Globalisation and Educational Restructuring in the Asia Pacific Region*, Basingstoke: Palgrave Macmillan.

Nichter, Mark (2002) 'Social relations of therapy management', in M. Nichter and S. Lock (eds) *New Horizons in Medical Anthropology*, London: Routledge: 81–110.

—— (2003) 'Paying for what ails you: sociocultural issues influencing the ways and means of therapy payment in South India', in Mark and Mimi Nichter (eds) *Anthropology and International Health. Asian Case Studies*. London: Routledge.

Nichter, Mark and Mimi Nichter (eds) (2003) *Anthropology and International Health. Asian Case Studies*. London: Routledge.

Oakes, Tim and Schein, Louisa (eds) (2005) *Translocal China*, London: Routledge.

OECD (2005) *OECD Economic Surveys China*, Paris: OECD.

—— (2006) *Education at a Glance 2006*, Paris: OECD.

Office of the Second China National Sample Survey on Disability (OSCNSSD) and the Institute of Population Studies (IPS), Peking University (2008) *Data Analysis of the Second China National Sample Survey on Disability*, Beijing: Huaxia Press.

Pahl, R. E. (1966) 'The rural–urban continuum1', *Sociologia Ruralis*, 6: 299–329.

Painter, M. and Mok, K.H. (2008) 'Reasserting the public in public service delivery: The de-privatization and de-marketization of education in China', *Policy & Society*, 27 (3): 137–50.

Pei, S. (2002) 'Xigang District establishes the Community Public Service Agency (Xigang qu jianli shequ gonggong fuwu she)', *Zhongguo Minzheng*, 4: 51.

People's Daily (2005) 'Intensified educational inequality in China', 12 February.

—— (2007) 'Heavy burden of higher education financing', 5 March.

People's Daily Online (2007) 'Intel to upgrade Dalian plan'. Online. Available HTTP: english.peopledaily.com.cn (accessed 1 March 2009).

Pierson, Christopher (1998) *Beyond the Welfare State: The new political economy of welfare*, London: Polity Press.

Pierson, P. (1994) *Dismantling the Welfare State? Reagan, Thatcher and the politics of retrenchment*, Cambridge: Cambridge University Press.

Price, Richard H. and Fang, Liluo (2002) 'Unemployed Chinese workers: The survivors, the worried young and the discouraged old', *Journal of Human Resource Management*, 13 (3): 416–30.

Qian, X.L. and Smyth, R. (2005) 'Measuring regional inequality of education in China: Widening cost-inland gap or widening rural-urban gap?', *ABERU Discussion Paper*, 12: 1–12.

Quinn, G. and Degener, T. (2002) *Human Rights and Disability: The current use and future potential of United Nations Human Rights Instruments in the context of disability*, New York: United Nations.

Raffaelli, M. (1997) 'The family situation of street youth in Latin America: A cross-national review', *International Social Work*, 40: 89–100.

Rawski, T. G. (1999) 'Reforming China's economy: what have we learned?', *The China Journal*, 41: 139–56.

Raymo, J.M. and Xie, Y. (2000) 'Income of the urban elderly in postreform China: political capital, human capital, and the State', *Social Science Research*, 29: 1–24.

Read, Benjamin L. (2008) 'Assessing variation in civil society organisations: China's homeowner associations in comparative perspective', *Comparative Political Studies*, 41 (9): 1240–65.

Reddy, Sanjay 2007 'Death in China: Market reforms and health', *New Left Review*, 45 (May/June): 49–65.

Rempel, H. and Lobdell, R. A. (1978) 'The role of urban-to-rural remittances in rural development', *Journal of Development Studies*, 14: 324–41.

Ren, F. (1995) *'Dalian shi chengshi jumin zuidi shenghuo baozhang xian zhidu jianjie'* (Opinions on the Dalian City Urban Resident Minimum Livelihood Guarantee Line System), *Zhongguo Minzheng*, 6: 27.

Rofel, Lisa (1999) *Other Modernities: Gendered Yearnings in China after Socialism*, Berkeley: University of California Press.

Rong, X.L. and Shi, T.J. (2001) 'Inequality in Chinese education', *Journal of Contemporary China*, 10 (26): 107–24.

Ruan, Y. (2007) 'Ministry of Construction: Migrant workers will be covered by housing provident fund', *China Newsnet*, 24 January. Online. Available HTTP: www.soufun.com/news/2007-01-24/932182.htm (accessed 28 April 2010).

Rural Household Survey Team of the National Statistics Bureau (2005) 'Dangqian nongmingong jiuye shuliang jiegou tedian' (Series of surveys: the employment structure of migrant workers). Online. Available HTTP: news.xinhuanet.com/employment/2006–02/14/content_4178450_1.htm (accessed 2 March 2007).

Saich, Tony (2008) *Providing Public Goods in Transitional China*, New York: Palgrave Macmillan.

Sato, Hiroshi and Shi Li (eds) (2006) *Unemployment, Inequality and Poverty in Urban China*, London: Routledge.

Saunders, Peter (2004) 'State and Family in the Living Conditions of the Aged in China: Changing Roles, Attitudes and Outcomes', in *ISA Research Committee 19th Annual Conference on Welfare State Restructuring: Processes and Social Outcomes*, Paris.

240 *Bibliography*

Saunders, Peter and Shang, Xiaoyuan (2001) 'Social security reform in China's transition to a market economy', *Social Policy & Administration*, 35 (3): 274–89.

Scheid, V. (2002) *Chinese Medicine in Contemporary China: Plurality and Synthesis*, London: Duke University Press.

Seeborg, M. C., Jun, Zhenhu and Zhu, Yiping.(2000) 'The New Rural-Urban Labour Mobility in China: Causes and Implications', *Journal of Socio-Economics*, 29: 39–56.

Segall, M. (2000) 'From cooperation to competition in national health systems – and back? impact on professional ethics and quality of care', *International Journal of Health Planning and Management*, 15 (1): 61–79.

Selden, M., and You, L. Y. (1997) 'The reform of social welfare in China', *World Development*, 25 (10): 1657–68.

Shan, F. (1995) 'Reform of mainland China urban old-age-pension system', *Issues & Studies*, 31 (11): 98–107.

Shang, X.Y. (2000) 'Bridging the gap between planned and market economies: employment policies for people with disabilities in two Chinese cities', *Disability & Society*, 15 (1): 135–56.

—— (2001) 'Moving towards a multi-level and multi-pillar system: Institutional care in two Chinese cities', *Journal of Social Policy*, 30 (2): 259–81.

—— (2002) 'Looking for a better way to care for children: Cooperation between the state and civil society', *Social Service Review*, 76 (2): 203–28.

—— (2008) *The System of Social Protection for Vulnerable Children in China*, Beijing: Social Sciences Academic Press (China).

Shang, X.Y. and Wu, X.M. (2003) 'Protecting children under financial constraints: the case of Datong', *Journal of Social Policy*, 32 (4): 549–70.

Shang, X.Y.,Fisher, K.R. and Xie, J.W. (2008) 'Discrimination against Children with Disability in China: A case study in Jiangxi Province', invited presentation paper, UN Convention on the Rights of Persons with Disabilities: a call for action on poverty, discrimination and lack of access, UNECA – Leonard Cheshire Disability Joint Conference, United Nations Conference Center, Addis Ababa, Ethiopia, 20–22 May.

Shang, X., Wu, X.M. and Wu, Y. (2005) 'Welfare provision to vulnerable children: the missing role of the state', *The China Quarterly*, 18 (1): 122–36.

Shanghai Research Institute of Educational Sciences (2005) 'The causes, implications and trends of the policy of transformation in public schools', *Education Development and Research*, 8B: 16–23.

Shi, D. (2002) *Kuashijide Zhongguo minzheng shiye: Shanghai juan* (China's trans-century civil affairs matters: Shanghai volume), Beijing: China Society Press.

Shi, Q.H., Wu, Mei, You, Shufen and Liu, Wenhua (2005) 'Affiliated colleges and private education development in China: Take independent colleges as an example'. Online. Available HTTP: ocair.org/files/presentations/Paper2003_04/forum2004/ChinaHE.pdf (accessed 19 May 2009).

Shirk, Susan (1993), *The Political Logic of Economic Reform in China*, Berkeley: University of California Press.

Shue, Vivienne (2006) 'The quality of mercy: Confucian charity and the mixed metaphors of modernity in Tianjin', *Modern China*, 32 (4): 411–52.

Shue, Vivienne and Wong, Christine (2007a) 'Introduction: Is China moving to a more equitable development strategy?', in V. Shue and C. Wong (eds) *Paying for Progress in China: Public Finance, Human Welfare and Changing Patterns of Inequality*, London and New York: Routledge: 1–11.

Bibliography 241

—— (eds) (2007b) *Paying for Progress in China: Public Finance, Human Welfare, and Changing Patterns of Inequality*, London and New York: Routledge.

Sidel, V. and Sidel, R. (1974) *Serve the People: Observations on Medicine in the People's Republic of China*, Boston: Beacon Press.

Skocpol, Theda (1994) 'From social security to health security? Opinion and rhetoric in us social policy making', *Political Science and Politics*, 27 (1): 21–25.

So, A.Y.C. (2005) 'Beyond the logic of capital and the polarisation model: The state, market reforms, and the plurality of class conflict in China', *Critical Asian Studies*, 37 (3): 481–94.

Solinger, D. J. (1991) *From Lathes to Looms*, Stanford: Stanford University Press.

—— (1999) 'Citizenship issues in China's internal migration: comparisons with Germany and Japan', *Political Science Quarterly*, 114: 455–78.

—— (2001) 'Why we cannot count the unemployed', *The China Quarterly*, no. 167: 671–88.

—— (2002) 'Labour market reform and the plight of the laid-off proletariat', *The China Quarterly*, no. 170: 304–26.

—— (2003) 'Chinese urban jobs and the WTO', *China Journal*, 49: 61–87.

—— (2004) 'State and society in urban China in the wake of the 16th Party Congress', *The China Quarterly*, no. 176: 943–59.

—— (2005) 'Path dependency re-examined: chinese welfare policy in the transition to unemployment', *Comparative Politics*, 38 (1): 83–101.

—— (2006) 'The creation of a new underclass in China and its implications', *Environment and Urbanization*, 18 (1): 177–93.

Song, Lina and Appleton, Simon (2008) 'Social protection and migration in China: What can protect migrants from economic uncertainty?', *IZA Discussion Paper* No. 3594.

Song, Shufeng (2003) 'Policy issues of China's urban unemployment', *Contemporary Economic Policy*, 21 (2): 258–69.

Song, S. F. and G. S. F. Chu (1997) 'Social security reform in China: The case of old-age insurance', *Contemporary Economic Policy*, 15 (2): 85–93.

SPRC CASS (2000a), 'Dalian shi 'Shequhua de zuidi zonghe shenghuo baozhang zhidu' fang'an' (Dalian City 'Socialising the minimum balanced livelihood guarantee system' plan), in SPRC CASS (ed.) (2003) *Zhongguo shehui baozhang zhidu zaizao – Dalian xiangmu pinggu cailiao*, Beijing: CASS: 7–8.

—— (2000b) 'Dalian Shi xigang qu wanshan shehui baozhang tixi shidian fang'an' (Dalian City Xigang District plan for perfecting the social security system experiment), in SPRC CASS (ed.) (2003) *Zhongguo shehui baozhang zhidu zaizao – Dalian xiangmu pinggu cailiao*, Beijing: CASS: 9.

—— (2001a), 'Dalian shi shequ gonggong fuwu she sheli fang'an (cao'an)' (Dalian City Community Public Service Agency set-up plan (Draft)), in SPRC CASS (ed.) (2003) *Zhongguo shehui baozhang zhidu zaizao – Dalian xiangmu pinggu cailiao*, Beijing: CASS: 10–11.

—— (2001b) 'Guanyu Dalian shequ gonggong fuwu she sheli fang'an de shuoming (Cao'an)' (Explanation regarding the Dalian City Community Public Service Agency set-up draft (Draft)), in SPRC CASS (ed.) (2003) *Zhongguo shehui baozhang zhidu zaizao – Dalian xiangmu pinggu cailiao*, Beijing: CASS: 12–15.

—— (2001c) 'Dalian shi Xigang qu gongrencun jiedao shequ gonggong fuwu she zhangcheng' (Dalian City Xigang District Workers Village Street Community Public Service Agency regulation), in SPRC CASS (ed.) (2003) *Zhongguo shehui baozhang zhidu zaizao – Dalian xiangmu pinggu cailiao*, Beijing: CASS: 16–17.

242 *Bibliography*

—— (2001d) 'Dalian shi Xigang qu gongrencun gonggong fuwu she guanli xise' (Dalian City Xigang District Workers Village Community Public Service Agency principles), in SPRC CASS (ed.) (2003) *Zhongguo shehui baozhang zhidu zaizao – Dalian xiangmu pinggu cailiao*, Beijing: CASS: 18.

—— (2003) 'Dalian shi shequ gonggong fuwu she zhengce yanjiu xiaojie' (Dalian City Community Public Service Agency Policy Research summary), in SPRC CASS (ed.) (2003) *Zhongguo shehui baozhang zhidu zaizao – Dalian xiangmu pinggu cailiao*, Beijing: CASS: 3–5.

—— (ed.) (2003) *Zhongguo shehui baozhang zhidu zaizao – Dalian xiangmu pinggu cailiao* (The Restructuring of China's Social Security System – Dalian Project Assessment), Beijing: CASS.

Stake, R. (2000) 'Case studies', in N.K. Denzin and Y.S. Lincoln (eds) *The Handbook of Qualitative Research,* 2nd edn, Thousand Oaks, CA: Sage Publications.

State Council (1994) '*Guowuyuan guanyu shixing fenshui zhicai zhengguanli de jueding*' (State Council decision to implement the divided-tax fiscal administration), in *China Financial Yearbook*, China Journal of Fiscal Press: 63.

—— (1997) '*Guowuyuan guanyu zai quanguo jianli chengshi jumin zuidi shenghuo baozhang zhidu de tongzhi*' (State Council Notice to establish a national urban residents' Minimum Livelihood Guarantee System), State Council's Document 29, 2 September. Online. Available HTTP: dbs.mca.gov.cn/article//csdb/zcfg/200711/20071100003522.shtml (accessed 3 October 1998).

—— (1999) '*Chengshi jumin zhuidi shenghuo baozhang tiaoli*' (Rules on the urban residents' minimum livelihood guarantee). Online. Available HTTP: dbs.mca.gov.cn/article//csdb/zcfg/200711/20071100003521.shtml (accessed 3 October 2008).

—— (2007) '*Guowuyuan guanyu zai quanguo jianli nongcun zuidi shenghuo baozhang zhidu de tongzhi*' (State Council Notice establishing nationally the rural Minimum Livelihood Guarantee System), State Council Document 19. Online. Available HTTP: www.gov.cn/xxgk/pub/govpublic/mrlm/200803/t20080328_32753.html (accessed 3 October 2008).

—— (2010) *The Outline of the National Educational Development 2010–2020*, Beijing: State Council, People's Republic of China.

Summerfield, Gale (1994) 'Economic reform and the employment of Chinese Women', *Journal of Economic Issues*, 28 (3): 715–32.

Sun, Liping (1994) 'Chongjian xingbie jiaose guanxi' (Re-establishing gender roles), *Sociology Studies*, 6: 65–68.

Sun, Qipan (2008) 'Nongcun jumin zuidi shenghuo baozhang zhidu de xianzhuang, wenti, yu duice' (Rural minimum livelihood guarantee system: current situation, problems and the countermeasures), *Zhongguo Minzheng* (China Civil Affairs), 6: 29–30.

Sun, Xiaoke and Liang, Qi (2000) 'Nanjingshi nügong xiagang yu zaijiuye xiangzhuang de tongji fenxi' (Statistical Analysis of Female Layoffs and Reemployment in Nanjing), *Journal of Nanjing University of Posts and Telecommunications* (Social Science), 2 (2): 43–46.

Sun, Xiaoyun Jakson, Sukhari, Carmichael, Gordon and Sleigh, Adrian C. (2009) 'Catastrophic Medical Payment and Financial Protection in Rural China: Evidence from the new cooperative medical scheme in Shandong Province', *Health Economics*, 18 (1): 103–19.

Swartz, D. (1997) *Culture and Power: the Sociology of Pierre Bourdieu*, London: University of Chicago Press.

Bibliography 243

Tacoli, C. (1998) 'Rural-urban interactions: A guide to the literature', *Environment and Urbanization*, 10: 147–66.

Tang, Jun (1992) 'Zhongguo de pinkun renkou he shehui jiuzhu zhibiao tixi' (Poverty population and social assistance indicators in China), *Social Sciences*, 5: 46–50.

—— (1994) 'Jianli pubian de shehui jiuzhu zhidu' (To set up a universal social assistance system), *Society*, 10: 23–26.

—— (2002a) 'The new situation of poverty and antipoverty', in Ru Xin, Lu Xueyi and Li Peilin, (eds) *2002 nian: zhongguo shehui xingshi yu yuce* (Year 2002: Analysis and Forecast of China's Social Situation), Blue Book on Chinese Society, Beijing: Shehui kexue wenxian chubanshe.

—— (2002b) 'The report of poverty and anti-poverty in urban China – the poverty problems in urban china and the program of minimum living standard' (unpublished manuscript).

—— (2003a) '*Zhongguo chengshi jumin zuidi shenghuo baozhang zhidu de tiaoyueshi fazhan*' (The leap forward style of development of Chinese urban residents minimum livelihood guarantee), in Ru Xin, Lu Xueyi and Li Peilin (eds) *2003 nian: zhongguo shehui xingshi fenxi yu yuce* (Year 2003 Analysis and Forecast of China's Social Situation), Blue Book on Chinese Society, Beijing: Shehui kexue wenxian chubanshe.

—— (2003b) *Zhongguo chengshi pinkun yu fupinkun baogao* (China Urban Poverty and Poverty Alleviation Report), Beijing: Huxia Publishing House.

—— (2004) 'Selections from report on poverty and anti-poverty in Urban China' (trans. William Crawford), *Chinese Sociology & Anthropology*, Winter/Spring.

—— (2006) '*Tiaozhengzhong de chengxiang zuidi shenghuo baozhang zhidu*' [The urban and rural minimum livelihood guarantee system in adjustment], in Ru Xin, Lu Xueyi and Li Peilin, zhubian (eds) *Shehui lanpishu: 2006 nian: zhongguo shehui xingshi fenxi yu yuce* [Social Blue Book: 2006 analysis and predictions of China's social situation], Beijing: shehui kexue wenxian chubanshe.

Tang, S. and Bloom, G. (2000) 'Decentralizing rural health services: A case study in China', *International Journal of Health Planning and Management*, 15: 189–200.

Tang, S., Meng, Q., Chen. L., Bekedam, H., Evans, T. and Whitehead, M. (2008) 'Tackling the challenges to health inequity', *The Lancet*, 372 (9648): 1493–1501.

Tartakovskaya, Irina and Ashwin, Sarah (2004) 'Who Benefits from Networks?', paper presented at the Employment Research Unit 19th Annual Conference, Cardiff, 3–5 September.

Taylor, J. E. and Wyatt, T. J. (1996) 'The shadow value of migrant remittances, income and inequality in a household-farm economy', *Journal of Development Studies*, 32: 899–912.

Tilky, L. (2008) 'Globalisation and educational disparity in Africa', paper presented at the International Conference on Education and Socially Disadvantaged Groups, National Chia Yi University, Taiwan, 5–6 December.

Titmuss, R. M. (1958) *Essays on the Welfare State*, London: Allen & Unwin.

Tudball, J., Fisher, K.R., Sands, T. and Dowse, L. (2003) *Supporting Families who have a Child with a Disability*, report for Families First Inner West, December 2002, Social Policy Research Centre Report 1/03, Sydney. Online. Available HTTP: www.sprc.unsw.edu.au/media/File/Report1_03_Supporting_Families.pdf (accessed 2 December 2010).

Uchimura, Hiroko and Jütting, Johannes (2007) 'Fiscal decentralisation, chinese style: good for health outcomes?', *IDE Discussion Paper* No. 111.

Unel, Bulent and Harm Zebregs (2006) 'The dynamics of provincial growth in china: a nonparametric approach', IMF Working Paper.

244   *Bibliography*

UN Committee on the Rights of the Child [UNCRC] (2005) 'Fortieth session consideration of reports submitted by states parties under article 44 of the convention concluding observations', UNICEF China.

—— (2006a) *Excluded and invisible: The state of the world's children 2006*, Geneva: UNICEF.

—— (2006b) 'General comment no. 9 the rights of children with disabilities', Forty-third session, Geneva, 11–29 September.

United Nations Committee on the Rights of Persons with Disabilities [UNCRPD] (2007) *Convention on the Rights of Persons with Disabilities (UNCRPD)*. Online. Available HTTP: www.un.org/disabilities/convention/conventionfull.shtml (accessed 4 January 2009).

UNDP (2008), *China Human Development Report 2008*, Washington, DC: UNDP.

UNICEF (2005) *Childhood under Threat: The State of the World's Children 2005* (Official Summary). Online. Available HTTP: www.unicef.org/sowc05/english/Table6_E.xls (accessed 5 January 2009).

Van Der Geest, Sjaak, Whyte, Susan Reynolds and Hardon, Anita (1996) 'Anthropology of pharmaceuticals', *Annual Review of Anthropology*, 25: 153–78.

Waldram, James 2000 'The efficacy of traditional medicine: current theoretical and methodological issues', *Medical Anthropology Quarterly*, 14(4): 603–25.

Wang, B. and Chen, J. (2005) 'Xibu nongcun jiben yiliao baozhang zhidu mianlin de wenti yu duice' (Primary medicare in Western China's rural areas: problems and countermeasures), *Journal of Sichuan University* (Social Science Edition) (Sichuan daxue xuebao, zhexue shehui kexue ban) 6: 20–28.

Wang, Shaoguang 2008 'State extractive capacity, policy orientation, and inequity in the financing and delivery of health care in urban China', *Social Sciences in China*, 29(1): 66–87.

Wang, X. (2005) 'Implications of social stratification for higher education enrolment', *Jiangsu Higher Education*, 3: 47–49.

—— (2005a) 'A study on higher education enrolment in Guangdong: A survey on a number of higher education institutions in Guangdong', *Higher Education Exploration*, 3: 11–13.

Wang, Y.B. (2007) 'China's higher education on an overpass of four fold transitions', paper presented to the video seminar series of 'Universities and Ideas', Zhejiang University, Hangzhou, China, 30 April.

Wang, Ya Ping (2004) *Urban Poverty, Housing and Social Change in China*, London and New York: Routledge.

Wang, Ya Ping and Murie, Alan (1999) *Housing Policy and Practice in China*. Basingstoke: Macmillan.

Wang, Zheng (2000) 'Gender, employment and women's resistance', in Elizabeth J. Perry and Mark Selden (eds) *Chinese Society: Change, Conflict and Resistance*, London and New York: Routledge: 62–82.

West, Loraine A. (1997) 'The changing effects of economic reform on rural and urban employment', paper presented at the Unintended Social Consequences of Chinese Economic Reform conference, Harvard School of Public Health and The Fairbank Center for East Asian Studies, Harvard University, 23–24 May.

—— (1999) 'Pension reform in china: preparing for the future', in S. Cook and M. Maurer-Fazio (eds) *The Workers' State Meets the Market: Labour in China's Transition*, London: Frank Cass.

White, Gordon, Howell, Jude and Shang, Xiaoyuan (1996) *In Search of Civil Society: Market Reform and Social Change in China*, Basingstoke: Macmillan.

Bibliography   245

White, S. (1998) 'From "barefoot doctor" to "village doctor" in tiger springs village: a case study of rural health care transformations in socialist China', *Human Organisation*, 57 (4): 480–90.

White Paper (2004) *China's Social Security System and Its Policy*, State Council Information Office Beijing: New Star Publishers.

—— (2006) *The Development of China's Undertakings for the Aged*, State Council Information Office, 12 December. Online. Available HTTP: www.china.org.cn/english/China/191990.htm (accessed 14 January 2009).

Whyte, S. (1997) *Questioning Misfortune: the Pragmatics of Uncertainty in Eastern Uganda*, Cambridge: Cambridge University Press.

Whyte, S., Van der Geest, S. and Hardon, A. (2002) *Social Lives of Medicines*, Cambridge: Cambridge University Press.

Wikimedia (2008), 'Administrative division of the People's Republic of China'. Available HTTP: upload.wikimedia.org/wikipedia/commons/archive/9/99/20081005212123!China_administrative.gif (accessed: 28 June 2010).

Wong, Chack-kie, Vai Io Lo and Tang, Kwong-leung (2006) *China's Urban Health Care Reform: From State Protection to Individual Responsibility*, Lanham, MD: Lexington.

Wong, Christine (2000) 'Central–local relations revisited: the 1994 tax-sharing reform and public expenditure management in China', paper presented at the International Conference on 'Centre–Periphery Relations in China: Integration, Disintegration or Reshaping of an Empire?', Chinese University of Hong Kong, 24–25 March.

—— (2007) 'Can the retreat from equality be reversed? An assessment of redistributive fiscal policies from Deng Xiaoping to Wen Jiabao', in Vivienne Shue and Christine Wong (eds) *Paying for Progress in China: Public finance, human welfare and changing patterns of inequality*, London: Routledge: 12–28.

—— (2009) 'Rebuilding government for the 21st century: Can China incrementally reform the public sector?', *The China Quarterly*, 200, December: .929–52.

Wong, Christine, Heady, Christopher and Woo, Wing T. (1995) *Fiscal Management and Economic Reform in the People's Republic of China*, Hong Kong: Oxford University Press.

Wong, L. (1998) *Marginalisation in Social Welfare in China*, London: Routledge.

Wong, L. and Flynn, N. (eds) (2001) *The Market in Chinese Social Policy*, Basingstoke: Palgrave.

Wong, L. and Poon, B. (2005) 'From serving neighbours to recontrolling urban society: the transformation of China's community policy', *China Information*, 19: 413–42.

Wong, L., and J. Tang (2006) 'Non-state old age homes as third sector organisations in China's transitional welfare economy', *Journal of Social Policy*, 35 (April): 229–46.

Wong, L., White, L. and Gui, X.S. (2004) *Social Policy Reform in Hong Kong and Shanghai*, Armonk, NY: M.E. Sharpe.

Wong, Yuk-Lin Renita (2002) 'Reclaiming Chinese Women's Subjectivities: Indigenizing "Social Work with Women" in China through Postcolonial Ethnography', *Women's Studies International Forum*, 25(1): 67–77.

World Bank (2002) *China National Development and Sub-National Finance: A Review of Provincial Expenditures*, World Bank: Poverty Reduction and Economic Management Unit, East Asia and Pacific Region.

—— (2008) *China: Public Services for Building the New Socialist Countryside*, Beijing: China CITIC Press.

World Health Organization (2000) *World Health Report, 2000 – Health systems: improving performance*, from www.who.int/whr/2000/en/.

246 Bibliography

Wu, B. (2001) 'Zhongguo 36 ge chengshi zuidi shenghuo baozhang biaojun shizheng fenxi' (Analysis of concrete evidence of 36 Chinese cities' minimum livelihood guarantee norm), *Shuliang jingji jishu jingji yanjiu* (Quantitative Economy Statistical Economic Research), 4: 36–39.

Wu, F. (2004a) 'Urban poverty and marginalization under market transition: the case of Chinese cities', *International Journal of Urban and Regional Research*, 28: 401–23.

Wu, H. X. and Zhou, L. (1996) 'Rural-to-urban migration in China', *Asian-Pacific Economic Literature*, 10: 54–67.

Wu, W. (2002) 'Migrant housing in urban China: choices and constraints', *Urban Affairs Review*, 38: 90–119.

—— (2004b) 'Sources of migrant housing disadvantage in urban China', *Environment and Planning A*, 36: 1285–1304.

—— (2006) 'Migrant intra-urban residential mobility in urban China', *Housing Studies*, 21: 745–65.

Xia, Guomei (2001) *The Stories of Unemployed Women in the City* (Hualuofengfei: chengshi nüxing shengcun fu), Shijiangzhuang: Hebei chubanshe.

Xiang, Biao (2007) 'Migration and health in China: Problems, obstacles and solutions', *Asian MetaCentre Research Paper Series* No. 17, www.populationasia.org/Publications/RP/AMCRP17.pdf (accessed 25 April 2010).

Xiao, J. A. (2006) 'Lack of rural–urban migrants' participation led to unenthusiastic responses to public housing for rural-urban migrants' (Nongmingong gongyu lengchang yuanyu quefa canyu jizhi), *New Beijing Daily* (Xin Jing Bao), 13 August.

Xinhua (20 Nov. 2005) 'Shanghai family spent 1/4 of their income in children's education'. Online. Available HTTP: news.xinhuanet.com/politics/2005–11/30/content_3855849.htm (accessed 14 May 2009).

Xu, D. (1998) 'Jiada gongzuo lidu, chengxiang quanmian tuijin – Guangdong sheng jianli chengxiang hu (cun) min zuidi shenghuo baozhang zhidu de zuofa' (Strengthen work, carry out fully in the cities and rural areas – Guangdong province establishes a method for an urban and rural (village) residents'' minimum livelihood guarantee system), *Zhongguo minzheng*, 3: 9–10, 15.

Xu, K. (1996) '*Jianli chengshi jumin zuidi shenghuo baozhang zhidu shizai bixing*' (*Establishing an urban residents' minimum livelihood guarantee system is imperative*), *Zhongguo minzheng*, 10: 12.

Xu, Qingwen and Jones, John F. (2004) 'Community welfare services in urban China: A public–private experiment', *Journal of Chinese Political Science*, 9 (2): 47–62.

Xu, Yanli and Tan, Lin (2002) 'Lun xiebiehua de shijian peizhi yu nüxing zhiye fazhan' (On Gendered Time Allocation and Women's Career Development), *Journal of China Women's College*, 14 (6): 1–7.

Xu, Yuebin, Liu, Fengqin and Zhang, Xiulan (2007) 'Zhongguo nongcun fanpinkun zhengce de fansi: cong shehui jiuzhu xiang shehui baohu zhuanbian' (Reflections on China's rural anti-poverty policies: transition from social assistance to social protection), *Social Sciences in China: A Bimonthly*, 3: 40–53.

Yang, D. P. (2004) 'The new development paradigm and China's education', in X. Yu *et al.* (eds) *Analysis and Forecast on China's Social Development 2005*, Beijing: Social Sciences Academic Press.

—— (2005) 'China's education in 2003: From growth to reform', *Chinese Education and Society*, 38 (4): 11–45.

Yang, H. *et al.* (2005) 'Workplace and HIV-related sexual behaviours and perceptions among female migrant workers', *AIDS Care*, 17: 819–33.

Bibliography 247

Yang, R. (1997) 'The debate on private higher education development in China', *International Higher Education*, Fall: 1–4.

—— (2002) *The Third Delight: Internationalisation of Higher Education in China*, London: Routledge.

—— (2007) 'Urban–rural disparities in educational equality: China's pressing challenge in a context of economic growth and political change', in A. Luke and M. Ismail (eds) *Handbook of Urban Education*, London: Routledge.

Yang, Z. and Zhang, Q (1999) 'Wuhanshi chengshi jumin zuidi shenghuo baozhang zhidu shishi zhuangkuang de diaocha fenxi' (Analysis of an investigation of the implementation situation of Wuhan's urban residents' minimum livelihood guarantee system), *Economic Review (Jingji pinglun)*, 4: 99–103.

Yin, R.K. (2003) *Case Study Research*, 3rd edn, Thousand Oaks, CA: Sage Publications.

Yu, D. (1992) 'Changes in healthcare financing and health status: the case of China in the 1980s', *Innocenti Occasional Papers, Economic Policy Series* 34 Florence: UNICEF: i-61. Online. Available HTTP: www.unicef-irc.org/cgi-bin/unicef/download_insert.sql?ProductID=155 (accessed 25 November 2003).

Yu, J. (2005) *Beijing, Zhuhai ji Guangzhou 'Chengzhongcun' gaizao mianlin de kunan ji gaizao banfa* (Difficulties and Suggestions in Regenerating Urban Villages in Beijing, Zhuhai and Guangzhou), Shenzhen: China Development Institute,

Yuan, L. and Lin, C. (1998) 'Ai ru chao yong – Qingdaoshi chengxiang zuidi shenghuo baozhang zhidu shishi jishi' (Love like a rising tide – a true reporting of the Qingdao city urban and rural minimum livelihood guarantee system), *Zhongguo minzheng*, 7: 10–11.

Zhang, Jie (1994) 'Guanyu jianli zuidi shenghuo baozhang zhidu de tansuo' (Exploring the establishment of the Minimum Livelihood Guarantee System), *Social Work Studies*, 6: 31–32.

Zhang, K. H. and Song, S. (2003) 'Rural–urban migration and urbanization in China: evidence from time-series and cross-section analyses', *China Economic Review*, 14: 386–400.

Zhang, L. (2001) 'Migration and privatization of space and power in late socialist China', *American Ethnologist*, 28: 179–205.

—— (2002) 'Spatiality and urban citizenship in late socialist China', *Public Culture*, 14: 311–34.

Zhang, L., Zhao, Simon X.B. and Tian, J.P. (2003) 'Self-Help in Housing and *Chengzhongcun* in China's Urbanization', *International Journal of Urban and Regional Research*, 27: 912–37.

Zhang, L. (2006) 'Contesting spatial modernity in late-socialist China', *Cultural Anthropology*, 47 (3): 461–84.

Zhang, Pengfei and Shih, Victor (2008) 'Deficit estimation and welfare effects after the 1994 fiscal reform in china: evidence from the county level', *China & World Economy*, 16 (3): 22–39.

Zhang, Qiujian (1999) 'Zhongguo shehui zhuanxingqi nügong jiuye bianqian' (Changes in Women's Employment during China's Social Transformations), PhD dissertation, Beijing: China's People's University.

Zhang, Xing Quan (2006) 'Institutional transformation and marketisation: the changing patterns of housing investment in urban China', *Habitat International*, 30 (2): 327–41.

Zhang, Y. (2002) *Kuashijiede Zhongguo zheng shiye: Liaoning juan* (Trans-global China Matters: Liaoning Volume), Beijing: Zhongguo shehui chubanshe.

248 *Bibliography*

Zhang, Y. (2003) 'Private education in China: issues and prospects', *Perspectives*, 4 (4).

Zhao, Yandong (2001) 'Shehui ziben, renli ziben yu xiagang zhigong de zai jiuye' (Social Capital, Human Capital and Reemployment of Laid-Off Workers), PhD dissertation, Chinese Academy of Social Sciences.

—— (2002) 'Measuring the social capital of laid-off Chinese workers', *Current Sociology*, 50 (4): 555–71.

Zhong, X. (2006) 'Analysis of the reasons about the impartiality deficiencies in China's higher education', *Journal of Jiangsu Polytechnic University*, 7 (3): 41–44.

'Zhongguo chengshi jumin zuidi shenghuo baozhang biaojun de xiangguan fenxi, jingji qita xiangguan lunwen', 'Chinese urban residents' *dibao* norm's relevant analysis; economic and other related treatises' (2006). Online. Available HTTP: www. ynexam.cn/html/jingjixue/jingjixiangguan/2006/1105/zhonggochengshijimin (accessed 18 August 2007).

Zhou, Yanqiu Rachel (2009) 'Help-seeking in a context of AIDS stigma: understanding the healthcare needs of people with HIV/AIDS in China', *Health and Social Care in the Community*, 17 (2): 202–8.

Zhu, Q.F. (2005) 'Social and economic indicators: Analysis and assessment', in X. Yu *et al.* (eds) *Analysis and Forecast on China's Social Development 2006*, Beijing: Social Sciences Academic Press.

Zhuang, H. (2002) 'The pension funding reforms in China', *China Perspectives*, 43: 17–25.

Index

Abu-Lughod, J. 160
Adams, Jennifer 10
Agesa, R. U. 160
Ali, Z. 195
All China Federation of Trade Unions 100
All China Women's Federation 100
Anagnost, A. 17
Anand, Sudhir 121
Anju Project 151
Appleton, Simon 1, 82
Arimah, B. C. 154
Arksey, H. 14
Ashwin, Sarah 96
Atuguba, R. A. 154

Baker, K. 195
Banks, M.E. 195
Baoma 106–7, 110–11, 116, 119
Basic Living Guarantee (XGBLG) 72, 73–4, 75, 77
Bauman, Z. 190
Baumgartner, F. 64, 81
Beijing: education 11, 13, 126, 131, 135–42 (Tables 7.3–10), 144–5 (Table 7.12), 146–7; housing 152; MLG (*dibao*) 42 (Table 3.1), 43 (Table 3.2), 45 (Table 3.5), 46 (Table 3.6), 47 (Table 3.7), 48 (Table 3.8), 54, 67, 80; older people 12, 171, 172, 175–6, 182–6, 188, 190; redundancy 82, 83, 87; social welfare provision 2, 9
Béland, Daniel 5, 173
Beresford, Peter 18
Bian, Yanjie 103
Blekesaune, Morten 17
Bloom, G. 108, 124
Blumenthal, David 7
Bo Xilai 12, 75, 79

Boermel, A.: (2008) 184, 191; (this volume) 3, 6, 7, 9, 12, 13, 15, 16, 17, 214, 221, 222
Borevskaya, N. 128
Bray, D. 174
Brockerhoff, M. 161
Bronfenbrenner, U. 195
Bureau of Statistics of County H: (2007) 196; (2008) 196

Cai, Y. 67, 73
cancer: rates 105, 107, 122–3; rejection of surgery 113, 115; surgery costs 111–12, 115, 120; surgery in rural Langzhong 105–6, 115–18; treatment 14
care, gendered informal 14
Carrillo, Beatriz: (2008) 7, 13; (forthcoming) 8
Carrin, G. 108, 109
Case, S. 195
Central Committee of the Chinese Communist Party (CCCCP) 16, 127, 147
central-local relations: actual authority relations 26; and cross-sectoral organizational relations 24–5; current characteristics in social policy process 26–9; financial responsibility relations 21 (Figure 2.1), 216; in governmental system today 22–6 (Figure 2.2); local government autonomy in social policy 26, 215–17; in Minimum Livelihood Guarantee 11–12, 29–34; responsibility relations 22–4; in social policy 20–2, 215–17; in social policy implementation 27–8; in social policy making 27; welfare provision 215–17
Central Party Committee and State Council (19 October 2002) 124

250 *Index*

Chan, A. 125
Chan, C.K. 13, 149
Chan, K.K.D. 128
Chan, K.W. 152
Chang, Kai 82
Chaoyang District Government 175
chemical industries 89, 90–1
Chen, B. 128
Chen, C.G 134
Chen, J. 107, 124, 205
Chen, Mengjuan 87
Chen, Shaohua 1
Chen, X. 132
Chen, X.M. 194
Chen, Y. 131, 133
Chen, Y. A. 194
Cheng, E. 143
Cheng, K.M. 128
children with disability: child rights 194–5;
 family support 13; hearing and speech
 impairment 196, 197–9; Jiangxi
 (County H) study 196–8; numbers
 194; social participation 193–4, 195,
 197–8; study of deaf child *see*
 Hengheng; support system 194
China Cooperative Medical Scheme
 (CCMS) 110
China Disabled Persons Federation
 (CDPF) 188, 195
China Education and Research Network
 (2006) 146, 147
China Higher Education Student
 Information (2007) 147
Chinese Academy of Social Sciences
 (CASS) 69, 132
Chinese Communist Party (CCP) 16, 127
Chinese Government web portal (2008)
 110
Chinese Service Centre for Scholarly
 Exchange 132
Chiu, Stephan W.K. 82
Chongqing: education 142 (Table 7.10);
 housing 152; MLG (*dibao*) 38, 39–40,
 41, 42–3 (Tables 3.1–2), 45–8 (Table
 3.5–8); redundancy 87
Chow, Nelson 11
Chu, G. S. F. 5
Comfortable Housing Scheme 151
commercialization 5–7, 87, 134, 214, 217
communes 4–5, 6
Confucianism 13, 14, 17, 117
Cook, Ian G. 124
Cook, Sarah: (2002) 86, 127, 213; (2007)
 110, 112, 120, 124; (this volume) 3;

and Jolly (2000) 82, 83; and Kwon
 (2008) 220
cooperative medical schemes (CMS) 6;
 rural (RCMS) 105, 106, 107, 108–10,
 112–13, 119–23
Costello, M. A. 161
Coyne, Joseph 1
CPSAs see Community Public Service
 Agencies
Crandon-Malamud, L. 106, 124
Croft, Suzy 18
Cultural Revolution 83, 84, 100–1, 103,
 108, 118
Cummings, W. 132

da Piedade Morais, M. 154
Dai, J.L. 132
Dalian: city 2, 67; CPSA policy 12, 64–7,
 79–80; CPSA policy sponsors 75–9;
 cross-city MLG comparisons 42
 (Table 3.1), 43 (Table 3.2), 45 (Table
 3.5), 46 (Table 3.6), 47 (Table 3.7), 48
 (Table 3.8); evolution of CPSAs 69–70;
 explaining emergence of CPSAs 70;
 and MLG background 67–9; model of
 MLG finance 12, 71, 74–5, 221; MLG
 funds-sharing formula 39; negative
 impact of *xiagang* and MLG policy
 73–4; negative views of MLG
 recipients 72–3
Davis, D. 5, 173
de Oliveira Cruz, B. 154
deaf people 202–4
Dean, H. 195
decentralization 10–11, 215–17
Degener, T. 194
Deng, Jingyuan 87
Deng Xiaoping 129, 214
Department for International
 Development (DFID), UK 70
Derleth, J. 65, 174
dibao see Minimum Livelihood
 Guarantee (MLG)
diet, Wuhan MLG study 57–8
disabled children *see* children with
 disability
disabled people (*see also* children with
 disability) 5, 9; Wuhan MLG study
 53–4
Disabled Persons Federation (DPF) 9,
 197, 204, 205–7, 208–9
Dixon, John 5
Dolan, L. 195
Donelly, M. 195

Dong, X. 117
Dong, Xiao-Yuan 86, 98
Dong, Z. 107, 108, 109
Dowling, M. 195
Duckett, Jane: (2002) 10; (2003) 1;
(2007a) 108, 109, 122, 124; (2007b) 7,
9; (forthcoming) 1, 6, 108, 109, 124;
and Hussain (2008) 5, 8, 82, 85, 87,
128
Duda, M.: and Li (2008) 160; *et al.*
(2008) 168; Li and (this volume) 3, 7,
13, 15, 214, 215, 217
Dummer, Trevor J.B. 124

'East-Central-West strategy' 141
economy, transitional 95, 101, 108, 127–9,
213–14, 217–18
education: adoption of fee-charging
principle 129–32; allocation of places
of study in Guangdong 143 (Table
7.11); annual school fees for migrant
children 145 (Table 7.12);
characteristics of survey sample 136
(Table 7.3); commercialization of
134–5; consequences of privatization
and marketization of 135–45; disabled
children 199–201, 208; families
reporting after-school tuition 138
(Table 7.6); family spending 13, 138
(Table 7.5); fees 7; funds per student
across regions 142 (Table 7.10);
hardship relating to education 139,
140 (Tables 7.7, 7.8); household
spending on 138 (Table 7.5);
inequalities 126; Maoist era 5, 126;
migrant children 144–5 (Table 7.12);
non-state grants 141 (Table 7.9);
privatization and marketization of
129–35; proliferating education
providers and the rise of the private
sector 133–4; public education
expenditure 130 (Tables 7.1, 7.2);
responses of urban residents 135–9;
restructuring 127–9; school staffing
and student enrolment 137 (Table
7.4); third sector 7–8; transformation
of system 126–7; widening regional
and urban-rural divide 140–5; Wuhan
MLG study 48–9, 54–6
Edwards, M. 154
employment (*see also* redundancy,
unemployment, *xiagang*): finding
work 95–101; full 4–5; migrant study
161–2; MLG role 72; negative impact

of *xiagang* policy 73–4; Wuhan MLG
study 49, 56–7
Esping-Andersen, Gøsta 15, 18, 19
Etkin, N. 124
Evers, Adalbert 18

family: growing responsibilities 13–14;
welfare role 1, 4–5
Fan, Ruiping 121
Fang, Jing 109, 124
Fang, Liluo 82
Farquhar, J. 125
Farmer, Paul 116, 121
Farrell, D. 143
Feng, L. 42, 145
Fitoussi, Jean-Paul 18
'five guarantee households' 5
Flower, J. 125
Flynn, N. 127
Fobil, J. N. 154
Fong, V. 190
Four-in-One system 68, 71, 74, 79
fraud, benefit 12, 66–7, 72, 78, 212, 221
Frazier, Mark L. 5, 173, 190
Froissart, Chloe 8
Funder, K. 194
Fuzhou 42

Gansu 127
Gao, Jun 6
Ge, D. 66, 70, 72, 74, 78
Gelissen, John 15
Geva-May, Iris 17
Gilbert, A. G. 154
Giles, John 82, 85
Glendinning, C. 14
Gmelch, G. 160
Gong, S. 151
Gong, Ting 84
Goodman, David S.G. 16
Gottdiener, M. 154
governmental system, central-local
relations 22–6
Gu, C. 152
Gu, Edward X. 18, 82, 85
Gu, T. 124
Gu, Zhaonong 89
Guan, Xinping: (1995) 1; (2000) 18;
(2001) 127; (2003) 31; and Solinger
(this volume) 86; and Xu (this
volume) 3, 9, 11, 64, 71, 216, 220
Guangdong 142–3
Guangzhou 11, 45–8 (Tables 3.5–8), 87,
144

252 *Index*

Handelman, H. 154
Hannum, Emily 10
Harbin 70
Harpham, T. 154
Hawkins, J.N. 128
He, L. 144
health care: cancer *see* cancer; commodified health and its consequences 113–18, 121; costs 105; evolution of system 107–10; family support 14; finance for rural health services 108–9; hospital ownership 7; Maoist era 5, 108, 118, 120, 121–2; marketization 6; rising costs 89, 108; rural Sichuan 104–6; Wuhan MLG study 53–4
Hindle, D. 1
Hong, Zhaohui 44
hospitals: autonomy 216; cancer treatment 14, 105, 107, 111–12, 115, 116–17, 123; costs 53–4, 89, 108–9, 112, 123, 198; healthcare structure 107–8, 112, 118; hearing impairment treatment 198, 204; Langzhong 'People's Hospital' 111–12, 113–14; ownership 7; perceptions of care at municipal hospital 104–6, 113–15, 120–1; private 6; RCMS 112, 120–1, 122, 123; urban public 6
Hou, Xiaohui 1
Household Registration System (*hukou*) 152–3
housing: choices in rapidly urbanizing cities 154; city policies 152–3, 168–70; costs 6–7, 127, 151; housing outcomes of migrant workers 160–1; housing providers and rent payment 162; migrant housing problem? 157–60; private sector 151; state policy 24, 168; subsidies 151–2; Taiyuan study 154–67 (Tables 8.2–7); work units 4, 84
Howell, Jude 2, 7, 9
Hsiao, William C. 7
Hu Jintao 16, 148, 188, 192, 215
Hu, Shanlian 6
Huang, Y. 152
Huberman, A. 197
Huchzermeyer, M. 154
Hunan Bureau of Education 131
Hung, Eva P. W. 82
Hurst, W. 190, 192
Hussain, Athar: (2007) 2; *et al.* (2002) 37, 39; Duckett and (2008) 5, 8, 82, 85, 87, 128

Ikels, C. 125, 176
Information Office of the State Council of the People's Republic of China (2004) 86
insurance: health (*see also* rural cooperative medical system) 2, 8, 9, 11, 89, 92, 104, 108–9, 112, 113, 121–2, 198; old-age 11, 92, 173–4; social 6, 8, 11, 14, 24, 31, 182–3; unemployment 8, 9, 11, 72, 85–6, 87, 92
Irwin, L.G. 196
Ismail, M. 143

Jenks, E.B. 195
Jiang, J. 112
Jiangxi: children with disabilities 11, 193, 194, 196, 198; education 142 (Table 7.10); social welfare provision 2; state and market 16
Jianwai: community activities 177–84, 185–9; older people 12, 171–3, 177–84, 190–1; re-development 172, 174–6, 186, 190
Jianwai Street Office (2005) 175
Jinan 42
Johnson, K. 194
Jolly S. 82, 83
Jones, B. 64, 81
Jones, John F. 7
Jütting, Johannes 18

Kahn, Joseph 16
Kamat, Vinay 124
Kelly, S. 195
Keng, C.W. 144
Khan, Azizur Rahman 1, 144
Kim, C. 154
Kim, S. 160
Kingdon, J. 64, 81
Kleinman, Arthur 124
Knight, J. 160
Kohrman, M. 195, 205, 209, 210
Kojima, K. 174
Kokubun, R. 174
Koldyk, D. 65, 174
Kwon, Huck-Ju 220
Kwong, Julia 6, 8, 128, 145

Lampton, D. 108
Lanzhou: education 11, 13, 127, 136–40 (Tables 7.3–8), 146; MLG (*dibao*) 11, 37, 38, 39, 40, 42 (Table 3.1), 43 (Table 3.2), 44–8 (Tables 3.5–8), 49–50, 63, 217, 221

Index   253

Lee, Ching Kwan 83, 85
Lee, Grace O.M. 11
Lee, P.N.S. 18
Legislative Affairs Office of the State
 Council (LAO) 25
Leonard, P. 125
Leung, Joe C.B. 1, 103, 127
Li, Bingqin: (2005) 152; (2006) 152;
 (2007) 170; and Duda (this volume) 3,
 7, 13, 15, 214, 215, 217; and Gong
 (2003) 151; *et al.* (2007) 153; Duda
 and (2008) 160; He and (2007) 144
Li, G. 128
Li, H. 161
Li, L. 153
Li, Peiling 103
Li, Qiang 82, 94, 95
Li, R. 129, 132, 148
Li, S. 124
Li, Shi 1
Liang, Qi 83, 87, 90
Liang, X. 151
Liaoning 2, 64, 67–8, 82
Lieberthal, K.G. 35, 64, 81
Lijphart, A. 197
Lin, J. 2, 133
Lin, Nan 83
Lin, T. 133
Liu, Houjun 86, 87
Liu, Jieyu: (2007) 97, 101, 103; (this
 volume) 3, 4, 5, 8, 12, 13, 14, 15, 17,
 214, 221
Liu, Jing 38, 49, 87
Liu, Y. 1
Liu, Zuo 21
Lobdell, R. A. 160
local economies, divergent 10–11
local government (*see also* central-local
 relations): autonomy in social policy
 26; CPSAs *see* Community Public
 Service Agencies; disability policy and
 organization 195, 205, 207–10;
 education provision 126, 131, 139, 149;
 fiscal decentralization and divergent
 local economies 10–11, 220; housing
 for migrants 152–3; implementation
 of policies 2, 3; MLG 9, 11–12, *see
 also* Minimum Livelihood Guarantee;
 older people policies 173, 177–84;
 private sector relations 16; reforms of
 structure 174; social insurance 6, 8;
 social welfare provision 5, 215–17;
 unemployment insurance 85; work
 unit reform 4, 6, 8–9, 86

Lora-Wainwright, A.: (2005) 114; (n.d.)
 125; (this volume) 3, 6, 8, 14–15, 17,
 214, 215
Lowry, I. S. 154
Luke, A. 143

Ma, L. J. C. 152
Mak, G. 143
Mann, Kirk 14, 15, 18
Mao Zedong 118, 122
marketization 5–7; of education 129–35
Maslove, Allan 17
Maurer-Fazio, Margaret 91
May, R. 157
Mcloughlin, C.S. 194
Meng, J. 39, 40
Meng, Qingyue 7
Meng, Xianfan 82
migrants: children's education 8, 144–5
 (Table 7.12); city housing policies 7,
 152–3, 169–70, 217; earnings 107,
 162; employment 156 (Table 8.1),
 161–2, 164; housing conditions 13;
 housing decisions 167 (Table 8.7);
 housing outcomes 154, 160–1, 167–70;
 housing providers and rent payment
 162–7 (Table 8.6); housing problem?
 157–60 (Tables 8.2, 8.3, 8.4), 167–70;
 life considerations and housing
 outcomes 160–1; mobility 162; rural
 to urban migration 151; social
 networks 13, 15; Taiyuan study 13,
 154–6, 161–7 (Tables 8.5, 8.6, 8.7),
 167–70
Miles, M. 195, 197
Minimum Livelihood Guarantee (*dibao*,
 MLG): amount 36–7; application for
 206; central-local relations 11–12,
 29–34; comparative study 40–50
 (Tables 3.1, 3.2, 3.5, 3.6, 3.7); Dalian
 67–9, 220–1; development 9, 220–1;
 excluded households 47–8;
 government spending 44 (Table 3.3);
 history and purposes 37–8, 213;
 implementation 221; issues (daily
 sustenance) 56–8; issues (illness and
 disability) 53–4; issues (schooling)
 54–6; negative impact of policy 73–4;
 negative views of MLG recipients
 72–3; number of participants 44
 (Table 3.4); opinions and feelings
 towards 59–63; rural 32–4, 35;
 structure of policy 71–2; studies 221;
 urban 29–31, 34–5; Wuhan

254 *Index*

programme 38–40, 220; Wuhan study 37, 53–63, 220–1
Ministry of Civil Affairs (MCA) 24, 30, 37, 68, 174, 195
Ministry of Education (MOE) 24, 131, 148
Ministry of Finance (MOF) 25
Ministry of Health (MOH) 24
Ministry of Housing and Urban-Rural Development (MHURD) 24
Ministry of Human Resources and Social Security (MHRSS) 24
Mitlin, D. 154
Moerman, D. 114, 124
Mok, K.H.: (1996) 132; (2000) 128; (2001) 6; (2005) 133; (2008b) 128, 133; (2009) 128; and Wong (this volume) 3, 4, 6, 7, 10, 13, 17, 218; *et al.* (2002) 82; *et al.* (2010) 127, 145; Painter and (2008) 146
Mountfield, E. 128
Murie, Alan 1, 7
Murphy, Rachel 17, 144, 190

Nanjing: enterprise restructuring 86–8; experiences of redundancy 88–91; MLG 42–3 (Tables 3.1–2), 45–8 (Table 3.5–8); redundant women workers 12, 14, 82–4, 87–8, 101–3; responses to redundancy 91–101, 102, 221
Nanjing Bureau of Statistics 90, 103
Nanjing City Environment Management Committee 99, 102
Nanjing Textile Bureau 92
Nanjing Women's Federation 91
National Bureau of Statistics of China (NBSC) 136; (1999) 85; (2005) 130; (2008) 87; (2009) 130
National Development and Reform Commission (NDRC) 25
National Grant Scheme 147
National Scholarship 147
Neighbourhood Offices 31
Neubauer, D. 149
Ngok, K.L.: (2005) 148; and Chan (2003) 128; and Kwong (2003) 128; Mok and (2008b) 128, 133
Nichter, Mark: (2002) 117; (2003) 113; and Nichter (2003) 121
Nichter, Mimi 121

O'Brien, K. 190, 192
OECD 130, 148

Office of the Second China National Sample Survey on Disability (OSCNSSD) and the Institute of Population Studies (IPS), Peking University (2008) 194
Oksenberg, M. 35, 64, 81
older people: community activities 179–82, 187; Jianwai study 171–3, 184–90; pensions 172, 173–4, 183, 190; 'people's livelihood' 184, 188, 191; self-reliance or care? 177–84; social services delivery 6, 9, 174; state policy 9; third-sector provision 8

Pahl, R. E. 160
Painter, M. 146
Pei, S. 65
pensions: delivery 174, 183; funding 214–15; life expectancy and 11; MLG (*dibao*) 58; policy innovation at the central level 173–4; redundancy 73, 88, 91–2; reforms 5–6, 173–4, 190, 214, 218; rural welfare 5, 8, 54; social policy 20, 172; state 88; urban 113, 173–4, 189; work units 4, 84, 190
Phillips, M. 107, 108, 109
Pierson, Christopher 218
Pierson, P. 64
political liberalization 7–8
Poon, B. 174, 192
Price, Richard H. 82
privatization of education 129–35

Qian, X.L. 143
Qingdao 39, 42
Quinn, G. 194

Raffaelli, M. 154
Ravallion, Martin 1
Rawski, T. G. 38
Raymo, J.M. 173
Read, Benjamin L. 2
Reddy, Sanjay 109
redundancy (*see also xiagang*): enterprise restructuring in Nanjing 86–8; experiences of 88–91; finding work 95–101; forms of 88–9; lay-offs 83, 84, 85; responses to 91–101; social support and networks 93–5; social welfare provision 84; state enterprise reform and 84–6; state workers 82; women in Nanjing 82–4
Re-employment Service Centres (RSCs) 8, 9, 72, 85–6, 87, 94

Index 255

Rempel, H. 160
Ren, F. 68
Residents' Committees 31
Riskin, Carl 1, 144
Rofel, Lisa 97
Rong, X.L. 143
Ruan, Y. 152
rural cooperative medical system (RCMS) 105–10, 112–13, 118–23
Rural Household Survey Team of the National Statistics Bureau (2005) 155

Saich, Tony 1, 2, 7
Saraceno, Francisco 18
SARS epidemic 109, 176
Sato, Hiroshi 1
Saunders, Peter 1, 15, 18
Scheid, V. 125
Seeborg, M. C. 151, 152
Segall, M. 109
Selden, M. 5
Shan, F. 5, 173
Shang, Xiaoyuan: (2000) 200; (2001) 195; (2002) 194; (2008) 194; and Wu (2003) 194, 207; *et al.* (2005) 194; *et al.* (2008) 207, 208; Fisher, Shang and Xie (this volume) 3, 4, 8, 9, 11, 13, 16, 214, 222; Saunders and (2001) 1, 18
Shanghai: education 133, 134, 140–1 (Table 7.9), 142 (Table 7.10), 144, 147; life expectancy 11; hospitals 198; migrant workers 144; MLG (*dibao*) 30, 32, 38, 42–3 (Tables 3.1–2), 45–8 (Tables 3.5–8), 64, 68, 71, 78; re-employmentservice 11; social welfare facilities 187
Shanghai Municipal Women's Federation 134
Shanghai Research Institute of Educational Sciences (2005) 133
Shanxi 32, 34, 153
Shen, J. 152
Shenyang 39, 42, 70, 87
Shenzhen 41
Shi, D. 71
Shi, Q.H. 133
Shi, T.J. 143
Shih, Victor 2
Shirk, Susan 35
Shue, Vivienne 17, 18, 191, 216
Sichuan: healthcare provision 110; healthcare study 14, 104, 105; living standards 106; redundancy 82, 87
Sidel, V. and R. 108

Skocpol, Theda 17
Smyth, R. 143
So, A.Y.C. 143
social institutions and child disability 207–10
social networks 14–15, 83, 95–7
social policy: central-local relations 20–2, 215–17; changing welfare geography 213–15; current characteristics of central-local relations 26–9; decentralization 215–17; evolving welfare mix 220–2; fiscal arrangements 28–9, 216; implementation 27–8; local government autonomy 26; making 27; Maoist era 127, 214, 215; national debates and global context 217–20; organizational systems 28; reform and modernization 211–13
Social Policy Research Centre (SPRC) 69
social support 93–5
socialization 181, 183, 217
Solinger, D. J.: (1991) 38; (1999) 7, 152; (2001) 5, 73, 82, 92; (2002) 1, 86, 103; (2003) 82, 86, 92, 94; (2004) 152; (2005)1; (2006) 85; (this volume) 3, 9, 10, 13, 14, 15, 65, 86, 214, 215, 217, 220, 221
Song, Lina 1
Song, S. F. 5, 82, 152
SPRC CASS: (2000a) 69; (2000b) 69; (2001a) 65, 70, 77; (2001b) 65, 70, 74; (2001c) 65, 77; (2001d) 66; (2002) 70; (2003) 66, 70, 78
Starlight (*Xingguang*) Project 174
state: changing role 8–9; decentralized 71; enterprise reform and redundancy 84–6
State Commission Office for Public Sector Reform (SCOPSR) 25
State Council 27–8; (1994) 22, 23, 28; (1997) 30, 71; (1999) 30, 71; (2007) 34; (2010) 148
Street Offices 31
Sun, Qipan 32
Sun, Xiaoke 83, 87, 90
Sun, Xiaoyun 124

Tacoli, C. 160
Taiyuan: city 154–5, 169; housing for migrants 7, 13; migrant employment distribution by industrial sector 156 (Table 8.1); migrant housing survey 153, 154–6, 161–7; MLG 45 (Table 3.5), 47 (Table 3.7), 48 (Table 3.8)

256 *Index*

Tan, Lin 97
Tan, M. 124
Tan, S. 125
Tan Z. 39, 40
Tang, Jun: (1992) 30; (1994) 30; (2002a)
40, 44; (2002b) 37, 38, 39, 40, 41, 45,
50; (2003a) 69, 73, 81; (2003b) 58;
(2006) 44; Wong and (2006) 2, 8, 18
Tang, S. 108, 124
Tartakovskaya, Irina 96
tax reform (1994) 21–2, 23 (Table 2.1)
Taylor, J. E. 160
textile industries 87–8, 90–1
third sector, emergence 7–8
'three new mountains' 127, 211
'Three Nos' 4–5, 29, 38, 74, 214
'Three Security Lines' 72
Tianjin: education 140–1 (Table 7.9),
144; migrant workers 144; MLG
(*dibao*) 38, 40, 41, 42–3 (Tables 3.1–2),
45–8 (Tables 3.5–8); philanthropy 13;
redundancy 87; variable welfare
provision 10
Tilky, L. 144
Titmuss, R. M. 18
Tudball, J. 195

Uchimura, Hiroko 18
UNCRC (2005) 194, 195
UNCRPD (2007) 194, 195
UNDP (2008) 142
Unel, Bulent 10
unemployment: increase in 5; lay-offs
and 84, 85; Wuhan MLG study 56–7
Unemployment Insurance (UEI) 72, 73,
85
UNESCO, Management of Social
Transition project (MOST) 70
UNICEF (2005) 194

Van Der Geest 106, 124

Waldram, James 124
Wang, B. 124
Wang, Shaoguang 108
Wang, X. 143
Wang, Y.B. 132
Wang, Ya Ping 1, 7, 37
Wang, Zheng 83
Ward, P. M. 154
Warner, Malcolm 11
welfare mix 1–2; evolving 220–2; from
plan to market 4–9; local variation
10–13; national debates and global

context 217–20; role of welfare system
222; societal consequences of
changing 13–15; towards an
understanding of China's welfare
regime 15–18
Wen Jiabao 38, 147, 148, 215
West, Loraine A. 5
White, Gordon 2, 7, Howell, Jude and
Shang, Xiaoyuan
White, S. 108
White Paper: (2004) 174; (2006) 174
Whyte, S. 124
women: constraints on finding work 14,
97–101; redundant workers in
Nanjing82–3, 88–91, 101–3; social
networks 95–7
Wong, Christine: (2000) 2; (2007) 10,
173, 192, 217; (2009) 29; *et al.* (1995)
10; Mountfield and (2005) 128; Shue
and (2007a) 17, 191, 216; Shue and
(2007b) 18
Wong, Hilda S.W. 1, 103
Wong, L.: (1998) 5; and Flynn (2001)
127; and Poon (2005) 174, 192; and
Tang (2006) 2, 8, 18; *et al.* (2004)
127
Wong, Yu Cheung 3, 4, 7, 10–11, 13, 17,
218
World Bank 218; (2002) 10, 22; (2008)
216
Wu, B. 41
Wu, F. 152
Wu, H. X. 160
Wu, W.: (2002) 152, 161; (2004b) 152,
155; (2006) 154
Wu, X.M. 194, 207
Wuhan: daily sustenance (work, food
and borrowing) 56–8; MLG (*dibao*)
programme 38–40, 63; MLG (*dibao*)
programme considered comparatively
40–50 (Tables 3.1–2, 3.5–8); MLG
(*dibao*) study 10, 11, 36–7, 50–3
(Table 3.9), 217, 220–1; opinions and
feelings towards MLG (*dibao*) 59–63;
redundant workers 82, 96; urgent
issues (illness, disability and
schooling) 53–6
Wyatt, T. J. 160

XGBLG *see* Basic Living Guarantee
Xia, Guomei 83
xiagang (laid-off) workers 38, 65, 73,
84–5, 88, 94
Xi'an 87

Index

Xiang, Biao 124
Xiao, J. A. 153
Xie, Y. 173
Xu, Bing 3, 9, 11, 64, 71, 216, 220
Xu, Qingwen 7
Xu, Yanli 97
Xu, Yuebin 11, 33

Yang, D. P. 131
Yang, H. 160
Yang, R. 127, 128, 143
Yang, T. 66, 70, 72, 74
Yang, Z. 38, 39, 41, 50, 54
Yin, R.K. 197
You, L. Y. 5
young people with disability 193–4
Yu, D. 109
Yu, J. 154
Yu, Ka Man 5, 173
Yu, Q.Y. 134
Yuan, Y. 151

Zahniser, S. 161
Zebregs, Harm 10
Zhang, Jie 30
Zhang, K. H. 152
Zhang, L.: (2001) 152; (2002) 152; (2006) 191; *et al.* (2003) 152
Zhang, L. 191
Zhang, Pengfei 2
Zhang, Q. 38, 39, 41, 50, 54
Zhang, Qiujian(1999) 88, 90
Zhang, Xing Quan 1
Zhang, Y. 68
Zhang, Y. 1
Zhang, Y. 124
Zhao, Yandong 95
Zhong, X. 143
Zhou, L. 160
Zhou, Yanqiu Rachel 7
Zhu, Q.F. 127, 132
Zhu Rongji 68–9, 72
Zhuang, H. 5, 173